THE SACRAMENTAL VISION OF
EDWARD BOUVERIE PUSEY

T&T Clark Studies in English Theology

Series Editors
Karen Kilby
Michael Higton
Stephen R. Holmes

THE SACRAMENTAL VISION OF EDWARD BOUVERIE PUSEY

T. A. Karlowicz

LONDON • NEW YORK • OXFORD • NEW DELHI • SYDNEY

T&T CLARK

Bloomsbury Publishing Plc

50 Bedford Square, London, WC1B 3DP, UK
1385 Broadway, New York, NY 10018, USA
29 Earlsfort Terrace, Dublin 2, Ireland

BLOOMSBURY, T&T CLARK and the T&T Clark logo are trademarks of
Bloomsbury Publishing Plc

First published in Great Britain 2022
Paperback edition published 2023

Copyright © Tobias A. Karlowicz, 2022

Tobias A. Karlowicz has asserted his right under the Copyright, Designs and Patents Act, 1988, to be identified as Author of this work.

For legal purposes the Acknowledgements on pp. viii–ix constitutes an extension of this copyright page.

Cover image: clairevis/iStock

All rights reserved. No part of this publication may be reproduced or transmitted in any form or by any means, electronic or mechanical, including photocopying, recording, or any information storage or retrieval system, without prior permission in writing from the publishers.

Bloomsbury Publishing Plc does not have any control over, or responsibility for, any third-party websites referred to or in this book. All internet addresses given in this book were correct at the time of going to press. The author and publisher regret any inconvenience caused if addresses have changed or sites have ceased to exist, but can accept no responsibility for any such changes.

A catalogue record for this book is available from the British Library.

Library of Congress Cataloging-in-Publication Data
Names: Karlowicz, Tobias A., author.
Title: The sacramental vision of Edward Bouverie Pusey / Tobias A. Karlowicz.
Description: London ; New York : T&T Clark, 2021. | Series: T&T Clark studies in English theology | Includes bibliographical references and index. |
Identifiers: LCCN 2021018911 (print) | LCCN 2021018912 (ebook) |
ISBN 9780567701633 (hb) | ISBN 9780567701688 (paperback) |
ISBN 9780567701640 (epdf) | ISBN 9780567701671 (ebook)
Subjects: LCSH: Pusey, E. B. (Edward Bouverie), 1800–1882. |
Church of England–Doctrines. | Oxford movement.
Classification: LCC BX5199.P9 K37 2021 (print) |
LCC BX5199.P9 (ebook) | DDC 230/.3–dc23
LC record available at https://lccn.loc.gov/2021018911
LC ebook record available at https://lccn.loc.gov/2021018912

ISBN: HB: 978-0-5677-0163-3
PB: 978-0-5677-0168-8
ePDF: 978-0-5677-0164-0
eBook: 978-0-5677-0167-1

Series: T&T Clark Studies in English Theology

Typeset by Newgen KnowledgeWorks Pvt. Ltd., Chennai, India

To find out more about our authors and books visit www.bloomsbury.com and sign up for our newsletters.

In memoriam
T. M. K.

CONTENTS

Acknowledgements	viii
Note on Text	x
List of Abbreviations	xi
INTRODUCTION: PERSPECTIVES ON PUSEY	1
Chapter 1 PUSEY REINTERPRETED	15
Chapter 2 ALLEGORY AND THE SACRAMENTAL VISION	55
Chapter 3 BAPTISM AND UNION WITH CHRIST	89
Chapter 4 COMMUNION AND THE REAL PRESENCE	119
Chapter 5 SACRIFICE AND THE ATONEMENT	149
Chapter 6 SACRIFICE AND THE SACRAMENTS	167
CONCLUSION: RECLAIMING PUSEY FOR THEOLOGY	187
Bibliography	195
Index	211

ACKNOWLEDGEMENTS

This book has been revised and expanded from a doctoral thesis completed at the University of St Andrews in 2013. My supervisor, David Brown, has played a significant role, not only in steering my research and stirring my thinking during my doctoral studies, but more importantly in shaping my development as a scholar, both at that time and since. My examiners, Geoffrey Rowell (d. 2017) and Mark Elliott, offered numerous insights and criticisms, which contributed substantially to the refinement of this work. My study of Pusey, however, began somewhat earlier, during my priestly formation at Nashotah House Theological Seminary. Among the faculty during my time there, Timothy Johnson first encouraged me to pursue further academic study, while Thomas Holtzen and Charles Henery guided the first steps of my research on Pusey and the Oxford Movement.

Much of the initial research for this book was conducted at the libraries of the University of St Andrews. Two other libraries, however, have been essential to its completion. The manuscript collections of Pusey House in Oxford were pivotal to my research; I am indebted to the chapter and to the current principal, George Westhaver, for permission to quote from these collections. George has also been a valuable source of expertise on Pusey's 'Lectures on Types and Prophecies in the Old Testament'. I am moreover grateful to the past principal and priest-librarians, Jonathan Baker, Barry Orford, William Davage and Philip Corbett, for their hospitality and assistance during my visits to Oxford; and to the present librarian, Jessica Woodward, for her assistance with 'remote' consultation of various archival materials. In addition, the past and present staff of the Frances Donaldson Library at Nashotah House, especially David Sherwood, Laura Groetsch and Bramwell Richards, have provided inestimable help in procuring any number of obscure sources during the completion of the project. Opportunities to teach at Nashotah House, both on Anglican history generally and on Pusey specifically, have helped significantly to broaden my historical perspective and refine my readings of Pusey. My conversations with Shawn McCain and Gary Ball were especially useful; Gary in particular helped prepare the ground for key developments in the way I articulate central aspects of Pusey's theology.

At various stages of this project, numerous others have provided advice, assistance, encouragement, or hospitality. Among them are Brian Douglas, Albrecht Geck, Carol Engelhardt Herringer, Ian McCormack, Rob MacSwain, Stephen Holmes, Alan Torrance, Stephen Presley, Shawn Bawulski, Sheree Lear, Sean Cook, Allen and Amanda Jones, Dru Johnson, Micah and Jennifer Snell, John Frederick, Gavin White (d. 2016), Ann Loades, Robin Ward, Keith Ackerman, Joel Scandrett, Charles Erlandson, Hans Boersma and Jim Packer (d. 2020). Above all, my family have supported me without fail over more than a decade of research, writing and revisions. My wife Becky has been unstintingly flexible in making the countless adjustments to work and family life necessary to the research and writing of this book: without her love and generosity, it simply would not have happened. My mother Sarah and my wife's parents Mark and Mary Kay have also contributed significantly both in encouragement and in various practical contributions over the years. To them, as to all who have made this work possible, I offer my heartfelt thanks.

NOTE ON TEXT

Many of the older works used in this book are available in electronic or reprint editions; where these editions have been used, this information is given in the bibliography but not in the notes. Likewise, the full form of many older titles shortened in the notes is given in the bibliography. All biblical quotations are from the Authorized Version.

ABBREVIATIONS

Works by Pusey

Baptism 1	*Scriptural Views of Holy Baptism* [1st edn]
Baptism 2	*Scriptural Views of Holy Baptism* [2nd edn and after]
'Comfort'	'The Holy Eucharist a Comfort to the Penitent'
Eirenicon I	*The Church of England a Portion of Christ's One Holy Catholic Church*
Eirenicon III	*Is Healthful Reunion Impossible? A Second Letter to ... Newman*
English Church	*The Real Presence ... the Doctrine of the English Church*
Enquiry I	*An Historical Enquiry into ... the Theology of Germany*
Enquiry II	*An Historical Enquiry into ... the Theology of Germany, Part II*
Fathers	*The Doctrine of the Real Presence, as Contained in the Fathers*
Jelf	*The Articles Treated on in Tract 90 ... in a Letter to the Rev. R. W. Jelf*
London	*A Letter to the Right Hon. and Right Rev. the Lord Bishop of London*
Oxford	*A Letter to the Right Rev. Father in God, Richard, Lord Bishop of Oxford*
Par. S. I	*Sermons during the Season from Advent to Whitsuntide*
Par. S. II	*Parochial Sermons*, vol. 2
PCS	*Parochial and Cathedral Sermons*
Pl. S.	*Plain Sermons, by Contributors to the 'Tracts for the Times'*
Richards	*The Church of England Leaves Her Children Free*
SR	*A Course of Sermons ... Chiefly Bearing on Repentance*
'Types'	'Lectures on Types and Prophecies of the Old Testament'
US I	*Nine Sermons, Preached ... between 1843–1855**
US II	*Sermons Preached ... between A.D. 1859 and 1872*
US III	*Ten Sermons Preached ... between 1864–1879**

* Sermons paginated individually in the editions used.

Other abbreviations

LBV	Liddon Bound Volumes, Pusey House
TFT	Tracts for the Times by Members of the University of Oxford

Introduction

PERSPECTIVES ON PUSEY

Edward Bouverie Pusey lived from 1800 to 1882; during his lifetime, his name became synonymous with a widespread theological movement which changed significant portions not only of the Church of England but of global Anglicanism. Indeed 'Puseyism' was the popular name of the Oxford Movement not only in England but across Europe. Within England, he became the central figure of the Movement, for both its admirers and its detractors. He was, by any measure, a major figure – not because of his office, nor because of his role as a party leader (which he steadfastly refused to countenance), but because of his theological writing. In England, he was recognized as a formidable scholar, even by his opponents; in America, the library of the Anglo-Catholic seminary at Nashotah House, built in 1910, inscribed his name on its facade together with other great doctors of the Church such as Athanasius, Augustine and Hooker. Today, however, his standing among theologians is somewhere between dismissed and ignored. Even in studies of the Oxford Movement, Pusey has fallen into a curious gap in scholarship. On the one hand, as Owen Chadwick noted, 'Newman scholarship is an industry.'[1] On the other, there has been a move away from study of the Movement's leading figures, to emphasize the broader spread and effect of Tractarianism.[2] In between these two tendencies, however, other prominent figures of the Movement have been nearly overlooked.

Pusey has been no exception. *The Life of Edward Bouverie Pusey, D.D.* was written by his disciple Henry Parry Liddon and published after Liddon's death in 1893.[3] Over the next few decades, there were a handful of biographies written by friends and admirers; but thereafter, nothing of substance was written until David

---

1. Owen Chadwick, *The Spirit of the Oxford Movement: Tractarian Essays* (Cambridge: Cambridge University Press, 1990), 319.

2. George Herring, *What Was the Oxford Movement?* (London: Continuum, 2002), 2–4. 'Tractarians' were adherents of the Oxford Movement, so-called after the Movement's influential series of 'Tracts for the Times'. A brief account of the Oxford Movement is given in Chapter 1.

3. Henry Parry Liddon, *The Life of Edward Bouverie Pusey, Doctor of Divinity, Canon of Christ Church; Regius Professor of Hebrew in the University of Oxford*, ed. J. O. Johnston and Robert J. Wilson, 3rd edn, 4 vols (London: Longmans, Green, 1893).

Forrester's Oxford doctoral thesis in 1967 (later published in revised form as *Young Doctor Pusey*).⁴ A handful of biographical studies and journal articles were published again in the years around the 1983 celebration of the 150th anniversary of the Oxford Movement. The most notable volume of this period, however, was the collection *Pusey Rediscovered*, which aimed to present a case for Pusey's historical significance, but which was on the whole (with a few notable exceptions) unduly overshadowed by Forrester's troubling account of Pusey's family life.⁵

A new phase of Pusey scholarship began, however, in the 1990s, with a pair of insightful (if overlooked) doctoral studies of Pusey's sacramental theology by Jonathan Naumann and John C. Calhoun.⁶ In 2002, David Brown published an article challenging the presumption that Pusey was a less insightful theologian than his friend John Henry Newman, and in 2009 Albrecht Geck published a volume of Pusey's German correspondence with his friend F. A. G. Tholuck, reflecting two decades of research.⁷ The 2012 volume *Edward Bouverie Pusey and the Oxford Movement* offers a refreshing look at a number of historical issues involved in studying Pusey – most notably a critical reassessment of Forrester's influence on the field.⁸ Since then, the pace of scholarship has quickened: George Westhaver's doctoral thesis (also 2012) provides a valuable introduction to Pusey's important, but unpublished, 'Lectures on Types and Prophecies in the Old Testament'; Mark Chapman has included substantive discussion of Pusey's ecumenism in several chapters of *The Fantasy of Reunion* (2014); and Brian Douglas has published several studies on Pusey, primarily on aspects of his eucharistic theology (most notably *The Eucharistic Theology of Edward Bouverie Pusey*, 2015).⁹ Pusey has also

---

4. David Forrester, *Young Doctor Pusey: A Study in Development* (London: Mowbray, 1989). For discussion of Forrester, see below in this chapter and in Chapter 1 under 'Two theories of Pusey's "revolutions"'.

5. Perry Butler, ed., *Pusey Rediscovered* (London: SPCK, 1983).

6. Jonathan Charles Naumann, 'The Eucharistic Theologies of Nineteenth Century Anglican and Lutheran Repristination Movements Compared' (PhD thesis, University of Glasgow, 1990); John Clay Calhoun, 'Edward Bouverie Pusey's Theology of Conversion' (PhD diss., Drew University, 1993).

7. David Brown, 'Pusey as Consistent and Wise: Some Comparisons with Newman', *Anglican and Episcopal History* 7 (2002): 328–49; Albrecht Geck, ed., *Autorität und Glaube: Edward Bouverie Pusey und Friedrich August Gotttreu Tholuck im Briefwechsel (1825–1865)* (Göttingen: V und R Unipress, 2009). Cf. Geck, 'The Concept of History in E. B. Pusey's First Enquiry into German Theology and Its German Background', *Journal of Theological Studies* n.s. 38 (1987): 387–408; and 'Friendship in Faith: Edward Bouverie Pusey und Friedrich August Gottreu Tholuck im Kampf gegen Rationalismus und Pantheismus', *Pietismus und Neuzeit: Ein Jahrbuch des neueren Protestantismus* 27 (2001): 91–117.

8. Rowan Strong and Carol Engelhardt Herringer, eds, *Edward Bouverie Pusey and the Oxford Movement* (London: Anthem, 2012).

9. George Westhaver, 'The Living Body of the Lord: E. B. Pusey's "Types and Prophecies of the Old Testament"' (PhD thesis, University of Durham, 2012); Mark D. Chapman, *The*

begun to attract the notice of other scholars, most notably Timothy Larsen and Hans Boersma, who have both written brief but insightful discussions of Pusey's understanding of Scripture.[10]

The study of Pusey and his theology, therefore, is more vibrant now than it ever has been; and it appears to be on the rise. To date, however, there has been no comprehensive introduction to Pusey's theology. This volume aims to remedy that omission. Despite the recent increase in Pusey scholarship, however, the study of Pusey remains a novelty. A century's neglect is its own tacit assessment of Pusey's worth. Thus, the case for Pusey's interest as a theologian needs to be presented, and the reasons for his neglect considered.

There are, as with many historical figures, a wide range of reasons for interest in Pusey. On the one hand, for ecumenists, there is what A. M. Allchin described as the 'prophetic' nature of Pusey's perspective on Newman's conversion, particularly in light of the changes which Pusey foresaw to the Roman Catholic Church which were fulfilled in Vatican II.[11] And, though it ultimately foundered on the rocks of Vatican I, Pusey's three-part *Eirenicon* was one of the earlier proposals for Anglican–Roman Catholic ecumenism, and one of the few before Vatican II to gain serious attention from parties in both churches.[12]

On the other hand, within Anglicanism, ongoing controversies over ordination and sexuality have revived, in some quarters, the fraught and sporadic alliance between Anglo-Catholics and Evangelicals. The old tensions and distrust between the two movements – born with Evangelicalism in the eighteenth century and exacerbated by the Oxford Movement's radical changes to Anglican high churchmanship in the nineteenth – remain. Pusey was, however, a high

Fantasy of Reunion: Anglicans, Catholics, and Ecumenism, 1833–1882 (Oxford: Oxford University Press, 2014); Brian Douglas, *The Eucharistic Theology of Edward Bouverie Pusey: Sources, Context and Doctrine within the Oxford Movement and Beyond* (Leiden: Brill, 2015); 'Pusey's "Lectures on Types and Prophecies of the Old Testament": Implications for Eucharistic Theology', *International Journal of Systematic Theology* 14 (2012): 194–216; 'Pusey, Poetry and Eucharistic Theology', *St. Mark's Review* 238 (2016): 87–105; 'Pusey and Transubstantiation: An Exploration of His Thinking and Ecumenical Implications', *New Blackfriars* 101, no. 1091 (January 2020): 85–100; 'Pusey and Scripture: Dead End or Fertile Ground?', *New Blackfriars* 101, no. 1096 (November 2020): 698–715; Brian Douglas and Jane Douglas, 'Pusey and the Romantic Poets: Some Links to Eucharistic Theology', *New Blackfriars* 98, no. 1077 (2016): 539–54.

10. Timothy Larsen, 'E. B. Pusey and Holy Scripture', *Journal of Theological Studies* n.s. 60 (2009): 490–526; cf. Timothy Larsen, 'Anglo-Catholics: E. B. Pusey and Holy Scripture', in *A People of One Book: The Bible and the Victorians* (Oxford: Oxford University Press, 2011), 11–42. Hans Boersma, *Scripture as Real Presence: Sacramental Exegesis in the Early Church* (Grand Rapids, MI: Baker Academic, 2017), 221–4.

11. A. M. Allchin, *Participation in God* (Wilton, CT: Morehouse–Barlow, 1988), 48–9.

12. For a robust discussion of Pusey's *Eirenicon* and its broader historical context, see Chapman, *Fantasy*, esp. chapters 3–4.

churchman with deep sympathy for Evangelicalism. Indeed, the Swedish scholar Yngve Brilioth even asked, in 1933, 'Is Pusey, then, one of the great Anglican Evangelicals?'[13] More recently, John Calhoun has concluded that Pusey's insistence that he believed everything the Evangelicals did (differing from them only in what they denied) was in fact true.[14] Pusey, he argues, despite his frequent role as a controversialist defending the emerging Anglo-Catholic movement, is 'too profound and comprehensive' for his theology 'to be adequately expressed by one category' and transcends party divisions between Anglo-Catholics and Evangelicals.[15] As such, he will likely unsettle partisans on both sides; but he may also offer a path to mutual understanding. Anglo-Catholicism itself stands at a critical moment in its own history, riven by competing self-conceptions and facing an uncertain future. This was noted during the sesquicentennial of the Oxford Movement; the years since have only deepened the crisis.[16] Pusey, as one of the defining figures of the Oxford Movement, represents a form of what he called 'English Catholicism', which challenges contemporary conceptions of Anglo-Catholicism, but which might also offer clarity regarding the nature of 'Catholic' identity within the Anglican heritage.

These, however, taken on their own, make only a limited case for Pusey's contemporary interest – a figure of some historical interest, perhaps, or of some practical use, but one whose relevance is constrained to the narrow confines of certain academic specializations or ecclesiastical parties. This study aims to make a bolder claim: that Pusey, despite a century and more of neglect, is in fact a deeply original theologian, who, in his own right, merits sustained engagement within contemporary theology. Christianity today, particularly in the West, faces mounting challenges from waning belief, rival spiritualities and questions about its own ongoing relevance. Such difficulties were not unforeseen in the nineteenth century (nor indeed foreign to it), but Pusey was, more than many of his contemporaries, keenly aware of what lay on the horizon. This awareness led him to a penetrating critique of contemporary defences of orthodoxy as brittle in their handling of doctrine and compromised in their uncritical acceptance of the Enlightenment's legacy in theology. Pusey found his remedy in an engagement

13. Yngve Brilioth, *Three Lectures on Evangelicalism and the Oxford Movement* (Oxford: Oxford University Press, 1934), 32–6; *The Anglican Revival: Studies in the Oxford Movement* (London: Longmans, Green, 1933), 125, 242–3; cf. Liddon, *Life*, 1:255, 2:400–1.

14. Calhoun, 'Conversion', 300–1.

15. Calhoun, 'Conversion', 90.

16. Louis Weil, 'The Tractarian Liturgical Inheritance Re-assessed', in *Tradition Renewed: The Oxford Movement Conference Papers*, ed. Geoffrey Rowell (Allison Park, PA: Pickwick, 1986), 110; W. S. F. Pickering, 'Anglo-Catholicism: Some Sociological Observations', in Rowell, *Tradition*, 153–72; Geoffrey Rowell, *The Vision Glorious: Themes and Personalities of the Catholic Revival in Anglicanism* (Oxford: Oxford University Press, 1983), v. Cf. Roger Greenacre, preface to *Confession and Absolution*, ed. Martin Dudley and Geoffrey Rowell (Collegeville, MN: Liturgical Press, 1990), xi.

with patristic theology focused on recovering the Fathers' allegorical hermeneutic. This led him, in turn, to a view of creation as (in varying degrees of fullness) participating in and manifesting the eternal Word, and thus to his soteriological emphasis on union with Christ. The emphasis he placed on this doctrine, in turn, contributed to a major shift in nineteenth-century Anglican theology. But beyond this historical contribution, Pusey remains theologically relevant today, because the 'sacramental vision' which he drew from the Fathers – and which this study unfolds – addresses very current questions in theology and anticipates similar projects of *réssourcement*, aimed at the same problems, in twentieth- and twenty-first-century theology. Pusey's 'sacramental vision' is, therefore, both the key to understanding his theology and the ground of the argument for his ongoing relevance to theology.

Despite these reasons for interest in Pusey, however, there remain the questions of Pusey's reputation and why, until recently, it has suffered so much. Ian McCormack has done Pusey scholarship a useful service in digging through many of the academic references to Pusey over the past half-century and tracing their sources. What he uncovered was a mutually reinforcing web of citations, which, in the end, stem primarily from a single source: David Forrester's study of Pusey's early development.[17] Forrester portrays Pusey as a bright young German-trained intellectual, who, driven by the psychological traumas of his personal life, develops a morbid obsession with his own sinfulness, abandoning his youthful creativity for a harsh, negative dogmatism and a joyless asceticism. That the scholarship of several decades would depend almost entirely on one perspective is itself troubling; that the perspective being repeated is as negative (and, as we shall see, as problematic) as Forrester's assessment of Pusey only adds to the discomfort. But the question here is why it has gotten that way. McCormack faults the sources he surveys for academic laziness; and this may be partially true.[18] However, more careful attention to the scholarly process suggests that the problem he identifies is more of a symptom than a cause. Deep research is given to topics thought to merit the energy that requires; peripheral topics are covered by quick reference to whatever secondary sources are available. Unless someone is researching Pusey *specifically*, one is not likely to sort through the archival material (or, for that matter, a four-volume *Life*) to form an independent perspective. Thus, while Forrester's influence has certainly reinforced the prejudice against Pusey, the lack of independent research indicates primarily a deeper disinterest.

---

17. Ian McCormack, 'The History of the History of Pusey', in Strong and Herringer, *Edward Bouverie Pusey*, 15–19. In many cases, Forrester is mediated through exclusive reference to Colin Matthew's equally problematic 1981 article. Both theories are discussed in Chapter 2 under 'Two theories of Pusey's "revolutions"'. H. C. G. Matthew, 'Edward Bouverie Pusey: From Scholar to Tractarian', *Journal of Theological Studies* n.s. 32 (1981): 101–24.

18. McCormack, 'History', 15, 19.

The lack of interest in Pusey, in my estimation, can be attributed in part to the inaccessibility of his work and in part to a reputation that makes him both personally unappealing and academically uninteresting. The most obvious of these, though also the least important, is Pusey's relative inaccessibility, both as an individual and as a theologian. The vast majority of Pusey's personal papers remain unpublished; while an ample survey is provided in the lengthy *Life* written by Pusey's disciple Henry Parry Liddon, even Liddon (or his editors) were compelled to omit a substantial amount of material. Liddon's work is, moreover, daunting enough on its own to deter all but the most determined of researchers. Owen Chadwick described it 'unreadable'; whether or not that is fair, it certainly has been *unread*.[19] The *Life* is full of counterexamples to the 'doom and gloom' parody of Pusey, which have been retrieved from time to time by Pusey's defenders, but this only highlights the degree to which Liddon's biography has been neglected.[20] Forrester suggests that Liddon paints a very 'heavy' portrait of Pusey, though a careful reading of the *Life* reveals frequent mention of Pusey's humour.[21] Forrester's impression is likely due to the nature of the work itself: a barrage of detail, in a narrative structure that serves more to conceal its subject than to reveal it. But the *Life* has deeper problems: Liddon's editors appear to have been more concerned with a particular (Anglo-Catholic) portrayal of Pusey than with the man himself and excised from Liddon's manuscript many interesting details of Pusey's earlier thought.[22] Together with a similar suppression of Pusey's 'Lectures on Types and Prophecies' – *the* key document for unlocking his theology – this raises the question of the extent to which Anglo-Catholic refashioning of the Oxford Movement and of Pusey (as, respectively, their 'origin story' and 'founding father') has contributed to his subsequent neglect.[23]

If Pusey's life is inaccessible, so too is his thought. His prose is often convoluted; Newman wrote of his first work, in 1828: 'It is *very* difficult, even for his friends and the clearest heads, to enter into his originality, full formed accuracy, and unsystematic impartiality … he is like some definitely marked curve, meandering through all sorts and collections of opinions boldly, yet as

19. Owen Chadwick, *Spirit*, 38, 171.
20. McCormack, 'History', 26–7; Allchin, *Participation*, 59–60; cf. Liddon, *Life*, 4:331–2, 376.
21. David W. F. Forrester, 'Dr Pusey's Marriage', in Perry Butler, *Pusey Rediscovered*, 120.
22. K. E. Macnab, 'Editing Liddon: From Biography to Hagiography?', in Strong and Herringer, *Edward Bouverie Pusey*, 31–48.
23. Westhaver, 'Living Body', 280–1. Cf. Peter G. Cobb, 'Leader of the Anglo-Catholics?', in Perry Butler, *Pusey Rediscovered*, 349–65. Recent historiography of nineteenth-century high churchmanship and early Anglo-Catholicism increasingly emphasizes that the Oxford Movement was simply a part, albeit an important one, of a larger shift in Anglican high churchmanship: one implication is that the Movement was not the sole (or even always the decisive) factor in shaping later Anglo-Catholicism, as earlier mythologizing of the Tractarians had tended to suggest. See Jeremy Morris, *The High Church Revival in the Church of England: Arguments and Identities* (Leiden: Brill, 2016), 1–38.

it seems irregularly.'²⁴ While his style did improve as he matured, it remains difficult, and often requires both careful attention and a deep familiarity with Pusey's peculiarities of syntax and terminology in order to understand him correctly. These difficulties are compounded by the fact that Pusey (as will be discussed more extensively in Chapter 2) was largely a synthetic rather than an analytic thinker: while possessed of profound analytic capabilities which are evidenced in his historical and biblical studies, he simply was not interested in developing a theoretical syntax for his own thought when the circumstances did not require it. In keeping with this (and also reflecting the nature of theological discourse during his lifetime), Pusey never produced a single comprehensive presentation of his thought, but instead wrote an enormous variety of occasional works. As a result, the majority of his larger works were controversial in nature and have not aged well, being tied to particular debates in his own time. These works are, moreover, consciously framed as reassertions of threatened dogma, or as arguments from precedent to justify the permissibility his own position. Neither approach provides a good venue for showcasing originality of thought – even before considering that to claim 'originality' was, in any case, anathema to the Tractarian *ethos*. A better source for his thought is therefore in his preaching, which, even when controversial, always aims at a positive presentation of doctrine. Consequently, although the themes identified in this study can be found in all of Pusey's published works over 100 pages, greater weight will be given (with a few exceptions) to homiletical material. This priority of sermons over book-length publications, however, inverts the common (though increasingly challenged) academic assumption that books are 'scholarly' (and therefore interesting), while sermons are 'practical' (and intellectually uninteresting).²⁵ Tractarian studies are giving increasing weight to sermon material, but it is hard not to think that Pusey's reputation has suffered in part from a lingering tendency to regard preaching as material of secondary importance.

These are minor difficulties, however. At least, difficulties of style have proven no obstacle to interest in any number of other thinkers; and other issues of accessibility are overcome easily enough. The deeper problems with Pusey's reputation are his perceived lack of personal appeal and academic interest. Pusey appears unappealing because of the dark portrait of him that has been handed down. Forrester, for instance, paints the grim picture of a man driven by his inner demons into a destructive and joyless obsession with religion, abusing his children and crushing the spirit of his wife in a frenzy of co-dependent religiosity. Such a person is unlikely to win much sympathy, even if his ideas have merit. This

---

24. Liddon, *Life*, 1:164; emphasis Newman's.

25. Jeremy Morris notes that 'it is often forgotten that the Oxford Movement was not so much written as *preached*'. Morris, *High Church Revival*, 175; emphasis Morris's. See also John Boneham, 'Tractarian Theology in Verse and Sermon', in *The Oxford Handbook of the Oxford Movement*, ed. Stewart J. Brown, Peter B. Nockles and James Pereiro (Oxford: Oxford University Press, 2017), 271–86.

portrait is not new: it likely owes much to polemical attacks made in his own day. Some Methodists, for instance, apparently made Pusey into a bogeyman to scare children into good behaviour; and early in the twentieth century, G. W. E. Russell felt the need to dismiss dark portrayals of the sort later reproduced by Forrester as no more accurate than rumours that Pusey sacrificed a lamb each year on Good Friday.[26] And indeed Forrester's representation of Pusey appears to rest on uncertain foundations. With regard to Pusey's family life, Forrester's slim basis for Pusey's abusive treatment of his children has been called into question, and his conclusions are directly contradicted by the testimony of Pusey's children themselves and their friends, who recalled him as the most lenient and indulgent of parents.[27] Pusey's wife Maria suffered from tuberculosis beginning in 1835; strangely, though Forrester notes the fact, he never considers whether the waning of her spirits from that year might have been caused by the disease rather than by Pusey's supposed 'oppression'.[28]

Pusey's spirituality has also been described as gloomy and oppressive; Forrester attributes this to Pusey's supposed deepening depression. Sufficient evidence of Pusey's humour (as has already been noted) is given in numerous places for this narrative to be discounted; indeed, Pusey (in his spiritual direction) even commended 'cheerfulness' and 'playfulness' as Christian virtues.[29] Nonetheless, Pusey indeed suffered severe emotional blows in his life, particularly in the deaths of his wife and three of his children. Statements made in the midst of deep grief, however, should not be used to judge his overall spirituality. In fact, Pusey's most shocking statements of apparent self-loathing are better understood as expressions

---

26. George W. E. Russell, *Dr. Pusey* (London: A. R. Mowbray), 46; Gordon S. Wakefield, '"A Mystical Substitute for the Glorious Gospel"? A Methodist Critique of Tractarianism', in Rowell, *Tradition*, 187.

27. Russell, *Dr. Pusey*, 45–8; Maria Trench, *The Story of Dr. Pusey's Life* (London: Longmans, Green, 1900), 381–5; McCormack, 'History', 23–7.

28. Forrester, *Pusey*, 65–7.

29. Sr Clara, Reminiscences, in Liddon Bound Volumes 78, Pusey House; McCormack, 'History', 23–7; Pusey to Clarissa Powell [later, Sr Clara], Advent 1846, LBV 76. Although they are easily overlooked among the mass of material provided, Liddon's *Life* contains too many instances to cite. The advice regarding 'cheerfulness' is particularly noteworthy, having been written within weeks of Pusey's proposed rule of life, which included his infamous proposal not to smile. In fact, Keble – his spiritual director – expressed reservations about this proposal, making it doubtful that Pusey ever adopted it; regardless, it is important to note that Pusey includes in the proposal not only the frequently mentioned exception for children but also an almost universally omitted exception for cases that are 'a matter of love' (a broad category!) He furthermore includes a bracketed comment connecting the practice to contemplation of the just deserts of sin. A later letter of direction which censures his correspondent for a '*conceited* smile' (emphasis mine) also likely pertains. In context, therefore, Pusey's proposal about smiling appears not to reflect a spirituality which rejects joy for gloom, but one which eschews superficial happiness or self-satisfaction for cultivation of penitence as the ground from which true joy (and indeed playfulness) might

of a broad ascetical tradition, which, in the context of that tradition, point to hope in the midst of suffering rather than depression. Pusey's severe characterization of himself, in the months following the death of his daughter in 1844, as 'scarred all over and seamed with sin, so that I am a monster to myself' issues in the prayer that Jesus would 'heal my leprosy ... and raise me from the dead'.[30] Benedicta Ward has noted that this paraphrases Anselm (in a work Pusey later edited for publication), and similar patterns can be found in the *Golden Epistle* of William of St Thierry and in the opening steps of the *Spiritual Combat*, which Pusey was beginning to recommend to those under his spiritual direction at this time.[31] Yet ultimately, the roots of Pusey's piety are not in the Middle Ages or the Counter-Reformation but in the early church. Rowell observes, 'In his sense of the genuine *grace* of penitence and sorrow for sin, Pusey stands in the tradition of the Fathers, who recognized the grace of compunction and the gift of tears as an important part of the Christian transfiguration into the likeness of Christ.'[32] Indeed, that one 'ought to give himself at all times to accusing his own soul' and that 'God has forgiven you ... but he leaves you in grief because that is good for your soul' are, to the Fathers, wholly a part of the endeavour for complete transformation into the love of God; and we should not be surprised to find the same ideas in Pusey, who set himself the same goal and whose reliance on the Fathers is unquestioned.[33] As

---

grow. Pusey to Keble, 7 December 1846, LBV 102; Keble to Pusey, [n.d.] December 1846, LBV 98; Pusey to Sr Clara Maria [Hole], 15 September 1880, LBV 125. Pusey's proposed rule is discussed in Liddon, *Life*, 3:105–11 but is not given in full.

30. Pusey to Keble, 26 September 1844, in LBV 101; Liddon, *Life*, 3:96–97; cf. Mt. 11.5.

31. Benedicta Ward, 'A Tractarian Inheritance: The Religious Life in a Patristic Perspective', in Rowell, *Tradition*, 220–1; William of St. Thierry, *The Golden Epistle of Abbot William of St. Thierry*, trans. Walter Shewring (London: Sheed and Ward, 1973), §6, 42; Lorenzo Scupoli, *The Spiritual Combat* (Mesa, AZ: Scriptoria, 2009), 5–7. Cf. Pusey, 'Justification' (Oxford: John Henry Parker, 1853), 39–41, in *Nine Sermons, Preached before the University of Oxford, and Printed, Chiefly between 1843–1855*, new edn (Oxford: James Parker, 1879), paginated individually (hereafter *US I*); 'The Doctrine of the Atonement', in *Sermons Preached before the University of Oxford between 1859–1872* (Oxford: James Parker, 1872), 237–8, 242 (hereafter *US II*); *The Real Presence of the Body and Blood of Our Lord Jesus Christ the Doctrine of the English Church* (Oxford: James Parker, 1869), 204–9 (hereafter *English Church*). William (a friend of Bernard of Clairvaux, whose *Sermons on the Song of Songs* informed Pusey's contributions to the *Sermons on Repentance* – see below n. 34) recommends that the monk think 'everywhere light save with thee' as the beginning of the road to being filled with the love of God. *The Spiritual Combat*, meanwhile, emphasizes distrust of self, and three of the four means given for attaining it involve the contemplation of sin; this is, however, only the *first* step in the whole of the Christian life and leads immediately on to trust in God.

32. Geoffrey Rowell, 'The Anglican Tradition: From the Reformation to the Oxford Movement', in Dudley and Rowell, *Confession*, 107.

33. Sayings of Abbas Ammonas and Apollo, given in Benedicta Ward, trans., *The Sayings of the Desert Fathers: The Alphabetical Collection* (Kalamazoo: Cistercian, 1975), 26, 36.

Allchin notes, it is telling that Pusey's most eloquent preaching on union with God (in the *Sermons on Repentance* of 1845) is found at the culmination of the most painful period of his life.[34]

Pusey's personality, then, was not so dark or repulsive as has been popularly believed. The deepest problem, however, for Pusey's reputation, lies in the question of his interest as a theologian. This can be divided into two parts. The first is a matter of accurate historical placement and assessment. Pusey is often seen as a mere 'conservative', simply defending an established theology, or as adopting an essentially Roman Catholic position. In either instance, Pusey is not interesting in himself, because his positions were formulated by others; at best, he becomes a minor historical case study. Or, in a related phenomenon, he is treated simply as a 'Tractarian'. Pusey features most frequently in studies of the Oxford Movement as a whole, either under Newman's shadow (Härdelin's study of Tractarian eucharistic theology, valuable though it is, falls into this category) or as merely one point of evidence for the broader tendencies of the Movement (thus Nockles, Herring and other more recent writers). Both versions of this treatment, however, have a flattening effect. As Owen Chadwick notes, 'In trying to represent the mind of a movement, we are faced with the difficulty that movements have no mind. … Even the closest of associates may sometimes contradict each other, and on matters which are not unimportant.'[35] In reality, Pusey held a mixture of appreciation and criticism both for the Protestant 'old' high church tradition within Anglicanism and for Roman Catholicism. Similarly, although he was clearly a 'Tractarian', the members of the Oxford Movement (to Chadwick's point) did not always hold a unified position, and Pusey in particular differed from many of his colleagues within the Movement – even, occasionally, from his dear friend John Keble. It

---

Another saying of Abba Ammonas (27) bears a striking correlation to Pusey's commitment not to use upper-class travel. There is some question whether Pusey specifically read the writings of early desert monasticism: there is no clear evidence to this effect, but Ward considers it probable, given the parallels in Pusey's spirituality. Benedicta Ward, 'Tractarian Inheritance', 221-2; cf. Pusey's Rule, in Pusey to Keble, 7 December 1846. LBV 102.

34. Cf. Allchin, *Participation*, 53-4, 61; E. B. Pusey, ed., *A Course of Sermons on Solemn Subjects Chiefly Bearing on Repentance and Amendment of Life* (Oxford: John Henry Parker, 1845), discussed in text as *Sermons on Repentance* (hereafter cited as *SR*). The period from 1839 to 1845 included the death of Pusey's wife and one daughter (another having died previously), his suspension from preaching in the University and Newman's secession to Roman Catholicism. It is worth noting that Pusey always uses language of 'chastisement' with regard to his personal misfortunes, which connotes God's loving correction, rather than punishment (Heb. 12:6); cf. E. B. Pusey, 'The Value and Sacredness of Suffering', in *Plain Sermons by Contributors to the Tracts for the Times*, [ed. Isaac Williams and W. J. Copeland] (London: J. G. F. and J. Rivington, 1841), 3:291-309 (hereafter *Pl. S.*). See also John Saward, *Perfect Fools: Folly for Christ's Sake in Catholic and Orthodox Spirituality* (Oxford: Oxford University Press, 1980), 204-7.

35. Owen Chadwick, *Spirit*, 21.

would be an even greater mistake to identify Pusey with the younger generation of ritualists – of whom he was highly critical – or later Anglo-Catholicism. Albrecht Geck has rightly complained that Pusey's early Protestantism has too often been overshadowed by his later (supposed) Anglo-Catholicism, but the solution is not merely to emphasize his early years while allowing this period to remain disconnected from his later development.[36] Rather, we should ask how his later Tractarianism was shaped by his earlier adherence to, and critique of, high church Protestantism. Such an historical assessment highlights Pusey's independence in driving an evolution of Anglican theology, which contrasts sharply with elements of later Anglo-Catholicism which *are* imported from other traditions.[37]

Second, there is the closely related question of Pusey's originality. Beginning with Newman's *Apologia pro vita sua*, Pusey has been characterized as contributing 'scholarship' to the Oxford Movement, rather than original thought – as better at reproducing the ideas of others than at thinking for himself.[38] Despite this negative portrayal of Pusey later in his life, Newman had earlier noted the 'largeness, profundity, and novelty' of Pusey's thought, and we should expect to be able to trace this throughout his work.[39] David Brown identifies points of continuity between Pusey's earlier and later thought, in his emphasis on human fallibility, a rough, crisis-driven view of history and his pattern of appealing to underlying principles, and argues that these characteristics make him both more original than Newman and more relevant to the present day: 'However apparently remote, Pusey's stern face and asceticism actually better anticipated the complexities of our current dilemmas.'[40] Setting aside, for the moment, the question of Pusey's relationship to Newman, this study, like Brown's essay, argues that Pusey's originality and ongoing relevance to theology lie in his engagement with 'underlying principles' of theology, in particular the hermeneutical questions which led him to what

36. Geck, 'Concept of History', 388.

37. Pusey, of course, edited a number of Roman Catholic spiritual works for Anglican use. His purpose in doing so was pragmatic: Tractarian spirituality had opened questions not adequately addressed in existing Anglican literature, so Pusey found sources to meet the need, but edited them to conform to his understanding of Anglican theology. These redactions, however, exasperated his antagonists – both Protestants, who thought the revised works were but lures to the full-fledged perfidies of Romanism, and Roman Catholics, who saw Pusey as misrepresenting the true nature of the works and doing violence to their tradition.

38. John Henry Newman, *Apologia pro vita sua and Six Sermons*, ed. Frank M. Turner (New Haven, CT: Yale University Press, 2008), 185; Henry Chadwick, 'The History of the Oxford Movement: 150 Years On', in *Lift High the Cross: The Oxford Movement Sesquicentennial*, ed. J. Robert Wright (New York: Forward Movement Publications, 1983), 72–3. The relationship between Pusey's and Newman's theological perspectives is discussed in more depth in Chapter 2 under 'Allegory and the Sacramental Vision'.

39. Quoted in Liddon, *Life*, 1:164.

40. David Brown, 'Pusey', 348.

I describe as a 'sacramental vision', which interprets creation, the Scriptures and the Christian life.

This work is primarily intended to address the question of Pusey's ongoing relevance to theology, though as an exposition of his theology it will of course make his thought more accessible. It may also be hoped that it will begin to address the negative caricature of Pusey's personality which has hitherto been popular: the power of Pusey's preaching, one contemporary noted, came not from any rhetorical skill but from its 'single-minded force of love'; and the extent to which this permeates his theology will be evident in what follows.[41] As a study which addresses Pusey's standing as a figure of theological interest, however, this work is primarily concerned with the intertwined questions of his originality and historical influence. To this end, Chapter 1 addresses the question of Pusey's development and the continuity of his thought with the theology of the older high church tradition in the Church of England. In doing so, however, it raises the question of the overarching 'project' of Pusey's theology. This, I suggest, is to be found in Pusey's opposition to rationalism, and specifically in his diagnosis of the Church's chief vulnerability to it: the dis-integration of a holistic approach to faith into disconnected and increasingly atrophied emphases on apologetic theology and moralistic practice. Chapter 2 continues this broad discussion of Pusey's theological project by outlining his subsequent engagement with Patristic allegory, from which he drew the elements of his renewed 'sacramental vision' of creation's participation in, and manifestation of, Christ; and which therefore entailed his emphases on the concreteness involved in the communication of both meaning and grace, and on the centrality of the doctrine of union with Christ. The remainder of the study expands on this foundation by examining the way in which this 'sacramental vision' reshaped the theology Pusey inherited from the high church tradition. Chapters 3 and 4 discuss, respectively, his teaching on baptism and the Eucharist; Chapter 5 considers the interaction between sacrificial types and communion in Pusey's understanding of the atonement; and Chapter 6 carries this discussion forward into the sacramental realization of Christ's sacrifice in the Christian life. The conclusion then steps back from this close examination of Pusey's theology to consider more broadly his relevance within theology today.

Before proceeding with the main body of this study, however, there are two clarifications I wish to make regarding the nature of this inquiry. First, though 'systematic theology' in the strict sense is (as will be evident) entirely alien to Pusey's theological vision, this study aims nonetheless to develop a 'systematic' presentation of the underlying structures and connections within Pusey's thought, not an historical view of his development. While I address Pusey's development as a matter of necessity, the sketch provided is necessarily partial and provisional. A full study of Pusey's development is beyond the scope of this discussion; and

---

41. J. B. Mozley, *Essays Historical and Theological* (New York: E. P. Dutton, 1879), 2:155; cf. Liddon, *Life*, 1:2, 3:60–1, 4:377–82.

indeed, much of the work needed for a complete picture of it has not been done. Forrester remains the only academic biography of any length: more careful and more comprehensive studies of Pusey's personal life are needed, together with in-depth investigations of his interactions with high churchmen and Evangelicals, his attitudes towards both Roman Catholicism and other Protestant churches, and the sources of his theology, before more definite conclusions can be offered. Second (and for the same reasons), I do *not* claim that this sketch represents a conscious process – only an implicit logic – of development in Pusey; nor do I identify the historical stimuli for his development in any conclusive way. What I hope to offer, however, is a comprehensive view of Pusey's theology and an account of his 'sacramental vision' as the defining element in it. This, I believe, reveals the value in reclaiming Pusey for theology.

Chapter 1

PUSEY REINTERPRETED

This study sets out to give a comprehensive account of Pusey's theology. Almost immediately, however, it faces an obstacle, in the question of his development. The two most prominent accounts of Pusey's theological evolution, to date, assert that Pusey's participation in the Oxford Movement is linked to either one or two dramatic revolutions in Pusey's thinking, from an early liberalism to a later conservatism. According to these theories, a comprehensive account of Pusey's theology is impossible: the task requires continuity, precisely where they assert discontinuity. Due to the occasional nature of many of Pusey's works, the task of assessing his theology often requires tracing the threads of his thought on a topic through intermittent references in disparate works, to piece together Pusey's perspective on a given topic – precisely the kind of work these theories call into question. Moreover, it is often assumed that Pusey's eventual conservatism was firmly anti-intellectual (and, thus, academically uninteresting). This effectively limits discussion of his theological contribution to a small number of works that predate his adherence to the Oxford Movement – a result which is at least counter-intuitive, since Pusey is known primarily *because of* his contribution to the Oxford Movement and the works that stem from his activities in it.

However, both theories have deep flaws; and upon reassessing the movement of Pusey's thought, it appears instead to be characterized by the evolution of a consistent set of principles and concerns.[1] This makes, admittedly, for a less dramatic narrative of Pusey's development, but it does better justice to the depth and subtlety of his theology. The consistency of Pusey's thought is evident with respect to both facets of this study's analysis: he is consistent in grounding his theology in Anglican high church orthodoxy, and he is consistent in his concern that theology required a radical shift in perspective if it were to withstand the

---

1. For an alternative discussion of the consistency of Pusey's thought to that advanced here, see Brian Douglas, *Eucharistic Theology*, 32–3. Douglas holds that the 'modern orthodoxy' Pusey encountered in Germany (discussed below, under 'Pusey the progressive?') provided the foundation for Pusey's later 'mediating style' which held together reason, tradition and feeling.

coming storm of rationalism.[2] This chapter, therefore, will review the two theories of Pusey's supposed 'revolutions' and the grounds on which they are advanced, in order to argue for an overall pattern of *consistency* (rather than revolution) in Pusey's development, and in particular to articulate his roots in the older high church tradition and the critique which drove his broader theological project. However, because this discussion hinges on a number of details in Pusey's life, it will be useful to begin with a brief biography.

Biographical overview

Edward Bouverie Pusey was born on 22 August 1800, the second son of an aristocratic family. He attended school at Mitcham and Eton; then, after a year of private tutoring, entered Christ Church College at the University of Oxford. He excelled in university, taking first class in 1822. In 1823 he became a fellow of Oriel College (and a roommate of John Henry Newman), and the following year he won the prize for the University's Latin Essay. The mid-1820s also brought him to the attention of the Regius Professor of Divinity, Charles Lloyd (later Bishop of Oxford), who included Pusey in private lectures as part of a hand-picked group of the University's brightest young scholars. At Lloyd's instigation, Pusey made two extended trips to Germany (1825 and 1826–7), in order to learn both Hebrew and the latest biblical criticism. These trips were amazingly productive: in a short time he mastered not only Hebrew but also several other Semitic languages; though Lloyd and other friends worried that his work habits – including working up to fourteen-hour days – risked damaging his health. In 1828 he published his first

---

2. The high church tradition in Anglicanism emerged following the Restoration settlement of 1660. The name, originally pejorative, refers to their 'high' views of episcopacy and the ordained ministry (derived from the '*avant garde* conformity' of the seventeenth century) and of the dogmatic authority of the formularies of the Church of England (principally the Articles of Religion, Prayer Book and Ordinal, although some also include the Catechism and/or the Homilies). Because of this, they viewed themselves as holding the 'orthodox' position within the Church of England and were consistently opposed to views that asserted the priority of reason over dogmatic authority in matters of religion, which they classified as 'rationalism'. Despite political disfavour under Whig governments through much of the eighteenth century, high churchmanship remained strong in the parishes and regained political influence with the return of Tory governance in the early nineteenth century. However, while it was united by a general theological viewpoint and given expression by various societies and certain more organized political networks (most notably the influential 'Hackney Phalanx' around the businessman Joshua Watson and his clergy associates in the Hackney district of London), the high church tradition was neither so monolithic nor so cohesive as occasional reference to them as a 'party' might suggest. For an overview of recent historiography on the relationship between the high church tradition and the Oxford Movement, see Morris, *High Church Revival*, 1–38.

book (*An Enquiry into the Rationalism Lately Predominant in the Theology of Germany* – the central work in this chapter's discussion), which involved him in a series of literary skirmishes with the Cambridge high churchman Hugh James Rose. The same year, courtesy of Lloyd's patronage, he was appointed Regius Professor of Hebrew, a position he held for the rest of his life.

His chief task, on taking the Hebrew professorship, was to correct and complete the catalogue of the Bodleian Library's Arabic collection. This took until 1835; as a consequence, he largely missed the opening phases of the Oxford Movement. The triumvirate at the core of the Movement – Newman, Hurrell Froude and John Keble – had forged their friendship at Oriel while Pusey was in Germany, and had tempered their alliance through several controversies after Pusey had returned to Christ Church to take up his professorship. He supported the political emancipation of Roman Catholics in 1828–9 (they were opposed), and though he found Parliament's 1833 suppression of ten Irish bishoprics concerning, his measured opposition contrasts with Keble's denunciation of the act as 'National Apostasy', which inspired Newman to begin the Tracts for the Times.[3] Pusey only contributed two tracts (one a brief post-script) to the earlier part of the series; despite this contribution, he continued to hold reservations about the Movement. Nonetheless, in late 1835, Pusey overcame these reservations and marked his adherence to the Movement with three massive 'tracts' on baptism. These both saved the faltering series and changed it: later entries were no longer *tracts* (though they kept the name), but scholarly treatises. In the later 1830s, Pusey became a leading defender of the Movement amid its increasing controversies, and in 1843 he himself came under attack after delivering a devotional sermon on the importance of frequent communions ('The Holy Eucharist a Comfort to the Penitent'), for which he was suspended from preaching in the University for two years, on suspicion of teaching Roman doctrine.

These years, however, were also marked by deep personal tragedy. In 1817, Pusey had fallen in love with the fiery Maria Barker; but political differences between their families had prevented their marriage for over a decade, during which time he suffered deep depression. They married at last in 1828, after a brief delay caused by the death of his father; but their family life was marked by loss. Their daughter Katherine died in 1832; Maria herself died of tuberculosis in 1839; and another daughter Lucy died in 1844. His son Philip, despite ill health which prevented his taking holy orders, became a fair scholar in his own right, travelling the world at his father's behest in search of obscure patristic manuscripts; yet he too died in 1880, two years before his father. In the end, Pusey was survived only by his daughter Mary.

---

3. John Keble, 'National Apostasy Considered in a Sermon, Preached in St. Mary's Oxford before His Majesty's Judges of Assize on Sunday, July 14th, 1833' (London: A. R. Mowbray, 1931).

Newman converted to Roman Catholicism on 9 October 1845; just nineteen days later, the new church of St Saviour's, Leeds, was consecrated.[4] Pusey preached the *Sermons on Repentance* over the course of the consecration octave; of the friends who were to have joined him, most were detained by ill health or pastoral emergencies. This was, perhaps, fitting, as a sign of what was to come: Froude had died in 1836, and Keble (though an active correspondent) had long since retired to parish life, so Pusey quickly became the Oxford Movement's primary figurehead and statesman. Despite – or perhaps because of – his personal suffering, Pusey had the strength to hold the Oxford Movement on course through the late 1840s, and again through another rash of secessions after the conclusion of the Gorham case (1850), though parting shots from some Roman converts led to Pusey's secret inhibition by the Bishop of Oxford, Samuel Wilberforce, for over seventeen months.[5] Thereafter, Pusey continued to steer the Movement and defend its principles. Throughout this time, he fostered the revival of the religious life in the Church of England, and served as general editor of the Library of the Fathers. He died on 16 September 1882 and was buried beside his wife and children at Christ Church on 21 September.

Two theories of Pusey's 'revolutions'

The year 1835, which marked Pusey's full adherence to the Oxford Movement, is the turning point in both accounts of Pusey's supposed revolutions. David Forrester, in *Young Doctor Pusey*, argues that Pusey went through two major revolutions in his thinking, driven by the crises of his personal life. The first, completed in 1835, marked a shift from the earlier liberalism of the 1820s to political and theological conservatism, from a more generous spirituality to moral rigorism, and from an orientation towards new ideas coming out of Germany to an engagement with the early Christian Fathers; this was driven, Forrester maintains, by guilt over the deaths of his father and his daughter Katherine.[6] The second revolution,

---

4. Pusey had built St Saviour's as a monument to his own penitence; his daughter Lucy had donated the communion silver from her deathbed. Pusey retained patronage of the church, but repeated difficulties with the clergy he appointed (younger Tractarians, of less moderate views) became an ongoing source of frustration and soured his relationship with Walter Farquhar Hook, the Vicar of Leeds.

5. George Cornelius Gorham, an Evangelical, had been refused institution to the parish of Brampford Speke by Bishop Henry Phillpotts of Exeter, a high churchman, for having allegedly rejected the Prayer Book doctrine of baptismal regeneration. Phillpotts's ruling was upheld on appeal by the church courts, but overturned by the Judicial Committee of the Privy Council. High churchmen objected both to the apparent overthrow of what they believed to be official Church doctrine and to the overruling of ecclesiastical authorities in a matter of doctrine by a secular court.

6. Forrester, *Pusey*, 63–5.

tied up with the deaths of Maria and Lucy, was completed in 1845. Although he does not state it explicitly, Forrester strongly implies that this was a rejection of Protestantism and an embrace of Roman Catholic doctrine: he highlights Pusey's increasing emphasis on the Eucharist, his shifting attitudes towards the Reformation and Rome, and juxtaposes Pusey's endorsement of private confession in his two sermons on the *Entire Absolution of the Penitent* (1846) with the moral rigorism and the rejection of easy penitence found in his works of the later 1830s. The views Pusey held by late 1845, Forrester concludes, were 'the ones he was to retain for the remainder of his life'.[7]

Colin Matthew's 'Edward Bouverie Pusey: From Scholar to Tractarian' offers a similar perspective in putting forward a radical discontinuity in Pusey's thought. However, it is a simpler two-part distinction, contrasting the (supposed) intelligent liberalism of Pusey's German *Enquiry* (1828), which critiques the rigidity of scholastic Lutheran orthodoxy, with the (supposed) anti-intellectual conservatism of *Daniel the Prophet* (1864), which argues for an early date of the book of Daniel. Matthew's link between the two is Pusey's Tractarianism: his retreat from creative thinking was driven by his association with the Oxford Movement, which gradually involved him more and more in theological controversy, hardening him into a statesman and a polemicist, at the expense of his intellectual freedom.[8] Thus, in Matthew's view, the period from Pusey's association with the Oxford Movement in 1835 to Newman's secession in 1845 represents a period of gradual theological ossification.

In contrast to these theories, the view that will be advanced throughout this study is that Pusey is best understood as developing, albeit at times quite dramatically, the theology of the earlier high church tradition. In fact, the identification of Pusey with the high churchmen can be traced back as far as Newman's belittling portrait in the *Apologia*. Newman clearly respects novelty of thought: Whately and Froude brought him to oppose establishment, while Keble taught him sacramentality and refashioned Butler's doctrine of probability. Newman paints himself as a bold explorer into new territories: his *Lectures on the Prophetical Office of the Church* are 'directly tentative' because his aim of establishing an Anglican theology was too large to be 'the work of one man'.[9] This contrasts with his assessment of the old high churchmen. Rose is well connected, with a prominent reputation, a conservative predisposition and an admirable spirituality. William Palmer (of Worcester College) is immensely learned and 'decided in his religious views', though spiritually shallow; his *Treatise on the Church of Christ* is recognized as a major piece of theology, but 'authoritative' and 'in no sense ... a tentative work'. Pusey is treated similarly. Newman calls him 'ὁ‘ μέγας‘ on account of his scholarship, but describes him as 'haunted by no intellectual perplexities' and as

---

7. Forrester, *Pusey*, 206–10.
8. Matthew, 'Pusey', 101–24.
9. Newman, *Apologia*, 141–3, 148–9, 187–8.

'possessed pre-eminently' of 'confidence in his position'.[10] As Henry Chadwick notes, Newman attributes to Pusey no new intellectual insight but a greater sense of gravity, deeper scholarship and public respectability – the same description with which he dismisses the high churchmen.[11] But although Newman apparently meant to trivialize his friend's contribution to the Oxford Movement, and to his own development, this parallel contains a measure of truth. Pusey's respect for the high churchmen contrasts with Newman's dismissive attitude. While Newman increasingly distanced himself from the high churchmen, Pusey was reconciled with his old antagonist Rose; and despite the discomfort felt by many high churchmen towards the Oxford Movement, Pusey was always eager to align himself with the tradition of the Hackney Phalanx.[12] At the end of his life, reflecting on the Oxford Movement, he offered affectionate tribute to the older churchmen:

> It was often on my lips 'This is the Lord's doing and it is marvellous in our eyes.' There was a little seed scattered, and what a harvest of souls! But God had prepared the soil, and the fields were white to harvest. There was however a great deal of heart's devotion before, which never talked but acted. *I remember it in those before me*, of whom I learned.[13]

Both Newman's faint praise and Pusey's own tribute indicate a deeper connection between Pusey's thought and 'old' high churchmanship than Forrester or Matthew allow. But before that connection can be pursued in more detail, the question of revolution and continuity in Pusey's thought must first be discussed.

***

Matthew's argument has at least some superficial appeal. Certainly, Pusey's major works after the second edition of Tract 67 increasingly take on the nature of historical studies, or even compilations of authorities, in defence either of his own controversial positions or of some newly threatened, though previously uncontroversial, orthodoxy. But to stop there ignores Pusey's substantial collection of published sermons and addresses (a total of eleven volumes), and betrays the absence of any effort to identify the key principles of Pusey's 'creative' theology and determine whether or not they appear in his later work. Beyond this, Matthew

---

10. Newman, *Apologia*, 163–8, 187–8. Palmer of Worcester is not to be confused with his contemporary, the Tractarian ecumenist William Palmer of Magdalen College. All references in this work are, however, to the former.

11. Henry Chadwick, 'History', 72–3. Newman, *Apologia*, 183–5.

12. See Peter Nockles, *The Oxford Movement in Context: Anglican High Churchmanship 1760–1833* (Cambridge: Cambridge University Press, 1994), 280, 302–6, for discussion of Hackney Phalanx attitudes towards the Oxford Movement.

13. Pusey to Sister Clara, 22 August 1882, LBV 77; emphasis mine. Quoted in Liddon, *Life*, 4:376.

makes two assumptions about theology which, when identified, raise further questions about his analysis. First, in framing Pusey's development as a shift from 'scholarship' to 'statesmanship', it is implied that theology is properly the province of isolated academics thinking in detachment from the life of the Church. Yet if controversy were inimical to theology, the theological *corpus* would be much more slender than it is; moreover, the separation between theology and the Church which Matthew implies is increasingly seen not as normative but as problematic. Second, if Pusey's transition from liberal to conservative is one from originality to uncreativity, a further element of prejudice is added: it must at least be *possible* to have uncreative liberals and creative conservatives. Finally, beyond these assumptions, the accuracy of Matthew's treatment of the *Enquiry* and of *Daniel* has been sharply questioned. Robert Crouse observes that 'the hypothesis of Pusey as a young liberal seems far-fetched, and the evidence of his early associations with German scholarship seems, in fact, to point in the opposite direction'.[14] More recently, Timothy Larsen finds Matthew's treatment of *Daniel* so problematic as to question if Matthew even read the work.[15] Matthew's contrast between Pusey's earlier and later years, however, and the works involved in it, will be considered in due course.

Forrester, in contrast, relies heavily on a psychoanalytic approach emphasizing the growing gloom of Pusey's personal outlook as the motivating factor in his intellectual shifts.[16] Forrester's study also includes useful chapters on Pusey's German studies and his links with Evangelicalism; unfortunately, the main argument of the book is driven by his troubling account of Pusey's family life and his attempt to link it to Pusey's theological development. As the previous chapter indicated, Forrester's account of Pusey's family life is open to serious question. And indeed, his account of Pusey's intellectual development fares no better.

As evidence for his theory, Forrester offers a theological analysis focused on Pusey's attitudes about sin and forgiveness. From 1828, Forrester quotes,

> Sorrow must indeed accompany us until we are finally freed from its parent, sin; yet the 'godly sorrow' which a Christian must daily feel, if he thinks daily upon himself need be no harrasing [sic] feeling ... his sorrow ... quickens his diligence, his anxiety, and petitions for assistance, but does not make him despond.[17]

---

14. Robert D. Crouse, '"Deepened by the Study of the Fathers": The Oxford Movement, Dr. Pusey, and Patristic Scholarship', *Dionysius* 7 (1983): 141.

15. Larsen, 'Pusey and Holy Scripture', 504.

16. The notion of Pusey as 'gloomy' is hardly new, as some of the anecdotes recounted in the introduction would indicate. It is difficult, of course, to reconstruct the attitudes of nearly a century in which little was written on Pusey. But the fact that, in the early twentieth century, Pusey's biographers continued to refute such portrayals suggests that Forrester may be at fault simply for reinvigorating a lingering bias, rather than for inventing a new one.

17. Pusey to Maria, 6 April 1828, LBV 23; quoted in Forrester, *Pusey*, 61.

And:

> The past must be to every Christian a source of sorrow; yet one knows that on repentance the past is forgiven us, that our sins are blotted out in the blood of Christ, that in the sight of God they are pardoned, as though they had never been … the sting of sorrow is removed, its fruits are not or need not be 'uneasiness'.[18]

These passages are contrasted with Pusey's language of the 'hard and toilsome way of Repentance' in the 1835 tracts on baptism, and, as further evidence that Pusey 'began to regret his former attitudes on the subject of sin and repentance', Forrester quotes a letter to Maria in which Pusey rejects the tendency to excuse or diminish past sin on the basis of some enjoyment or strong emotion mingled with it, and refers to the ten years before their marriage as an example:

> Had they been years in which I had waited patiently on God's will, then I might have had a right to refer to them with joy: as it is, shame ought to mix itself with the joy and thankfulness that God did, notwithstanding, bestowe you on me; and so though one may refer to it with gratitude … yet I could not, without doing harm to myself, refer to it without the solemn memory of past sinfulness.[19]

This contrast between 1828 and 1835 forms Forrester's first 'revolution' in Pusey's theology. Whereas this shift is concerned with the increasing rigour (in Forrester's analysis) of Pusey's attitude towards sin, the second 'revolution' involves means of addressing sin: Pusey's increasing emphasis on the real presence of Christ in the Eucharist and his endorsement of private confession, both of which are tied to his attitudes towards the Reformation and Roman Catholicism. To focus at present on confession – the other topics will be discussed in depth later in this chapter – Forrester contrasts statements Pusey made in 1835 and 1839 with statements from his 1846 sermons on absolution.[20] In 1835, Pusey held that the Roman practice of confession amounted *in practice* to a second baptism, restoring man to a perfect state of grace, with little effort or cost to the sinner.[21] Similarly, in 1839 Pusey protests against any system – Protestant or Roman – which is more concerned with easing the conscience than with teaching the gravity of sin.[22] In 1846, however, Pusey preached: 'Consciences *are* burdened. … They wish to be, and to know that they are in a state of grace. God has provided a means, however deeply

---

18. Pusey to Maria, 16 May 1828, LBV 23; quoted in Forrester, *Pusey*, 61.
19. Pusey to Maria, 6 November 1835, LBV 24; quoted in Forrester, *Pusey*, 67–8.
20. Forrester, *Pusey*, 197–9.
21. E. B. Pusey, *Scriptural Views of Holy Baptism*, TFT 67–9 (London: J. G. and F. Rivington, 1836), 58–9 (hereafter *Baptism 1*).
22. E. B. Pusey, *A Letter to the Right Rev. Father in God, Richard, Lord Bishop of Oxford* (Oxford: J. H. Parker, 1839), 83–8 (hereafter *Oxford*).

any have fallen, to replace them in it.'[23] This newfound emphasis on sacramental grace, Forrester argues, indicates Pusey's acceptance of the Roman Catholic views on confession that he had rejected only a few years earlier.

The most critical flaw in Forrester's analysis is that his second 'revolution' in Pusey's thought relies on a chronological error: by Pusey's own account (given at least twice), he was hearing confessions a year before his protest against facile forgiveness in 1839 – and he could hardly be arguing against his own practice.[24] And indeed, the 'contrasts' Forrester brings forward are not as dramatic as he would have us believe. In 1828, Pusey maintained that ongoing sorrow for past sin is necessary, although its 'sting' is eased by the assurance of God's mercy; in 1835, he protested against the tendency to excuse sin to avoid that sorrow, and observed that a decade of his life would have been happier had he trusted in God rather than becoming self-destructive in his understandably depressive emotional state.[25] In 1839, Pusey's objection to shallow notions of repentance is softened by rejecting the notion that to 'revert to past sin, is to doubt of Christ's mercy'; and while he insists that 'there are but two periods of *absolute* cleansing, Baptism and the day of judgment', he is equally clear that the emphasis on continual penitence and sorrow for sin in the liturgies of the Church of England are the means by which 'our Church sets' a penitent sinner 'in the way in which God's peace may descend upon him'.[26]

What Forrester sets before us, then, is not in fact a pair of dramatic shifts in Pusey's theology, as he would have us believe, but the uninterrupted evolution of a consistent perspective. This culminates in 1846:

> In Baptism, sins are suddenly and painlessly blotted out through grace; deep sins after Baptism are forgiven, but upon deep contrition which God giveth: and

---

23. E. B. Pusey, 'Entire Absolution of the Penitent [I]' (Oxford: James Parker, 1866), 52; in *US I*, paginated individually.

24. E. B. Pusey, *A Letter to the Right Hon. and Right Rev. the Lord Bishop of London*, 7th edn (Oxford: John Henry Parker, 1851), 3 (hereafter *London*); *The Church of England Leaves Her Children Free to Whom to Open Their Griefs*, 2nd edn (Oxford: John Henry Parker, 1850), 134 (hereafter *Richards*).

25. Forrester, *Pusey*, 61–8, 186–202; Liddon, *Life*, 1:41–44. At several points in the 1820s, Pusey worked himself to the point of physical collapse; in Germany, he is recorded to have worked fourteen-hour days (and longer), prompting several friends to express concern for his health. Liddon later notes that Pusey 'dreaded his love of occupation, as a diversion from … close dealing with conscience'. In light of this observation (which Liddon describes as a paraphrase of Pusey's own words), it is likely the overwork which characterized Pusey's studies in Germany (and at other points in the 1820s) was a similar avoidance of the emotions caused by his parentally enforced separation from Maria, and may well be the 'past sinfulness' to which he refers in the 1835 letter quoted above. Forrester, *Pusey*, 45; cf. Liddon, *Life*, 1:112–13, 3:95.

26. Pusey, *Oxford*, 83–4, 92–3.

deep contrition is, for the most part, slowly and gradually worked into the soul, deepening with deepening grace, sorrowing still more, as, by God's grace, it more deeply loves; grieved the more, the more it knows Him Whom it once grieved, and through that grief and love inwrought in it by God, the more forgiven. So then, by the very order of God with the soul, (except when He leads it in some special way, and by the Cross and His own overflowing love blots out the very traces of past sin and its very memory,) continued sorrow is not only the condition of continued pardon, but the very channel of new graces, and of the renewed life of the soul. Sorrow, as it flows on, is more refined, yet deeper. To part with sorrow and self-displeasure would be to part with love; for it grieveth, and is displeased because it loves.[27]

In this sermon, Pusey repeatedly emphasizes that the condition of forgiveness is ongoing sorrow for sin; and as absolution is ultimately dependent upon Christ's judgement of the penitent's sincerity, 'continued sorrow' – even *after* absolution – is a necessary aspect of true penitence.[28] Pusey's penitential doctrine thus exhibits not 'revolution' – from laxity to rigour and thence from rigour to the acceptance of sacramental grace – but the gradual deepening of a continuous emphasis on the necessity of sorrow for sin, which persists from his early correspondence with Maria through to his mature doctrine.

To be clear, this assertion of continuity does not exclude development: Pusey's preaching in the 1830s often strikes a stern note, which contrasts with the warm fervour of his later sermons.[29] Nonetheless, even late in his life, the concerns of 1839 are echoed in Pusey's advice that private confession to a priest should be regular but not too frequent: frequent confessions, he thought, tended to bolster self-confidence by a superficial reliance on the rite, whereas the right use of confession should leave time for real penitence.[30] Indeed, Pusey's position in 1846

---

27. Pusey, 'Entire Absolution I', 23–4. Given that Pusey is arguing for confession as the *ordinary* means established by God for the comfort of penitents within the Church – even if it had been neglected – the exception Pusey mentions appears to reflect appreciation for the Evangelical 'conversion experience'. Pusey's language of 'deep' repentance in this quotation represents another thread of continuity in addition to those discussed here: compare, from 1827, 'the further a Christian actually advances, … the stronger will be the sense of his deficiencies, the deeper … sense of sin will he have; yet he will not be disheartened nor discontented'; and from 1835, 'We are in a lethargy. … *Until we lay deeper the foundations of repentance, the very preaching of the Cross of Christ becomes but a means of carnal security.*' Pusey to Maria, 4 October 1827, LBV 23; *Baptism 1*, 61–2, emphasis Pusey's.

28. Pusey, 'Entire Absolution I', 24. This theme is shared with Keble, who describes a 'calm deep loving sorrow' for past sin as a 'privilege of the blessed', given by God 'after deep penitence'. John Keble, 'Hell', in Pusey, *SR*, 88.

29. See Chapter 6 under 'Baptism, sacrifice and communion'; and cf. Chapter 3, n. 140.

30. Pusey to Sr Clara Maria, n.d. [1877], LBV 125; Pusey to Sr Clara, [April] 1882, LBV 77.

is not too far removed from his position in 1828, that 'the past must be to every Christian a source of sorrow; yet one knows that on repentance the past is forgiven us, ... the sting of sorrow is removed.'[31] If there is a difference, it is that his tone is deeper, his eloquence higher and his theology more explicitly grounded in love. As Geoffrey Rowell notes, 'Penitence is not punishment, it is at its heart an expression of love, a response to the greatness of the love of God, in creation, redemption, and sanctification. The reality of that grace, the reality of the penitence which it calls forth, and the reality of the salvation God offers are the true themes of Pusey's teaching.'[32]

These points of continuity, however, also provide the first topics for considering Pusey's relationship with the old high churchmen. Forrester suggests that (according to his theory) Pusey's newfound rigour with regard to post-baptismal sin was a product of his recently initiated acquaintance with the Fathers, begun under Newman's influence in the early 1830s. It is, however, likely that Pusey's knowledge of the Fathers began somewhat earlier: upon finishing his undergraduate degree, Pusey had received a folio collection of John Chrysostom and other Fathers; his mentor Charles Lloyd placed considerable emphasis on the importance of reading primary sources which Pusey clearly acquired; and Pusey is known to have attended the Patristics lectures of August Neander during his visits to Germany.[33] In any case, Pusey's opinions on baptism probably come from another source. Baptismal regeneration was a characteristic doctrine of the high churchmen. As early as 1823, he had defended it in friendly debates with Newman (then an Evangelical).[34] The main thrust of Pusey's teaching on baptismal regeneration was widely appreciated by high churchmen.[35] While the strength of Pusey's language on post-baptismal sin in Tract 68 shocked some of the older school – Rose, in particular, thought his language far too strong – Pusey's realism about dying to sin in baptism is itself a part of the high church perspective which he inherited.[36] Pusey's notes from Lloyd's lectures on Romans do not mince words about the gravity of post-baptismal sin:

---

31. Calhoun observes the structural continuity of Pusey's thought on baptism and repentance, noting that the difference between 1835 and 1846 is rather in the balance of optimism assigned respectively to the possibility of maintaining baptismal grace versus that of restoring it. J. B. Mozley thought Pusey's development on this point displayed 'a regular, continuous, and successive progress'. Calhoun, 'Conversion', 172; J. B. Mozley, *Essays*, 2:157–8.

32. Rowell, *Vision*, 79–80.

33. E. S. Ffoulkes, *A History of the Church of S. Mary the Virgin* (London: Longmans, Green, 1892), 401; Liddon, *Life*, 1:85–7.

34. John Henry Newman, *Autobiographical Writings* (New York: Sheed and Ward, 1957), 203.

35. See, e.g., Henry Phillpotts to Pusey, 10 November 1849, LBV 59.

36. Liddon, *Life*, 1:351–2.

Unless the Divine nature be itself changed, sin must remain equally odious in the sight of God, and Christians who relapse into sin after being called to Christianity must still remain liable to the divine wrath. The first principle indeed of the Christian Faith is surely this: that the Lord hateth iniquity with a perfect hatred, and, he who in consequence of his adoption of this principle, and the conviction of his own sin has taken refuge in the remedy, which Christianity has provided for him, will surely be acting against the first principle of his Faith, if he falls back into those sins, which made him first embrace the Christian faith.

This conclusion is stated to be 'beyond all controversy'. The consequence of this, the continuing discussion makes clear, is that, while forgiveness is possible upon repentance, any post-baptismal sin amounts to a voluntary renunciation of baptism.[37]

Confession and absolution form a second link back to the high churchmen. Forrester holds that this is a later development in Pusey's thought, influenced by patristic teaching and by John Keble, who had begun hearing confessions as early as 1826.[38] However, although Pusey himself only began hearing confessions in 1838, and only made his first confession (to Keble) in 1846, the idea was not a new one. Keble's practice is the first indication that this was not solely a Tractarian novelty, as it predated the tracts by seven years, and the impetus towards confession within the Movement (driven by Pusey's works on baptism) by more than a decade.[39] Nor was Keble idiosyncratic except in *doing* what others only talked about. In fact, both the continental and English reformers had been ambivalent towards private confession, valuing it as an ascetical tool and an assurance of the Gospel promise of forgiveness, while criticizing various abuses and the Roman *requirement* of auricular confession; this attitude was held more or less consistently in the English church up to the eve of the Oxford Movement.[40] Forrester also acknowledges the encouragement given by Walter Farquhar Hook – a conservative high churchman, though often sympathetic to the Tractarians – to Pusey's interest in absolution, during the controversy over his views on post-baptismal sin.[41] Several others can be added: Rose had similarly pointed to absolution in responding to Pusey's tracts on baptism, and Edward Churton wrote appreciatively of Pusey's sermon of January 1846.[42] In 1832, William Palmer of Worcester College had emphasized the continuity of the provisions for

---

37. Charles Lloyd, Lectures on Romans, in Pusey Papers – Notebooks, Pusey House, 6:1, 4, 12–13. The notes are undated, but in a notebook with an 1823 watermark; although clearly written in Pusey's hand, Liddon remarks, 'In many cases the strong, clear sentences are evidently Dr. Lloyd's.' Liddon, *Life*, 1:62–3. This document will be cited by reference to chapter and verse in Romans.

38. Forrester, *Pusey*, 200.

39. J. B. Mozley, *Essays*, 2:157–8.

40. Geoffrey Rowell, 'The Anglican Tradition', in Dudley and Rowell, *Confession*, 91–106.

41. Forrester, *Pusey*, 200, 205.

42. Liddon, *Life*, 1:351–2, 3:69.

confession in the Prayer Book office for the visitation of the sick with the wider Western tradition dating back to at least 494.[43] Absolution was, in fact, not a foreign idea even to pre-Tractarian Evangelicals. In the same year, Pusey's former undergraduate tutor, Thomas Vowler Short, wrote, 'Confession to a priest is no where [sic] mentioned [in Scripture] as absolutely necessary; but reason, as well as the word of God, strongly points out, that to acknowledge our faults, especially to one vested with spiritual authority over us, must be a most effectual means of restraining us from the commission of sin.' Short concludes that the neglect of confession is 'a misfortune to our church'.[44] Later high church objections to Pusey's practices as a confessor, which emerged especially in response to the attacks made on Pusey in the wake of the Gorham judgement, were focused not on theology but on more practical matters. Bishop C. J. Blomfield of London worried that Pusey's ministry as a travelling confessor violated diocesan and parochial jurisdiction; Samuel Wilberforce of Oxford maintained that private confession should be occasional – either in extreme cases of conscience or on the deathbed – rather than regular. Phillpotts of Exeter shared these concerns and doubted whether sins needed to be enumerated, as long as there was evidence of repentance.[45] Nonetheless, this pre-Tractarian interest in private confession and absolution, and the acceptance of Pusey's theology (if not of his practice) among the older school of high churchmen, suggest that Pusey's own views represent a theological deepening of his inherited high church theology, not a new discovery or a departure from it.

Pusey the progressive?

Forrester's theory thus appears to do no more justice to Pusey's development than Matthew's; specifically, the topics of post-baptismal sin and private confession have suggested both that his development should be considered more as a gradual process of deepening than as one or more 'revolutions', and that his intellectual roots remain, throughout his life, firmly planted in the old high church tradition. This suggestion, however, needs further examination; and the fundamental question on this point is, how 'liberal' was Pusey in his early years, how 'conservative' in his later years, and how do we connect the two periods? This question has both political and theological dimensions, and at least in Pusey's early life (before 1829

---

43. William Palmer, *Origines Liturgicae, or Antiquities of the English Ritual, and a Dissertation on Primitive Liturgies* (Oxford: The University Press, 1832), 2:228. This provision in the office for the visitation of the sick was the foundation of later Anglo-Catholic arguments for the legitimacy of private confession within the Church of England. (This work is drawn partially from Lloyd's notes on the same subject.)

44. Thomas Vowler Short, *A Sketch of the History of the Church of England to the Revolution of 1688* (Oxford: S. Collingwood, Printer to the University, 1832), 254–5.

45. Blomfield to Pusey, 3 December 1850, LBV 40; Phillpotts to Pusey, 20 and 23 October 1850, and n.d. [1853?], LBV 59; Liddon, *Life*, 3:309.

and the Catholic Relief bill) it is possible to draw connections between the high churchmen and the Tories as 'conservatives', and the latitudinarians and the Whigs as 'liberals'. After 1829, the political landscape shifted, and there was much less of an identification between political and theological parties.[46] Pusey's theological development will be discussed in due course; for the moment, Pusey's political views will further illustrate the evolution – not revolution – of his thought.

Forrester in particular has identified an early liberal streak in Pusey's politics, which he attributes to a youthful reaction against the extreme conservatism of Pusey's father. Pusey expressed sympathy for Queen Caroline during her 'trial', for instance, and supported Catholic Emancipation – the removal of political disabilities for Roman Catholics – as early as 1825.[47] Support for the queen, however, was widespread; and despite the use of her cause by radicals, the accusations of infidelity hurled at both parties were equally, if not more, verifiable with regard to her husband George IV. Pusey's views may well have been a reflection of the broader public sympathy for the queen, rather than an indication of radicalism.

Emancipation is also less of a political index than might be thought. It proves certainly that Pusey was not an ultra-Tory, and that he was not of the most rigid high churchmanship. Beyond eliminating that extreme position, however, it proves little. While the cause had been raised repeatedly by reforming politicians since at least the end of the eighteenth century, the developments leading up to its approval in 1829 show that by the 1820s, some conservatives had reconciled themselves to the idea. The legislation was proposed by the Duke of Wellington's Tory government, admittedly in reaction to the election in 1828 of the Roman Catholic political activist Daniel O'Connell as MP for County Clare, Ireland. But even before O'Connell's election, Phillpotts – the 'most militant of Tory clergymen' – had privately suggested conditions under which Emancipation might be acceptable to high church principles.[48] The vast majority of high churchmen

---

46. The Tory government of the Duke of Wellington passed the Catholic Relief Bill, granting political emancipation to Roman Catholics, in 1829. The legislation was, however, at odds with traditional Tory value for the 'Protestant Constitution' and deeply divided the party; its political power collapsed the following year, to be replaced, after a few years, by Robert Peel's Conservative Party. The Whigs faded more gradually, but by the end of Pusey's life had been replaced by the Liberal Party, led (through much of the later nineteenth century) by William Ewart Gladstone.

47. Forrester, *Pusey*, 14. Caroline had married the future George IV in 1795 to effect an alliance between the United Kingdom and Brunswick during the Napoleonic Wars. The marriage was unhappy from the beginning, and upon George's accession in 1820 he attempted to divorce her by Act of Parliament; these proceedings (which ultimately failed) came to be referred to as her 'trial'. She died shortly after his coronation – which she was barred from attending – in 1821.

48. E. A. Varley, *The Last of the Prince Bishops: William Van Mildert and the High Church Movement of the Early Nineteenth Century* (Cambridge: Cambridge University Press, 1992), 129; Owen Chadwick, *The Victorian Church*, 2nd edn (London: Adam and Charles Black, 1970), 1:10.

still opposed the bill; nonetheless, the leading ecclesiastical contenders both for and against it were high churchmen: Pusey's own mentor Charles Lloyd, Bishop of Oxford, and the formidable William Van Mildert, Bishop of Durham. Van Mildert had previously committed himself to oppose any form of emancipation as a matter of principle. Lloyd, however, had been the tutor of Sir Robert Peel, home secretary in Wellington's government (and a future prime minister); both personal loyalty to his pupil and his more pragmatic temperament led him to support the bill. Their arguments for and against the bill can help to illuminate the nature of the debate within high church circles, and (most importantly with regard to Pusey) the grounds on which a high churchman might have supported Catholic Emancipation.

Lloyd spoke in support of the bill on 2 April 1829. He argued that emancipation was both necessary and inevitable; necessary, to prevent a civil war, and inevitable, due to the 'progress of public opinion' throughout the UK, especially as reflected in 'the course which has of late years been taken by the talent and education of the country'.[49] He was clear in expressing his regret at this progress, and his affection for the existing form of the Establishment, but

> the stream has passed into a different channel, and is, in my judgment, uncontrollable by any human power; and it remains only for those who, like myself, behold these things with fear, and agony, and sorrow, to rely upon that wise and bounteous Providence, who can turn all things unto good, can bring light out of darkness, and order out of anarchy.[50]

Nonetheless, the tensions of the time raised the spectre of war; and as the changing public mood made emancipation inevitable, war to prevent it could not be *just*, according to the understanding of Christian moral theology. Moreover, delaying the passage of emancipation would exacerbate the political pressures of the debate and lead, in the end, to worse consequences for the Church of England.[51] Considered in such a light, passage of the bill became a moral duty.

The next day Van Mildert offered a rebuttal. He had been absent the day before and had only been informed of Lloyd's speech by hearsay. Consequently, he mistook several of Lloyd's arguments in his rebuttal.[52] A recurring theme

49. *Hansard's Parliamentary Debates* (London: C. C. Hansard, 1829), n.s. 21:76.
50. *Parliamentary Debates*, n.s. 21:77.
51. *Parliamentary Debates*, n.s. 21:76–80.
52. Lloyd objected specifically to five of Van Mildert's allegations against him as mistaken: that he (Lloyd) had argued that state policy should be determined by pragmatic rather than moral considerations; that he believed the past abrogation of penal laws against Roman Catholicism to have predetermined (effectively) the question of the Protestant Constitution; that he supported the change in opinion to which he alluded in his arguments; that he had claimed that Rome had surrendered the temporal claims of the papacy; and that he had deprecated the character of an individual from whose arguments he had dissented. *Parliamentary Debates*, n.s. 21:156–7.

of his speech was the warning that although some – including Lloyd – were supporting the bill as a means to defend the church's Establishment, it was highly unlikely that the church's political opponents would respect that intent once given political power.[53] 'It was proposed to put a powerful lever in their hands, and it was expected that they would not make use of it.'[54] As evidence, he drew attention to the unlikely coalition of 'the Catholics and the Liberals, as they were called, of every description, down to the lowest grade of Socinians' who joined in supporting emancipation.[55] This reads now as an unpleasant polemic; but beneath the harsh rhetoric lies an ecclesiological concern about the identity of the Church of England as the nation's church and the integrity of Parliament's role, at the time, as its sole governing body.[56]

These arguments provide a background for locating Pusey's positions on this question, and similar reforms, on the British political spectrum of the 1820s and 1830s. His support for Emancipation, though it predated Lloyd's, was founded on similar grounds. Pusey thought the political disabilities of Roman Catholics were a cause of grievance against the Church of England; their removal would remove the grievance, thereby benefitting the established church.[57] This is a more optimistic outlook than Lloyd's, but still similar in principle to the argument that maintaining the status quo would in the long run be detrimental to the church. In contrast, however, although Pusey was less moved by Keble's Assize Sermon than Newman, by 1833 he nonetheless had come to oppose the new Whig government's reforms of the Irish church.[58] By then, Van Mildert's warnings had, to all appearances, come true: the whiggish coalition which so worried Van Mildert had *not* been content with the removal of political disabilities but *had* continued to make increasingly intrusive reforms to the church's structure. This does not mean that Pusey was opposed to reform, however. The same year saw his publication of *The Prospective and Past Benefits of Cathedral Institutions*, which addressed the proposed (and much needed) restructuring within the Church of England and put forth moderate proposals for repurposing Cathedrals as centres for training and mission, instead of either leaving them to patronize sinecures or abolishing them completely.[59]

53. *Parliamentary Debates*, n.s. 21:146–56.
54. *Parliamentary Debates*, n.s. 21:150.
55. *Parliamentary Debates*, n.s. 21:149.
56. Historically, the Church of England was governed by the Convocations of the Provinces of Canterbury and York. Convocation, however, had been suspended since the early eighteenth century and was not restored until 1852.
57. Forrester, *Pusey*, 15; Pusey, like many high churchmen, also opposed sacramental 'tests' of church membership for political purposes (repealed the year before emancipation), as sacrilegious; he repeated this view in 1835. Liddon, *Life*, 1:132–3; E. B. Pusey, *Subscription to the Thirty-nine Articles* (Oxford: J. H. Parker, 1835), 11–12.
58. Forrester, *Pusey*, 138–44; cf. Liddon, *Life*, 1:276.
59. E. B. Pusey, *Remarks on the Prospective and Past Benefits of Cathedral Institutions, in the Promotion of Sound Religious Knowledge and of Clerical Education*, 2nd edn (London: Roake and Varty, 1833).

Within a few years, Blomfield had taken charge of the Church Commissioners charged with reforming the Church of England and steered ecclesiastical reforms in accordance with high church principles.[60] The contrast between Pusey and Newman in their attitudes towards his leadership is telling: Newman remained hostile to reform and transferred this hostility to Blomfield. Pusey, however, remained on amicable terms with the Bishop of London until the controversies of the 1850s and donated £5,000 (more than either the King or the Archbishop of Canterbury) to Blomfield's fund for the building of London churches.[61]

Later in life, Pusey's attitude towards reform was often pragmatic. For instance, he opposed secularizing the Universities; but while he preferred to preserve their ecclesiastical character as training centres for the established church, he thought multi-denominationalism within the Universities, each denomination retaining its internal vitality, an acceptable alternative to the tepidity of making theology merely academic.[62] And he was highly adaptable, even in defeat: after opposing the expansion of professorial roles in the University, he nonetheless became one of the new professorial members of the Hebdomadal Board and carried out his duties with considerable skill and zeal.[63] Regarding party affiliation, Pusey commented in his later years: 'I could have been a Tory; but 1830 ended Toryism. I could not be a mere Conservative, i.e. I could not bind myself, or risk the future of the Church on the fidelity or wisdom of persons whose principle it is to keep what they think they can, and part with the rest.'[64] Rather, he chose to support those whom he trusted to have the best interest of the Church at heart. So, despite numerous practical differences, he was an ardent supporter of Gladstone, even after the latter's adoption of political liberalism; and though their friendship chilled somewhat on Gladstone's appointment of Frederick Temple as Bishop of

---

60. Robert Andrews notes that high churchmen had, in fact, been active in church reforms in the years before 1830. His observation with regard to that period also applies more broadly and is appropriate both to Blomfield and, indeed, to Pusey: 'The reform of existing structures not only appealed to their [high churchmen's] innate conservatism, it played to the high church strength of being able to work productively within the confines of the Established Churches of England and Ireland, especially in cooperation with the episcopate.' Robert M. Andrews, 'High Church Anglicanism in the Nineteenth Century', in *The Oxford History of Anglicanism*, ed. Rowan Strong, vol. 3, *Partisan Anglicanism and Its Global Expansion, 1829-c. 1914*, ed. Rowan Strong (Oxford: Oxford University Press, 2017), 146–7.

61. Newman, *Apologia*, 157; Liddon, *Life*, 1:330; S. A. Skinner, *Tractarians and the 'Condition of England': The Social and Political Thought of the Oxford Movement* (Oxford: Oxford University Press, 2004), 243.

62. Liddon, *Life*, 4:200–1.

63. Pusey's business acumen surprised many of his colleagues. Ieuan Ellis, 'Pusey and University Reform', in Perry Butler, *Pusey Rediscovered*, 315–19.

64. Liddon, *Life*, 4:199. Although it continued to exist for some time afterwards, the Tory party's influence collapsed in 1830, amid the upheaval following Catholic Emancipation.

Exeter in 1869, Gladstone nevertheless served as a pall-bearer at Pusey's funeral.[65] The well-being of the Church also guided his views on Establishment – in 1842, and again in 1850-1, he would express a classic high church belief in the benefits of Establishment for the nation, so long as the church remained free to guide the national conscience; but unlike more conservative churchmen, he was also willing to raise the possibility that disestablishment might be necessary to the preservation of the church: 'Better disestablishment than corruption.'[66]

Aside from the strictly political, it should also be noted that (contrary to widespread belief) the Tractarians had deep social concerns which were rooted in their sacramental theology. The more theological aspects of Pusey's social concerns will be treated in Chapter 3; for the moment it might be worthwhile to consider Pusey's attitudes towards women. This could, in fact, overlap with social critique: a caustic treatment of the gender difference in standards of sexual morality provided his rebuttal to the supposed moral superiority of the upper classes.[67] Beyond such critiques, his wife Maria fit poorly with Victorian expectations of women, due to a strong personality and a lack of patience for the frivolities of polite society, but was a competent Latinist who was able to assist with his textual criticism of Augustine for the Library of the Fathers; both her earnestness and her intellect seem to have contributed to his devotion to her.[68] Later in life, one of the more prominent aspects of Pusey's work was his support for the renaissance of Anglican religious orders, especially among women. While he was concerned not with feminism but the evangelization of the cities, this activity repeatedly brought him into conflict with fathers whose only vision for their daughters was for them to marry well, and it was founded on the conviction that women could have a vocation to God's service, which paralleled male vocations to the ordained ministry.[69] At least in this case, Pusey's concerns for the Church entailed the rejection of established social norms.

---

65. Liddon, *Life*, 4:196-7. Temple had been a contributor to the highly controversial broad church manifesto *Essays and Reviews*; though Temple's essay was in itself inoffensive, Pusey thought his connection with the volume made him unacceptable, particularly as a successor to Henry Phillpotts, the bastion of high church orthodoxy.

66. E. B. Pusey, *A Letter to His Grace the Archbishop of Canterbury, on Some Circumstances Connected with the Present Crisis in the English Church*, 3rd edn (Oxford: John Henry Parker, 1842), 13-14; *The Royal Supremacy Not an Arbitrary Authority* (Oxford: John Henry Parker, 1850), 208-15; *London*, 193-4; Pusey to Liddon, 6 April 1871, LBV 68; cf. William Palmer, *A Treatise on the Church of Christ*, 3rd edn (London: J. G. F. and J. Rivington, 1842), 1:372-6; 2:233-78; Peter Nockles, 'Pusey and the Question of Church and State', in Perry Butler, *Pusey Rediscovered*, 275-6.

67. E. B. Pusey, *Marriage with a Deceased Wife's Sister Prohibited by Holy Scripture* (Oxford: John Henry Parker, 1849), x-xii.

68. Maria to Pusey, 9 February 1828, LBV 21; Owen Chadwick, *Spirit*, 214.

69. E.g., Pusey to Sr Clara Maria, 19 April 1875, LBV 125.

Politically and socially, then, it appears that the distinctions between Pusey's earlier and later views cannot be drawn so sharply as has been suggested. In his early years, Pusey indeed saw the need for reform. But this was hardly unique to 'liberals', though he was perhaps more optimistic about such changes than others, such as Lloyd, who supported reform. And this attitude towards reform is not inconsistent with his later years. The most prominent change in him is the loss of his earlier optimism, though this should be interpreted in light of the century's shifts, both in politics and in churchmanship, which left high church Anglicans far less secure at the end of the century than under the Tory–high church alliance of the 1820s. Nonetheless, as his attitude towards women in the religious life demonstrates, he continued to be willing to break with the status quo where he believed it necessary for the good of the Church and the salvation of souls.

Continuity and evolution I: The Reformation and Rome

Pusey's views on confession and his political outlook both suggest that his development is best characterized by continuity of thought and purpose, accompanied however by increased caution and a more critical attitude, which replaced an earlier and less guarded optimism. Two further topics will serve as test cases to support this analysis: his attitudes on Protestantism and Roman Catholicism, and his views on ecclesiastical authority.

It is implied in Forrester's work, and in many others, that Pusey began his life a firm Protestant and ended it a Roman Catholic in all but name.[70] However, these shifts in Pusey's thinking may in fact be understood in a way parallel to what I have already argued with regard to his theological inheritance from the high church tradition and his social and political views: Pusey exhibits a deepening criticism of the Reformers and of anti-Roman polemic on the one hand, and an increasingly nuanced understanding of Roman Catholicism on the other; but does not abandon his own position which is, from very early on, best described as a form of 'Reformed Catholicism' – a theology grounded on broadly Reformed (though high church Anglican, and not strictly Calvinist) principles, while Catholic (again, in a broad sense) in outlook and orientation. Pusey's own theology is addressed in the remainder of this study; what will be examined here is the way in which his theological continuity is expressed in ongoing appreciation for the Reformation and reticence towards Rome, beneath his increasing critical nuance.

Pusey's shifting attitudes on the Reformation can be reviewed, in part, through his attitude towards Luther. In the *Enquiry*, Luther is a hero, someone who restored the spirit of true religion, only to have his renewal of the faith thrown off course by later systematizers and polemicists who drew narrow points of dogma from the reformer's every off-hand statement.[71] This early admiration for Luther

70. Forrester, *Pusey*, 206–10; Matthew, 'Pusey', 118.

71. E. B. Pusey, *An Historical Enquiry into the Probable Causes of the Rationalist Character Lately Predominant in the Theology of Germany* (London: C. and J. Rivington,

is often contrasted with Pusey's supposed 'unchurching' of Lutheranism and his increasing pessimism about the German church, especially after 1840 (as in, for instance, his opposition to the proposal for a joint Anglican–Lutheran bishopric in Jerusalem); these supposed 'reversals', however, are connected to nuances in his development and, as will be shown, do not reflect the 'revolutions' that Forrester and Matthew would suggest.[72] In contrast to Pusey's supposed rejection of Luther, there are many references which show a continuing appreciation lasting late into his life. In his work on baptism, foreshadowing the interpretations of the 'Finnish school', he cited Luther's commentary on Galatians as containing the very doctrine of union with Christ that he himself taught; in the second edition this is slightly strengthened, possibly as a quiet defence of the reformer from the assault of Newman's *Lectures on Justification* (published, in defence of Pusey's baptismal theology, in the intervening years).[73] In the mid-1850s, however, Pusey begins to discuss Luther's fallibility. In *The Real Presence of the Body and Blood of Our Lord Jesus Christ the Doctrine of the English Church*, he admits that the source of Lutheran 'errors' regarding the Eucharist is in Luther himself.[74] But, while denouncing the ubiquity of Christ's body as heretical, Pusey also defends Luther as holding a correct understanding of the *communicatio idiomatum*, being guilty only of exaggeration in his controversy with Zwingli.[75] Likewise, Luther's emphasis on the sacrament as kindling faith is not wrong, only incomplete. On both points, however, blame (again) falls more heavily on followers who systematized Luther's partial or exaggerated statements into dogmatic pillars of Lutheranism.[76] What these comments show is an increasing admission of Luther's fallibility as an individual teacher, within the consistent framework of his earlier critique – if systems built on Luther were flawed, he must himself have been imperfect. Still, beside the criticism, Pusey continues to show a lingering personal regard for Luther which lasts late into his life.

1828), 19–20 (hereafter *Enquiry I*); *An Historical Enquiry into the Probable Causes of the Rationalist Character Lately Predominant in the Theology of Germany. Part II. Containing an Explanation of the Views Misconceived by Mr. Rose, and Further Illustrations* (London: C. J. G. and F. Rivington, 1830), 367–70 (hereafter *Enquiry II*).

72. On the Jerusalem bishopric, see Liddon, *Life*, 2:248–60.

73. Pusey, *Baptism 1*, 28–30; *Scriptural Views of Holy Baptism, as Established by the consent of the Ancient Church, and Contrasted with the Systems of Modern Schools*, TFT 67, 4th edn (London: J. G. F. and J. Rivington, 1840), 120–4 (hereafter *Baptism 2*); Carl E. Braaten and Robert W. Jenson, eds, *Union with Christ: The New Finnish Interpretation of Luther* (Grand Rapids, MI: Eerdmans, 1998). Newman notices at least one similar passage, perhaps influenced by Pusey's work, but counts it as an exception in Luther's thought. J. H. Newman, *Lectures on Justification*, 2nd edn (London: J. G. F. and J. Rivington, 1840).

74. Pusey, *English Church*, 318–29.

75. For discussion of Pusey's views on Luther's eucharistic theology, see below in Chapter 4, under 'Real presence I: Pusey's reformed framework'.

76. Pusey, *English Church*, 96–109, 112–25.

While Pusey's lasting affection for Luther suggests that he had not entirely rejected the Reformation by the early 1840s, his attitudes towards one man offer only a narrow perspective. A broader view might be gained from surveying his appreciation for the English Reformation. There is little mention of the English reformers in his earliest writings, although we might assume that he gave them a standing similar to that of the continental reformers. By 1837, however, a note of criticism is introduced: Pusey sees Cranmer as weak-minded and too easily influenced by the continental refugees to whom he extended hospitality. He retains a high estimate of Ridley, however, and he makes the claim that Anglicanism had retained its catholicity because (unlike Lutheranism and Calvinism) it did not follow the teachings of any one man – a view which complements his developing critique of scholastic Lutheranism as a systematization of Luther.[77] Pusey, in contrast to Newman and Keble, initially thought the proposed Oxford memorial (1838; built 1841–3) to the martyrs of the English Reformation unobjectionable in principle, despite the fact that it was put forward as an anti-Tractarian polemic. The concerns he did have concerned the political nature of the proposal and his ongoing objection (first stated in the work on baptism) to glorifying individual *reformers*. As such, he offered a counter-proposal (which, however, received little support from any quarter) to build a church in thanksgiving for the benefits of the English *Reformation* as a whole.[78] Indeed, from the 1830s on, the catholicity of the Church of England – including its Reformation-era formularies – is a recurring theme in Pusey's work, and as late as 1865 he would refer to members of the Church of England as 'English Catholics' without distinguishing between parties.[79] While this approach demonstrates Pusey's tendency to take a 'long view' of the church, emphasizing its official core doctrine, apart from any temporary phases, controversies or personalities, it also demonstrates an appreciation for the Church of England that lasted throughout his life. Pusey could be increasingly critical of elements in the Church of England's past, as he was indeed of much in its present, without rejecting the Church of England itself.

On the other hand lies the question of Pusey's attitudes towards Roman Catholicism. If the supposition that Pusey turned his back on the Reformation in fact relies upon evidence which is better understood as indicating increasing criticism *together with* long-standing appreciation, the simplistic assumption that he abandoned Protestantism for an essentially Roman Catholic theology is also in need of significant reappraisal. It has been more accurately stated that his position after Newman's secession in 1845, like Keble's, was one of neutrality

---

77. E. B. Pusey, *Testimony of Writers of the Later English Church to the Doctrine of the Eucharistic Sacrifice, with an Historical Account of the Changes Made in the Liturgy as to the Expression of that Doctrine*, TFT 81 (London: Gilbert and Rivington, 1838), 15–17, 24–7.

78. Liddon, *Life*, 2:64–76.

79. E. B. Pusey, *The Church of England a Portion of Christ's One Holy Catholic Church, and a Means of Restoring Visible Unity. An Eirenicon, in a Letter to the Author of the Christian Year* (Oxford: John Henry and James Parker), 275 (hereafter *Eirenicon I*).

towards Rome; but this was not merely institutional neutrality from a position of theological agreement.[80] Rather, as the muscular ecumenism of the *Eirenicon* (three volumes, 1865–70) shows, it was a neutrality that balanced increasing institutional engagement with theological criticism. This criticism has its roots in the 1830s: in 1837, Pusey cites the doctrines of transubstantiation and purgatory as the primary contributors to the medieval corruption of the doctrine of the eucharistic sacrifice; in 1839, he not only repeats these claims but also faults Rome for substituting confession in place of repentance, for lowering its estimate of baptism and for withholding the eucharistic cup from the laity; in 1843, his sermon on the Eucharist specifically rejects theorizing as to the nature of Christ's sacramental presence – a jab at transubstantiation, spelled out more fully in 1853.[81]

But the roots of his engagement with Rome also run deep. The distinction of Newman's Tract 90 between the official doctrine of Rome and its popular theology – the 'received system', in Tractarian parlance – goes back at least to the 1820s. Lloyd had distinguished between official Roman teaching on images and popular idolatry in his defence of Catholic Emancipation; Pusey utilized a similar distinction between the official 'system of' and the popular 'system in' a church in 1830, and again appealed to this distinction in 1839 as the basis for his criticisms of Roman teaching on baptism and absolution.[82] In the 1860s, he employed the same distinction as the foundation of his engagement with Rome: the challenge of the *Eirenicon* was to separate official teaching from the errors of popular devotion.[83] Regarding the Eucharist, Pusey concludes, drawing on arguments by Robert Wilberforce, that the doctrine of transubstantiation which he (and the other Tractarians) had criticized as excessively physical in its conception was not so: rather, Anglicans had a more physical understanding of 'substance' than many Roman Catholic theologians, but when that was understood, he concluded, 'I know not what could be included in our term "substance," which the English Church affirms to remain, which is not included in the Roman term "accidents", which they also affirm to remain.'[84] Pusey still disliked the theory – in 1867 he made it clear to Newman that his inquiries about transubstantiation were in order

---

80. Rune Imberg, *In Quest of Authority: The 'Tracts for the Times' and the Development of the Tractarian Leaders, 1833–41* (Lund: Lund University Press, 1987), 173–6; Nockles, *Context*, 178–80.

81. Pusey, *Eucharistic Sacrifice*, 7–10; *Oxford*, 86–8, 114–17, 135–9; 'The Holy Eucharist a Comfort to the Penitent' (Oxford: John Henry Parker, 1843), 3 (hereafter 'Comfort'), in *US I*, paginated individually; 'The Presence of Christ in the Holy Eucharist' (Oxford: James Parker, 1871), 33–6, in *US I*, paginated individually.

82. *Parliamentary Debates*, n.s. 21:80–5; Pusey, *Enquiry II*, 41–5; *Oxford*, 86–8, 114–17.

83. Pusey, *Eirenicon I*, 98–9.

84. Pusey, *Eirenicon I*, 24; see also *Is Healthful Reunion Impossible? A Second Letter to the Very Rev. J. H. Newman, D.D.* (Oxford: James Parker, 1870), 75–90 (hereafter *Eirenicon III*). Cf. Robert Isaac Wilberforce, *The Doctrine of the Holy Eucharist* (London: John and Charles Mozley, 1853), 123–8.

to describe it properly, not as a matter of his own belief – but the two positions could be explained to one another.[85] In order for 'explanation' to proceed between the two sides, however, certain objectionable beliefs had to be cleared away. This took the form of putting the objections to Roman Catholic doctrine as strongly as possible.[86] This muscular approach to ecumenism was successful in drawing the desired response. Newman quipped, 'You discharge your olive-branch as if from a catapult'; but he also clarified that many of Pusey's quotations on devotion to the Virgin Mary were outside mainstream Roman theology.[87] But, besides the timely topics of the Immaculate Conception and Papal authority, several of the issues Pusey raises show a continuity with his criticisms of the 1830s.[88] So, for instance, while Pusey can reconcile himself with an intermediate state in which the deceased

---

85. Pusey, *Eirenicon I*, 228–9; cf. *On the Clause 'And the Son'* (Oxford: James Parker, 1876), 2; cf. Liddon, *Life*, 4:168. Brian Douglas argues that at the end of this correspondence with Newman, Pusey 'is prepared to use the term transubstantiation' and has come to a position 'in harmony' with the doctrine of Trent, albeit *without* accepting a change in the substance of the elements. This interpretation is, however, very hard to reconcile with the fact that the Council of Trent specifically anathematizes any position which *does not* set forth a change in substance of the elements (a difficulty of which Pusey, who discusses the Council at length in his *Eirenicon*, was surely aware), as well as with Pusey's stated personal indifference to transubstantiation as a theory, and the fact that he never uses the term with reference to his own position, even in writings after this correspondence. *Pace* Douglas, a more nuanced interpretation of Pusey's position in this correspondence (which also draws on his argument in the *Eirenicon*) is that Pusey believed, in light of Robert Wilberforce's questions about the definition of 'substance', that transubstantiation was capable of being explained by the Roman church in a fashion compatible with Anglican reservations regarding a change in substance, *should competent Roman authority choose to do so*. Despite this disagreement as to Pusey's final position, Douglas's overall account of Pusey's development with regard to transubstantiation generally supports the pattern described here, of increasing critical nuance in his engagement with both Anglican and Roman Catholic theology. Douglas, *Eucharistic Theology*, 143; 'Pusey and Transubstantiation', 93, 97; cf. Council of Trent, Session 13, 'Decree Concerning the Most Holy Sacrament of the Eucharist', chapter 2 and canon 2, http://www.thecounciloftrent.com/ch13.htm.

86. This is ironic, given Pusey's acceptance of Keble's cautions about such endeavours following the *Enquiry*; but his challenges were not directed against anything *he* saw as core matters of dogma, and this approach shows that Pusey's appreciation for academic debate continued nearly four decades later: it had not been extinguished, only muted on certain matters due to pastoral concerns.

87. Pusey, *Eirenicon I*, 257–8; *First Letter to the Very Rev. J. H. Newman, D.D.* (Oxford: James Parker, 1869; = *Eirenicon II*); J. H. Newman, *A Letter to the Rev. E. B. Pusey, D.D. on His Recent Eirenicon* (London: Longmans, Green, Reader, and Dyer, 1866), 9; Rowell, *Vision*, 196.

88. The Immaculate Conception was defined as Roman Catholic dogma in 1854; papal infallibility in 1870.

Christian grows in love for God through a period of longing before entering heaven, he still objects to more penal versions of purgatory; and when contemplating the possibility of reunion between the English and Roman churches, he insists that Anglicans should keep their own practices, including the administration of the cup to the laity.[89] In the end, however, criticism won out over engagement: the decision of Vatican I in favour of Papal infallibility (though it was foreseen) and the subsequent excommunication of Ignaz von Döllinger – 'Germany's ablest theologian', in Pusey's estimation – were, for Pusey, an infuriating disappointment, after which he abandoned any thoughts of reunion.[90]

Once again, the pattern that has emerged in other aspects of Pusey's development holds true: his shifts of opinion are more subtle, and contain a higher degree of continuity, than the theories of Pusey's 'revolutions' allow. It is true that after 1835 Pusey would not have thought of himself as a 'Protestant' – in part because the theological responsibility he felt was wider and older than merely the sixteenth century, but also because, having already identified polemicism as a distorting influence on theology, mere 'protest' was not sufficient for him. With regard to both the Reformation and Roman Catholicism, his subsequent development can be regarded as the gradual realization of this shift: a move from polemical support and opposition towards critical engagement with both. What his lingering affections and criticisms, however, suggest – and what the following study of his theology will show – is that as he built towards this position of critical engagement, his foundations nonetheless remained securely in high church Protestantism. While he saw himself, after 1835, as an 'English Catholic' rather than as a Protestant, his English Catholicism was not an Anglicized Roman Catholicism, but was in fact a critical engagement with, and development of, his own Protestant heritage.

Continuity and evolution II: Authority and the Church

In contrast with Forrester, Matthew grounds his account of Pusey's early theology on his *Enquiry* into German rationalist theology. This was written as a response to Hugh James Rose, who had in 1825 delivered a series of lectures at the University of Cambridge, published as *The State of the Protestant Religion in Germany*. Rose's lectures were addressed to ordinands, encouraging them to lives of practical devotion, rather than idle speculation, and warning them away from the errors of private judgement and scepticism, and the reading of pernicious German rationalist theology.[91] By his own admission, Rose lacked an adequate knowledge

---

89. Pusey, *Eirenicon III*, 96–122, 328–31.

90. E. B. Pusey, 'This Is My Body' (Oxford: James Parker, 1871), 7; in *US III*, paginated individually.

91. Hugh James Rose, *The State of the Protestant Religion in Germany; in a Series of Discourses Preached before the University of Cambridge* (Cambridge: J. Smith, Printer to the University, 1825), v–viii, 20–4, 110–12. 'Rationalism' in theology, characterized by the appeal to reason over (or even apart from) the dogmatic authority of revelation and

of the historical causes that had produced German rationalism, but this had not kept him from discussing its formative ideas. The work was ill-received in Germany. Pusey's German friends thought that Rose had painted with too broad a brush; many feared that an apparently ignorant and antagonistic work from a prominent English theologian was certain to harm the cause of Christianity in Germany. Pusey noted in early 1827 that Schleiermacher was the only theologian in Germany known to have a good opinion of Rose's book, and that 'the strongest against it are the most Christian'. He himself thought the negative reaction was excessive but an inevitable consequence of Rose's historical errors.[92]

Despite urgings from his German friends, Pusey was reluctant to respond; by 1827, he had finally decided to write a brief introduction for a response to be produced by Professor Karl Heinrich Sack; in the end, Sack's letter became the introduction to Pusey's historical study. The *Enquiry* was published in May 1828, a week before Pusey's diaconal ordination. Whereas Rose had attributed the corruption of German theology to the lack of adequate formularies (specifically, the absence of a uniform liturgy and the neglect of too-detailed confessional documents) and the lack of episcopal 'controul' to enforce doctrinal compliance, Pusey argued that Christianity had failed in Germany, not from lack of defences but through the subversion of its protectors.[93] As he would describe his view decades later, 'The rationalists ... were the lineal descendants not of the assailants of Christianity, but of its defenders.'[94] In Pusey's theory, the narrow, polemical scholasticism or 'orthodoxism' of the post-Reformation era produced a twofold reaction.[95] Intellectually, the narrowness and rigidity of confessional Lutheranism drove away those who could not easily fit within it; spiritually, the emphasis on polemical controversialism reduced the faith to an intellectual exercise

---

church doctrine, developed in reaction to the religious wars of the seventeenth century. The Romantic reaction to Enlightenment thought had both rationalist and anti-rationalist dimensions, reflected in (for instance) critical efforts to 'get behind' historical texts (notably the search for the 'historical Jesus') or (conversely) the search for modes of perception beyond mere reason (exemplified by the Romantic poets, as well as by the aspects of the Oxford Movement discussed in the following chapter).

92. Liddon, *Life*, 1:150–1. Matthew asserts that Pusey was deeply influenced by Schleiermacher during his time in Germany. Whatever influence he may have had, Pusey's statement suggests that his view of Schleiermacher was not uncritical. Cf. Matthew, 'Pusey', 106–9.

93. Rose, *Protestant Religion*, 14–20.

94. E. B. Pusey, *Collegiate and Professorial Teaching and Discipline* (Oxford: John Henry Parker, 1854), 53. Cf. *Daniel the Prophet: Nine Lectures Delivered in the Divinity School of the University of Oxford, with Copious Notes*, 3rd edn (London: James Parker, 1869), xxv–xxvi.

95. 'Orthodoxism' may be defined, parallel to rationalism (and pietism), as an approach to theology characterized by a preoccupation with narrow and overly defined standards of orthodoxy. This is exemplified in the *Enquiry* by the *Formula of Concord*.

disconnected from practical Christianity.[96] And so, on the one hand, those who were intellectually repelled by orthodoxy rejected not only its excesses but any certainty in the faith at all; on the other, the reforming movement of Arndt and Spener attempted to restore balance between practice and doctrine, but in the end the Pietists also slipped away, emphasizing morality at the expense of doctrine. Subsequent generations of apologists, however, learned from these reactions a faith grounded in reason and concerned primarily with morality. In the end, they could only defend Christianity, on principles adopted from its critics, as a system of rational morality; and so the faith lay helpless before the assault of secular philosophy.[97] However, Pusey closed on a hopeful note: his friends in Germany were engaged in an attempt to rescue the practical orientation of pietism and the intellectual openness of rationalism from their respective errors and turn them to the service of orthodoxy; although it was too soon to judge, he was optimistic about the future.

Albrecht Geck has noted that Pusey's position, and that of his German friends, is not so much liberal Protestantism, but a 'modern orthodoxy' aimed at 'a synthesis of "faith" and "understanding"' – a position represented, for instance, by Pusey's language about 'animated science'.[98] The modern orthodox position was a dialectical one: whereas orthodoxism and rationalism had their respective errors, modern orthodoxy aimed to use the best of 'science' to recover a vigorous orthodoxy.[99] This dialecticism does have 'progressive' overtones, since the rise of rationalism, though corrosive in itself, nevertheless provided the means ('science') to correct orthodoxism. But any apparent 'progressivism' is mitigated by the fact that Pusey's *Enquiry* narrates the *decay* of systems rather than their progress; and he specifically rejects the 'progress of humanity', criticizing the notion that Christian

---

96. Although Pusey ceased to use the terminology of 'orthodoxism' after the *Enquiry*, the concern it identifies recurs throughout his work. See Pusey, *Cathedral Institutions*, 37–40; 'Introductory Essay', in *Essays on Re-union*, [ed. Frederick George Lee] (London: Gilbert and Rivington, 1867), 11, 20–2.

97. Pusey's account of 'orthodoxism' and its consequences bears broad similarities to more recent accounts which likewise fault reductionist handling of doctrine for contributing both to the disjunction between Christian doctrine and practice, and to the eventual rise of relativism and secularism. For further discussion see the Conclusion. Cf. Hans Boersma, *Nouvelle Théologie and Sacramental Ontology: A Return to Mystery* (Oxford: Oxford University Press, 2009), 2–3; *Heavenly Participation: The Weaving of a Sacramental Tapestry* (Grand Rapids, MI: Eerdmans, 2011), 166–7; James K. A. Smith, *Introducing Radical Orthodoxy: Mapping a Post-Secular Theology* (Grand Rapids, MI: Baker Academic, 2004), 99–100.

98. Albrecht Geck, 'From Modern-Orthodox Protestantism to Anglo-Catholicism: An Enquiry into the Probable Causes of the Revolution in Pusey's Theology', in Strong and Herringer, *Edward Bouverie Pusey*, 54.

99. Geck, 'Modern-Orthodox', 56–7; *Autorität*, 48–52; cf. Leighton Frappell, '"Science" in the Service of Orthodoxy: The Early Intellectual Development of E. B. Pusey', in Perry Butler, *Pusey Rediscovered*, 1–33.

morality could be established by mature reason as much as by revelation.[100] To the Pusey of the *Enquiry*, 'science' is a good which God brings out of the evil of rationalism, not the engine of inevitable progress.

The *Enquiry*'s German roots, however, contributed to misunderstanding. Phrases such as the 'freedom of the gospel' and a 'new era in theology', though popular among his German friends, were easily misunderstood in England. There are also stylistic flaws. In many places Pusey's syntax seems more German than English, hampering the clarity of his language; and his coining of new words, most notably the pejorative 'orthodoxism', led to further confusion. Newman observed that it was 'sadly deformed with Germanisms', adding, 'It is a very valuable sketch, and will do good, but will be sadly misunderstood both from his difficulty of expressing himself, the largeness, profundity, and novelty of his views, and the independence of his radicalism.'[101] Pusey was well aware of the work's flaws: not long after the book was published, he observed,

> I have, in fact, been unlike other people in my language as in everything else. … I do not expect a very merciful handling from reviews. The sentiments scattered up and down [the book] will fare still worse than the style; and I expect to be thought one-third mystic, one-third sceptic, and one-third (which will be thought the worst imputation of all) a Methodist, though I am none of the three.[102]

In fact, repeated misunderstandings of the book led him ultimately to issue a retraction and to forbid its republication in his will. Despite this retraction, however, and regrets over his handling of particular topics (such as inspiration), he always maintained the accuracy (and orthodoxy) of the book's main argument.[103]

Misunderstanding, combined with cynicism about the future of German theology, stirred a high church reaction against Pusey. Rose extensively revised and enlarged his work in line with Pusey's criticisms, but he also issued a rebuttal.[104] His reply to Pusey dismisses the *Enquiry* as 'only a sort of excrescence from Professor Sack's Letter, a child which has outgrown its parents, and unintentionally thrown them into the shade' and accuses Pusey of wilfully misunderstanding his earlier work (though his revisions suggest a tacit acknowledgement to the contrary), while raising doubts as to Pusey's orthodoxy.[105] Moreover, although Pusey quite

---

100. Pusey, *Enquiry I*, 133–47, 162–3.
101. Liddon, *Life*, 1:164.
102. Liddon, *Life*, 1:152–3.
103. Liddon, *Life*, 1:173–6.
104. H. J. Rose, *The State of Protestantism in Germany, Described: Being the Substance of Four Discourses Preached before the University of Cambridge in 1825*, 2nd edn, enlarged, with appendix (London: C. J. G. and F. Rivington, 1829).
105. H. J. Rose, *A Letter to the Lord Bishop of London, in Reply to Mr. Pusey's Work* (London: C. J. G. and F. Rivington, 1829), 7–8.

openly acknowledged the influence of both Neander and August Tholuck on his thinking, the latter had asked not to be named; yet notes from Tholuck's own lectures on the same subject surfaced not long after Pusey's work was published. Despite private correspondence in which Pusey clarified that Tholuck was the anonymous friend he had cited, Rose nonetheless seized the opportunity to raise the spectre of plagiarism.[106]

Pusey had not intended to write on Germany beyond the original volume of the *Enquiry*, but his own misgivings about the work were confirmed with the publication of Rose's response, and he set about to defend his reputation. The second part of the *Enquiry* appeared in 1830; in it, Pusey clarified his arguments, defended certain other remarks he had made (most notably on inspiration) which Rose had attacked and added several substantial chapters of historical material which are most notable as an expression of his deep admiration for Spener.[107] Helpfully, he imposes a unifying lens on his earlier argument: the common cause for the collapse of orthodoxy, as of pietism, was the general tendency of renewal movements to lapse, through the pressures of partisan controversy, into 'formularism', either of doctrine or practice, whereby beliefs or practices originally meant for the revitalization of the whole Church are reduced to mere badges of party membership.[108]

In his initial lectures on German rationalism, Rose had emphasized the importance of articles and episcopacy. For Matthew, Pusey's refusal to acknowledge that these were effective defences of the Church displays a latitudinarian or 'low church' sentiment, and his adherence to the Oxford Movement, with its dogmatism and strong emphasis on apostolic succession, indicates a significant reversal in his thought. As with the topics that have been discussed above, however, Pusey's development is less dramatic than often supposed; but the question of authority in the Church can nonetheless help clarify Pusey's relationship with the high churchmen, while elucidating his stance on a key tenet of Tractarianism.

Pusey's early views on episcopacy should be stated precisely. He did not de-value the episcopate, but rather he maintained that its existence was not

---

106. Rose, *Reply to Pusey*, 105–6. Rose printed Pusey's explanatory letter (see Liddon, *Life*, 1:161–3), ostensibly to let the reader draw their own conclusions.

107. Pusey, *Enquiry II* (London: C. J. G. and F. Rivington, 1830), 314–61.

108. Pusey, *Enquiry II*, 392–7. 'Formularism' thus articulates Pusey's model for understanding the Reformation (discussed above under 'Continuity and evolution I: The Reformation and Rome') as a necessary correction to the errors of the medieval church, but one which in turn needed correction. Although Pusey abandons the term after *Enquiry II*, the evolution described above suggests that the theory it describes mutated from a particular theory about the evolution of German (and English) theology in a specific period and became something like a universal theory of the inevitable corruption of the temporal church, in which every reform generates the next error. This view explains in part Pusey's appreciation for the emphasis on self-doubt that he found in the *Spiritual Combat*, noted in the introduction.

sufficient to preserve a church from error: episcopal churches in Scandinavia had become as rationalist as non-episcopal churches in Germany, but the presbyterian Church of Scotland had remained as orthodox as the episcopal Church of England.[109] When challenged by Bishop Blomfield, he professed his own deep appreciation of episcopacy but was unwilling to relinquish his conviction that its absence was unrelated to the growth of rationalism in Germany.[110] This rather weak statement has been contrasted with Rose's stronger position to conclude that Pusey held a 'low church' *bene esse* view of the episcopate, versus Rose's high church *esse* position and thus that Pusey was not a high churchman.[111] This contrast, however, reads pre-Tractarian high churchmanship through the lens of the Oxford Movement. In reality, the high church tradition held the *bene esse* position and were unwilling to unchurch foreign protestants who lacked bishops (local non-episcopal bodies were viewed as schismatic, but primarily because the Church of England was understood to be the Catholic Church *in* England).[112] Rose, in fact, holds that bishops make a very specific contribution to the well-being of the Church. Pusey at this time also held that bishops existed for the well-being of the Church, but he rejects this specific benefit and is vague as to what benefits he affirms.[113]

With his involvement in the Oxford Movement, Pusey adopted the Tractarian belief that bishops were essential to the Church. Rune Imberg has traced how, in Pusey's tracts, the continental protestants referred to as 'churches' in earlier editions become 'bodies' in later versions, and Pusey is known to have occasioned some consternation by refusing communion to a Lutheran colleague visiting at

---

109. Pusey, *Enquiry II*, 15–21.

110. Pusey to Blomfield, n.d., LBV 40.

111. This distortion, in fact, appears to derive from Liddon. Liddon, *Life*, 1:171.

112. Nockles, *Context*, 146–52.

113. The high church view of the episcopate as pertaining to the *bene esse* of the Church, derived from Hooker and shaped by the 'avant garde conformity' associated with Archbishop Laud, originally understood this in an ontological sense, as pertaining to the wholeness of the Church. By the time of Rose's argument, however, this appears to have shifted to a more pragmatic understanding of the 'well-being' of the Church. Pusey's later views, as discussed here, seem to go well beyond the earlier position, but certain aspects of his later thought (e.g., his refusal to 'unchurch' the German Lutheran churches) would appear to be consistent with an 'ontological' *bene esse* view of the episcopate. Richard Hooker, *Of the Laws of Ecclesiastical Polity*, in *The Works of That Learned and Judicious Divine Mr. Richard Hooker*, ed. John Keble, 7th edn (Oxford: Clarendon Press, 1888), 3.2.1, 7.5.2, 7.5.8, 7.11.10, 7.14.11; William Laud, *A Relation of the Conference between William Laud, Late Archbishop of Canterbury, and Mr. Fisher the Jesuit, by the Command of King James, of Ever Blessed Memory*, in *The Works of the Most Reverend Father in God, William Laud, D.D., Sometime Archbishop of Canterbury* (Oxford: John Henry Parker, 1847–57), 2:143–4; and 'The Answer of the Most Reverend Father in God, William, Lord Archbishop of Canterbury, to the Speech of the Lord Say and Seal, Touching the Liturgy', in *Works*, 6:134.

Oxford.[114] A late work considering the role of the episcopate makes it *the* sole ruling organ of the Church.[115] And, in an oft-quoted statement, Pusey named a 'high estimate of Episcopacy, as God's ordinance' as a main feature of 'Puseyism'.[116] While this certainly represents a much stronger position than that shown in his early years, there is also continuity. Even as a Tractarian, Pusey thought the doctrine of apostolic succession dull and uninteresting. And while defending the doctrine in 1839, he nonetheless refused to unchurch continental Protestants, insisting that the questions the Tractarians raised regarding non-episcopal ordinations were meant to emphasize the blessings of the Church of England, not to deny God's grace to other bodies.[117] As late as 1870, he wrote to Liddon, about the days leading up to Newman's secession,

> Dear J. H. N. [Newman] said to me one day at Littlemore, 'Pusey, we have leant on the Bishops, and they have given way under us.' Dear J. K. [Keble] and I never did lean on the Bishops, but on the Church. We, or rather the whole Church, have had plenty of scandals as to Bishops, and always shall have them.[118]

Clearly, he had not lost his earlier views on the episcopate as a defence of the Church. In fact, there appears to be a certain ironic logic when these various

---

114. Imberg, *Quest*, 172–6; Geck, 'Modern-Orthodox', 61–3; *Autorität*, 86, 93–4; Pusey's reasons for this action are unclear, but may be connected to episcopal nature of confirmation in the Church of England, and the requirement, discontinued in the twentieth century, for confirmation prior to communion. While it is somewhat hazardous to read back later Anglo-Catholicism onto the Tractarians (especially Pusey), this reasoning was articulated in the early twentieth century by Charles Gore, in his response to the controversy generated by the participation of two Anglican bishops in the 1913 Kikuyu interdenominational communion service. Charles Gore, *The Basis of Anglican Fellowship in Faith and Organization* (London: A. R. Mowbray, 1914), 35.

115. E. B. Pusey, *The Councils of the Church from the Council of Jerusalem A.D. 51, to the Council of Constantinople A.D. 381* (Oxford: John Henry Parker, 1857). In Pusey's argument, priests and deacons are admitted to synods only as theological advisors to the bishops, and laity are excluded.

116. Liddon, *Life*, 2:140–1.

117. Pusey, *Oxford*, 146–82: Pusey writes,

> While maintaining that they only are *commissioned* to administer the Sacraments, who have received that commission from those appointed in succession to bestow it, we have never denied that God *may* make His own Sacraments efficacious, even when irregularly administered; we should trust it might be so: some of us are bound up by ties of affection to those very Protestant bodies, which it is supposed we should so harshly and wantonly cut off from the Church of Christ

– a clear reference to his German friendships (152, emphasis Pusey's).

118. Liddon, *Life*, 4:231.

statements are taken together: bishops, if they are important to the Church, must constitute an essential organ of it, since it is not clear that they necessarily contribute to its well-being.

The other topic raised by Pusey's dispute with Rose is his attitude towards articles of faith. Rose had maintained that the rise of rationalism had been allowed in part by the neglect of the Lutheran confessional statements; Pusey maintained that over-adherence to them had narrowed the vision of German theology and provoked an anti-dogmatic reaction. This has been coupled with some statements in Pusey's letters to Maria during their engagement, which Forrester paraphrases as stating that 'differences of outlook among the principal bodies of dissenters were akin simply to the varying degrees of emphasis placed on certain doctrines by the high church and Evangelical parties, in the Church of England; and as such, were neither of vital importance nor to be confused with the truth itself'.[119] Taken together, these have been used to suggest that Pusey had a latitudinarian disregard for doctrinal differences.

It is important, however, to acknowledge the context for Pusey's statements. In the latter case, he was answering Maria's question, why differing beliefs between denominations were not cause to disbelieve Christianity.[120] He was not setting out his general views on doctrine or the Church, but was explaining that the diverse positions held within Christianity did not disprove the claims of Christianity to be a revealed religion; so for instance, Anglicans and Baptists might disagree as to their doctrine of baptism, but 'the main principle that persons should be baptized is admitted by both'.[121] That is, certain things (e.g., the principle of baptizing) have been revealed, and those are held in common; the precise explanations for them might still be disagreed upon. In context, this statement need not entail indifference to doctrine.

So too the *Enquiry*'s argument that overly detailed formularies provoke an anti-dogmatic reaction suggests a desire to preserve dogma, rather than indifference to it. As with his position on episcopacy, when pressed, Pusey reaffirmed his appreciation of the English Articles of Religion. The difference between the Articles and, for instance, the Formula of Concord was that the Articles were brief and allowed for some breadth of interpretation, while the Formula is detailed, requiring assent to each particular – a requirement that was particularly generative of formularism.[122] Or, to put it somewhat differently, but in a way that makes the idea easier to trace in Pusey's later thought, the Articles set boundaries for belief,

---

119. Forrester, *Pusey*, 19–20.

120. M. R. Barker to Pusey, 3 October 1827, LBV 21.

121. Pusey to M. R. Barker, 4 October, 1827, LBV 23.

122. Pusey, *Enquiry I*, 19–25, *Enquiry II*, 30–4, 45–7. Pusey's dislike of the Formula of Concord is repeated in 1857, where his discussion of the Lutheran doctrine of the ubiquity of Christ's body makes this doctrine a specific instance of the general process outlined in the *Enquiry*. Pusey, *English Church*, 119–25; cf. Yngve Brilioth, *Eucharistic Faith and Practice Evangelical and Catholic*, trans. A. G. Hebert (London: SPCK, 1930), 110.

while the Formula states beliefs that require assent. In the period of the tracts, this can be seen in Pusey's allowance for differing interpretations of the Articles. Unlike Newman's position in Tract 90, Pusey never argues that his beliefs are merely permissible; he insists rather that his position is the correct interpretation of the Articles, when read precisely and in the context of both their history and the Prayer Book, Catechism and Homilies.[123] But despite this insistence, he always allowed his opponents a place in the Church.[124] Again, although he served as a theological advisor to Phillpotts during the Gorham case, he regretted the prosecution, believing that the cause of truth was better served by persuasion and mutual explanation than coercion.[125] Later, an evolution of the *Enquiry*'s understanding of the Articles as boundaries shapes the ecumenical proposals of his *Eirenicon*. Here, he suggests that the Articles and the Council of Trent both set boundaries – but different ones, with room between them. The Tridentine decrees state the minimum for belief, while the Articles set a maximum. So, for instance, Trent insists that Christ is present in the Eucharist, but the Articles state that this is 'only after an heavenly and spiritual manner', not by a physical change in the elements. Or again, Trent holds that the Eucharist is a sacrifice, while the Articles insist that it may not in any way interfere with the one sacrifice of Christ.[126] Between these two limits, mutual explanation (perhaps even agreement) was possible.

So, in Pusey's understanding of ecclesial authority, what we have found is that his understanding of episcopacy started at a position similar to the high churchmen, though less defined than the position held by Rose. His association with the Oxford Movement produced a shift towards a stronger understanding of the episcopate; but this stronger view of the role of bishops was, ironically, consistent with his earlier reservations about the benefits of episcopacy, which he continued to hold. On the other hand, he developed early on an understanding of ecclesiastical articles as boundaries for faith, rather than as propositions to be adhered to, which clearly continued throughout his life. Thus, Pusey's views on ecclesial authority once again exhibit not revolution but a balance of continuity and development.

---

123. Pusey, *English Church*, 161–239.

124. Pusey, *Oxford*, 122–3. Both Pusey and Newman allow that a range of positions is allowed by the Articles, but for Newman it is because they are vague, whereas for Pusey it is because they are precise; Newman thought their original intent anti-Catholic, but Pusey took a longer view, emphasizing the various revisions of the Articles and the necessity of taking them in the larger context of other Anglican formularies, regardless of the views of any individuals involved along the way. J. H. Newman, *Remarks on Certain Passages in the Thirty-Nine Articles*, TFT 90, 4th edn (London: J. G. F. and J. Rivington, 1841), 4, 80–2; cf. Roderick Strange, 'Reflections on a Controversy: Newman and Pusey's "Eirenicon"', in Perry Butler, *Pusey Rediscovered*, 336–7.

125. Liddon, *Life*, 3:217–19.

126. Pusey, *Eirenicon I*, 23–31. *Eirenicon III*, 75–90. For an extended discussion of the *Eirenicon* see Chapman, *Fantasy*, especially chapters 3–4.

The German Enquiry and the renewal of theology

In order to understand the central concern of Pusey's theology, however, it is necessary to move past questions of authority to the main argument of the *Enquiry*. Despite Matthew's assertions, it is clear, even on a superficial reading, that Pusey's sympathy for rationalism only extends as far as a certain optimism about modern orthodoxy's salvage effort and, perhaps, an excessive need to point out the good intentions of the figures he studies, even when he is critical of the ultimate effects of their thought.[127] He and Rose are agreed in opposing rationalism; their differences are primarily as to its cause.[128] In contrast to Rose's emphasis on episcopacy and doctrinal documents, Pusey's account is a history of attempts to hold together the intellectual and practical (including both emotional and moral) aspects of faith, within an orthodox framework. The heroes of his story are Luther and Spener, with their respective attempts to unite this triad. The tragedy of his narrative is the decay of each system due to 'formularism'. After Luther, confessionalism lapsed into orthodox formularism, clinging to a narrow orthodoxy that stifled the intellect, while Christian practice slipped away. After Spener, pietism lapsed into practical formularism, in which a rigid emphasis on personal morality was accompanied by an ever more tenuous grasp of orthodoxy and a disregard for intellectual inquiry. Naturally, the third erroneous approach to Christianity is rationalism, focused on the activity of the intellect, capable of addressing practical morality, but at odds with Christian orthodoxy. Pusey's modern orthodox friends had seized upon its ability to connect intellect and Christian practice, and hoped on these grounds that 'science' could be rescued from rationalist influence as a unifying element.

This conceptual analysis can provide a tool for understanding Pusey's evolution. Pusey's later pessimism about the German churches was grounded primarily in disillusionment: 'science', unsurprisingly, had proven unreliable as a mediating principle, as his German friends slipped either towards rationalism or towards orthodoxism; only Tholuck continued to maintain the modern orthodox position.[129]

---

127. Pusey had, in fact, travelled to Germany to learn the best way of combating rationalism. Brian Douglas (following Frappell) argues that any 'liberalism' on Pusey's part was solely 'a conservative tactic', although he notes that Pusey's thought on the whole should be characterized more as 'cautious' (as in David Brown, 'Pusey') than 'conservative'. Liddon, *Life*, 1:44–9, 77, 88–9; Douglas, 'Pusey and Scripture', 704–5.

128. This opposition to rationalism was characteristic of high churchmanship, which had insisted, since the early eighteenth century, that mere unaided reason was blind to the deeper realities of faith. Richard Sharp, '"The Communion of the Primitive Church"? High Churchmen in England, c. 1710-1760', in Stewart J. Brown, Nockles and Pereiro, *Handbook*, 30–1.

129. Pusey to Tholuck, 24 March 1865, in Geck, *Autorität*, 180; cf. Frappell, '"Science"', 22–3. Geck holds that Pusey quickly turned his back on the modern orthodox project as this disillusionment set in. Douglas, however, 'disputes Geck's position' arguing that Pusey maintained throughout his life a 'mediating style' like that of the modern orthodox perspective, which reflected an epistemological value for a balance of reason, tradition

But even before these shifts began to appear, it is likely that the mediating role of 'science' had received a fatal blow. 'Scientific' inquiry relies heavily on academic dispute to contest findings and test positions. Accordingly, Pusey had written, 'The enquiries in Germany, though occasionally carried on wrong principles, seem generally to have had truth for their object, have contributed to the firmer and better-grounded establishment of several books [of Scripture], and to the better classification of all', adding, 'where doubts have acquired a general prevalence, it is an unquestionable service to collect those doubts as strongly as they are capable of being put; the only result of the desultory answers with which, till this is done, vindicators often content themselves, is to produce an unjustified and unconvinced conviction'.[130] When Pusey, in the process of preparing the second part of the *Enquiry*, asked Keble for his input, Keble insisted that no practical good could come of raising doubts about the faith, in any context. Error was to be put down as soon as it raised its head, rather than debated.[131] Keble's sentiment apparently took hold of Pusey, as his attitudes from the 1830s onwards indicate – for instance, in his support for the campaign against Renn Dickson Hampden's appointment as Regius Professor of Divinity.[132] This did not end Pusey's appreciation of dialogue, however: he supported mutual explanation between high church and Evangelicals, and between Anglicans and Roman Catholics, over the course of his life. It was only dialogue with those who compromised the faith which was excluded.

Despite the collapse of 'science' as a mediating principle, however, there are signs that Pusey's concern for the union of an intellectually vibrant orthodoxy with faithful practice continued to influence his thought. Within a few years, Pusey began a *ressourcement* of patristic allegory as a step towards a symbolic and sacramental principle which would unify the intellectual and practical aspects of Christianity (discussed in the next chapter). Even beyond that project, the union of orthodox doctrine and faithful practice is a central concern throughout his theological writing; and his understanding of dogma (as discussed above) allows a certain intellectual freedom, within boundaries. Moreover, Pusey's concern in the *Enquiry* is not primarily with German history but with English theology: 'orthodoxism' and

---

and feeling. My assessment mediates between the two: Pusey did indeed abandon modern orthodoxy and its particular project of salvaging 'science' for orthodoxy. Nonetheless, he maintained the principles he had found in modern orthodoxy, and – as the next chapter will show – his search for an alternative vehicle for these principles, once 'science' had been abandoned, ultimately pushed him to a much more radical re-envisioning of theology. Geck, 'Modern Orthodox', 57–8; Douglas, *Eucharistic Theology*, 32–3.

130. Pusey, *Enquiry I*, 153–5.

131. Keble to Pusey, 19 April 1829, LBV 50; Pusey to Keble, 13 May 1829, LBV 101.

132. Pusey to Tholuck, 30 July 1836 and 6 March 1837, in Geck, *Autorität*, 162–9. Hampden, later bishop of Hereford, had advocated the position that doctrinal statements, including the Creeds, were constructions of merely human authority. His appointment, in 1836, by the Whig prime minister Lord Melbourne, aroused fierce opposition among high churchmen, including the Tractarians.

'pietism' correspond respectively to high churchmanship and Evangelicalism; and he squarely acknowledges the English roots of rationalism. From this perspective, the Oxford Movement itself can be characterized as a movement of intellectual creativity and scholarship, in the service of orthodoxy and faithful practice. Its various members doubtless came to this position for different reasons: in Pusey, it was the addition of Evangelical feeling and piety to high church orthodoxy; in Keble and Froude, it was the addition of Romantic emotion to the high church tradition of both piety and asceticism; for Newman and the Wilberforces (Robert and Henry), it was the fusion of high church principles with Evangelical character.[133] Despite their different approaches, their common position in uniting these principles was doubtless part of Pusey's attraction to the Movement. Moreover, Pusey's critique of orthodoxism and pietism corresponds, in some ways, to the Tractarians' tensions with both 'old' high churchmen and Evangelicals. Newman had thought the *Enquiry* would 'do good': seen in that light, this parallel raises the possibility that it may, in fact, have contributed at least indirectly to the formation of the Tractarian position.[134]

Not only does the *Enquiry* explain, in part, Pusey's adherence to the Oxford Movement, its central theory of the decay of renewal movements through partisan 'formularism' appears to have had a lasting effect on his perspective. His hesitation about fully committing to the Movement can be seen (in part) as caution with regard to its partisan nature. In fact, despite the accusations of William Palmer and others, and despite the widespread perception (indeed, the reality) of his leadership in the Movement, Pusey always insisted that he was never a party leader.[135] In

---

133. Beyond these high-profile individuals, there were a number of erstwhile Evangelicals who adhered to the Oxford Movement. This was in part a consequence of a fracture within Oxford Evangelicalism following the emergence of a handful of extreme Evangelical factions in the Church of England, which had a presence in Oxford beginning in the 1820s. This fragmentation left more moderate or 'churchly' Evangelicals looking for an alternative foundation on which to found their resistance to the rising threats of liberalism and state intrusion into the church, which they found in the Oxford Movement. Grayson Carter, 'The Evangelical Background', in Stewart J. Brown, Nockles and Pereiro, *Handbook*, 42–3.

134. Cf. Richard Hurrell Froude, 'Essay on Rationalism, as Shown in the Interpretation of Scripture', in *Remains of the Late Reverend Richard Hurrell Froude, M.A.: Fellow of Oriel College, Oxford*, ed. J. Keble and J. H. Newman (London: J. G. and F. Rivington, 1839), Part 2, 1:2. Froude's distinction between two opposed classes of rationalist – intellectualist and supernaturalist – also correlate loosely to a collapsed orthodoxism and a decayed pietism in Pusey's model, and bear even more directly on the allegorical concerns discussed in the next chapter.

135. William Palmer, *A Narrative of Events Connected with the Publication of the Tracts for the Times* (London: Rivingtons, 1883), 240; Owen Chadwick, *Spirit*, 37. Chadwick notes, 'If [Pusey] had thought a party to be following him, he would have shut himself in his house, said his prayers, and continued with his studies.' The point here is that this is not merely a matter of temperament; it is also a matter of principle reflecting his life-long worry about 'formularism', and in particular the way that concern took shape in his repeated

keeping with that principle he resisted joining the English Church Union until 1866, when he took the position of vice president, which had been Keble's until his death that year, in memory of his departed friend.[136] In that role, however, he was frequently at odds with the more audacious of the ritualists, and used the threat of resignation as an effective bludgeon to enforce moderation on their proceedings.[137] In these disputes he insisted, for instance, that private confession was beneficial but ought not be mandatory, and that liturgical innovations, as optional (not necessary) expressions of theology, should be regulated by the needs and desires of the congregation.[138] In light of the *Enquiry*, we might understand this as his resistance to the descent of Tractarian sacramentalism into ritualist formularism.

Matthew opposes the *Enquiry* to Pusey's *Lectures on Daniel the Prophet* (1864).[139] But here again, more careful reading offers a different perspective. An early date of the book of Daniel, which Pusey defended, is no longer widely accepted. But to emphasize the current rejection of Pusey's position risks overlooking the fact that it was only decades later, after Pusey's death, that his position was definitively defeated; at the time it was a massive contribution to an ongoing scholarly debate.[140] Larsen finds Pusey's philological scholarship 'brilliant' and 'persuasive', concluding that 'Matthew never bothered to read this volume before denouncing and dismissing it', and that 'it is Matthew who did not face the scholarship in Pusey's *Daniel the Prophet* but rather evaded it; and Matthew who attempted to answer Pusey's learned efforts by ignoring them'.[141] Brian Douglas similarly emphasizes the quality of Pusey's scholarship and concludes that the true 'takeaway' from *Daniel* is Pusey's ongoing rejection of orthodoxism and the moderation of his claims for critical methodology.[142] In Pusey's day, his argument was seen as unanswerable; it was only with the publication of S. R. Driver's commentary on Daniel in 1900

---

arguments concerning the errors that grew from making a single figurehead the source of a theological system.

136. The English Church Union formed in 1859 out of local 'Church Unions' formed by high churchmen in response to the Gorham controversy earlier in the decade. It took a leading role in defending Anglo-Catholics through the controversies and prosecutions of the following decades.

137. The ritualists were high churchmen (or early Anglo-Catholics) who sought to express Tractarian theology through the recovery of medieval liturgical practices. They were influenced not only by the Oxford Movement but also by the nineteenth century's general fascination with the Middle Ages and by the liturgical researches of the Cambridge Camden Society (later, the Ecclesiological Society) associated with John Mason Neale.

138. Cobb, 'Leader', 353-61; Robert Mackley, 'Dr Pusey and the SSC', in *In This Sign Conquer: A History of the Society of the Holy Cross 1855-2005*, ed. William Davage (London: Continuum, 2006), 54-62; cf. Liddon, *Life*, 4:271-91.

139. Matthew, 'Pusey', 115-16.

140. Larsen, 'Pusey and Holy Scripture', 507.

141. Larsen, 'Pusey and Holy Scripture', 504-6.

142. Douglas, 'Pusey and Holy Scripture', 707-11.

that 'Daniel scholarship slipped out of Pusey's range of fire' – showing remarkable longevity (thirty-six years) in a hotly contested field.[143] Driver himself, though disagreeing with Pusey, singles out Pusey's lectures as 'extremely learned and thorough' among other works on Daniel.[144]

To compare *Daniel* to the *Enquiry*, however, more specific points of inquiry are needed. Christopher Seitz identifies four aspects of Pusey's argument in *Daniel*, which can be used for a deeper analysis: piety as the guarantor of orthodoxy, a miraculous understanding of prophecy, the interpretation of the Old Testament by the New and the doctrine of Christ as an infallible teacher who interprets the Old Testament (Seitz offers these as criticisms of Pusey; I repurpose them here to show the originality of Pusey's own critique).[145] The key to understanding Pusey's position on these topics lies in the second point, prophecy as a miracle. Pusey concedes that belief in the supernatural is something that follows from faith, so he is not concerned to preserve a definition of prophecy as supernatural prediction which thereby provides 'proof' of Christianity.[146] Rather, given that prophecy *is* supernatural prediction – both for Pusey and for those he critiques – the fundamental reason for denying the prophetic nature of the book of Daniel is the tacit assertion that there is no supernatural, and therefore no prophecy.[147]

---

143. Christopher Seitz, *Figured Out: Typology and Providence in Christian Scripture* (Louisville, KY: Westminster John Knox, 2001), 30.

144. S. R. Driver, *The Book of Daniel* (Cambridge: University Press, 1900), ciii–civ; cf. Larsen, 'Pusey and Holy Scripture', 518. Driver retained this assessment of Pusey's work in the 1912 edition, despite making editorial changes to the passages immediately surrounding it.

145. Seitz, *Figured Out*, 17.

146. In a University Sermon of this decade, he concedes that while some miracles might be seen as essential to the Gospel, many miracles in Scripture are not so closely tied to the fundamental tenets of Christianity, and 'for the most part … we believe those other miracles, because we believe the Gospel', rather than the reverse. Prophecy, like other miracles, may prepare someone for faith, but it cannot produce faith – faith is entirely the gift of God. The distinguishing feature of prophecy is that whereas other miracles happen, and then might be recorded, prophecy's miracle is in its recording, and so it provides an enduring testimony to which any reader might be a witness, not just those present for a particular event. Nonetheless, as the necessity of faith in understanding miracles would suggest, the use of miracles (especially prophetic prediction) as 'proof' of Christianity was in fact antithetical to Pusey's theology. E. B. Pusey, 'Prophecy, a Series of Miracles which We Can Examine for Ourselves', in *US II*, 53–77; and see Chapter 2, under 'Allegory and scripture'.

147. *Daniel*'s emphasis on prophetic prediction should not be taken to exclude Pusey's interest in allegory discussed in the next chapter. The essay to which Pusey was responding not only criticized traditional views of the book of Daniel but also displayed negative attitudes towards both allegory and sacramentalism; his emphasis in *Daniel* on miraculous prophetic prediction is merely the vehicle for critiquing a set of principles which also had

Those who use the argument [against the prophetic understanding of Daniel] call themselves 'unprejudiced,' simply because they are free from what they call *our* prejudices. But of course one who lays down, that such a book cannot have been written at a given time, *because*, in that case, it would contain definite predictions of the future, as much prejudges the question on the ground of his antecedent anti-doctrinal prejudices, as he can allege of us, that we decide it on our doctrinal prejudices, i.e. on our previous belief.[148]

That is, there is no progressive ability to transcend past prejudices and obtain 'objective' scholarship; there is only scholarship that proceeds from prior principles, which either include or exclude faith. Accordingly, Pusey states his own bias and sets about the task of revealing his opponents', by dismantling the arguments with which they would conceal it. Despite aiming to address every argument raised on Daniel's date, he admits, 'my own conviction is, that the point really at issue remains, when they are answered.'[149] His aim is less to prove his position than to expose the 'point really at issue' – the clash in opposing systems. The other points Seitz mentions are properly understood in light of this. The interpretation of the Old Testament by the New, centring on Christ, *is* a principle outside the text (as Seitz objects) – but so too, ironically, is the rejection of this hermeneutic. Piety, meanwhile, relates to formation in the tradition which bears the interpretive principles.[150] Pusey was intimately familiar with the good intentions of many critics. His concern, however, was not with their intent but with the effects of their principles, both in the *Enquiry* and in *Daniel*. The difference between the two is not in his argument: in fact, he repeats the thesis of the *Enquiry* in the introduction to *Daniel*: 'Rationalism was the product, not of the attacks on the Gospel but of its weak defenders.'[151] The difference lies, rather, in his attempt to distinguish intent from principle in the *Enquiry*, absent in *Daniel*. But such niceties had obscured Pusey's argument in the *Enquiry*; he was not likely to repeat the mistake.

Daniel, rather than supplying a contrast to the *Enquiry*, shows that its concerns and concepts continued to shape his thinking throughout his life. He agreed with Rose in his opposition to rationalism; where they differed was that Pusey believed that a radical renewal of theology was needed to combat it – reliance on

---

consequences for these other emphases in his theology. Rowland Williams, 'Bunsen's Biblical Researches', in *Essays and Reviews*, 2nd edn (London: John W. Parker, 1860), 64–5, 86–7.

148. Pusey, *Daniel*, 7; emphasis Pusey's. Pusey's belief in the miraculous nature of prophecy dates at least as early as the *Enquiry*: in defending his theological positions to Bp. Lloyd, he describes his understanding of biblical inspiration as consisting primarily in the general inspiration of the authors as religious teachers but excludes prophecy as a special case: 'Prophecy of course stands by itself.' Pusey to Lloyd, 6 October 1828, LBV 108.

149. Pusey, *Daniel*, xiii–xiv.

150. Piety is intimately connected with the Tractarian concern for *phronesis*. See discussion of Keble and Isaac Williams in Chapter 2 under 'Allegory and theology'.

151. Pusey, *Daniel*, xxv–xxvi.

formularies and episcopacy would not be enough. Although his initial optimism about his German friends' 'modern orthodoxy' faded quickly, the concerns that drove it remained; and his involvement in the Oxford Movement can be seen as a continuation of that reforming impulse. There are parallels here with his political development. Both politically and theologically, it is highly doubtful that Pusey was ever a 'progressive' or a liberal, though he did see the need for reform. Where Pusey changed was in his optimism about reform, which shifted under the course of events and the stern counsel of Keble, and under the inherent pessimism of his own theory of formularism, towards a more critical and cautious attitude. Indeed, with the political changes of his lifetime, this caution very nearly became resistance to many of the changes proposed by governments that were increasingly secular in their outlook, though Pusey remained adaptive. Theologically, however, this caution enabled him to criticize and in some measure restrain the excesses of his own party: despite deep differences in strategy and the mutual distrust that resulted, after Pusey's death William Palmer credited Pusey with having guided the Oxford Movement to the kind of revitalized churchmanship he and other high churchmen of the old school had hoped for.[152]

***

Despite, therefore, the received views of Pusey's 'revolutions', Pusey's development shows much more subtlety than simplistic contrasts between his earlier and later attitudes have suggested. There is change – if there were not, he could truly be charged with intellectual stagnation – but underneath the change is a strong element of continuity. The change itself is best characterized, in light of this continuity, as a deepening of his views, rather than as a reversal. Practically, this often shows itself as a form of pessimism (especially about the trustworthiness of government in effecting reform); but beneath the surface the shifts in his thought were produced by the consistent application of deeply held principles. Pusey had criticized Luther's followers in 1828; it was only natural, later in life, to criticize in Luther the seeds of the theology which they developed: Luther had been exempted from criticism, at first, because of his heroic status, but the logic of Pusey's critique already implicated him. German modern orthodoxy was an attempt at renewal; but in an analysis where the principle of every renewal degenerates into a lifeless formula, what chance does a renewal have, which depends on the attempted salvage of a principle already adverse, in the modern orthodox analysis, to living faith? Such logical implications are at the roots of Pusey's evolution. This deepening can be traced – as in this chapter – through various aspects of Pusey's thought: political and ecclesiastical reform, the nature of authority in the Church, his attitudes on the Reformation. But these are peripheral to Pusey's central goal of renewing theology to serve a holistic vision of the Christian life. The modern orthodox attempt to use science as a mediating principle did not survive long in

---

152. Palmer, *Narrative*, 240–1.

Pusey's thought. Rather, by the mid-1830s, he had turned to a *ressourcement* of Patristic thought, focussing (as was natural, given his concern for the authority of Scripture) on a bold engagement with the allegorical hermeneutic. That younger generations of Tractarians slipped towards their own formularisms even during his lifetime suggests that there is no simple solution: the lapse of revival into party spirit proved more inevitable than the young Pusey had thought, a matter of human nature rather than of theological approach. Nonetheless, as we shall see, the particular problems posed by 'orthodoxist' and pietist formularisms spurred Pusey to a radical re-envisioning of theology, which in many ways anticipates important discussions in twentieth- and twenty-first-century theology.

Chapter 2

ALLEGORY AND THE SACRAMENTAL VISION

Pusey's early *Enquiry* into German theology analysed the collapse of theological renewals into a barren 'formularism', producing a theory which is evident in his works as late as *Daniel the Prophet*. This analysis, however, posed a problem. Orthodoxism and pietism were the failed remnants of past renewals: if, as Pusey eventually concluded, the modern orthodox use of 'science' as a mediating principle was unreliable, what could provide the holistic revitalization of faith and practice he thought was needed? This chapter will argue that Pusey found his answer in a sacramental vision of creation drawn from the allegorical reading of Scripture found in many of the early church fathers and in a corresponding theology, which, in its emphasis on concrete images – and indeed, physical sacraments – both opens a depth of meaning and addresses elements of the human psyche that are inaccessible to more discursive approaches to theology.

Allegory and scripture

Pusey published the second part of the *Enquiry* in 1830; the years that followed were almost entirely consumed by his work on the Arabic catalogue. As he emerged from that task in the mid-1830s, however, he began two concurrent studies: the patristic use of biblical allegory and the doctrine of baptismal regeneration. The timing of these projects – as Pusey's next major studies after the Enquiry – suggests that together they provide the solution to the *Enquiry's* problem. They produced, respectively, the unpublished 'Lectures on Types and Prophecies of the Old Testament' and the *Scriptural Views of Holy Baptism* (which, not surprisingly, also contains a great deal on the subject of allegory; the second edition is almost entirely a study of baptismal types in the Old Testament). The 'Lectures on Types', which will be the particular focus of this chapter, were written in the summer of 1836 as Pusey's part in a collaboration with Keble aimed at understanding patristic exegesis and were delivered, beginning in the following Michaelmas term, to a newly formed Tractarian theological society.[1] Keble expressed his appreciation for

---

1. Westhaver, 'Living Body', 12; Keble to Pusey, 18 January and 28 March 1837, and from 6 October to 10 December 1840 in LBV 50. Keble's contribution was eventually published in 1840–1 as TFT no. 89, *On the Mysticism Attributed to the Fathers*, discussed below.

the work, while Newman hailed it as an antidote to the views of David Friedrich Strauss.[2] Despite this praise, however, and numerous revisions continuing into the 1840s, the work was not published in Pusey's lifetime; and after his death, it appears to have been suppressed by the early librarians of Pusey House as being potentially too controversial.[3] Since its rediscovery by Alf Härdelin in the 1960s, however, it has received increasing attention as a key Tractarian document.[4] It is also the key to understanding Pusey's subsequent theology.

During Pusey's studies in Germany, his apologetic concerns had directed him to the study of the Old Testament, which culminated, on his return to England, in his appointment as Regius Professor of Hebrew. The *Enquiry* reflects Pusey's preoccupation with the interpretation of Scripture; in it, he criticizes 'orthodoxism' for a use of the Bible which made the 'plain meaning' of the text (according to a given author's reading) a polemical weapon against competing interpretations. In Pusey's analysis, this approach sapped Scripture of its vitality, by flattening its rich complexities into one-sided arguments: it was precisely this reductionist polemicism which set in motion the series of reactions that led, ultimately, to the rise of rationalism.[5] Pusey's critique foreshadows, in some respects, more recent theological discussions which argue, more broadly, that similarly flat or one-dimensional (in their terminology, 'univocal') views of truth and being inevitably fail to account for the complexity of reality, and thus give way to relativistic (equivocal) perspectives.[6] Pusey, however, approaches the problem primarily from the standpoint of biblical interpretation. The use of Scripture, therefore, lay close to the heart of the *Enquiry*'s problem and could also point towards a solution: if a narrow and wooden mode of interpreting Scripture was so detrimental to faith, what hermeneutic might provide an alternative?

In the 'Types', the *Enquiry*'s concerns continue to drive Pusey's thought. He is concerned with the rise of rationalism and with the way unbelief is fostered by a compromised orthodoxy. He approaches the topic, however, through the narrower question of the New Testament interpretation of Old Testament prophecy, which

---

2. Newman to Pusey, 12 September 1839; given in J. H. Newman, *The Letters and Diaries of John Henry Newman*, ed. Gerard Tracey (Oxford: Clarendon Press, 1995), 7:145. Strauss appeals to allegory as evidence for seeing the biblical accounts of Jesus as fictionalized or 'mythologized'. This is the opposite of Pusey's approach, in which the (un-fictionalized) historical account is the foundation on which allegory rests. David Friedrich Strauss, *The Life of Jesus Critically Examined*, trans. George Eliot, ed. Peter C. Hodgson, 4th edn (Philadelphia, PA: Fortress Press, 1972), 65.

3. Westhaver, 'Living Body', 280-1.

4. Andrew Louth, 'The Oxford Movement, the Fathers, and the Bible', *Sobornost*, 6 (1984): 31. A. M. Allchin, 'The Theological Vision of the Oxford Movement', in *The Rediscovery of Newman*, ed. John Coulson and A. M. Allchin (London: Sheed and Ward, 1967), 51.

5. Pusey, *Enquiry I*, 26-35.

6. Smith, *Radical Orthodoxy*, 99-100; Boersma, *Nouvelle Théologie*, 108.

2. Allegory and the Sacramental Vision

was increasingly becoming an intellectual difficulty with regard to the faith. The problem, he argues, is with the apologetic use of prophecy pioneered by William Paley (and popular with some high churchmen, such as Rose): that miraculous predictions are 'evidences' or proofs of Christianity. This requires that prophecy *clearly* foretell the future – specifically with regard to Christ – but Old Testament prophecies are *not* clear, with dire consequences for a faith based on such 'proof'. As a side effect of such 'evidences', however, the definition of prophecy was narrowed. All that did not *clearly* predict the New Testament, or at least have New Testament authorization, was not prophetic; and the meaning of prophecies was narrowed to their 'direct' predictive value. The elimination of any prophecies outside these strictures, and the narrowing of those that remained, led to an impoverished theology – theologians 'were content with nothing but the mid-day sun, and so lost all sympathy for the refreshing hues of its rising and setting light, and those glimpses into a far distant land, which, indistinct though they may be, open a wide range of vision'.[7] This represents a development of Pusey's earlier critique of orthodoxism: the *Enquiry* was concerned with narrow (univocal) approaches to theology, which involved a polemical use of Scripture that limited its use to the proof of doctrine.[8] The 'Types', while focused specifically on Scripture, considers that subject more broadly, both as to the apologetic use of Scripture as 'proof of faith' (not just of doctrine) and the wider effects of such reading of Scripture, which include a narrowing perception of theology.[9] As in the *Enquiry*, Pusey's concern is not to overturn orthodoxy but to preserve it against the threat of rationalism (reflected particularly in the nascent higher critical methods he knew from his studies in Germany). If the sole purpose of Scripture is to prove faith (or doctrine), criticism can disprove it. Pusey's solution, however, is not to reject reason per se in defence of Scripture but to seek a reading of Scripture which places reason in right relation to faith.[10]

In order to do this, Pusey looks first to the example of the New Testament. The New Testament writers use prophecy to direct faith, rather than to create or support it, Pusey argues, and we need to adopt their approach. This is 'a system

---

7. Pusey, 'Lectures on Types and Prophecies of the Old Testament', Pusey House, 2 (hereafter 'Types').

8. Allchin, 'Theological Vision', 56–7.

9. This is not a reversal of his earlier position (that narrow theology results in reading Scripture as 'proof'); rather, they are mutually reinforcing tendencies. See discussion of phronesis below in this chapter under 'Allegory and theology'.

10. Douglas, 'Pusey and Scripture', 702–3, 712, 714. The more recent critiques noted above ground their arguments in a critique of univocal ontology, for which they provide an historical analysis reaching back to the high Middle Ages; they also address different (primarily twentieth-century) manifestations of it. Nonetheless, the overarching account of the reduction of Scriptural exegesis to 'proof of doctrine' and its deleterious effects in modern and postmodern responses to faith is consistent with Pusey's analysis. Smith, *Radical Orthodoxy*, 89–100; Boersma, *Nouvelle Théologie*, 149–50, 215; *Heavenly Participation*, 2.

wholly different from our own', he warns, and those who too casually criticize the Apostles' reading of Scripture will find themselves criticizing the Apostles themselves, a pattern found in the previous century of German theology.¹¹ The approach he sees in the New Testament relies not on historical contextualization but on larger patterns evident across the whole of Scripture; which, however, in any given instance, might rely on details that are incidental to the immediate passage's 'direct' meaning. On the one hand, this allows for an infinite interplay of resemblances, imagery and ideas, within the Scriptural framework; on the other, it often results in vague, indefinite or highly personal interpretations of Scripture. This indefinite quality, however, is not theologically inappropriate, because 'God and his ways and his nature we can of course know but in part, and our highest knowledge must be our indistinctest'.¹² Pusey does not allow for mere fancy however. In the first edition of *Baptism*, he had employed a similar critique of the rationalists' tendency to reduce ideas or objects to their scientifically observable 'essentials' and, as a remedy, insisted on a reading of Scripture which was both *literal* and *comprehensive*.¹³ Comprehension, in addition to reflecting the influence of Article 20 (that the Church may not 'so expound one place of Scripture, that it be repugnant to another'), balances the distortions introduced by personal emphases with a broader perspective founded on Pusey's belief that whatever is given by God must, in virtue of that fact, be significant, even if we cannot discern how.¹⁴ This corresponds to the emphasis in the 'Types' on the harmony between

11. Pusey, 'Types', 9–11.

12. Pusey, 'Types', 2. Pusey here appears to be referring to what Boersma describes as the 'analogy of truth' (parallel to the better-known 'analogy of being' or *analogia entis*): God being wholly other, our understanding of him is purely analogical rather than direct. Boersma, *Nouvelle Théologie*, 108; *Heavenly Participation*, 166–7. Cf. discussion of Soskice below, in this chapter, under 'Allegory and theology'.

13. Pusey, *Baptism 1*, ix, 37, 78, 148–53. This is connected to Pusey's rejection of the superficial mindset that assumes nature and mystery to have been explained away by science. E. B. Pusey, preface to Augustine, *The Confessions of St. Augustine*, trans. E. B. Pusey (London: J. M. Dent, n.d.), xxii–xxiv.

14. Pusey, *Baptism 1*, 1–6. In the *Enquiry*, Pusey's allowance of historical inconsistencies in Scripture had necessitated a clarification of his understanding of inspiration – he held a common high church theory (shared by Blomfield, among others) that Scripture was inspired, because its authors were themselves inspired teachers of religious truth (thus, for instance, Paul's letters are not an inspired exception in his otherwise uninspired ministry, but reflect his general oral teaching as an inspired apostle); inspiration as to religious matters, however, need not translate into a divine superintendence over the transmission of superficial historical details. *Enquiry II*, 54–87; On Inspiration, Pusey Papers – EBP Biblical MSS, Pusey House; Blomfield to Pusey, 16 January 1830, LBV 40; cf. Palmer, *Treatise*, 2:5. Understood in light of his earlier perspective, Pusey's turn to allegory in the late 1830s appears to maintain a view of inspiration which retains its focus on religious truth over historical accuracy (although history, if anything, increases in importance), while simultaneously shifting towards a belief in the full verbal inspiration of Scripture.

Scripture's larger patterns and its minute details; but the important constraint is in the requirement for literalism. Literalism here means that passages which speak of spiritual operations (such as baptismal regeneration) or which recount miracles are not to be explained away by elaborate reinterpretations but are to be taken as stating the real events or effects.[15] It is on this basis that, at one point in the 'Types', Pusey criticizes a passage of Augustine (which the latter had, later in life, retracted on the same basis) as mere fancy, not grounded in the literal meaning of the text.[16]

In the later version of *Baptism*, these themes are expanded in a lengthy investigation of baptismal types. Of particular interest, however, is the way in which Pusey elaborates his conceptual framework for understanding types in a way which highlights the implications for his theology. First, he expands on his earlier insistence on the harmony of Scripture, and the importance of each detail, no matter how small. All events in Scripture

> have bearings every way, all belong to a vast system of which we have some glimpses, which we cannot construct as a whole, nor, consequently tell *all* the bearings of the several parts: yet, by reason of this oneness of the whole system, all of its parts, as being parts of one, have some relation to the other, and we ... have principles enough given to us, to enable us to understand and interpret some of those relations.[17]

Moreover, even the smallest details in Scripture are deeply meaningful and can be more meaningful than larger events:

> Thus, His earthly sun, as it draws and disposes our clouds around himself, and gives to each their due form, and a portion of his own brightness, imparts to each tiny speck the richness of his glory, and most often bathes and envelops those with his lustre, while those earthborn masses, which would claim to themselves more of solidity, and a more distinct existence, can receive but a slighter tinge, and in their outskirts only, testify his presence. In like way, it may be, that those human things, which have a more substantial existence, are less fitted to be

---

15. Pusey, *Baptism 1*, 16–17; cf. John Keble, *On the Mysticism Attributed to the Early Fathers of the Church*, TFT no. 89 (London: J. G. F. and J. Rivington, 1841), 38–52. So Christ's baptism 'with the Holy Spirit and with fire' was followed by a *literal* descent of the Holy Spirit with fire on Pentecost; in light of Jewish baptisms and John the Baptist's ministry, Jesus' teaching on regeneration by 'water and the Spirit' (Jn 3.5-6) is meant literally. The importance of literalism was also emphasized by Keble.

16. Westhaver, 'Living Body', 195. Put in terms of univocal and equivocal approaches, a comprehensive reading of Scripture guards against the univocal tendency to isolate particular passages for the sake of a narrow literalism, while literalism guards against an equivocal tendency to draw overarching morals or narratives from a 'comprehensive' reading of Scripture while sitting light to the actual text.

17. Pusey, *Baptism 2*, 272.

symbolical of Him, while the mean things of the world, and things despised in man's eyes, may be made the vehicles of His mysteries, or point to them.[18]

Pusey roots this in the inspiration of Scripture by God and his presence in 'every jot and tittle'.[19] The language that Pusey uses, however, of 'things despised in man's eyes' becoming the vehicles of God's glory, also points strongly towards the incarnation. He acknowledges that the Fathers' emphasis on what appear to be mere details may produce readings that seem 'fanciful' to modern readers, but he notes (with a rather postmodern self-awareness) that this could be as much a fault on our part, as on theirs: 'Either we must see too little, or they too much; and we have taken upon ourselves to decide in our own favour.'[20]

Pusey is not technically precise in his discussion – he is concerned more with a recovery of the Fathers' theological vision than analysis of it – but his account is consistent with the analysis of Henri de Lubac's magisterial *Medieval Exegesis*, which can help articulate the structures Pusey is engaging.[21] De Lubac sees pre-Reformation exegesis as making a fundamental distinction between the literal and the 'allegorical' sense of Scripture.[22] Allegory must be grounded in the literal sense of the text – that is, in an accurate understanding of the biblical history as

18. Pusey, *Baptism 2*, 273–4.

19. Pusey, *Baptism 2*, 274–5; cf. n. 14 above. This is much stronger than Pusey's earlier views, but the change should not be overstated: his earlier belief that Scripture reflected a broader inspiration of the apostolic witness as religious teachers was regarding *facts*, that is, that their teaching was guaranteed in its religious, not historical, content. This statement pertains to the verbal symbolism of Scripture, and the two positions are not necessarily mutually exclusive, although the later statement marks a dramatic change of interest in Pusey's thought.

20. Pusey, *Baptism 2*, 273. Alister McGrath argues that one of the benefits of postmodernism for theology is the reclamation of a sense of historical location. Alister E. McGrath, *The Genesis of Doctrine: A Study in the Foundation of Doctrinal Criticism* (Grand Rapids, MI: Eerdmans), 82–92.

21. Thus Pusey's argument for becoming 'acquainted' with patristic interpretation is not merely a matter of proper understanding but is concerned with learning, *for ourselves*, 'how things abstract may be studied devotionally'. In contrast, although Keble is sympathetic to Pusey's critique of rationalism and is favourable towards Patristic exegesis, he is more concerned with a proper reverence for the interpretative approach of Scripture and Christian antiquity than with its recovery; in several places, he admits the difficulty posed by allegory to modern minds and hesitates as to whether it could be adopted. Pusey, preface to *Confessions*, xxiv–xxv; contrast Keble, *Mysticism*, 8–14, 70–105, 160–2.

22. Henri de Lubac, *Medieval Exegesis: The Four Senses of Scripture*, trans. Mark Sebanc and E. M. Macierowski (Grand Rapids, MI: Eerdmans, 1998–2009), 1:144–5, 225–6, 266. De Lubac's work explicates the 'four senses of Scripture': literal, allegorical (pertaining to Christ and the Church, or roughly the New Testament fulfilment of the Old Testament), moral and anagogical (roughly, mystical or eschatological). The moral and anagogical senses however are expansions or applications of the allegorical sense, and it is the more

it is presented to us – because salvation and God's revelation were worked out *in history* as *historical facts*. De Lubac emphasizes that allegory, applied to the Old Testament, is not a fanciful play on words but an understanding of the theological significance of *what was done* – it is *allegoria facti*.[23] This is precisely Pusey's reason for emphasizing the literal meaning of the text. The meaning of the Old Testament, however, is found in the New, which means that the two testaments share an organic unity.[24] And in keeping with the infinity of the One subject and author of Scripture, the interpretation of Scripture is 'indefinite' and 'inexhaustible'.[25]

There is, however, a question of terminology which might be addressed. Pusey refers to his topic as 'types'; or with the adjective 'typical' which corresponds roughly to the modern 'typological'. Since the middle of the twentieth century, the propriety of a distinction between 'typology' (concerned with clear historical foreshadowing) and 'allegory' (concerned with a broader range of spiritual signification) has been debated.[26] But, as George Westhaver notes, such a distinction is opposed to the idea Pusey is formulating – Pusey admits different degrees of strength and clarity between types, but to his mind they are all different degrees of the same phenomenon; indeed, the limitation of what he calls 'types' to clear historical anticipations is precisely the point he was arguing against. If Pusey avoids the term 'allegory', it is not to distinguish 'allegories' from 'types', but because 'allegory', in the early nineteenth century (as today), was usually associated with arbitrary or fanciful interpretations – a connotation Pusey is keen to avoid. Accordingly, it is proper to understand his project as 'allegory' in the broad sense de Lubac describes.[27]

Before continuing on to consider the content of Pusey's engagement with the Fathers, it should be noted that while the particulars of Pusey's engagement with allegory (discussed in the remainder of this chapter) were deeply original, his reliance on types was itself not a novelty within Anglicanism: rather, it provides both another connection with the old high church tradition and a point of tension with them. High churchmen typically exercised a degree of reticence in

---

fundamental twofold distinction – literal and allegorical (in the broader sense) with which Pusey is concerned.

23. De Lubac was primarily opposed to a *reduction* of biblical meaning to the literal sense. Boersma, *Nouvelle Théologie*, 156–9.

24. De Lubac, *Medieval Exegesis*, 1:25–6, 144–5, 225–47, 266; 2:59–63, 88–9 (*allegoria facti*), 107–17.

25. De Lubac, *Medieval Exegesis*, 1:77; c.f. also 1:80–1, 214, 258–9.

26. This distinction was introduced by de Lubac's student Jean Daniélou but was opposed by de Lubac, whose rejection of the distinction now appears to be widely accepted. Boersma, *Nouvelle Théologie*, 180–90; *Scripture as Real Presence*, 24–5, 95.

27. Westhaver, 'Living Body', 200–2. In this discussion, I will use 'allegory' and 'allegorical' to describe the general process or its principles (Pusey's word is 'typical', which, however, in current usage is open to misinterpretation); 'type' will be used, following Pusey's usage, for specific institutions, events or images which fit this scheme.

avoiding the over-definition of certain theological topics, such as the atonement. Discussions of Old Testament types provided a means of entering into such subjects, while evading the theological narrowing that otherwise might occur – concerns at least partially shared by Pusey. While Paley's 'evidences' were popular as a form of apologetics with some high churchmen, the use of Old Testament types in theology had a long history in high church tradition (going back at least to Lancelot Andrewes at the turn of the seventeenth century) and was particularly favoured by high churchmen of the 'Hutchinsonian' school, such as William Jones of Nayland.[28] But the same reticence that made the use of types appealing could also restrain over-exuberant spiritualizing of the biblical text: Daniel Waterland, for instance, limited the category of types to what was clearly used as such in Scripture – the position rejected by Pusey.[29] Even Waterland, however, could take the time to write several lengthy essays on the proper relation of the Old Testament's sacrificial rites to Christianity.[30] Pusey's engagement with patristic allegory thus fits within the perspective on Pusey's development maintained throughout this study, as a critical re-envisioning of an inherited approach to theology, rather than a radical departure from earlier high churchmanship.

Allegory and theology

Pusey's turn to the Fathers, and specifically his investigation of allegory, is a rich subject which could be examined from a number of perspectives. The question in view here, however, is its role in shaping his wider theological project. The *Enquiry*

---

28. Westhaver, 'Living Body', 270–3; William Jones, *Course of Lectures on the Figurative Language of the Holy Scriptures* (London: J. F. and C. Rivington, 1787). John Hutchinson (1674–1737) was an anti-Newtonian natural philosopher, who sought to provide a biblically grounded and theologically oriented account of physics. His work inspired a group of eighteenth-century conservative churchmen, including Jones, who protested vigorously against the latitudinarian theology often associated with Newtonian philosophy; elements of this 'Hutchinsonian' school were influential on the later high church 'Hackney Phalanx', with which Van Mildert and Lloyd were associated. Hutchinson's connection between the natural world and theology, coupled with his speculations about the Hebrew language, provided a natural ground for interest in spiritual readings of the Old Testament. Westhaver sees the Hutchinsonians as providing precedent for Tractarian theology, but notes that the Tractarians made a stronger connection between orthodoxy and biblical allegory. George Westhaver, 'Mysticism and Sacramentalism in the Oxford Movement', in Stewart J. Brown, Nockles and Pereiro, *Handbook*, 264.

29. Westhaver, 'Living Body', 146–7.

30. Daniel Waterland, 'The Christian Sacrifice Explained', in *The Works of the Rev. Daniel Waterland, D.D.*, ed. William Van Mildert, 3rd edn (Oxford: University Press, 1856), 5:121–84; 'Distinctions of Sacrifice', in *Works*, 5:231–96; 'Christ's Sacrifice of Himself Explained; and Man's Duty to Offer Spiritual Sacrifice Inferred and Recommended', in *Works*, 5:737–46.

had faulted 'orthodoxism' for its flat, polemical reading of Scripture; but it had also traced, from that starting point, the growing separation between doctrine and practice, which cleared the way for the rise of rationalism. A hermeneutical defect, of course, calls for a hermeneutical solution, but Pusey was searching specifically for a hermeneutic that would reintegrate faith and life. In allegory, he found not just an interpretive theory, but just such a comprehensive spiritual world view.[31] This is, in turn, deeply entwined with his theology of baptismal union with Christ, as well as with the broader Tractarian discussion of the moral aspect of theological understanding. Understanding, however, is given form by language, and language seeks to express reality, so Pusey's discussion moves beyond spirituality, through linguistic considerations, to questions of ontology.

Pusey's study of baptism was conducted over the same period as his investigation of allegory, and firmly established union with Christ as the central pillar of his soteriology. Union with Christ, however, is not just a soteriological doctrine: it is the foundation of his whole theology and is essential, therefore, to understanding the function of allegory in his thought. This can be seen, for instance, in his treatment of natural types. For Pusey, the allegorical relationship of image and spiritual meaning extends beyond Scripture into the natural world. These spiritual meanings in the created order, however, are not immediately or superficially obvious. The 'book of creation', Pusey wrote, 'is best read by the purest & most divine. ... To the worldly or sensual it is a sealed book. What is Divine in it can be read only by what is Divine in man. To those of the earth, it is earthly; the Spirit in man decyphers to man what is spiritual in nature.'[32] 'What is Divine in man' is, to be clear, not intrinsic to humanity, but is a gift of participation in God by grace. This understanding of union with God as the source of allegorical

---

31. The link Pusey makes between hermeneutics and the integration of doctrine and spirituality once again foreshadows, at least in part, more recent projects. De Lubac traces the decline of allegory to the growing separation of theology and spirituality, in a process reaching back to the Carolingian period, and his study is motivated in part by a concern to find an alternative, spiritually integrative, path between modernity and the arid orthodoxy of neo-Thomism. Similar analyses can be found in Boersma's critique of modern and postmodern Evangelicalism and in the more sweeping analysis of Radical Orthodoxy. These accounts (especially that of Radical Orthodoxy) prioritize discussion of participatory ontology. As the discussion in this chapter indicates, such an ontology is, in fact, integral to Pusey's thought. Nonetheless, insofar as ontology is largely theoretical, it is insufficient. What is at stake for Pusey is not merely theory but lived reality: the hermeneutical aspect, which he prioritizes, both forms and is formed by elements of Christian *practice*, and is, therefore, closer to the heart of the issue. De Lubac, *Medieval Exegesis*, 1:48–73, 2:194–7; Boersma, *Nouvelle Théologie*, 2, 149–50; *Heavenly Participation*, 2, 21–5; Smith, *Radical Orthodoxy*, 89–100.

32. Pusey, 'Types', additional fragments. Westhaver notes that for Pusey, theological knowledge is grounded in a 'participation in divine life'. Westhaver, 'Living Body', 81–5; cf. Douglas, *Eucharistic Theology*, 184–5.

discernment and theological understanding, however, closely involves the moral condition of the person: participation is not something static but a process of growth and movement, moving into nearer union with God in Christ through increasing holiness.

The relation of holiness to baptism will be considered in the next chapter; at present, it may be noted that the connection between sanctification and understanding was a shared theme of the Oxford Movement. This is stated most clearly in Isaac Williams's two tracts on reserve.[33] Williams notes, for instance – once, with direct reference to allegory – that although the most faithful Christians are not necessarily those with the best grasp of theology, their faithfulness enables them to see God's work around them, giving them a support for their faith to which someone more learned but less faithful would be oblivious.[34] Likewise, there are two kinds of knowledge indicated by Scripture, one which is public, the other secret; 'a knowledge which without charity puffeth up' and 'that which is truly Divine and inseparable from charity; where to know and to love God, is one and the same thing, and both of them eternal life'.[35] It is this knowledge, the knowledge of faith which sees God at work in Scripture, history and the world around us, in which we ought to grow.[36]

Without this loving knowledge of faith, however, Scripture becomes correspondingly opaque. In allegory, the revelation of the New Testament is *hidden* in the Old; Williams notes that whereas books are generally intended to convey their meaning as clearly as possible, 'We cannot say this of God's written word. It may have other objects quite of another kind, which its very obscurity serves, better than its distinct meaning would do.'[37] So too, Jesus' parables have an element of 'darkness' which repels the understanding; his most important teachings were given, and many of his miracles performed, in secrecy; God in the Old Testament veils himself from sight; Jesus never calls himself the 'Christ' – this is left to those who, like Peter, are guided by the Holy Spirit, or who, like Mary, 'ponder in their hearts' the manifestations of his divinity.[38] Within the Church, God approaches

---

33. Reserve had some precedent in the high church 'reticence' concerning theological over-definition discussed above (under 'Allegory and scripture', and see below, Chapter 5, under 'The atonement and the sacrificial types'). For Williams, however, it is more narrowly concerned with what Jeremy Morris describes as the principle, that 'proper teaching adjusted religious truth to the capabilities of those to whom it was addressed'. Morris, *High Church Revival*, 175.

34. Isaac Williams, *On Reserve in Communicating Religious Knowledge*, TFT 80 (London: J. G. and F. Rivington, 1838), 29–32, 78. Hereafter *Reserve I*.

35. Isaac Williams, *On Reserve in Communicating Religious Knowledge* [Conclusion], TFT 87, 2nd edn (London: J. G. F. and J. Rivington, 1840), 85. Hereafter *Reserve II*.

36. Keble, *Mysticism*, 137–43. Keble notes, similarly, that as natural philosophy cannot lead us to God, or explain God's actions, the Fathers accordingly considered it a distraction from the work of growing in love and knowledge of God.

37. Isaac Williams, *Reserve I*, 4–8.

38. Isaac Williams, *Reserve I*, 11, 13–20, 21–5.

hidden in the sacraments, which are not outwardly divine; and by the same token, the Kingdom of God is hidden within the Church.[39]

This obscurity serves a dual purpose. It may challenge an inquisitive mind to a deeper engagement with holy things.[40] But it also protects those who are morally unfit from the dangers of God's revelation. Therefore, religious teaching should be geared to the Christian maturity of the recipients, and Christian conduct should be characterized by self-effacing humility.[41] Neglect of such reserve, however, has led to the decline of Christianity (Williams argues): publicly through fostering irreverence; privately, by sowing an individualism which recreates the biblical God according to subjective imagination – a 'puffing up', which deceives itself by substituting feeling and persuasion for 'any really deep and true sense, of religion'. Obedience without humility follows, seeking attention as a prop to this self-deception.[42]

Undergirding this principle of reserve is the Aristotelian concept of *phronesis*: action both shapes and flows from character, which determines understanding. Joseph Butler had applied this to the reception of Christian doctrine – a moral character would be receptive to Christian revelation, an immoral character averse to it.[43] Beginning in 1814, and developing through sermons in the early 1820s, Keble adapted Butler's theory to the divide between orthodoxy and heresy. This produced 'an ascending spiral movement' between morality and truth: truth, especially Christian truth, shapes action; repeated faithful acts make one more receptive to a deeper understanding of the truth, and so forth. Higher truths, however, can be misunderstood and misused by those not ready for them – hence the principle of reserve. In Keble's formulation, *phronesis* became a central idea for the Tractarians. In the formative years before the tracts, it led Newman and others to introduce a spiritual dimension to their tutorials at Oriel College, causing considerable controversy. In later years, the connection between morality and orthodoxy became a staple of Tractarian polemics.[44]

Accordingly, Williams insists on a stern moralism.

Good works, being nothing else but the exercise of a good principle, will make a good man (as far as, humanly speaking, a man can be called good), and those are not good works which will not make a man good; and he is not a good man,

39. Isaac Williams, *Reserve I*, 33, 65–8; *Reserve II*, 86–98.
40. Isaac Williams, *Reserve I*, 8–11; *Reserve II*, 45–7.
41. Isaac Williams, *Reserve I*, 34–54.
42. Isaac Williams, *Reserve I*, 55–8.
43. James Pereiro, *'Ethos' and the Oxford Movement: At the Heart of Tractarianism* (Oxford: Oxford University Press, 2008), 91–3. Butler was popular during the Tractarians' formative years at Oriel and was introduced to the Oxford curriculum in 1832. Boyd Hilton, *The Age of Atonement: The Influence of Evangelicalism on Social and Economic Thought 1785–1865* (Oxford: Oxford University Press, 1988), 172.
44. Pereiro, *'Ethos'*, 93–9.

who does not love God with all his heart, and depend on the aid of the blessed Spirit, and trust in Christ.[45]

He insists (not without merit) that when Paul speaks of preaching 'Christ crucified' he is more often speaking of being crucified with Christ than of the atonement; concluding (less convincingly) that although the cross necessarily involves the atonement, it is better to preach dying with Christ, leaving the atonement implicit, than to preach the atonement itself.[46] 'So far therefore as we keep the commandments we shall embrace the atonement, and so far only, whether we speak of it or not.'[47] It is better to preach God's judgement, drawing men to repentance, but 'to suppose, therefore, that a doctrine so unspeakable and mysterious as that of the atonement, is to be held out to the impenitent sinner, to be embraced in some manner to move the affections, is so unlike our Lord's conduct, that it makes one fear for the ultimate consequences of such a system.'[48]

Pusey thought Williams's tracts the most valuable contribution to the series, but it is in fact Williams who most points out Pusey's divergence from the Tractarian norm.[49] James Pereiro notes that, in the assessment of several Tractarians, Pusey was 'not a Butlerian'.[50] He had read Butler and had recommended the *Analogy of Religion* to Maria during their engagement.[51] However, he was in Germany during the formative time when Keble's ideas spread to the other central figures of the Movement and, unlike them, never had the opportunity to test Keble's theories as a tutor. His understanding of Christian holiness incorporates elements of *phronesis*, especially regarding the role of good works in Christian growth; but he places a much stronger priority on the work of Christ within the Christian than on individual moral effort.[52] He would likely agree with Williams's suggestion that the difficulty of Jesus' parables (for instance) was intended at least in part to challenge the understanding of those who were seeking God, and thence to draw them nearer; and the principle of adapting one's teaching to the maturity of the audience is also perfectly compatible with his thought. Likewise, the interior disciplines of his rule of life suggest agreement with the sentiment that proper personal reserve is best shown not in outward reverence but by the principles 'not

---

45. Isaac Williams, *Reserve II*, 62.
46. Isaac Williams, *Reserve I*, 74–7.
47. Isaac Williams, *Reserve II*, 72. The surrounding context makes it clear that he is emphasizing the two great commandments, to love God and neighbour.
48. Isaac Williams, *Reserve II*, 61, 65.
49. Westhaver, 'Living Body', 266.
50. This reflects the assessment of William John Copeland and Frederick Oakeley. Pereiro, 'Ethos', 127–8; 'The Oxford Movement's Theory of Religious Knowledge', in Stewart J. Brown, Nockles and Pereiro, *Handbook*, 197.
51. Maria Barker to Pusey, 18 October 1827, LBV 21.
52. See discussion of Pusey's understanding of holiness in Chapter 3 under 'Holiness, sin and repentance'.

to seek to remedy by external effects, that which can only come from within; to think less of appearance, more of the reality; to be natural, serious, forbearing, as considering what, and where we are, and what we are coming to.'[53]

However, Williams is apparently uncomfortable with much of Pusey's contribution to the Oxford Movement. Pusey's tracts on baptism and on the eucharistic sacrifice are singled out as apparent violations of reserve, explained (rather weakly) as necessary reminders of forgotten doctrine: 'reserve' had supposedly been maintained by marking the title pages '*ad clerum*'![54] Williams cautions that renewed studies of allegory – Pusey again the instigator, with support from Keble – should not be undertaken from mere curiosity but with humility and devotion; and he emphasizes the necessity of exercising reserve in the renewal of ascetic practices, particularly fasting – the topic of Pusey's first two tracts.[55] That Pusey is singled out in such a way, and that the majority of his tracts – including all of his most notable contributions – appear suspect, suggests a deep divergence between Pusey and the other Tractarians.

This difference is particularly notable in the later version of *Baptism*, in which Pusey has clearly moved away from any sort of argumentative demonstration of his subject. He laments the loss of allegorical thinking within the Church, and the resulting loss of appreciation for the theological value of types:

> We are obliged to detect, by analysis, what was to them transparent; and such 'demonstrations,' as compared with their perception, are much what the operation of the anatomist, in detaching the several sinews and muscles, is to their action in life. … Still even under these disadvantages, it will probably be *felt*, that this system of the Ancient Church does perceive a harmony in Holy Scripture, to which we are strangers.[56]

Pusey laments the loss not only of a practical appreciation of allegory but of an entire way of thinking. He disparages analytic 'demonstrations' in favour of a synthetic 'perception' of the harmony of Scripture. Pusey, in fact, adopts a similar approach: he does not argue in favour of allegory but describes it and hopes its value will be 'felt'. While the importance given to the details of Scripture in this system can produce interpretations bewildering to the modern reader, 'to judge from experience, they will, to anyone who does not rudely reject them, gradually recommend themselves more and more.'[57] Pusey, from his own statements, simply

---

53. Pusey to Keble, 7 December 1846, LBV 102; Isaac Williams, *Reserve II*, 102–3.

54. Isaac Williams, *Reserve II*, 98–9.

55. Isaac Williams, *Reserve II*, 103–12; E. B. Pusey, 'Thoughts on the Benefits of the System of Fasting, Enjoined by Our Church', TFT 18, 3rd edn (London: J. G. and F. Rivington, 1838); 'Supplement to Tract XVIII. On the Benefits …' TFT 66, new edn (London: J. G. and F. Rivington, 1838).

56. Pusey, *Baptism 2*, 389; emphasis mine.

57. Pusey, *Baptism 2*, 366.

aims to unfold his theological vision, so that it might attract adherents by its own beauty, comprehensiveness and what we might call 'fittingness'. This puts him in direct contrast with Williams. People *do* come to a deeper understanding of theological truth through spiritual growth. But that truth, as the revelation of God's love, also has attractive power to draw people to faith. While reminders of the Last Judgment may, on occasion, be useful – and Pusey certainly believed this to be the case – they are not the primary means of drawing people to obedience. The greater revelations of God's mercy may be the seed, and not just the fruit, of increasing sanctification.[58] There is no hint in Pusey's work of Newman's decree, that '*we require the Law* not the Gospel'.[59]

Just as the topic of reserve shows Pusey's similarities and differences from the rest of the Oxford Movement, so too it shows his continuity with, and departure from, the old high churchmen. Williams's idea of 'reserve' articulates and develops the theological reticence found in the older high church tradition. Van Mildert, for instance, had preached a series of sermons on 'Cautions respecting subjects of theological discussion', which outlined several areas of theological inquiry that could not be narrowly defined, without risk either of heresy or, at least, unnecessary division within the Church – dangers Williams attaches to lack of reserve.[60] Pusey's emphasis on the eucharistic presence of Christ and on Christ's indwelling of the Christian clearly exceeds what would have been comfortable for many in the older school (and perhaps even more conservative Tractarians like Williams), although (as will be discussed in the following chapters) his high church lineage is still clear in both of those doctrines. However, it is notable that elsewhere Pusey follows the high church practice of teaching doctrine through the use of Old Testament types (as in, for instance, his teaching on the atonement and the eucharistic sacrifice, discussed in Chapters 5 and 6).

The aesthetic or affective element in Pusey's thought, however, points us towards his psychology of faith. In the 'Types', he wrote,

---

58. Similarly, Pusey saw the doctrine of eternal punishment primarily as a stumbling block on the road to perdition: it could arrest an individual's descent into sin, but it could not, of itself, foster growth in holiness. E. B. Pusey, *What Is of Faith as to Everlasting Punishment?*, 3rd edn (Oxford: James Parker, 1880), 3–4.

59. Newman to Samuel Wilberforce, 4 February 1835; quoted in David Newsome, 'Justification and Sanctification: Newman and the Evangelicals', *Journal of Theological Studies*, n.s. 15 (1964): 43. Pusey's attitude, that true doctrine will ultimately prove attractive in its own right, likely influenced his later allowance of divergent doctrinal views within the Church of England (discussed in Chapter 1 under 'Authority and the Church'). Undoubtedly, this was in part political tact. Yet this belief in the attractiveness of true doctrine provides the ground on which he could argue only for Tractarian views to be *permitted*, without giving way to doctrinal relativism.

60. William Van Mildert, *Sermons Preached before the Honourable Society of Lincoln's Inn, from the Year 1812 to the Year 1819* (Oxford: S. Collingwood, Printer to the University, 1831), esp. 1:94–114; cf. Isaac Williams, *Reserve I*, 45–50.

> A man's simple belief, as it does not appeal to the understanding, so it cannot be rejected by the understanding: it lies altogether in a different province. Belief also (not *conviction* produced by argument whereby a man is as the word expresses 'convicted' rather than led to believe – but) [*sic*] unreasoning belief is, as well as unbelief, deeply rooted in the human mind; and whenever witnessed it appeals to an original principle of our nature, which, because pure and from God, and a relic of our uncorrupted nature, and a consequence of our original derivation from the breath of God, that we recognize our Father's and Maker's voice – has a mysterious, talismanic control over our souls; while, therefore, they who are yet blessed with it, should not go about to seek for any other argument, but rest content with or rather cherish this; lest in the multitude of words or of proofs they lose it; yet others, who may have, in any degree lost it, must beware how they take it up in their mouth, simply because they are convinced that it ought to be in the heart. For this forced reassumption of it, will be unreal and hollow and is but self-deceit; but it will be answered as a reward to the return by God's blessing to that simplicity.[61]

This is not, as a superficial reading might suggest, mere anti-intellectualism. Rather, Pusey observes that the predisposition to belief or unbelief is psychologically prior to intellectual inquiry; winning an argument will not necessarily lead to either faith or doubt. But this pre-intellectual disposition is not a static quality. In adopting a critical quest for proof, a believer is opening the door to doubts, although they might not necessarily follow; conviction does not necessarily lead to faith, but it *can* if it produces not just a change in position (e.g., from atheism to theism), but humility before God.[62] In addressing this pre-intellectual aspect of our minds, then, the affective power of imagery becomes pivotal. The ubiquity of imagery in poetic and religious language testifies to its importance in this respect; even the sacramental nature of words as material objects, marks on a surface, vibrations in the air, which somehow bear meaning, underscores the fundamentally concrete, rather than abstract, nature of communication.[63] Because we think, at the most basic level, in terms of concrete objects, images and objects become powerfully significant, not just intellectually but on an emotional or inarticulable level. Accordingly, an abstract, critical or argumentative approach to matters of faith is a methodological error, an application to theology of means not suited for it.[64] Faith bears with it

---

61. Pusey, 'Types', 42.

62. Pusey, 'Types', 4–6; cf. *Everlasting Punishment*, 45. Compare with Pusey's assessment that the 'point really at issue' in the debate over the book of Daniel is not primarily the date of the biblical text, but divergent prior principles that shape interpreters' views on that question. See above, Chapter 1, under 'The German *Enquiry* and the renewal of theology'.

63. Pusey, 'Types', additional fragments.

64. Pusey here has parallels with Radical Orthodoxy, which insists similarly that all reason is undergirded by prior religious commitments, and which thus, in place of apologetics, places a priority on the affections and on the role of the senses and imagination in epistemology, and thus on the 'sensible world' as a 'sacrament or image that points us

a sense of wonder, purity and infinity.⁶⁵ This is foreign to the dryness of abstract argumentation. 'Clarity and intelligibility are of course in themselves good', but the wrong approach risks 'seeking to grasp divine truths from the outside, when in fact they are realities which can only be understood in so far as we are entering into them and being grasped by them'.⁶⁶ Images may 'grasp' us where arguments do not, and so, in Pusey's theology, it is often as important (and sometimes more so) to read the images as to read the arguments.⁶⁷ This approach to theology provides intelligibility, which, precisely because it is non-analytic in nature, not only addresses the deeper needs of human psychology but also carries with it both a deep reverence for divine mystery and an inexhaustible depth of meaning.

***

Underlying this view of theology is a sophisticated and radical epistemology. Pusey holds that material or visible things are more readily apprehended by humans, and are more immediate and concrete in the impressions they make, than abstract reasoning. These images or surface meanings point to deeper, veiled meanings; although the surface meanings are intended, the veiled meaning is, in fact, primary: every part of creation is, in its deepest significance, an image which speaks of God, though God is himself always beyond the image.⁶⁸ Indeed, the ultimate source of every type, biblical or natural, is in the eternal Word – an ontological priority which Pusey indicates by the use of 'archetype' to describe Christ's relationship to the types (in preference to the more usual 'antitype') throughout the lectures.⁶⁹ The relation between type and archetype, the surface and the veiled meanings, is not arbitrary but is based on analogies actually present in the images or objects involved; the way in which this is expressed is a natural use of language.⁷⁰ The recognition that allegory is, therefore, not merely poetic

to God'. Radical Orthodoxy draws this perspective from Augustine and also, in part, from Bernard of Clairvaux, who were both sources of Pusey's theology. There are also parallels with the interest of Eliade and Daniélou in natural symbolism as revelatory. Smith, *Radical Orthodoxy*, 146–8, 180–2, 224–9, 244–5; Boersma, *Nouvelle Théologie*, 171–2.

65. Pusey, 'Types', 6.
66. Allchin, 'Theological Vision', 58.
67. For Isaac Williams (as well as for other Tractarian poets), the poetic use of imagery was able to convey 'concepts which could never be adequately explained in prose' while also presenting deep theological themes beneath a veil of poetic complexity, allowing such concepts to be developed and in a sense discussed, in a fashion which was nonetheless 'reserved' from the casual reader. Pusey was not a poet, but appears to use a similar 'poetic' approach to theology throughout his work. Boneham, 'Tractarian Theology', 274.
68. Pusey, 'Types', 16.
69. Pusey, 'Types', 19; Westhaver, 'Living Body', 170. This use of 'archetype' has been adopted by Boersma, who discusses Pusey's usage in *Scripture as Real Presence*, 24–5, 222–4.
70. Thus, 'the province of the true poet has been … to *trace out the analogies* which are *actually impressed* upon creation'. Pusey, 'Types', 15, emphasis added; cf. Douglas, 'Pusey, Poetry and Eucharistic Theology', 96, and see above in this chapter at n. 12.

or theological artifice, but based on a real analogy between type and archetype, provides for a richer theological understanding.[71]

As this engagement with the way in which imagery conveys meaning might suggest, Pusey is interested in the nature of figurative language and its role in theology. This is an interest shared with Keble, who defines poetry as 'the expression of an overflowing mind, relieving itself' of its over-full thoughts and emotions, 'more or less indirectly and reservedly' by the use of a symbolic system of associations. Biblical allegory is the poetry of the Church; creation itself is a kind of divine poetry.[72] For Keble, '*poetical forms of thought and language*' are therefore 'the channel of supernatural knowledge to mankind. Poetry ... may almost seem to be God's gift from the beginning ... the ordained vehicle of revelation, until God Himself was made manifest in the flesh.'[73] Pusey's perspective is similar, maintaining that 'creation was God's speech'.[74] He discusses the use of figurative language for God's attributes and the relations within the Trinity, and considers, on several occasions, the structural parallels between types and figurative language.[75] He even finds a providential aspect in the Old Testament's use of Hebrew – which by its structure is highly susceptible to figurative use – and the way in which these Hebrew metaphors are taken up into the Greek of the New Testament.[76]

Two recent analyses of the nature of figurative language can help clarify this aspect of Pusey's discussion. Janet Martin Soskice has argued for an understanding of figurative language analogous to scientific 'models', which allow something more elusive or less understood to be spoken of in terms of something that is

---

71. Pusey, 'Types', 21.

72. Keble, *Mysticism*, 144, 148; cf. Douglas, 'Pusey, Poetry, and Eucharistic Theology', 91.

73. Keble, *Mysticism*, 185–6; emphasis Keble's. Geoffrey Rowell argues that the Tractarians, especially Pusey, were particularly influenced by Ephraim Syrus, precisely because of this poetic approach to theology. Geoffrey Rowell, '"Making [the] Church of England Poetical": Ephraim and the Oxford Movement', *Hugoye* 2 (1999): 111–29.

74. Pusey, 'Types', additional fragments. For further discussion, see below under 'Allegory and the Sacramental Vision'.

75. Pusey, 'Types', 17, 21, 24; and various additional fragments.

76. Pusey, 'Types', additional fragments:

> The peculiarities of the Hebrew language are its picture-character and its undefinedness. Thus, even where metaphor is not prominent, it's [sic] language not being bound to one meaning, is applicable, with different degrees of precision, to different though allied subjects. This admission of degrees furnishes the very character of a type. It gives, as it were, a nearer and a background; a nearer to which the words might superficially appear to bear the closer resemblance, and a further and deeper to which, on account of their indefiniteness they would correspond, and which in that it is deeper, does in fact more fully correspond with them.

more concrete and better understood.⁷⁷ However, because the image being used as a model is complex, having 'a duality, or indeed a plurality, of associative networks', it suggests extensions in the understanding of whatever is being modelled, which is precisely its importance for science – for instance, if the brain is modelled as a computer, there is not only that basic image: experiences become 'data input', and various aspects of our psychology are 'wiring' or 'programming'. This not only gives us a language for various aspects of the mind's workings but also suggests the ways in which those parts might interact.⁷⁸ As the scientific use of models would indicate, however, they are not always perfect and might need to be revised, or even discarded, as our understanding grows, and *this is an indispensable quality of the model*. Models do not have to be 'perfect' to do their job, because they are aimed at advancing our understanding, not at producing absolute knowledge of a thing in itself.⁷⁹ Similarly, Robert Lakoff and Mark Johnson develop the idea of a 'metaphorical concept', roughly equivalent to Soskice's 'model'. Through an extensive investigation of how overarching 'metaphorical concepts' shape our everyday thought and language, they argue that root metaphors generate further metaphors, in a process that pervades our everyday speech. Different metaphors can interact with each other in a systematic fashion, through their shared structural elements. For instance, both quantity and quality are associated with metaphors of vertical orientation (e.g., 'rising numbers', 'higher quality') and can combine using this shared 'vertical' orientation to produce the maxim, 'bigger is better'.⁸⁰

There are several aspects of these theories which recommend them as tools for analysing Pusey's thought. Soskice is explicitly concerned with the infinity and unknowability of God – concerns which Pusey shares – and argues that the effectiveness of models, despite a lack of perfect correspondence to their subjects, suggests the particular propriety of figurative language for talking about God. (Pusey's types, however, unlike Soskice's models, exist 'as is' and cannot be revised or discarded, though they may be complementary.) Lakoff and Johnson's demonstration of how deeply ingrained metaphors are in our speech supports Pusey's supposition that imagery functions on a deeper psychological level than abstract 'direct' discourse.⁸¹ Both theories also emphasize the way images network and interact with one another for their significance, and so elucidate why Pusey thought that the system of types might allow for deeper theological understanding than 'clearer' language does. Beyond this, in Pusey's theory, 'types' function much like 'models' or

77. Janet Martin Soskice, *Metaphor and Religious Language* (Oxford: Clarendon Press, 1985), 50–1.

78. Soskice, *Metaphor*, 51, 99–101.

79. Soskice, *Metaphor*, 130–41.

80. George Lakoff and Mark Johnson, *Metaphors We Live By* (Chicago: University of Chicago Press, 2003), 14–24.

81. Indeed, it is a recurring theme in both Soskice and in Lakoff and Johnson that figurative speech is necessary and inevitable; Lakoff and Johnson go so far as to argue that all speech is figurative, and that direct speech is impossible. Soskice, *Metaphor*, 99–136; Lakoff and Johnson, *Metaphors*, 110–14, 159–88, 210–22.

root-level 'metaphorical concepts', as flexible means of understanding one thing in terms of another, and allowing that structural relationships between types can allow those images to build on one another and enrich each other, perhaps even to point beyond themselves together in a way in which they would not individually. Two adaptations, however, need to be introduced from the principles of the allegorical tradition. First, in accordance with the concreteness of the *allegoria facti*, it is not only imagery, wordplay and conceptualizations that can function in this way, but objects, institutions and events as well (especially those in Scripture). Second, each of these things is to be given a Christological orientation in its significance. This produces a dramatic shift, reversing the directionality between the signifier and the signified, not in terms of epistemological access but in terms of the way in which the two, between themselves, are related.[82] We still grow in our understanding of Christ by means of the 'type', but the type is not merely something that *we* use to explain some aspect of Christ's person or ministry, due to some resemblance (as in the historicist account). Rather, Christ defines the type, because he is the origin and archetype of all that points to him; the types are, in Pusey's words, '*logoi* proceeding from and setting forth the *logos*'.[83]

***

Pusey's emphasis on the theological significance of images invites a further comparison, earlier in the twentieth century, with Austin Farrer. Farrer rejects the ideas of biblical revelation as either mere dictation or mere historical event, proposing instead that revelation consists in the events of the incarnation being framed in images, which were then 'unfolded' in apostolic thought by the mind of Christ in the Church, his body: 'The great images interpreted the events of Christ's ministry, death, and resurrection, and the events interpreted the images; the interplay of the two is revelation.'[84] So far, Farrer and Pusey are much alike. But there are also differences, where Farrer appears more limited. Some of these are due to the constraints of his topic (specifically *biblical* revelation) and the boundaries of his project (to approach revelation through 'the natural knowledge of God', rather than 'by the direct road of revealed truth').[85] But, although he acknowledges the growth of images beyond the New Testament, there is no discussion of the mind of Christ in the post-apostolic church, and consequently the role of tradition (the ongoing reflection of the Church) in understanding Scripture appears much weaker.[86] Moreover, the absence of the Tractarian interest in *divine* poetry weakens

---

82. Cf. Alan J. Torrance, *Persons in Communion* (Edinburgh: T&T Clark, 1996), 176. Gottlob Frege had theorized that the 'sense' of a word determines what it refers to; Torrance suggests a theological reversal in which language referring to God in fact has its sense conditioned by its 'reference'.
83. Pusey, 'Types', 24.
84. Austin Farrer, *The Glass of Vision* (Westminster: Dacre Press, 1948), 36–43.
85. Farrer, *Glass*, 96.
86. Farrer, *Glass*, 49–50.

his view of prophecy and of creation. Similarities between prophecy and poetry are noted, but poetry is confined to being merely human making.[87] Likewise, created objects *may* speak of God, but this is not inherent to creatureliness; creation is not God's speech.[88] So, for Farrer, 'the Bible-reader', unlike the theologian (who analyses and risks confusing the images), 'will immerse himself in the single image on the page before him, and find life giving power in it'.[89] Pusey would certainly agree as to the life-giving power of the biblical image, but the image *is* never, and never can be, 'single'. It is precisely *because* 'creation was God's speech' that he sees the vitality of the image as dwelling in its poetic interplay with other created images, which Farrer thinks risks confusion. And so, for Pusey, the material world is much more vibrant than Farrer allows – though only if we have the spiritual eyes to see.

Beyond this comparison, it is possible to draw from the preceding discussion a broader outline of Pusey's approach to theology. The idea of mutually informing images in networks of meaning, as it involves *different* images and significances interacting with one another, appears to set forth an alternative to the overly narrow 'systems' he rejects in the *Enquiry*.[90] But it is also possible to connect it with later statements. His belief that Catholic truth required holding together apparently divergent realities (for instance, regarding the coexistence of the eucharistic elements with the real presence of Christ) shows a similar character; and his formula for 'explaining' the Articles and the Tridentine decrees to each other as minimum and maximum boundaries on doctrine can easily be understood as a particular instance of this tendency in his thought.[91]

Pusey's concept of doctrinal authority can be understood in the same light. His conception of the episcopate, collectively, as an organ of the Church, is analogous to this emphasis on interactive networks of ideas, and contrasts with Newman, who emphasized the role of individual bishops.[92] Similar principles influenced his attitudes towards the Church of England's Reformation inheritance, as it stands in relation to the broader Christian tradition. Pusey's attitudes towards the Reformers differed from some of his more conservative high church friends – as emerged, for instance, in his controversy with Hook over the practices at St Saviour's, Leeds. But these differences do not imply that the Reformers held no authority for Pusey.

87. Farrer, *Glass*, 113–31.
88. Farrer, *Glass*, 85.
89. Farrer, *Glass*, 51.
90. Boersma notes that multiplicity of meaning is inherent in allegory, but does not give way to purely equivocal readings of Scripture. Boersma, *Nouvelle Théologie*, 152–4, 164; *Heavenly Participation*, 147–9.
91. E. B. Pusey, *The Doctrine of the Real Presence, as Contained in the Fathers* (Oxford: John Henry Parker, 1855), 75–119 (hereafter *Fathers*); *Eirenicon I*, 266–7. For Pusey's discussion of the Articles in relation to Trent, see Chapter 1 under 'The Reformation and Rome'.
92. See above in Chapter 1, under 'Continuity and evolution II: Authority and the Church'.

Rather, the distinction was that they held a different kind of authority. Whereas Hook insisted that loyalty to the Reformation required loyalty to the doctrines of the Reformers, Pusey emphasized instead the degree to which the Reformers themselves turned to the Fathers – a significant portion of his discussion with Keble regarding communion of the wicked, for example, concerned Archbishop Matthew Parker's reading of Augustine and the way in which that influenced his editing of the Articles.[93] This suggests that, for Pusey, loyalty to the Reformation meant doing what the reformers did – turning to Scripture and the Fathers in order to revivify and cleanse the Church – and not merely thinking what they thought. Indeed, such a loyalty might entail theological differences, given the emergence of new sources, improved textual criticism since the sixteenth century and (not least) a different historical context with profoundly different world views (whether Enlightenment or Romantic) and an equally different set of theological challenges. It is also possible, however, within this broader framework of 'boundaries' and 'networks', to see his refusal to privilege the doctrines of the Reformation over earlier centuries as an unwillingness to de-contextualize the Reformers, or to separate their teaching from wider 'networks' of theology.

In contrast, Pusey clearly does privilege the patristic era. The patristic reading of Scripture, he argues, is closest to the hermeneutic exemplified in the New Testament itself (which emphasizes that, for all the stress Pusey places on tradition, it is never more than a secondary, interpretive authority compared to the primary authority of Scripture).[94] History, for Pusey, is oriented towards the New Testament, and in particular the life and self-oblation of Jesus Christ.[95] The present has no privileged perspective on the past, but is bound to its own historical context, and stands at a distance, both chronologically and intellectually, from that focal point.[96] The Fathers are, therefore, the most reliable interpreters of Scripture: not only does their closer historical proximity to Jesus and the New Testament suggest a closer continuity between their teaching and its apostolic source, but their use of allegory itself testifies to a continuity of perspective with the New Testament which has since been lost, while their creeds and definitions of the faith stand as a testament to their authority.[97]

93. Liddon, *Life*, 3:120; Pusey to Keble, 19 August to 10 October 1856, LBV 104; Keble to Pusey, 20 August to 8 October 1856, LBV 99; given in Liddon, *Life*, 3:460–9. For discussion of communion of the wicked, see below, Chapter 4, under 'Real presence II: Ascent and descent'. Matthew Parker (Archbishop of Canterbury, 1559–75) was the first Archbishop of Canterbury following the Elizabethan Settlement and thus exercised significant influence on the final versions of the English Reformation's theological formularies.

94. Pusey, 'Types', 38–9; *Deceased Wife's Sister*, 6.

95. De Lubac, *Medieval Exegesis*, 1:xiv–xviii, 2:69–76. Boersma notes that at the heart of Pusey's argument in the 'Types' is a distinction between historical and Christological readings of prophecy. Boersma, *Scripture as Real Presence*, 222–4.

96. Pusey, 'Types', 91; Louth, 'Oxford Movement', 40.

97. This entails scepticism towards any dogmatic additions or subtractions in later centuries, whether by Moderns, Reformers or Roman Catholics, though this scepticism

This, however, raises the problem of what Pusey and the other Tractarians referred to as the 'patristic consensus'. The idea of patristic unanimity has been criticized as naïve.[98] Westhaver notes, however, that not only the Tractarians but also their opponents (e.g., R. D. Hampden) treated the Fathers monolithically – a tendency inherited from Anglican divines of the seventeenth and eighteenth centuries.[99] But in Pusey, the idea may be more complex than is frequently assumed. If his understanding of a patristic consensus is informed by the ideas just discussed – of mutually informing images and doctrine defined by boundaries rather than positions – we should expect it to be a 'consensus' which nonetheless contains great variety; a broad spectrum of *different* opinions, which nonetheless *together* point towards an ineffable, mysterious reality.[100] It is worth observing that in contrasting the 'consent of the ancient Church' with 'the systems of modern schools', the subtitle of *Baptism*'s later editions not only opposes antiquity to modernity but 'consent' to 'systems'; and if (as the work's allegorical emphasis would suggest) 'systems' are characterized by excessive clarity and definition, 'consent' might be expected to be less defined, less precise, but richer and more various.[101] Indeed, if the flaw of formularism lies in its reductionist narrowing of

does not rule out changes in the outward expression of the faith, or development through the clarification or re-articulation of core doctrine. Cf. n. 105 below.

98. Brilioth, *Three Lectures*, 60–1; Carol Engelhardt Herringer, 'Pusey's Eucharistic Doctrine', in Strong and Herringer, *Edward Bouverie Pusey*, 102–3.

99. Westhaver, 'Living Body', 139–40; H. R. McAdoo, *Anglicans and Tradition and the Ordination of Women* (Norwich: Canterbury Press, 1997), 16, 19; Sharp, '"The Communion of the Primitive Church"?', in Stewart J. Brown, Nockles, and Pereiro, *Handbook*, 27.

100. Although dealing with English divines rather than the early Fathers, the same principle is evident in Tract 81. The sources provided in this *catena patrum* (compiled for Pusey by Benjamin Harrison; Pusey supplied the introduction) come from what Waterland had identified as two different schools of thought. This suggests that the point in presenting them is therefore *not* to set forth a single, uniformly held Anglican theology of the eucharistic sacrifice, but to show an historical Anglican acceptance of such a doctrine (i.e., as within the doctrinal 'boundaries' of the formularies), across varying theological presentations. Imberg, *Quest*, 37–8; Waterland, 'Christian Sacrifice', 5:134–5.

101. In a letter to Tholuck, Pusey specifically delineates between the varied individual opinions of the Fathers (which are not binding) and the broad 'catholic' contours observable across their thought (which are). Similarly, Pusey writes concerning the Eucharist, 'however different the occasions may be, upon which the truth is spoken of, *in whatever variety of ways* it may be mentioned, the truth itself is one and the same, one uniform, simple *consentient* truth' concerning the real presence. Demonstrating such 'consent' is the point behind Pusey's somewhat tedious compilations of historical (usually patristic) sources. This more complex notion of 'consent' fits broadly with Pusey's notion of doctrinal statements as setting boundaries for belief, rather than stating precise theories that must be held (discussed in Chapter 1 under 'Authority and the Church'), and roughly parallels his insistence on a *comprehensive* reading of Scripture (discussed above in this chapter, under

theology, the true alternative is to be found not in some equally narrow alternative but in a complex and multifaceted consent.[102]

The recovery of patristic theology, however, is not merely an academic question of defining the boundaries of patristic consent. Such definition is, rather, both a source for, and a rule to guide and evaluate, a theology grounded not so much in the doctrine but in the lived reality of the baptismal gift of union with Christ. The reality of this gift is reflected in the practical holiness of the Christian, and accompanied by the gift of faith.[103] Through the mutual coinherence of holiness and faith, the Christian's growth in holiness enables, by faith, a clearer perception of the types given by God in Scripture and creation. The faith received in baptism, however, is, for Pusey, specifically *the faith of the Church*. The deepening understanding of the images given by God, then, is a matter of inhabiting, and becoming habituated in, the tradition of the Church, working between the figures to draw out their relations, within and alongside patterns already drawn between them.[104] This is, however, emphatically a matter of *perception*. Leighton Frappell observes that 'Pusey repaired to the Fathers originally in search of a method rather than an authority.'[105] While this is accurate as a statement about Pusey's *turn* to Christian antiquity, the reference to 'method' can mislead if applied to what he found there. Boersma notes that patristic exegesis is not based upon methodology but is in fact 'a form of contemplation' or '*theōria*'.[106] And indeed, what Pusey

'Allegory and scripture'). Pusey to Tholuck, 19 November 1839, in Geck, *Autorität*, 176–7; Pusey, *Fathers*, 719.

102. This is not to say that there cannot be degrees of 'consent', some of which indicate a closer agreement than what has been argued here. In his correspondence with Keble regarding eucharistic reception by the wicked, Pusey notes that Augustine was out of step with 'the consent of the Fathers' on this subject, seeming to mean a close agreement among the majority of the Fathers: the discussion demonstrates, however, that even in this narrow sense, consent is not a naïve assumption of patristic uniformity. But Pusey also (one year prior, but during the period in which he was weighing the former question) includes Augustine in his demonstration of patristic consent regarding the real presence, implying a broader sense in which consent on primary issues nonetheless allows for divergence on subsidiary questions. Pusey to Keble, 19 August and [27?] September 1856, in LBV 104; Pusey, *Fathers*, 497–543.

103. For discussion of faith and holiness in relation to baptism, see below in Chapter 3 under 'Union with Christ I: Faith, justification and glorification' and 'Union with Christ II: Holiness, sin and repentance'.

104. Pusey does not explicitly discuss doctrinal development, but the model suggested here – which is also logically consequent upon the historical narrative implicit in his theory of formularism – is a recursive model in which development occurs through the 'filling in' or elaboration of existing doctrine by repeated correction of theological distortions, rather than the linear progression set forth in Newman's *Essay on the Development of Doctrine*.

105. Frappell, '"Science"', 22–3.

106. Boersma, *Scripture as Real Presence*, 255. Cf. Andrew Louth, *Discerning the Mystery: An Essay on the Nature of Theology* (Oxford: Oxford University Press, 1983),

gained from the fathers was not a theological 'method' for doctrinal science but a theological *vision* – specifically, as the next section will argue, a *sacramental* vision – offering 'glimpses into a far distant land'.

Allegory and sacramentalism

Both the dual nature of biblical types as historical events or institutions which set forth an eternal archetype, and the broader lessons Pusey drew from imagery and figurative speech point to the idea of a sacrament, defined in the Prayer Book Catechism as an 'outward and visible sign of an inward and spiritual grace'. The catechism adds further qualifications which narrow its discussion to the two dominical sacraments, Pusey's treatments of which are discussed in the next two chapters. However, there are also, in Pusey's theology, broader principles of sacramentality, which are shaped by the allegorical considerations just discussed – in particular Pusey's doctrine of creation and the intimacy of God's involvement in the world which results from it.[107]

Keble's suggestion that creation was a kind of divine poetry, '*verba visibilia*' revealing God to those who sought him, highlights the sacramentality of creation in Tractarian thought.[108] For Keble, this is implicit in Scripture's use of natural imagery – the New Testament makes as much use of natural imagery as it does of Old Testament types, and often in similar ways: Heaven is the 'true sanctuary', but Christ is the 'true vine'. This suggests as much revelatory divine intent in creation as in Hebrew Scripture.[109] Moreover, natural imagery has networks of signification, similar to those of institutions or events: reference to a field opens up the whole realm of agriculture, even aspects not explicitly mentioned; and the

59–64. Louth argues, drawing on Gadamer, Polanyi and Hort, that despite popular notions concerning the 'scientific method', the sciences in fact depend on internalizing a tradition, just as much as more 'subjective' disciplines.

107. The Catechism (which dates, in its final form, from 1604) reflects earlier discussions in the Articles of Religion (Article 25) and the 'Homily of Common Prayer and Sacraments', the latter of which however recognizes a broader sacramentality beyond the narrowest technical definition. Pusey's theology is consistent with the homily's approach, which lies behind his preference for the term 'sacramental' to 'sacrament' for rites other than baptism and the Eucharist. 'An Homily Wherein Is Declared That Common Prayer and Sacraments Ought to Be Ministered in a Tongue That Is Understood of the Hearers', in *Certain Sermons, or Homilies, Appointed to Be Read in Churches* [...] (London: Prayer-Book and Homily Society, 1852), 328–9. For Pusey's usage of 'sacramental' see below in this section.

108. Keble, *Mysticism*, 148. This perspective is at least indirectly attributable to Butler, who cites Origen's use of allegory as providing the principle for his own 'analogy'. Joseph Butler, *The Analogy of Religion, Natural and Revealed, to the Constitution and Course of Nature*, in *The Works of Bishop Butler*, ed. David E. White (Rochester, NY: University of Rochester Press, 2006), 153.

109. Keble, *Mysticism*, 162–8.

combined regularity of many images, together with the complexity of their use (as, e.g., the Holy Spirit being described variously in terms of fire, water and breath), adds further support to this parallel.[110]

The same theme also plays an important role in Pusey's theology. 'The world then is our word of God; by His speech was it made'; 'To speak was to create; and so creation was his speech, as re-creation shall be another word.' And again,

> that which is of God, and wherein, according to their measures, God is, must in some finite way, express the character of God, which is in them, and must bear some relation to the other offspring of God. What God hath created, must, one may boldly say, express God; since God has no copy external to Himself, … human making must be after a pattern without him, although received in his mind, because he is finite and being created, createth not; Divine Creation must be the expression of something within God, because he is infinite.

Pusey has, however, a caveat to this analogy between human and divine making: because of sin, the reflection of divinity in human making 'is, in a measure, *de*faced' though 'not *e*ffaced; as far as it has life and remains good, it retains the impress of God'. In creation, however, insofar as all things continue to be upheld by God's spirit, they therefore 'breathe something divine'.[111]

The Tractarians were deeply influenced by the Romantic Movement (particularly the early Romanticism of the Lake Poets). Romantic ideas shaped Tractarian views on tradition and (later) the aestheticism and medievalism of the ritualists; and Keble and Newman both drew on Romantic thought for more particular purposes.[112] Pusey was no exception, and this discussion of divine communication in nature is the point at which the Romantic influence on his thought is most evident: both Wordsworth and Coleridge thought that nature conveyed the divine, and Coleridge in particular spoke of the natural world as God's 'eternal language'.[113] The Tractarian handling of the concept is more theologically rigorous, in ways that are not trivial: Pusey's description of *creation* as divine *speech* refers precisely to the creation account of Genesis 1, which Coleridge's somewhat pantheistic description of *nature* as divine *language* does not. A similar theological sharpening of Romantic thought can be seen in the importance the Tractarians attributed to poetry, and indeed to the role of the imagination in theology, which, while clearly influenced by the Romantics, was different in two important respects. First, the

---

110. Keble, *Mysticism*, 168–71, 179–85.

111. Pusey, 'Types', additional fragments.

112. Stephen Prickett, *Romanticism and Religion: The Tradition of Coleridge and Wordsworth in the Victorian Church* (Cambridge: Cambridge University Press, 1976), 91–119, 152–210, 249.

113. Douglas, 'Pusey, Poetry, and Eucharistic Theology', 89–90, quoting Coleridge, *The Complete Poems*, ed. William Keach (London: Penguin Press, 2004), 232; Douglas and Douglas, 'Pusey and the Romantic Poets', 541–8.

Tractarian understanding of tradition introduces a communal element (as, e.g., in Pusey, where it is understood precisely as historical *consensus* in the faith) which balances the potentially egocentric tendencies of creative imagination, which they rejected in the Romantics.[114] Second, the Tractarian understanding of imagination as 'a capacity for recognition' is distinct from the (quasi-divine) 'creative power' given to that faculty in Romanticism.[115] This is the point particularly in view here: for Pusey, it is not too much to say that 'imagination' is simply the act of faith in perceiving God's speech.

Pusey finds evidence for this understanding of creation in the fact that various images communicate the same meanings across cultures. 'Thus a broken flower, as designating one untimely cut off; mown corn as manhood cut down; the course of a river as cleansing ...; a bubble, as vanity; spring, as youth, winter as old age; and the like, will be found in every language, i.e. by every nation these analogies have been perceived and held to be true.'[116] For Pusey, the principle that 'creation was God's speech' applies also to the interpretation of human society: God is revealed to a limited extent, even in 'heathen' cultures. Secular or pagan histories or philosophies can outline certain characteristics of human nature, or of morality and the consequences of good or evil, and thus to a certain extent provide patterns of history which we can learn from. However, this has two important qualifications that distinguish such revelation from that contained in Scripture. First, they are imperfect, though even that imperfection points by its lack to the perfection of God. And second, 'what is typical in the world's history' is not in the details or particular persons, but in the broad outlines of events. Though this contrasts with his observations of biblical types, which often depend on details or particulars, it is nonetheless similar to the tendency, which he observes in the Old Testament histories, to strip away 'all peculiarity of character ... from those whom the world counts great', so that they appear 'in the one single character of haughty and unconscious instruments of God's will'.[117] So too, God reveals himself, not only through the faithful characters in Scripture but also through the ungodly (e.g., Pilate in writing the inscription on the cross) – 'guiding, empowering, and acting in the free-will of His servants, overruling the enslaved minds of His enemies, so that the one acted and spoke by His Spirit, the other, acting and speaking by the evil spirit which possessed them, yet both in words and actions, portrayed an ideal more finished than themselves'.[118]

---

114. Louth, 'Oxford Movement', 34–6.

115. Allchin, 'Theological Vision', 64; cf. David Jasper, 'Pusey's "Lectures on Types and Prophecies of the Old Testament"', in Perry Butler, *Pusey Rediscovered*, 56; Douglas and Douglas, 'Pusey and the Romantic Poets', 548.

116. Pusey, 'Types', additional fragments. The context for this observation is a discussion of Arabic poetry.

117. Pusey, 'Types', additional fragments.

118. Pusey, 'Types', additional fragments.

Implicit in this vision of creation, however, is an analogy between types – of all kinds – and the sacraments. The outward type relates to its allegorical meaning in a way that parallels the relation of the outward and inward parts of the sacrament. Pusey suggests that this is a structural principle in creation. The outward–inward relation can be seen in the natural world, as in Scripture; it is also reflected in the 'compound nature' of humanity – body and soul – and in language: 'our very words are two-fold; they are taken from material things, have a material substance, yet act invisibly, bear an un-material meaning, as they are received by the eyes and ears but act on the soul, so that we may in some states of mind, lose all consciousness of seeing or hearing them'. This sacramental duality of creation reaches its pinnacle in the incarnation: God revealed in a material human body.[119]

The philosophical perspective underpinning this 'sacramental vision' is a mystical materialism, which Pusey believes to be inherent both in the beliefs of the early church and in the theology of the Prayer Book.

> It may be remarked (and misapprehension may thereby be saved, and our own Liturgy illustrated) that in this history, and elsewhere, there is in the Ancient Church what by moderns would be condemned as Realism, or Materialism, or Mysticism. Their view seems to have been of this sort; that, since God had appointed the use of water for Baptism, there must have been an appropriateness in it, which there was in no other element; that there was an analogy between His physical and moral Creation, and that not only imaginative but real; that in forming the Physical, He had respect also to the purposes which He designed in His Moral creation, and imparted to the physical agent properties corresponding to its moral uses; that in His own earlier dispensations He had regard to the latter, and not only taught man beforehand what should be, but, in a manner, by employing His creature in the subordinate offices of the former, imparted to it a fitness to serve in the latter and greater.[120]

119. Pusey, 'Types', additional fragments. These sacramental 'parallels' are described in their patristic origin by de Lubac, *Medieval Exegesis*, 1:150; 2:4–27, 59–63, 83–5, 107–17.

120. Pusey, *Baptism 2*, 361. 'Realism' posits the real existence of external reality; 'mysticism' concerns the participation of that reality in God. Both of these are clearly elements in Pusey's thought. The inclusion of 'materialism', however – denoting the view that reality is entirely made up of matter – is problematic, since Pusey clearly believes in the existence of immaterial or spiritual reality (in this passage corresponding to the 'moral creation'). One reading would see this as simply a loose usage, meant, in conjunction with 'realism', to indicate realism with regard to the existence of matter. A stronger (and more likely) reading, however, would interpret Pusey as using something like the technical definition, but with three implied corollaries: the limitation of materialism to the 'physical creation', the existence of a distinct 'moral' or spiritual creation, and the participation of the physical (material) in the moral (spiritual). On this reading, the force of 'materialism' would therefore exclude dualism or primarily abstract conceptions of reality (especially, in Pusey's historical context, idealist views which assert the ontological priority of an immaterial mind and its thoughts or perceptions) from the this-worldly (physical) aspect of creation: God did

Pusey clearly favours this mystical 'materialism'; the reality of the material object or substance is given deeper significance by its higher meaning, much like the 'literal' sense of the biblical types. This reflects a Platonic metaphysic of participation, perhaps latent, to some extent, in Pusey's Anglican education (Westhaver traces it to Richard Hooker), but more likely acquired from his immersion in the Fathers.[121] This is most evident in the hierarchical relations (redolent of Neo-Platonism) that Pusey sees between the various types; and in particular, between the various classifications of types and sacraments.[122] Natural or historical types speak less clearly of Christ than biblical types; 'sacramentals' (such as marriage, absolution or preaching) point us to Christ, but do not communicate *him* personally in the same degree as the dominical sacraments. 'Things, words and persons' all have 'inherent' hierarchical relations to each other; and according to their various qualities 'stand in different degrees of nearness' not only to each other, but to their archetype. Conversely, a prophecy (or a natural type) may also have 'a manifold sense and fulfilment', the highest being the most real.[123]

The 'materialism' described here is the first of two crucial points on which Pusey differs from Newman: in direct contrast to Pusey, Newman professes his own philosophical idealism and belief in the 'unreality of material phenomena'.[124] These statements reflect the view, rooted in empiricist philosophy, that things cannot be known in themselves, but only through the mind's experience of them. Newman combines this perspective with reference to 'objective ideas' and 'objective facts'.[125] This use of 'objective' as a qualifier indicates Newman's belief in a reality that is independent of the mind – an important consideration, in light of his idealism. But it also marks another contrast with Pusey. According to an 'objective' conception, reality exists passively, is subject to rational discovery and verification (often through the application of an appropriate method) and therefore exists in itself. (Truth, on this view, concerns the correspondence between statements and reality – a notion which de Lubac contrasts with an earlier understanding,

---

not create minds and spirits, but bodies and spirits, and the spiritual is therefore conveyed in bodily, rather than abstract, form.

121. Douglas, 'Pusey's "Lectures on Types"', 196; Westhaver, 'Living Body', 216–17; Smith, *Radical Orthodoxy*, 73–7; Boersma, *Nouvell Théologie*, 86–7; *Heavenly Participation*, 22–5.

122. Cf. Boersma, *Heavenly Participation*, 34–5; *Scripture as Real Presence*, 113.

123. Pusey, 'Types', additional fragments; cf. *The Minor Prophets* (New York: Funk and Wagnalls, 1888–9), 1:159–92, 2:47–51, 64, 236.

124. Newman, *Apologia*, 140–1, 148. Cf. J. M. Cameron, 'Newman and the Empiricist Tradition', in Coulson and Allchin, *Rediscovery*, 77. Härdelin argues that Newman, like Pusey, acquired a kind of Platonism from reading the Fathers; *if* this is the case, their different metaphysical and epistemological frameworks gave it very different results. Alf Härdelin, *The Tractarian Understanding of the Eucharist* (Uppsala: Almquist & Wiksells, 1965), 70.

125. J. H. Newman, *An Essay on the Development of Christian Doctrine*, 11th impression (London: Longmans, Green, 1900), 34, 55.

in which truth is an 'assimilating force that transforms the very intelligence', not gained through methodology but conveyed by the rule of faith.)[126] Insofar as it focuses on the existence of things in themselves, an 'objective' view of reality clearly clashes with Pusey's understanding of creation as participating in Christ; indeed, it corresponds to the flat, reductionist or 'univocal' views of meaning and existence which he specifically rejects. In fact, Pusey's only prominent use of the term is to refer to the 'real objective presence' of Christ in the Eucharist; and he carefully excludes any wider metaphysical implications from his usage: he uses the phrase *'not as wishing to obtrude on others a term of modern philosophy*, but' – simply – 'to express that the Life-giving Body ... is, by virtue of the consecration, present without us, to be received by us'. Similarly, Pusey's introduction to *Daniel* appeals to 'definite' rather than 'objective' truth.[127] This divergence, in particular, can account (at least in part) for the stylistic contrast between the two friends: Newman, in his prose theology, relies on the classification and definition of concepts; Pusey on the accumulation and interplay of images.

This sketch of the philosophical divergences between Pusey and Newman, brief as it is, should suggest the care needed – which has not always been exercised – in determining where their theologies are compatible and where they are not.[128] The full ramifications of these differences cannot be explored here. With regard to Pusey's 'sacramental vision', however, they point to a stark contrast between the friends' respective treatments of sacramentalism. For Newman, spiritual ascent can be characterized (in the terminology of his empiricist idealism) by the loss of

---

126. De Lubac, *Medieval Exegesis*, 1:xv–xvi, 3:96; cf. Louth, *Mystery*, 26–8. The concept is perhaps best understood through the parallel usage in grammar: the subject acts; the object is acted upon. The view de Lubac articulates is therefore described by Louth as 'subjective truth'. For an 'objective' theory of meaning, see description in Lakoff and Johnson, *Metaphors*, 185–9.

127. Pusey, 'Presence of Christ', vi–vii; 'This is My Body', 40 (emphasis added); *Daniel*, xxvii. This phrase is not original to Pusey – it appears earlier in Robert Wilberforce's *Doctrine of the Incarnation*, and Pusey refers to it in correspondence with Keble as common terminology among the Tractarians. R. I. Wilberforce, *The Doctrine of the Incarnation of Our Lord Jesus Christ, in Its Relation to Mankind and to the Church* (London: John Murray, 1848), 433–5. Cf. Pusey to Keble, 24 December 1854; 15[?] August 1856; and 27[?] September 1856, LBV 104; and 29 December 1858, LBV 105.

128. Though not necessarily consequent on the differences noted here, other contrasts have been made which are beginning to disentangle Pusey's theology from Newman's. Thus, David Brown argues that Newman's theory of development displays 'too much of Victorian over-confidence in the inevitability of progress' whereas Pusey places a more appropriate emphasis on human fallibility and sinfulness. Mark Chapman, meanwhile, makes an apt contrast between Pusey's 'Catholicism of the Word' and Newman's 'Catholicism of devotion', though his description of Pusey's approach to Christianity as 'dry' and 'rational', while justifiable perhaps as a narrow assessment of the *Eirenicon*, fails to account for Pusey's wider spirituality or theology. David Brown, 'Pusey', 334–5; Chapman, *Fantasy*, 70–99.

'material phenomena' – this is, in fact, his description of Jesus' post-resurrection appearances – and in the same way, sacramentalism involves moving *past* the (unreal) phenomena of the sign to the (objective) reality of the thing signified.[129] Pusey, however, insists that it is just as idolatrous to dispense with the sign, as to stop short in it:

> It has been well said that God has appointed, as it were, a sort of sacramental union between the type and the archetype, so that as the type were nothing, except in as far as it represents, and is the medium of conveying the archetype to the mind, so neither can the archetype be conveyed except through the type. Though the consecrated element be not the sacrament, yet neither can the soul of the Sacrament be attained without it. God has joined them together, and men may not and cannot put them asunder.[130]

Both the 'carnal' idolater and the 'pseudo-spiritualist' see the type and the sacramental elements as bare, and thereby lose their spiritual benefit:

> the carnal would live on bread alone, the pseudospiritualist [*sic*] without it; the carnal man mistakes the clouds of darkness for Him who is enshrouded within it, the pseudo-spiritualist would behold Him, Whom 'man cannot see and live', the 'light inapproachable, Whom no man hath seen or can see'; the carnal neglects the revelation, the pseudo-spiritual would know the unveiled God.[131]

For Pusey, the concrete image, with its richness of meaning, is the indispensable, sole means of revelation; for Newman, it is a 'material phenomenon' – at best to be surpassed, at worst a misleading snare to the understanding. The two friends seem not to have noted the seeds of this divergence between them in the 1830s (or if they did, they chose not to stress it for reasons of friendship), and Newman may not yet have fully realized the implications of his own philosophy. After his conversion to Roman Catholicism, however, he appears to have adopted a theory of transubstantiation profoundly shaped by his idealism. This contrast seems to have caused some misunderstanding in their 1867 correspondence on the Eucharist, where Pusey's concern is to understand how the *matter* of the eucharistic elements fares in Roman Catholic doctrine, but Newman rejects the question as falling outside proper theological inquiry.[132]

129. Newman, *Justification*, 235–6.
130. Pusey, 'Types', 23–4.
131. Pusey, 'Types', 23–4, quoting Exod. 33.20, 1 Tim. 6.16.
132. Liddon, *Life*, 4:166–72. The nuances of the correspondence are difficult to interpret: Newman's *explicit* response to Pusey's question about 'matter' ('I do not think it is a theological word') refers to its omission from the Catechism of the Council of Trent and the Thirty-nine Articles. This is, of course, a point of which Pusey would have been aware – it is likely the very motivation behind his question. However, though Newman's reply does not explicitly broach the subject of idealism, he identifies the 'accidents, species' and even

2. Allegory and the Sacramental Vision

For Pusey, the essence of revealed religion, especially the religion of the incarnation, is that we do not comprehend God; rather, God makes himself known to us. Thus the life of the Church, the life of the sacraments and the language of Scripture – the concrete, tangible aspects of religion, *by which* God makes himself known – cannot be set aside:

> Neither the letter without the Spirit, nor the Spirit without the letter – prayers, which God giveth into the midst of us to hear; earthly Sacraments yet full of Heaven, earthly words, yet full of the Word, *logoi* proceeding from and setting forth the *logos*. And we, as we walk still by faith and not by sight, must be constant to see still the reflected light, 'as in a glass darkly,' not 'face to face,' that we be not guilty of the folly which the Heathen fable was intended to reprove, when she (the soul) who would see the Father of all, unveiled, had her request and perished.[133]

This emphasis on the sacramental and other aspects of outward religion is also implicit in a note to this discussion, on translations that 'substitute abstract, and as they would fain have it, clearer terms for the types or typical language of the Old Testament', but 'uniformly by this transmutation evaporate much of their meaning. … Men think that we gain in clearness, but they lose in depth; nay, we employ definite terms, in order to comprehend that which is infinite!' The particular examples he has in mind are quite specific:

> We have not, it is true, visible propitiatory sacrifice or a visible theocracy, a visible temple, but it is still through the medium of these figures that we understand, (as far as we do understand,) the reality: we have no better way of understanding the main truths of the Gospel than through these very figures, 'the sacrifice of Christ' 'the kingdom of God' 'the temple of the Holy Ghost;' and he who would lay aside these types and typical language, and understand the mysteries of God without them, would be acting contrary to the teaching of Scripture and so very wrongly and foolishly.[134]

Given that the text above this note explicitly refers to the Eucharist and the liturgies of the Church, it is clear that Pusey is thinking not only of the biblical images of sacrifice, the kingdom of God and the temple, but the sacramental manifestations of those images within the Church.

---

the 'physis' of the elements as 'phenomena', and he concludes that their difficulty reaching an understanding in this exchange is due to 'some radical differences of thought'. It is likely, therefore, that his resistance to considering Pusey's question is informed by his idealism.

133. Pusey, 'Types', 23–4, quoting 1 Cor. 13.12 and referring to the Greek myth of Semele; cf. Exod. 33.20. For Pusey's views on types in non-Christian cultures, see above in this section.

134. Pusey, 'Types', 24.

A deeper understanding of Pusey's sacramentalism can be gained from two of what he called 'sacramentals' or 'mysteries', absolution and marriage. 'Sacramentals' – an open-ended category for Pusey, not limited to the five 'sacraments of the Church' – are placed distinctly below baptism and the Eucharist. Nonetheless, they convey more than just gifts to the understanding: they do not directly communicate union with Christ, but they can convey real, practical grace to assist in faithful Christian living and in spiritual growth.[135] Absolution has some resemblance to baptism, 'restoring the returning penitent to the state of grace from which he had fallen, cleansing anew the white robes which he had defiled, remitting the guilt, and opening the avenues to the full inflow of grace which sin had choked'.[136] It is a restoration, however, not a second beginning; it is not a new life in Christ, but the removal of the cancerous growth of sin. 'In Baptism, a man becomes a new self, and being another man, has no more to do with his former sins, than if they had been committed by another, except to love and thank God who had freed him from them; by Absolution, pardon is given, life is renewed, but the penitent is the same as the sinner.'[137] Marriage, on the other hand, is an exercise in love in preparation for heaven – its vocation, for both husband and wife, is to imitate the love of Christ for his Church, despite its faults. Christ loves with the power to remove those faults, and though 'we cannot imitate the power, we can, through His grace imitate the love'.[138]

In a certain sense, these 'mysteries' are closer to types than to baptism and the Eucharist, because while the dominical sacraments convey what they signify, these lesser rites point beyond themselves to greater gifts, as 'shadows of things unseen, the foretaste, in some measure, of things eternal'.[139] So, the Old Testament observances of the Day of Atonement 'did cleanse from sins', but only in a legal and

---

135. E. B. Pusey, *The Articles Treated on in Tract 90 Reconsidered, and Their Interpretation Vindicated in a Letter to the Rev. R. W. Jelf, D. D.* (Oxford: John Henry Parker, 1841), 39–42 (hereafter *Jelf*). Pusey accepts a general use of the term 'sacraments', but prefers to use it specifically to refer to the dominical sacraments; 'mystery' in patristic usage included the dominical sacraments, but Pusey applies it to other sacramental aspects of Christian practice in order to distinguish them from the dominical sacraments. Preaching, fasting, the Creed, prayer – especially the Lord's Prayer – Scripture and martyrdom are all elements of Christian practice which, Pusey argues, ought to be seen as 'mysteries'. Pusey sees his position as moderating between rejection of any sacramentality in these things (which he thinks stems from too low a conception of the grace given in baptism and the Eucharist), and the Roman Catholic system, which by emphasizing confession and transubstantiation *in practice* risked throwing baptism into the shade. See *Baptism 2*, 190; *Oxford*, 114–17; cf. Palmer, *Treatise*, 1:173–4; and see above in this chapter, n. 107.

136. Pusey, 'Entire Absolution I', 30.

137. Pusey, 'Entire Absolution I', 22–3.

138. E. B. Pusey, 'The Sacredness of Marriage', in *Parochial Sermons*, vol. 2, 3rd edn (Oxford: John Henry Parker, 1857), 391–3 (hereafter *Par. S. II*).

139. Pusey, 'Marriage', 387.

therefore 'outward and inadequate and transitory' way, while foreshadowing the greater reality of redemption in Christ.[140] Absolution not only forgives sins in the present life, but foreshadows Christ's declaration of forgiveness of the penitent at the last judgement: 'the judgment, ... is an earnest of the judgment of Christ, and is confirmed by Him'.[141] Thus the image of the Last Judgement is, for the sincere penitent, not one of fear but of hope: our judge is our redeemer. Marriage, meanwhile, signifies 'the mystery of holy union'.[142] It reflects the Trinity, through the union of man with woman who 'was formed not apart ... but of the very substance ... of the man'.[143] And it reflects the 'three-fold union of God with man' in the incarnation, in Christ's union with the Church as his 'one mystical body' and in his union with each Christian, 'since what Christ does for the whole Church, He, through His indivisible love, does for every soul which He makes His, ... He ... espoused [sic] to himself each single soul which, by His love, He should draw unto Himself'.[144] As an image of divine unity-in-love, marriage is therefore a foretaste of heaven.

> This love shall not decay, much less dies [sic], even after the body's death. For souls which are united in Christ, shall not be separated from Christ; they shall live on still, one in the one love of Christ. In heaven there shall be 'neither marrying nor giving in marriage,' but there shall be love; love, pure, holy, happy, like that of the angels of God in heaven, who are ever filled with the love of God, ever behold the Face of God, are ever over-streamed with the radiancy of that love, which issues forth from the eternal Fountain of love.[145]

A final distinction lies in a certain degree of uncertainty as to whether the grace signified in them is conveyed: they '*may be*' – not *are* – 'and *some* certainly are, ... means of grace'.[146] It is not that Pusey doubts God's willingness to give grace by any means available, but whereas Christ himself had promised his presence in the dominical sacraments, there is no such guarantee in these other mysteries. Unlike baptism and the Eucharist, the grace of such rites depends at least in part

---

140. Pusey, 'Types', 97–8; cf. Waterland, 'Christian Sacrifice', 148.

141. Pusey, 'Entire Absolution I', 24. Cf. 'Entire Absolution of the Penitent, Sermon II' (Oxford: John Henry Parker), 37–9; in *US I*, paginated individually. Pusey's second sermon on absolution uses the same imagery of the Last Judgment, in connection with the season of Advent.

142. Pusey, 'Marriage', 387. The language of 'mystery' is drawn from the sermon's text (Eph. 5.32); but it is no accident that the term which Pusey connects in *Baptism* with these sacramental rites becomes a recurring theme in the sermon. Note that the three doctrines signified by the 'literal' union of man and woman in marriage correspond (respectively) to de Lubac's anagogical, allegorical, and moral forms of interpretation.

143. Pusey, 'Marriage', 387–8.

144. Pusey, 'Marriage', 389–90.

145. Pusey, 'Marriage', 393–4.

146. Pusey, *Jelf*, 35; emphasis mine.

on the participants. Absolution only remits sin 'if the penitent be sincere', and the reality of its grace is therefore in some degree contingent on the minister's judgement: 'the same penitent has yet to appear before the Judgment-seat of Christ, that, according to his sincerity, the Lord may ratify *or annul* the judgment of His servants'.[147] Likewise in marriage, the unspoken qualification is that its grace depends, to some degree, on the human will to grow in it: we *can* imitate Christ's love, by his help; doing so, and the transformation that comes from such imitation, is possible, but not automatic. This qualified nature of the grace given in these 'mysteries' again places them between the types and the dominical sacraments: it is a higher grace than that of the Law, and directly connected to the Christian life, but more contingent than the realities contained in baptism and the Eucharist. What this intermediate status shows, however, is the strength of his sacramental vision of creation: all things are instruments of God; nothing (save sin) is apart from him.

***

Understood through the lens of the earlier *Enquiry* into German theology, Pusey's interest in allegory is not just an historicist preoccupation, but his answer to the urgent problem of renewing the Church and its theology which had been posed by the *Enquiry*. In expanding an approach used (though in a limited way) within the older high church tradition, Pusey was able to find principles which allow an imaginatively rich and engaging approach to theology, while providing for considerable complexity when the relation and interaction of images and types is translated into theological practice. While many of Pusey's longer works are controversial in nature and therefore utilize other modes of argumentation, allegory continues to be evident throughout much of his later work, particularly in *The Minor Prophets* and in his homiletical material, where it can provide either the subject matter or indeed the medium of Pusey's discussion. The heart of this vision, however, is Pusey's belief that all things – nature, history and more particularly Scripture and the life of the Church – participate in and set forth the incarnate Christ, the archetype and subject of all creation.

---

147. Pusey, 'Entire Absolution I', 24; emphasis mine.

Chapter 3

BAPTISM AND UNION WITH CHRIST

Pusey's *Enquiry* into German rationalism had highlighted the dangers of a narrowly dogmatic or apologetic approach to theology, and of a merely moralistic approach to the Christian life. As discussed in the previous chapter, Pusey found his corrective in a turn to the Fathers and in a sacramental vision of creation drawn from their allegorical hermeneutics. This addressed the concerns of the *Enquiry*, first by providing the principles (expressed in patristic allegory) for a rich and complex theology; and second, by placing Christian living on the foundation of a robust doctrine of union with Christ. These themes not only share an ontological root but are connected, as has already been noted, through the Tractarian emphasis on the necessity of holy living for theological discernment, and (for Pusey especially) in the theological importance given to types, both in Scripture and the natural order, as created and *concrete* communications of Christ, their archetype. The intertwining of union with Christ and the concrete communication of him to the faithful points, in turn, to the sacramental life of the Church and, above all, to the two sacraments of baptism and the Eucharist. In these sacraments, Pusey insists, God unites us to himself in his Son, which places them at the very centre of the Christian life. As Westhaver notes, in Pusey, 'the exposition of the Incarnation becomes the exposition of the sacraments and of the sacramental union of the mystical body of Christ with the Head'.[1]

Pusey's sacramental theology also provides a fruitful opportunity, however, for examining his development of the theology of the high church tradition. Baptism and the Eucharist were already central to high church thought; Pusey's 'sacramental vision' only reinforced a perspective inherited from the older tradition. Union with Christ was, again, not a new doctrine. The weight Pusey gave to it, however, produced a new intensity in Tractarian views on baptismal holiness and Christ's presence in the Eucharist, which startled some churchmen of the older school. This intensity, however, reflected Pusey's concern, beginning with the *Enquiry*, for a holistic approach to Christianity which united doctrine and practice: it is above all in the concreteness of the sacraments that the doctrines of salvation *touch* the Christian life. Baptism, as the foundational sacrament of the Christian life, naturally comes first.

1. Westhaver, 'Mysticism', 261.

Baptism and regeneration

Pusey's fullest discussion of baptism comes in the *Scriptural Views of Holy Baptism*, published, in the first edition (1835–6), as three tracts (numbers 67–69) totalling roughly two hundred pages and, in later editions (from 1839), as one tract (number 67) of roughly four hundred pages.² Both versions, written concurrently with Pusey's study of allegory, engage in lengthy discussion of the biblical types of baptism; in the later version, this occupies the majority of the work. The Flood receives differing interpretations in the two editions: in the first, the ark (as the Church) is the vessel which saves from destruction, while the waters (foreshadowing baptism) are the occasion for entering it; in the second, the waters themselves are the focus, destroying the old world that it may be renewed, just as in baptism the 'old Adam' is destroyed and replaced by the new.³ The crossing of the Red Sea is, likewise, a deliverance from evil and destruction into a new life. It is followed by the desert, foreshadowing the difficulties of the Christian life and the danger of falling away, though the heavenly manna (foreshadowing the Eucharist) is given for sustenance.⁴ Circumcision serves as a symbol of 'spiritual mercies' and 'spiritual duties', though as being merely symbolic (and not, as the Flood and the Red Sea, a redemptive event in itself) it is of weaker force in its application to the reality of baptism.⁵ The Levitical washings before worship, or to cleanse leprosy, symbolize baptism as the means of entering the Church, and as our cleansing from sin.⁶ Following these types which are specifically mentioned

---

2. The three tracts address different topics related to baptism: Tract 67 discusses baptismal regeneration, Tract 68 addresses the spiritual consequences of post-baptismal sin and Tract 69 presents a polemic against Calvinist views of the sacrament. This chapter is primarily concerned with the contents of Tracts 67 and 68; Tract 69, as a negative polemic, does not offer as much insight into the workings of his theology. Moreover, Pusey's charge that Calvin allegedly sees baptism as a mere sign must be regarded as mistaken: Calvin, like Pusey, sees baptism as conferring union with Christ and regeneration. This was, however, the nadir of Pusey's views of Calvin, which continued to evolve: he was likely unduly influenced in his views both by Newman's antipathy for the Genevan master and by the equation, in nineteenth-century polemical usage, of 'Calvinism' with Evangelicalism. Pusey revised (and substantially expanded) Tract 67, but revisions to the other two tracts were never completed, and they were omitted from the later editions of the Tracts for the Times. Jean Calvin, *Institutes of the Christian Religion*, ed. John T. McNeill, trans. Ford Lewis Battles (London: SCM Press, 1961), 4.16.1–6, cf. Mark A. Garcia, *Life in Christ: Union with Christ and Twofold Grace in Calvin's Theology* (Eugene, OR: Wipf and Stock, 2008), 127–8, 151; Pusey, *Baptism 1*, 111–24. For discussion of Pusey's views on Calvin, see Chapter 4 under 'Real presence I: Pusey's reformed framework'.

3. Pusey, *Baptism 1*, 44–5; *Baptism 2*, 303–5.
4. Pusey, *Baptism 2*, 312–20.
5. Pusey, *Baptism 2*, 320–3.
6. Pusey, *Baptism 2*, 340–1.

in the New Testament, Pusey also discusses several identified by the early Fathers, although he argues not so much for the reception of every one, as for the value of being alive to the spiritual meanings of Scripture: 'it is a cold, stiff, and lifeless system, so to bind ourselves to take the letter of Holy Scripture, as to refuse to stir hand or foot, even when that Scripture seems to beckon and invite us, and point the way'.[7] Similarly, he argues that baptismal meanings can be drawn from many of Christ's miracles – such as the pool of Siloam – which, though occurring in the New Testament, are open to allegorical interpretation as acts of physical, rather than spiritual, deliverance.[8]

Natural types are also important. Marriage (which is perhaps both a biblical and a natural type) is one such: Pusey uses the language of becoming 'one flesh' more frequently with reference to the Eucharist, but he occasionally applies it to baptism as the beginning and source of the Christian's union with Christ.[9] Likewise, although baptismal regeneration is generally discussed as a doctrine, it is also a type (new birth) – and Pusey considers both aspects. Thus, approaching it doctrinally, he maintains that baptism

> is our new birth, an actual birth of God, of water, and the Spirit, as we were actually born of our natural parents; herein then are we also justified, or both accounted and made righteous, since we are made members of Him who is Alone Righteous; freed from past sin, whether original or actual; have a new principle of life imparted to us, since having been made members of Christ, we have a portion of His life, or of Him who is our Life; herein we also have the hope of the resurrection and of immortality, because we have been made partakers of his resurrection, have risen again with Him.[10]

However, considered as a type, the imagery of birth also adds to our understanding of baptism. Birth is a past event, but one which implies present life: 'Birth is one gift, though it would not profit us to have been born, unless the being, thus bestowed, were afterwards upheld by His Fatherly care.'[11] And like natural birth, spiritual rebirth is mysterious. 'How the Sacraments effect this we know not: we understand not the mysteries of our first, how should we then of our second, birth? Of both rather we confess, that we are fearfully and wonderfully made, but how we were fashioned, we know not.'[12] Indeed, consideration of regeneration as a type – and the interpretation of that type through the further natural type of the seed – exercises considerable influence on Pusey's articulation of regeneration as a

---

7. Pusey, *Baptism 2*, 344.
8. Pusey, *Baptism 2*, 344–67.
9. Pusey, *Baptism 2*, 101–2; 'Bliss of Heaven – Glory of the Body', in *SR*, 303.
10. Pusey, *Baptism 2*, 23–4.
11. Pusey, *Baptism 2*, 155.
12. Pusey, *Baptism 1*, 113–14.

doctrine, concerned with the beginning of growth in the Christian life rather than its fulfilment (a view discussed more fully below).

However, despite the importance of types in Pusey's understanding of the sacraments, and indeed the deep significance of the material elements in them, the sacraments are more than just types. There is a correlation between the symbolic and spiritual aspects of the types, and the outward and inward parts of the sacraments. However, they are differentiated by the foundational distinction within the allegorical hermeneutic, between type and reality. The Old Testament types foreshadow the future realities of the New Testament; the sacraments participate in the realities of Christ's death and resurrection, and are themselves realities prefigured in the old covenant. They are symbolic, indeed, but they are also much more.

> They are mystical representations to the soul: they are props of faith: they are visible seals of God's promises: they are images of things invisible: they are instruments to lift up our hearts to communion with God in Christ: but they are more; ... They are channels of Divine grace to the soul, which are closed up indeed by unfaithfulness, yet are efficacious, not simply by animating our faith; but the one, by actually incorporating us into Christ, and creating in our souls a new principle of life, and making us 'partakers of the Divine nature'; the other, imparting to us increased union with Christ.[13]

Because they are *realities*, and not mere figures, Pusey insists on the reality of the grace given in the sacraments, and the reality of the change that grace can bring. The sacraments are 'full of life and honour and immortality, for that they are full of Christ'.[14]

***

In baptism, the reality of this sacramental grace entails, however, that the Christian's baptismal death and resurrection with Christ (Rom. 6.3-6) is not merely a moral teaching. That the Christian *ought* to die to sin and live in Christ is implicit in the passage, but its point is that this death and resurrection *has been given* in baptism:

> 'We have been all baptized into Christ,' i.e. into a participation of Christ, and His most precious death, and union with Him, we, i.e. our old man, our corrupted selves, *have been* buried with Him, by Baptism, into that death, *that we may* walk in newness of life. Again, we *have been* planted in the likeness of His death *that we may* be of His resurrection. Again, our old man *has been* crucified – that the whole body of sin *may be* destroyed. And so, throughout, there are two

---

13. Pusey, *Baptism 1*, 113–14. Reflecting on 1 Jn 5.6-8, Pusey comments that the sacraments 'are the visible tokens of His invisible Presence; the means of our adoption; the "pledges of His love;" the witnesses that He "is come in the flesh"'. Pusey, *Baptism 2*, 299–300.

14. Pusey, *Baptism 2*, 128.

deaths, in one of which we were passive only; we were baptized, buried, planted, crucified; the very language marks that this was all God's doing, in us, and for us: there remains the other death, which we must continually die. Sin has once been remitted, slain, crucified; we must, [sic] henceforth watch that it live not again in us, that we extirpate all the roots thereof, that we serve it not again, that we live through its death.[15]

Paul's language is both past and passive – what God *has done* to us, in baptism. Our union with Christ's death and life, the guarantee of our own resurrection, is entirely God's work through the sacrament.[16] Pusey finds this point important enough that he substantially expands it in the later edition: we *were* circumcised without hands, and buried and raised with Christ (Col. 2.10-13, 3.1); we *were* sealed or anointed; the Church *was* cleansed (Eph. 5.26) – all *past* actions of God, which produce the *present* reality of life in Christ.[17] In the Christian life, Pusey argues, the past event is baptism, its present consequence is union with Christ.

So, in Galatians 3.27 ('For as many of you as have been baptized unto Christ, have put on Christ'):

Whoever of us has been baptized, was thereby incorporated into Christ, and so being made a portion and member of the Son of God, partakes of that sonship, and is himself a child of God: so that henceforth the Father looks upon him, not as what he is in himself, but as in, and a part of, His Well-beloved Son, and loves him with a portion of that ineffable love with which He loves His Son. St. Paul speaks then not of duties, (though every privilege involves a duty corresponding,) but of privileges, inestimable, inconceivable, which no thought can reach unto, but which all thought should aim at embracing, – our union with God in Christ, wherein we were joined in the Holy Baptism.[18]

These 'privileges' of baptism and God's inestimable love for all who, through it, are in Christ are the major theme of the work in both its earlier and its later form. In this we can see the *Enquiry*'s concerns lurking in the background – Pusey stresses the *privileges* of baptism, against the rationalism which would sever the grace from the sacrament as impossible or unbelievable, against a 'Pietist' Evangelicalism which gave undue weight to the personal and affective, and against an 'orthodoxist' high churchmanship which held the truth of the doctrine, but 'coldly', setting forth the duties rather than the gifts that regeneration implies. Pusey insists, rather, that in baptism, everything signified by the baptismal types, or by the rite itself, has in fact been given to us by God.

---

15. Pusey, *Baptism 1*, 22–3; emphasis Pusey's. Cf. also 31–4.
16. Pusey, *Baptism 1*, 26–8.
17. Pusey, *Baptism 2*, 93–109 (Romans); 124–33 and 175–87 (Colossians); 155–75 (on 'sealing'); and 190–1 (Ephesians).
18. Pusey, *Baptism 1*, 28; cf. *Baptism 2*, 109–24.

However, just as prophetic types might have differing degrees of fulfilment, the gifts of baptism are fulfilled in different degrees of perfection. First is the 'perfection in our home ... whereby they who shall attain, shall be perfected in Him Who Alone is Perfect, our Father Who is in Heaven'. Then comes the perfection of baptism: 'Perfect must be the gift of The Perfect', although we receive it imperfectly; 'Perfect is the principle of life imparted to us, but we receive it in "a body of death."' But last, there is the perfection of this life, which consists in yielding completely to God's will: 'And as we are thus perfect in the purpose of God, so have we a sort of relative, an imperfect perfecting, in faith, in will, in temper, in love, if we give up ourselves without reserve to receive that perfect gift of God. It is a sort of perfection, to hold nothing back from the perfecting grace of God'.[19]

The latter two of these 'perfections', however, are mixed. Our imperfect receiving of God's perfect gift and the 'imperfect perfection' of Christian growth both reflect the reality of sin. Natural types prove their usefulness in grappling with this tension. Pusey was well aware of the ambiguities surrounding the word 'regeneration', but his own understanding of the term is literal – *re-birth*, a new beginning. Regeneration is therefore the gift of grace in a 'seminal' form, which grows when nourished. Pusey does not make a sharp distinction between planting the seed and its later growth, however: 'in Scripture, and by the ancient Church, the latter is regarded as included in the former'.[20] Christian holiness, then, is the growth and realization of baptism's gifts. But this imagery helps to account for post-baptismal sin. Christians are not born full-grown. And for some the 'gift' may be 'rendered useless for want of cultivation' – either through removal from the Church or through the Church's neglect – though God, in his faithfulness, may yet provide means of growth and restoration that are beyond our understanding.[21] The image of the seed also proves useful in distinguishing infant and adult baptisms. Regeneration is a gift that needs to be received, a seed that needs to be planted and nourished, and so there is a measure of human passivity in receiving sacramental grace: a sacrament conveys the grace associated with it, so long as 'no obstacle is placed in its way by the unworthiness of the recipient'.[22] Infants are passive by nature, and so there is no question of whether they receive grace, only of how it is nurtured.[23] An adult, however, *can* oppose God's gift if they come to baptism with false motives; Pusey concludes, by analogy to the Eucharist, that this must be

---

19. E. B. Pusey, 'Progress our Perfection', in *SR*, 315–16. Similarly, Pusey interprets 1 Jn 3.9 as saying that we do not sin, 'in whatever degree we are realizing the life, which was in Baptism conferred upon us ... our sins are a portion of our old man, our corruption, our death; and so far, we are not living'. *Baptism 1*, 166–70.

20. Pusey, *Baptism 1*, 148–53.

21. Pusey, *Baptism 1*, 164–6.

22. Pusey, *Baptism 1*, 83.

23. Pusey, *Baptism 1*, 84.

spiritually dangerous, although even then, God can work through the sacrament and grant repentance for receiving it unworthily.[24]

***

The doctrine of baptismal regeneration thus provides a further example of the importance of allegory in Pusey's theology, but it also shows his close theological ties with the older high churchmen. Members of the older school were appreciative; Henry Phillpotts was particularly admiring (though he complained of the small print in the edition Pusey sent him) – as his prosecution of Charles Gorham shows, he was not one to take this doctrine lightly.[25] In his assessment, the Tractarian doctrine of baptism was the same as that held by the older school; and so, for instance, addressing the clergy of his diocese in the aftermath of the Gorham Judgment, he excused a reluctant quotation from Newman on the basis of the latter's conformity (on the question of baptism) with the eighteenth-century high churchman Daniel Waterland.[26] Waterland will thus serve as a useful point of comparison with Pusey: Phillpotts clearly saw him as a doctrinal authority, and could appeal to him as such without controversy in a predominantly high church diocese; moreover, with the publication of Van Mildert's edition of Waterland's *Works* in the 1820s, he was a relatively accessible source. So, although high churchmanship was far from uniform, comparing Pusey with Waterland will provide a sense of Pusey's relationship with a significant strand of high church thought.

In fact, Pusey's understanding of baptism bears a strong resemblance to Waterland's. Waterland emphasizes that God's grace is given apart from 'any righteousness which *we* have done' and rejects attempts to sever inward regeneration from the outward sacrament, as a 'modern' innovation.[27] Regeneration itself is a change wrought by the Holy Spirit in baptism, by which a person 'is translated from his *natural* state in *Adam*, to a *spiritual* state in *Christ*'.[28] This change is permanent and carries with it numerous privileges, which, however, can be summed up in the forgiveness of sins and a '*covenant claim ... to eternal happiness*'.[29] These privileges can be forfeited through rebellion against God – he (again) rejects the 'modern'

---

24. Pusey, *Baptism 1*, 170–6; *Baptism 2*, 229–37. With regard to receiving unworthily, cf. 1 Cor. 11. Pusey also draws on the traditional story of Simon Magus, derived from Cyril of Jerusalem's Sixth Catechetical Lecture. This appears to have been a frequent test case in high church discussions of baptism; cf. Daniel Waterland, 'Regeneration Stated and Explained According to Scripture and Antiquity, in a Discourse on Titus III. 4, 5, 6', in *Works*, 4:442–4.

25. Phillpotts to Pusey, 10 November to 5 December 1849, LBV 59. On Gorham, see above, Chapter 1, n. 2.

26. Henry [Phillpotts], *A Pastoral Letter to the Clergy of the Diocese of Exeter, on the Present State of the Church* (London: John Murray, 1851), 23–6.

27. Waterland, 'Regeneration', 427.

28. Waterland, 'Regeneration', 429.

29. Waterland, 'Regeneration', 433; emphasis Waterland's.

position that 'the *regenerate* can never *finally* fall from grace' – but the original gift is not lost; and if the person is moved to repentance, it is because of the regeneration already received, not through a new grant of it.[30] This, however, highlights the importance of our role in receiving God's gift, which leads him to the distinction (based on Tit. 3.4-6) between regeneration, the spiritual state given by God, and renewal, the disposition of heart and mind formed by cooperation between the human and the Holy Spirit. Like Pusey, he also concludes that the necessity of human receiving of God's grace entails that in adult baptism (not infant baptism), it is possible for the candidate to be baptized unworthily – to salvation nonetheless if they repent, but to condemnation if they do not.[31]

Pusey's strong resemblance to Waterland on the doctrine of baptism indicates his continuity with the high church tradition, if not of a direct influence from Waterland himself (whom Pusey thought 'cold').[32] Indeed, baptismal regeneration provides perhaps the best proof of his high church roots – as early as 1823, his defence of the doctrine was sufficient to shake Newman's opposition.[33] But comparison with Waterland also shows some differences. Waterland's work is characterized by an admirable doctrinal clarity; Pusey is less clear, but his tone is deeper. Unlike other Tractarians, he resists Waterland's distinction between regeneration and renewal, perhaps because it risks distancing the seed of regeneration from its fruits.[34] Waterland admits the privileges of baptism; Pusey spends much of his work emphasizing their greatness. Waterland, in closing, urges renewal through a 'sedate, regular, and uniform obedience to God's commandments'.[35] Pusey would doubtless advocate a regular and uniform practice of obedience, but he is less sedate – were he to write a similar sentence, he would likely say 'whole-hearted' or 'vigorous' instead. With Waterland, he is sceptical of the attempt to ground God's grace on individual emotions; but Pusey does not shy away from rapturous meditations on God's love. This difference in tone lies beneath the criticisms Pusey received from his high church contemporaries: when the privileges of baptism shine with such a brilliant light as Pusey would show, the sin which rejects them must appear the darker. But it was on this point that he was criticized – his language on post-baptismal sin was thought too strong.

This emotional depth in Pusey, however, brings in a subjective element that points to his relationship with Evangelicalism. Calhoun notes that Pusey's insistence on the utter depth of sin is a point of commonality with Evangelicals, as is his emphasis on the importance of conversion.[36] In fact, during the heat of the

30. Waterland, 'Regeneration', 433–7; emphasis Waterland's.

31. Waterland, 'Regeneration', 442–4.

32. Liddon, *Life*, 2:33.

33. Newman, *Autobiographical Writings*, 203–4. Newman was at the time an Evangelical.

34. Newman, *Justification*, esp. 81, 94–106, 112–15; R. I. Wilberforce, *The Doctrine of Holy Baptism*, 2nd edn (London: John Murray, 1849), 10. Hereafter, 'renewal' is used in a general sense, not in the technical sense given by Waterland.

35. Waterland, 'Regeneration', 457.

36. Calhoun, 'Conversion', 174–8, 245.

Gorham controversy, Pusey argued for a 'way of peace' between high churchmen and Evangelicals, by emphasizing the necessity of *both* conversion and sacraments; and he defended Evangelicals as objecting primarily to a system in which conversion was *replaced* by sacraments, rather than one in which they are complementary – he agreed that holy living (as a result of conversion) was necessary to the fruitfulness of the sacraments.[37] Pusey had stated this position more than a decade before, in *Baptism*. In the first edition, Pusey noted that there was considerable value in a mature 'conversion experience', as an awakening to God, and a rejection of sin, and even allowed that in *strength* the term regeneration would be appropriate, if it did not risk obscuring God's mercies in baptism.[38] In the revised version, this appreciation has been more fully synthesized into his baptismal theology. Here, he insists that 'our justification is imputed to us, not through the feelings, but *through* Baptism', against the tendency to emphasize personal commitments of faith to the exclusion of baptism; but he also insists that the opposite error lacks the 'vivid perception that by abiding faith only can that gift be retained'.[39] 'Thus in the words "justification by faith," all the Christian privileges and gifts are indeed included, since they are all part of the faith, bestowed on one who *embraces* the mercies of God in Christ, and is *through the Sacraments* made a member of Him.'[40]

Pusey's tensions with the 'old' high churchmen over post-baptismal sin, and the resonances Calhoun notes between Pusey's baptismal doctrine and Evangelicalism, both pertain primarily to the relation between baptism and holiness. Pusey's approach to this subject aims to combine high church doctrine with Evangelical practice – a combination which, in turn, reflects once again the *Enquiry*'s concern with the disjunction between 'orthodoxism' and 'pietism'. As the foregoing discussion has described, Pusey found his resolution to this disjunction in the doctrine of union with Christ; and this is, once again, the anchor for his understanding of baptismal holiness. For Pusey, giving weight to the doctrine of union with Christ is an evangelical and apologetic necessity, because it concerns the deepest longings of humanity. We were made to be united with God, and only God can satisfy our deepest longings. Because of these longings, we have an insatiable desire to be united to *something*.

---

37. Calhoun, 'Conversion', 175; cf. Pusey, *Royal Supremacy*, 188, 254–8. Pusey's sympathy for the Evangelical position is likely shaped, at least in part, by his insistence on keeping Christian growth as an element of regeneration. For the same reason, Pusey was appreciative of the ambiguities surrounding the word 'regeneration'. In addition to his general dislike of Phillpotts's prosecution, he also thought it mistaken to have built the case on the less stable ground of regeneration, rather than on the more definite creedal statement, 'one Baptism for the remission of sins'. Pusey to Keble, 7 February 1850, LBV 103; Bourchier Wrey Savile, *Dr. Pusey: An Historic Sketch* (London: Longmans, Green, 1883), 37–8; Liddon, *Life*, 1:17.

38. Pusey, *Baptism 1*, 71–2.

39. Pusey, *Baptism 2*, 20; emphasis Pusey's.

40. Pusey, *Baptism 2*, 20; emphasis mine.

'Union with God.' Yes, this is the almost inextinguishable longing of man, created, as he is, in the image and likeness of God, unless he brutalize himself; ... David uses the most fiery longing of our volcanic frame, to express the soul's burning desire for union with its God. And this God must long to give, since He has implanted the desire for it. Only from God could we have this longing for God.[41]

If this desire 'find not its satisfaction in faith', human nature turns to pantheism, 'glad to merge its own personality in the ocean of the being of an impersonal god, of which it thought itself a part, sooner than be for ever an isolated existence, separate from its god'. This is the true alternative to Christianity; deism, atheism and all other forms of unbelief inevitably slide towards that end. 'Many clouds have rolled away, many more are rolling away; half-faith and half-unbelief are disappearing; and the deadly antagonism is unveiling itself: "Is Jesus God, or is man a part of God?" "Has he no God but himself, but humanity?" ... There remains only one consistent choice, the Catholic Faith ... or Pantheism.'[42]

Although these passages are taken from Pusey's later sermons, there is early evidence for this concern. In the 'Types', he was careful to contrast his sacramental perspective, in which 'Divine Creation must be the expression of something within God, because he is infinite', and which allows that, as all things are upheld by God's spirit, they therefore 'breathe something divine', with pantheism, which 'confines the Infinite within the finite, the spiritual within the natural, and made [sic] the Creator coexistent with the created.'[43] When Yngve Brilioth dubbed Pusey the 'doctor mysticus' of the Oxford Movement, it was not intended as a compliment (a point which subsequent Anglo-Catholic writings on Pusey have tended to overlook). It was, rather, a title latent with the accusation that Pusey's sacramentalism was pantheistic.[44] The principles of Pusey's 'sacramental vision', however, show that sacramentalism, for Pusey, is what *distinguishes* Christianity from pantheism.[45] Whereas pantheism erases the distinction between creator and

41. Pusey, 'This Is My Body', 42.
42. E. B. Pusey, 'Will Ye Also Go Away?' (Oxford: James Parker, 1880), 15; in US III, paginated individually.
43. Pusey, 'Types', additional fragments.
44. Brilioth, *Anglican Revival*, 298–305.
45. It is worth comparing Pusey on this point with the ontological critique of modernism made more recently within Radical Orthodoxy. Radical Orthodoxy holds that the inevitable consequence of univocal ontology has been the emergence of nihilism. While Pusey's argument concerning pantheism is obviously different in certain respects, the parallels between the arguments should also be noted: both draw out spiritual consequences from the abandonment of a participatory or sacramental world view, and both reject atheism as the true antagonist of Christianity. The difference appears to lie in psychological versus ontological approaches to the argument. Thus, Pusey is concerned with the human desire for belonging, whereas Radical Orthodoxy addresses the logical consequences of a metaphysical perspective. And indeed, Radical Orthodoxy's account of nihilism is one

created by merging the world with an abstract deity, the sacraments involve us in an intensely personal union of love with the Incarnate Lord. The centrality of the incarnation to Pusey's allegorical system assures this. If types (in Scripture or in nature) reveal something of God, if the sacraments communicate grace, it is only because these are, as it were, the concentric circles by which God draws us nearer to Jesus Christ, the revelation of God not in words or abstract thoughts, but tangibly, in the flesh – the greatest revelation of God's love, uniting humanity to himself.

The centrality of the incarnation, however, highlights another aspect of Pusey's thought. His contrast between the 'old man' and Christ is the classic language of recapitulation: Christ by the incarnation recreates humanity, replacing the humanity of Adam which is corrupted by sin. However, Christ's recreation of *humanity* needs to be translated to the renewal of *each human*. Christ's acts in the incarnation, cross, resurrection and ascension all transform humanity – man was united to God, died to sin, received new life and was taken into heaven. 'Yet it was our nature still, not ourselves'; all of these things were done 'out of us', to our nature generally, not to each of us in particular. The particular renewal of each Christian comes in the gift of the Holy Spirit at Pentecost.

> Whit-Sunday is the filling up of the Ascension. The wondrous exchange was half made on the Ascension, when Man in God was taken up into Heaven, and sat on His Father's Throne; the day of Pentecost fulfilled the promise of the Father, and as man now dwelt in God, so God, in a New and Ineffable Way, dwelt thenceforth in man.[46]

This gift, however, is specifically communicated in baptism. 'Our nature had been raised from the dead, had been sanctified, but not we ourselves; for us then it was further necessary that we should be individually made partakers of that cleansing, and this St. Paul says had been done for them; their hearts *had been* cleansed from an evil conscience, as their bodies cleansed by pure water.'[47] It is because the sacraments form the link between the general gifts of the incarnation and each Christian that Pusey connects them to *theosis*; they impart, as he puts it, 'a deifying influence, … to "be as Gods," being partakers of the Son of God'.[48]

This distinction between the renewal of humanity generally and the salvation of each person provides the framework for a distinction in his soteriology between,

---

in which humanity takes the place of God – just as in Pusey's account of pantheism. The claim, for Radical Orthodoxy explicitly and almost certainly for Pusey as well, originates in Augustine. Smith, *Radical Orthodoxy*, 99–101, 137, 186–9.

46. E. B. Pusey, 'The Christian the Temple of God', in *Sermons during the Season from Advent to Whitsuntide [Parochial Sermons*, vol. 1], 4th edn (Oxford: John Henry Parker, 1852), 345–6 (hereafter *Par. S. I*).

47. Pusey, *Baptism 2*, 186; emphasis Pusey's.

48. Pusey, *Baptism 1*, 113–14.

as Pusey puts it, Christ's work *for us* and *in us*.⁴⁹ So, for instance, interpreting Romans 4.25, Pusey writes, 'The sacrifice on the Cross perfected our redemption to Godward, but there was a further act to complete it toward, and in, us. "He was delivered for our offenses," and so completed the atonement; but "He was raised for our justification," to communicate its fruits to us.'⁵⁰ This death–resurrection pairing occurs frequently in Pusey's thought. The *for us–in us* duality in fact characterizes *each* of Christ's acts, using his death *for us* and his resurrected life *in us* as an abbreviation of the larger pattern. 'The Birth was for Suffering, Atonement, and Death' but also 'imparted Divinity to humanity'; 'on the Cross He bore our sins' to make atonement 'and by Death destroyed death' in humanity. 'In the Resurrection He imparted life to our whole nature', but through it 'He giveth Himself to us'; 'in the Ascension He placed it' – our nature – 'in Himself, at God's Right Hand', fulfilling the union of God and man, 'there to intercede for us' as our priest. 'At Pentecost He imparted to the Church, and to us individually in our measure, that Life and those Graces, which He, in His Human Nature, had "received for man," and which as yet dwelt in Him, our Head, only.'⁵¹

Likewise, commenting on Ephesians 5.25-27, Pusey draws a parallel between the statements (as he paraphrases them) that Christ 'gave Himself for' the Church and that 'He cleansed her, that he might sanctify her', in order to link the Passion with baptism, respectively the external winning of benefits for us and the internal application of them.⁵² Pusey warns that 'whoever would meditate, speak, preach, on the Passion of our Lord, thinking that It alone could touch men's consciences, would act, as if man could give himself love, or that unloving hearts must melt at once at the hearing of so great love.'⁵³ 'Yet not the doctrine of the Cross alone' externally 'but He Himself Who for us hung thereon must impart its virtue to us' internally; 'Himself, who bore the Cross to atone for us, applying its saving efficacy to our souls; Himself, our living Pattern, tracing His own Divine Image on all who "look to" Him.'⁵⁴ Pusey could elaborate on the distinction between Christ's outward and inward work with considerable detail and eloquence:

> Great need have we, indeed, to look to Jesus! As Man, our Way and Pattern and Guide; as God, our Home, to Whom we are going; without, the Image Which, day by day, we should seek to have traced upon ourselves; within, the Giver of that Holy Spirit Who traces it; without, in His Life, Death, and Passion, the Object of our Love; within, He poureth in that love wherewith we love Him,

---

49. E. B. Pusey, 'The Cross Borne for Us and in Us', in *Pl. S.*, 3:1–18.

50. Pusey, *Baptism 2*, 100.

51. E. B. Pusey, 'Christ Risen Our Justification', in *Par. S. I*, 217, 221–226; cf. 'The Resurrection of Christ, the Source, Earnest, Pattern of Ours', in *Parochial and Cathedral Sermons* (London: A. D. Innes, 1892), 453-4 (hereafter *PCS*).

52. Pusey, *Baptism 2*, 196-7.

53. E. B. Pusey, 'Looking unto Jesus, the Groundwork of Penitence', in *SR*, 180.

54. Pusey, 'Looking unto Jesus', 181.

through the Holy Spirit which He hath given us: His Passion melteth into love those whose thoughts dwell upon It. And He by His Fire first melteth our stony hearts within, and upholdeth our heavy thoughts that they may rest on Him. He is our Teacher, without, by His gracious and Divine Acts; within, by pouring into us His Light and Love: our Redemption by His Death, our Righteousness by His indwelling; Himself in Himself the Eternal Righteousness and Wisdom, for Which we thirst; our Righteousness here in the way, in that we thirst for Him; hereafter in His Fulness, when they who thirst for Him, shall be filled.[55]

Taken on its own, this quotation, for all its eloquence, simply articulates a traditional theory of recapitulation. What is notable, however, is that Pusey (in the same sermon) not only connects the incarnation and resurrection to Christ's work 'for us', as one might expect, but also incorporates Christ's Passion and death, not merely as aspects of the incarnation (recapitulation theories characteristically account for the Passion by emphasizing that Christ redeems the whole of the human experience, *including* death) but specifically as an atoning sacrifice. This synthesis of patristic theology with later Western thought (discussed more fully in Chapter 5) again points towards Pusey's creativity and has historical significance in the developments of nineteenth-century theology. The remainder of this chapter, however, will consider Pusey's understanding of Christ's work *in* us, with relation to faith, justification, repentance and the glorification of the human body.

Union with Christ I: Faith, justification, glorification

Faith, in Pusey's thought, unlike justification and repentance, is not itself an aspect of Christ's indwelling. Nonetheless, it is closely related to union with Christ: first, because he holds that it is given, with the gift of union, in baptism; and second, because it enables and actualizes the love that flows from union with Christ. As with the graces given in baptism, faith is a gift of God, not something we have in ourselves. This gift of faith is given (primarily) in baptism, 'the depository, as it were, and guardian and perpetuator of sound faith in the Church'.[56] For this reason, the faith *of the Church* is important in infant baptism, rather than that of the child.[57] Pusey does not directly address the case of adult baptism, where faith is necessary prior to receiving the sacrament; but there are grounds to think that he would class faith before baptism as a prevenient grace from God, and yet as being so far superseded by the faith given *in* baptism that *by comparison*, it seems to be no faith at all.[58]

---

55. Pusey, 'Looking unto Jesus', 173.
56. Pusey, *Baptism 2*, 200–5.
57. Pusey, *Baptism 1*, 153–64.
58. This is by analogy to Pusey's discussion of non-Christian holiness, discussed in this chapter under 'Holiness, sin, and repentance'.

For Pusey, faith is prior to works, because works come from love; love is directed, ultimately, to God; and without faith, we do not know God so as to love him. 'Faith, in one sense, goes before love, because, unless we believed, we should have none to love. Faith is Divine knowledge. As in human love we cannot love unless we have seen, heard, or in some way known, so, without Faith, we cannot know aught of God, or know that there is a God Whom to love.'[59] 'Faith … goes before love, in thought; for we love, because we believe, not believe, because we love.'[60] Faith is therefore, in Pusey's understanding, a faculty which enables us to know and love God. At the same time, however, faith is a gift from God, which *accompanies* our own renewal by Christ's indwelling; and being thus renewed, knowing God by faith *in* our renewal, faith is in fact inseparable from, and inheres in, love.[61] 'Faith goes even before love, in thought, but not in deed.'[62] Indeed, faith without love is no faith at all: 'Faith which loves not, is not faith; it is dead. And what is dead, hath ceased to be.' This is, in fact, rooted in the very nature of faith as a divine gift.

> Where love is not, there is not the Holy Spirit, Who is Love, and Who 'shed abroad love in our hearts'. And without the Holy Spirit there cannot be faith, since faith is the gift of the Spirit. A dead body is a body without a soul; a dead soul is a soul without God. A 'dead faith' is a 'faith without love'.

So devils are without faith. They may know *that* God exists, but 'neither devils nor bad men can "believe *in* God." For "to believe in God," says a holy man, "is by believing to love, by believing to go into Him, by believing to cleave unto Him and be incorporated among His Members."'[63] This relationship between faith and love can be seen again in their relation to knowledge of God. So, Pusey says, 'Faith is instead of eyes. By Faith we see Him who to our eyes of sense is unseen. We behold both backwards and forwards, and round about us, and every way we behold the love of God.'[64] But at the same time, the way to understanding is through the submission of human reason to divine love. 'The key to the supernatural system is

---

59. E. B. Pusey, 'Faith', in *Par. S. II*, 4.
60. Pusey, 'Faith', 1.
61. Pusey, 'Faith', 5.
62. Pusey, 'Faith', 1.
63. Pusey, 'Faith', 12–13; referring to Jas 2.15-20 and quoting Rom. 5.5 and S. Laurence Justinian, *De fide*, c. 3. In contrast to Pusey, Newman holds that devils *can* have faith: faith is mere belief, and is not saving without other graces to condition it. Newman's objectivism lies at the root of this difference. Newman, *Justification*, 287–92; and see above, in Chapter 2, under 'Allegory and the Sacramental Vision'.
64. Pusey, 'Faith', 1. This connection between faith and sight is Augustinian in its roots and finds expression among the radical German Pietists, whom Pusey had studied for the *Enquiry*. Hans Boersma, *Seeing God: The Beatific Vision in Christian Tradition* (Grand Rapids, MI: Eerdmans, 2018), 113–14; Smith, *Radical Orthodoxy*, 151–3.

love, as that of the natural is intellect, One, All-wise and All-loving, guiding us in both. Love, and thou wilt find nothing hard. Love God, and thou wilt understand of Him all which can be understood in the flesh.'[65]

Thus, although faith is prior 'in thought', the emphasis of the Christian life must be on works of love, for two reasons. First, faith makes love possible, but growing love produces growing faith, and love grows through works. 'Acts of love do not prove only that we have a living faith, they increase it. For to do good is to use the grace of God; and on the faithful use of grace, more grace is given.'[66] 'Faith and deeds of faith are, both of them, graces of this passing world. Yet God hath appointed that not only shall they be inseparable, but that they shall strengthen one another.'[67] This reflects, once more, the Tractarian understanding of *phronesis* discussed in the previous chapter; and as such, it bears directly on the question of theological understanding: if 'faith is instead of eyes', and acts of love are the means of strengthening faith, then charity is the means by which to nurture a keener perception of the sacramental nature of both Scripture and creation; and this more penetrating spiritual 'sight' should spur the Christian on to further acts of deepened charity.

Second, faith is elusive, and easily confused with emotion; while emotions, in turn, are unreliable. Thus,

> God assigns to us works as the test of our faith, not faith as the test of our works. And this, because it is easy to deceive ourselves as to our faith or our feelings; it is not so easy to deceive ourselves as to our deeds, if we will but look into our consciences by the light of the law of God. It is easy to say, 'Lord, Lord;' it is *not* easy, but of the power of the grace of God, to 'deny ourselves and take up our cross and follow Him.' … It is an easy, costless confession, to own ourselves what we are, 'unprofitable servants;' it is hard, first to labour with our whole strength, through the grace of God, to 'do all things whatsoever He hath commanded,' and then, and then only, it will be the fruit of God's grace to own it.[68]

Works, therefore, have an inverted sacramentality about them. Whereas a sacrament is a visible sign that conveys an invisible grace, works of love are the signs which flow from the unseen faith that has been received.

This discussion of faith and works, however, raises in turn the topic of justification. In the sermon just cited, Pusey compares the theology of the Jacobean Calvinist divine and English bishop, John Davenant, with the decrees of the Council of Trent, demonstrating (in a manner which foreshadows the *Eirenicon*) that the difference is one of emphasis: Protestantism and Romanism aim their arguments, respectively, against Pelagianism and Antinomianism, but

---

65. Pusey, 'Will Ye?', 18–19.
66. Pusey, 'Faith', 14.
67. Pusey, 'Justification', 29–30.
68. Pusey, 'Justification', 44–5, quoting Lk. 6.46, 9.23, 17.10, and Mt. 28.20.

actually teach the same necessity of a faith characterized by works.[69] Beyond the question of faith and works, however, there is the question of what it means, in itself, to say that God 'justifies'. Pusey offers a definition, in two parts: to justify is '1, to declare the soul righteous or acquit it, and 2, to make it what He declares it. To "justify" is, in what is called a "forensic" sense, to pronounce just, or to acquit. But *the word of God is power*.' Thus, in creation, or in Christ's pronouncement that the leper be clean, what God declares, *is*. So, too, with justification.[70] In baptism, God imputes Christ's righteousness to the sinner, but it is what might be called an 'effective imputation' that brings about what it declares.

This imputation, like the gift of faith, takes place in baptism. Justification is, therefore, one aspect of baptismal regeneration: 'This is our new birth; herein then are we also justified, or both accounted and made righteous, since we are made members of Him who is Alone Righteous.'[71] Consequently, much of Pusey's argument parallels his discussion of baptismal regeneration. Rather than making justification 'consequent' upon Christians' ongoing and simple 'present act of casting themselves on the Redeemer's merits', Pusey notes that Scripture speaks of justification as *past* when discussing individuals, and present only when discussing God's agency, or justification considered abstractly, as in baptism.[72] Just as he emphasizes the reality of grace in baptism, the real effect of this imputation, actually making the baptized members of Christ, and righteous in him, is crucially important. As humanity is in Adam by nature, and not just by imputation, 'so, on the other hand, are we *in* Christ, not merely by the imputation of His righteousness, but by an actual, real, spiritual origin from Him'. 'It is ... no outward imputation of righteousness; no mere ascription of His perfect obedience in our stead; ... none of these things come up to the reality of being "*in* Him."'[73]

However, Pusey's twofold definition of justification gives it a dual nature. Not only at baptism but throughout the life of faith, and even at the Last Judgment, the Christian has both an external and an internal righteousness, both of which derive from union with Christ.

---

69. Pusey, 'Justification', 11–16, 34–5. This again reflects Pusey's notion of doctrinal standards as boundaries; see above, Chapter 1, under 'Authority and the Church'.

70. Pusey, 'Justification', 18–19, emphasis added.

71. Pusey, *Baptism 2*, 23–4.

72. Pusey, *Baptism 2*, 156–9.

73. Pusey, *Baptism 2*, 116–17, emphasis Pusey's; Pusey is commenting on Gal. 3.27–28. Cf. E. B. Pusey, 'God is Love', in *Parochial Sermons Preached and Printed on Various Occasions* (London: Walter Smith, 1884), 1–2:

> What is man's Righteousness, but Christ Himself? or Grace, but His indwelling Spirit, shed abroad within the heart? or Love, but God? Herein is the exceeding love of God, not only that He has made and remade us; not only that, being sinners, He accounts us righteous, but that He is our righteousness; not that He gives us strength, out of Himself, but that Himself is our strength within us.

As the first act of God's love in justifying us is two-fold: 1. forgiving, 2. hallowing; so, 'since in many things we all offend,' we have need of both to the end. To the end, our Lord has taught us to pray always for daily bread of life, and daily forgiveness; to the end, and in the end, our Father to Whom we pray, continually pardons, continually pours in His grace into our souls, and in both ways upholds us in that state of justification, in which He placed us.[74]

The differing perfections of baptism pertain here: a perfect righteousness in the end, the perfect gift of Christ who is righteous within and an 'imperfect perfection' in righteousness as the Christian continually grows in him. Yet, as the baptized receive Christ imperfectly, and do not reach full maturity in this life, they still need God's forgiveness and his *external* declaration of righteousness while returning to him in penitence, that declaration making them to be more and more righteous. Although the holiness of the saints has a 'likeness' to Christ's holiness, 'it could not stand before the Holiness of God', and their obedience is 'acceptable only through the Obedience of Him Who had no sin'.[75] Consequently, Pusey is critical of any approach which overemphasizes either the external or internal aspect of justification, to the neglect of the other. So, for instance, he faults Alexander Knox – who was much admired by Newman – for emphasizing imparted grace, but neglecting judicial absolution such that 'what Christ worketh *in* us' could 'cast a shade over what He did and suffered *for* us'.[76]

Pusey's distinction between Christ's work *for us* and *in us* thus reappears as a structural element in his soteriology. Both must be held together, rather than set in competition with one another. Yet in justification, what connects them is a progression through the various aspects of Christ's righteousness. Pusey notes the different dimensions of Jesus' explanation that his own baptism was necessary 'to fulfil all righteousness'. First, as John the Baptist was sent by God to the Jews, it is an act of submission by Christ, as a Jew, to an ordinance of God. Second, in that Christ identifies himself with sinners who are in need of baptism, we can see in Christ's baptism God's love as the fulfilment of the Law. Third, Christ's baptism so consecrated the waters of baptism as to communicate to individuals the righteousness which he, by his incarnation, had communicated to human nature as a whole. And finally, this same consecration introduces an 'everlasting righteousness' because it is by the water of baptism that 'the justifying efficacy of His meritorious Cross and Passion was to be conveyed to all believers'.[77] These layers of meaning present a New Testament application of the principles Pusey discussed in the 'Types' with

---

74. Pusey, 'Justification', 26–7.

75. Pusey, 'Union with Christ Increased through Works Wrought through Him', in *SR*, 218.

76. Pusey, *Baptism 2*, 19–20; emphasis Pusey's. While Newman technically admits something similar to Pusey's 'effective imputation', his emphasis also falls much more strongly on the internal aspect of justification. Newman, *Justification*, 92, 116–43.

77. Pusey, *Baptism 2*, 277–80.

regard to prophecy, and demonstrates the way in which the multiple bearings of a single image or event work together to provide a richer vision of the whole. In this case, the varied significances of Christ's obedience work together to demonstrate the unity of the two aspects of Christ's work. His obedience *for us* in the incarnation is fulfilled by his righteousness *in us* through baptism.

***

The indwelling of the resurrected Christ, however, is the source not only of justification but of new life. When, 'by the Spirit of Holiness', the Father 'raised' Christ's human nature 'from the dead, he made it not only "the first fruits," but the source of our Resurrection, by communicating to our nature His own inherent Life'.[78] This is not, however, just a gift of spiritual life, but of physical life, and the renewal of the human body, which is fulfilled ultimately in the general resurrection. Again, sacramental union with Christ is central. 'He Himself is' our resurrection.

> He gives it us not, as it were, from without, as a possession, as something of our own, but Himself is it to us: He took our flesh, that he might vivify it; He dwelt in it, and obeyed in it, that He might sanctify it; He raised it from death by His quickening Spirit that He might give it immortality ... And we in His Church being incorporated into Him, being made members of His Body, flesh of His Flesh, and bone of His bone, through His Sacraments, partake of His Life and immortality, because we partake of Him; we are made members of Him, He dwelleth in us, and is our Life; 'Because I live, ye shall live also'.[79]

The importance of not just spiritual but bodily life emerges in three sermons on the 'Bliss of Heaven' which form the climax of Pusey's *Sermons on Repentance*. Pusey repeats that the future blessed state is the result, not merely of grace, but of the indwelling of God himself, which replaces the original righteousness lost by sin.[80] The beatific vision is the fulfilment of this indwelling, because the

---

78. Pusey, *Baptism 2*, 101.

79. Pusey, *Baptism 2*, 101–2. This passage was reused in an 1871 sermon with minor grammatical alterations that considerably improve its readability. A larger change, however, is where 'and we in His Church ... partake of Him', is instead written, 'And we, in his Church, being incorporated into Him, being made members of His Body, flesh of His Flesh and bone of His Bones, through His Sacrament, partake of Him'. This makes communion with Christ much more direct and personal. The singular 'Sacrament' is also notable – 'flesh of His Flesh and bone of His Bones' is a frequent eucharistic phrase in Pusey, and this could be a modification in that direction, shifting the meaning of 'partake' from *participation* to *eating*. The published sermon, however, has many typographical errors, which make it unclear whether this change is intended. In any case, the main idea of the passage remains unaltered. Pusey, 'The Resurrection of Christ', 453.

80. E. B. Pusey, 'Bliss of Heaven, "We Shall Be Like Him"', in *SR*, 255–67.

transcendent God cannot be known or seen but by God in us; and cannot be known or seen 'as He is' but by God *perfected* in us.[81] But even the beatific vision is, in some sense, incomplete: the martyrs under the altar cry out with longing for the fulfilment of God's will for the Church, at the general resurrection – the saints, as humans (both spiritual and material), are not perfect without the restoration of their bodies; bodies which, however, because of the deification of humanity in Christ, are themselves glorified.[82]

> Great is the gift, that we should not again be liable to corruption, dishonour, weakness, but, instead, have bodies whose beauty can have no decay, whose glory cannot be dimmed, obedient to the spirit, and so themselves spiritual, excelling in might, mighty as the Angels. But how much more that this beauty and glory and might and spirituality of our bodies shall be the likeness to the glorious Body of Christ; that they shall shine with His brightness, be spiritual through His indwelling love, be incorruptible through His life in the spirit, be swift through His drawing to Himself![83]

Moreover, the transfiguration and the resurrection appearances of Christ were given to foreshadow the Christian's own glorification:

> Not for His own sake was that glory which ever resided in Him, the Glory of His Divine Person, allowed once to pierce through the Flesh which He for us had taken; nor for Himself after His Resurrection, was His Body, Which, before, once only walked on the water, removed above the laws of natural bodies ... not being merely Spirit but 'Flesh of our flesh, Bone of our bone,' as we are now by union with Him 'members of His flesh and His bones.'[84]

This transformation, in some measure – if not in the fullness it will have in the resurrection – can be seen even in this life. So, at Stephen's martyrdom, his face appeared like 'the face of an angel' (Acts 6.15). But there is also an analogy of opposites to be drawn: sinful or sensual living has observable physical effects in this life (most obvious, perhaps, with certain forms of gluttony); and so, Pusey argues, holy and spiritual living likewise have present physical effects, however difficult to perceive or describe.[85]

---

81. E. B. Pusey, 'Bliss of Heaven, "We Shall See Him as He Is"', in *SR*, 272–88.
82. E. B. Pusey, 'Bliss of Heaven – Glory of the Body', in *SR*, 289–304.
83. Pusey, 'Bliss of Heaven – Glory of the Body', 301.
84. Pusey, 'Bliss of Heaven – Glory of the Body', 303; paraphrasing Eph. 5.20.
85. E. B. Pusey, 'The Transfiguration of our Lord the Earnest of the Christian's Glory', in *Pl. S.*, 223–40. Contrast with Newman's view of Jesus' post-resurrection appearances as exhibiting Jesus' loss of 'material phenomena'. Newman, *Justification*, 235–6; discussed above, in Chapter 2, under 'Allegory and the Sacramental Vision'.

Union with Christ II: Holiness, sin and repentance

While faith, justification and the glorification of the human body address the subject of baptismal holiness from a doctrinal standpoint, there are also practical questions, especially concerning its relationship to sin and repentance. For any reader of Pusey's sermons, it is immediately clear that his foremost concern is the pursuit and encouragement of *practical* Christian holiness.[86] This concern for holiness drove the Tractarian preoccupation with diligence in pastoral care and catechesis.[87] The subject even found its way into Pusey's ecclesiology. In contrast with the high church 'branch theory' which made the Church of England a coequal 'branch' of the Church Catholic, together with the Churches of Rome and of Constantinople, the Tractarians have been identified as emphasizing a more critical attitude towards Anglicanism.[88] But in Pusey, at least, this is linked to an increasingly critical stance towards the differing churches without distinction (outlined above in Chapter 1). In his revision of branch theory, the emphasis shifts from a polemical defence of the Church of England's catholicity, to a criticism of how *each* branch has fallen away from true catholicity. These schisms are themselves sinful, falling short of the wholeness to which the Church is called, but they are also (perhaps more importantly) the *result* of sin. Consequently, the pursuit of holiness is the foundation of all Christian unity.[89]

But what is holiness? Commenting on the parable of the vine (Jn 15.1-17) – a natural type – Pusey maintains (as we would expect) that the spiritual life, and any ability Christians have to 'bear fruit', are the result of union with Christ, being 'grafted into Him', and his life within, through the gift of the Holy Spirit – so long as the gift of grace is not shut out by 'dead works'.[90] The indwelling Christ, however, is not only life but the life of the God who is love. Love is the very foundation of

---

86. This is the case even in more doctrinal sermons: Pusey, 'Presence of Christ', 10–12, 68–74; 'The Doctrine of the Atonement', in *US II*, 261–2.

87. Pusey, *Baptism 1*, 201–8.

88. C. Brad Faught. *The Oxford Movement: A Thematic History of the Tractarians and Their Times* (University Park: Pennsylvania State University Press, 2003), 43; cf. Nockles, *Context*, 178–80.

89. Pusey, *Eirenicon I*, 44–66; 'Introductory Essay', 3–9. Though he had long since abandoned the language of 'formularism' in the works in question, this view represents the implications of that early theory. Formularism treats as essential certain characteristics of a revival (in its original formulation) or (more broadly) of a particular part of the Church, which are in themselves only instrumental in their significance. It can thus be considered theologically as revival, or church, *incurvatus in se*. If, however, this is the root of division, unity is not attained through doctrinal agreement but through corporate ascesis, achieved in the Church's corporate pursuit of love, humility and self-denial. This not only addresses the root cause of ecclesial division in human sin but also (according to Tractarian theology) grants clearer theological perception, from which agreement might eventually arise.

90. Pusey, 'Union with Christ', 214–16.

God's indwelling the Christian through Christ; that 'Love communicates Itself' is the fundamental reality of the Trinity.[91] Love flows out from the inner life of the Trinity, even before creation.

> He saw each one of us, just as He should create us … the individual object of His love. But each one made, to communicate Himself and His love to each … Himself the only adequate repose and joy of our souls; Himself the unceasing, overflowing, transporting contentment of our being, our God and our All: Himself to be united with us, and we with Him: to … be transported with and penetrated with His Love, and for ever thrill with the beatitude of the Beatific Vision.[92]

Love, however, is active. If Christians are indwelt by the divine love, that love will show itself in obedience to God, and flow through them, as it flowed out from God, to others.[93] Union with God is the root of Pusey's challenge, 'Where [is] the Gospel measure of self-denying, self-sacrificing charity?'[94]

But there is a need to distinguish between Christian holiness and other virtue. While the holiness of regeneration, the new birth as sons of God, is reserved to the Church, sanctification extends beyond the Church, in various degrees as another sort of hierarchy: it describes 'the imparting of all holiness, from the faintest spark that ever purified the benighted heart of a benighted heathen, to the holiest Angel who stands before the throne of God'.[95] Even without accompanying holiness, the 'virtues and wisdom which were granted to the Heathen world' are 'an effluence from Him who filleth all in all, as so many scattered rays from the Father of lights' and, though they might be used in the service of sin (as, for instance, wisdom in pursuing pleasure, or self-denial for the sake of pride), are nonetheless 'faint emblems of that concentrated glory which was to be shed upon the world through the Sun of righteousness'.[96] One step nearer to Christian holiness are the patriarchs and Job, who were sanctified, but not regenerate: 'They were the faithful servants, but not as yet the sons, of God. Christ had not died: our nature was not yet placed at God's right hand: the ever-blessed Son of God had not yet become man, that

---

91. Pusey, 'The Love of God for Us', in *PCS*, 442.

92. Pusey, 'The Love of God for Us', 447–8; cf. 'The Mystery of the Trinity, the Revelation of Divine Love', in *PCS*, 493–502.

93. Pusey, 'Union with Christ', 228–9; cf. Jn 14.15.

94. E. B. Pusey, 'Victory over the World', in *Pl. S.*, 84.

95. Pusey, *Baptism 1*, 137. Similarly, Pusey argues that inspiration was given in the Old Testament not just to prophets but even to (e.g.) the craftsmen employed in the construction of the Tabernacle. Both his discussions of holiness and of inspiration appear to reflect the hierarchical ordering of types discussed above in Chapter 2, under 'Allegory and the Sacramental Vision'.

96. Pusey, *Baptism 1*, 137–8; 'The Love of God for Us', 475; 'God's Condescending Love in Restoring Man by His Own Indwelling', in *PCS*, 459–61.

we, whom "He is not ashamed to call brethren," might be sons of God, as being in and of Him.'[97] Even after the resurrection, Cornelius the centurion (Acts 10) was sanctified before his baptism by God's grace but not as a Christian: 'He was, then, as a Heathen, sanctified'; but 'the sanctification of a Heathen who feared God, fell far short of the holiness following upon the Christian birth.'[98] 'Cornelius had faith … he had love; he had self-denial; he had had the power to pray given to him; but he had not Christian faith, nor love, nor self-denial, nor prayer; for as yet he knew not Christ: he could not call God Father, for, as yet, he knew not the Son.'[99] So, being sanctified but not regenerate *before* his baptism, he was regenerate and further sanctified *by* baptism.[100] Meanwhile, above mere virtue, and above the degrees of sanctification which pertain to non-Christians and to Christians, stands the holiness of Christ living in the Church through the sacraments.

With regard to practical holiness, however, the one virtue which colours all other Christian virtues, which removes selfishness from Christian love, is humility.[101] This, too, is derived from the incarnation, in which Christ set aside his divine glory and power, in order to embrace human frailty and weakness. 'Nothing was lacking to His Perfection, as God; nothing of man's infirmities, which flow from sin, though without touch of sin, was lacking that He should be Perfect Man. Our imperfect nature He took perfectly.' Even Christ's dependence on the earthly food and drink – given by God to humanity – is a sign of humility in embracing human weakness and in submitting to his Father.[102]

Charity and humility exist, above all, in actions. They are cultivated, therefore (especially humility), through spiritual disciplines. Pusey's earliest contribution to the tracts was on fasting; and voluntary self-denial (especially in keeping the fast days of the Church) remained an important part of his spiritual teaching throughout his life. Occasions of self-denial should lead to charity, but, to foster humility, lesser denials are preferred to greater ones.[103] Interior mindfulness of one's own sin provides an antidote to outward recognition or honour.[104] Pusey,

---

97. Pusey, *Baptism 1*, 135, cf. Heb. 11.39-40: 'These all, having obtained a good report through faith, received not the promise; God having provided some better thing for us, that they *without us* should not be made perfect' (emphasis added). Pusey does not deny the *ultimate* regeneration of the Old Testament patriarchs, only that they were regenerate within their earthly lives.

98. Pusey, *Baptism 1*, 139.

99. Pusey, *Baptism 1*, 141.

100. Pusey, *Baptism 1*, 140; cf. *Baptism 2*, 225-7. In the second edition, Pusey concedes that Scripture is unclear as to whether or not regeneration was imparted to Cornelius before baptism. Even if it were, Pusey argues, Cornelius's baptism should be understood in light of other baptisms in the New Testament, and baptism is, in this narrative, still inextricably linked with conversion and spiritual rebirth.

101. E. B. Pusey, 'The Incarnation, a Lesson of Humility', in *Par. S. I*, 70-1.

102. Pusey, 'The Incarnation, a Lesson of Humility', 67.

103. Pusey, 'The Cross Borne for Us, and in Us', 15-17.

104. Pusey, 'The Incarnation, a Lesson of Humility', 72.

mindful of his own social standing as an aristocrat by birth and as Regius Professor, was even at one point inclined to make outward expressions of humility towards those of lower social standing than himself, though Keble, as his spiritual director, worried this would cause social disruption (he recommended that Pusey confine himself to inward acts of self-humiliation).[105] Even so, the Church has a special duty of service to the poor, who reflect Christ's own humility. Just as Christ has declared himself to be present in his sacraments, he has also declared himself to be present in the poor. Therefore, 'the poor of Christ are the Church's special treasure … for they are what Christ for our sake made Himself'. 'Realize we that they are Christ's, yea, that we approach to Christ in them, feed Him, visit Him, clothe Him, attend on Him, and we shall feel … that it is a high honour to us to be admitted to them.' We should show charity to the poor, 'not relieving them coldly', but with humility and love, such as we would show to Christ himself.[106]

These themes – concern for holiness; God's love shown through Christian action, especially towards the disadvantaged of society; and humility – are not surprising, though the brief account given here certainly contrasts with the forbidding tales of Pusey's spirituality that have often been told. But they also bring us back to his reforming instinct. In a striking sermon, originally preached at a collection for a women's penitentiary (i.e., for prostitutes), Pusey delivers a sharp critique of the social conditions which produce sin, and Christian complicity in this system. On the one hand, there are those 'who for want or homelessness or friendlessness broke the law of God', but who 'may yet turn to God; and if there be a penitent sinner, over whom Angels may rejoice, surely it may well be such as these, who fell through others' sin even more than through their own, and who seem to have been dragged on to their misery, than themselves to have sought it'. On the other, there are the sinful 'others' who have caused their fall, the 'man, who makes light of other breaches of God's law, who forgives himself any breaches of the law of God'; but who 'fulfils in them the righteous judgment of God, and, as it were, outlaws them'.[107]

> We shall not always, I trust, be more moved by the exciting tales of misery, than by a holy jealousy and tender love for souls, to keep for our Redeemer those His yet untainted temples. We shall not for ever, I trust, look on unheeding, unmoved, with a sort of fatalist indifference, as though sin must have its course, although Christ died, and rose, and ascended, and sent down the Holy Ghost, to efface the guilt of sin and conquer its dominion over us. We shall not for ever pass by on the other side, while thousands upon thousands, still pure, still, like your own sisters or daughters, capable of becoming virtuous wives and loving mothers, are plunged, heap after heap, in their yet white garments, into that black, loathsome, defiling, stifling pool of sin, and then congratulate ourselves

---

105. Pusey to Keble, 7 December 1846, LBV 102; Keble to Pusey, December 1846, LBV 98.
106. E. B. Pusey, 'God with Us', in *Par. S. I*, 58–60; cf. Mt. 25.34-46.
107. Pusey, 'God's Condescending Love', 467–8.

and plume ourselves and thank God, as though we had done Him good service, if, here and there, we drag one or other with difficulty to the shore, soiled, begrimed, half-dead, if so be Christ will yet restore life and cleanse them. 'This ought ye to have done, and not have left the other undone.'[108]

Here, beginning from a concern to preserve the baptismal purity ('white garments') of society's vulnerable, Pusey shifts the guilt of prostitution away from the women caught up in it to the capitalists who put them in such desperate straits, the men who take advantage of them and the society which faults women for their acts of desperation while condoning – or even applauding – those who have caused, or taken advantage of, it. Genuine love, in fact, looks not to self-congratulatory sensationalism (which, in reality, merely cloaks a deeper complacency) but to the decidedly less glamorous work of socio-economic reform: the humbler act of charity prevails over the flashier one. In his own life, Pusey founded a printing press at the Ascot Priory orphanage in order to teach the girls living there a trade which would provide economic stability once they were on their own.[109] More broadly, however, his judgement on society's role in bringing about the destruction of human dignity, and his sharp attack on the superficial sensationalism that masks complacency about deeper ills, outlines a social critique which applies to a range of present social issues, not least those which touch on questions of poverty and racial inequality.[110]

***

Though the Christian is called to holiness, inevitably, sin rears its head. One of the most controversial aspects of Pusey's teaching in his own day was his emphasis on the gravity of post-baptismal sin. This, however, is a direct consequence of his understanding of baptism. The baptismal union with Christ unites Christians to Christ's death, so 'our life from Baptism to our death should be a practice of the Cross, a learning to be crucified, a crucifixion of our passions, appetites, desires, wills, until … we have no will, but the will of our Father which is in Heaven'; having the 'old man' crucified in us by God, 'we must, by the strength given us, keep it crucified; see that it strive not, rebel not, break not its bonds, much less ourselves seek to undo them'.[111] Moreover, the privileges given in baptism, and implicitly renounced by subsequent sin, are unutterably high. All the gifts of regeneration, holiness, justification and glorification which lie in baptism are

---

108. Pusey, 'God's Condescending Love', 469–70, quoting Mt. 23.23. 'White garments,' Eccl. 9.8, Rev. 3.4, 7.14; cf. 1 Cor. 6:18-19 and Lk. 10:31-2, 16.14-17.2.

109. Leonard Prestige, *Pusey* (London: Philip Allan, 1933), 120–1.

110. Skinner notes that the various oft-recounted acts of Pusey's charity are best seen as 'necessary expressions of his churchmanship', and Pereiro notes that Pusey's decision to build St Saviour's, Leeds, was in part driven by the social concerns connected to the location of the church. Skinner, *Tractarians*, 14; Pereiro, ' "A Cloud of Witnesses": Tractarians and Tractarian Ventures', in Stewart J. Brown, Nockles, and Pereiro, *Handbook*, 208.

111. Pusey, 'Cross Borne for Us, and in Us', 5.

recklessly hazarded by sin; and what is more, the root of those gifts is in union with God himself – something far higher than Adam's original state of righteousness before the fall.[112] And there can be no second baptism. As Christ died 'once for all', the Christian dies and rises again *once* with Christ in baptism, and death comes but once: repeated baptisms (were they effective) would invalidate previous baptisms, offending against the grace of the sacrament.[113] God, by his grace, might yet restore through repentance, yet 'man has no means to restore such; for man it is impossible'.[114] And the consequences too are grave: 'branches really withered are not in the Vine, but cast forth; those dead in trespasses and sins, though they may yet be brought back to life, are not now *in* Christ'.[115]

Stated in its starkest form, in Tract 68, Pusey's emphasis on the gravity of post-baptismal sin raised an outcry. Even sympathetic readers thought he denied forgiveness for sins committed after baptism. But this was not his intent, as the passages just cited show. In reality, his aim was to emphasize the uniqueness of baptism in the Christian life, the greatness of God's gift in it and the gravity of sin, in light of that gift.[116] There is forgiveness for sins after baptism, but in contrast to the renewal given in baptism, the healing received in penitence is incomplete. This is a practical observation on Pusey's part: whereas baptism is the new beginning of the Christian life, subsequent repentance is a process of recovery. In baptism we are given, spiritually – and perhaps, in an adult, even psychologically (if the break with the past is as dramatic as Pusey's theology says it should be) – a 'clean slate'; once sin is readmitted, it must be uprooted and guarded against. While baptism gives complete healing, the healing of repentance leaves spiritual 'scars:' 'there remaineth no more such complete ablution in this life'.[117] It is 'to be received

---

112. Pusey, *Baptism 1*, 59.

113. Pusey, *Baptism 1*, 51–3, on Heb. 6.1-6; Pusey follows a widespread Patristic interpretation of the passage. A hint of his intent shows in that he does not quote rigorist interpreters like Tertullian, who denied the possibility of repentance for post-baptismal sin: instead, he draws on Chrysostom's account which moves directly from the impossibility of a second baptism to the role of repentance. Erik M. Heen and Philip D. W. Krey, eds, *Hebrews*, Ancient Christian Commentary on Scripture, ed. Thomas C. Oden, New Testament 10 (Downers Grove, IL: InterVarsity Press, 2005), 83–7.

114. Pusey, *Baptism 1*, 51.

115. Pusey, *Par. S. I*, ix; emphasis Pusey's.

116. This likely reflects an influence of St Augustine on Pusey's thought. Pusey, in the preface to his translation of Augustine's *Confessions* (published 1838, but begun in the year following the publication of *Baptism 1*) notes Augustine's strong views of his past sin, which however are of no concern to the saint because they had been washed away in baptism. Pusey makes the same comparison in *Baptism 1*, but with regard to post-baptismal, rather than pre-baptismal, sin – for which, necessarily, baptism cannot provide the same security. Pusey, preface to *Confessions*, xxviii.

117. Pusey, *Baptism 1*, 54–7, 63. Thomas Mozley notes that, in Pusey's doctrine, sin 'leaves its consequences in heart, mind, body, and soul, and in those who share it or suffer from it. This is not a truth of revelation, but a natural fact.' While the penitent is forgiven

gratefully, as a renewal of a portion of that former gift; to be exulted in, because it is life; but to be received and guarded with trembling, because it is the renewal of what had been forfeited; not to be boasted of, because it is but the fragment of an inheritance, "wasted in riotous living".[118] Because of the difficulty of spiritual combat against sin, penitence is slow, 'rugged and toilsome and watered with bitter tears'.[119] And it is not the emotion of a brief moment; it is, rather, the continuous work of a lifetime:

> Were the repentance at once perfect, so, doubtless, would the pardon be; but it is part of the disease, entailed by grievous sin, that men can but slowly repent; they have disabled themselves from applying completely their only cure: the anguish of repentance, in its early stages, is often the sharpest; it is generally long afterwards that it is in any real degree purified and deepened.[120]

The long and arduous work of true repentance leads Pusey to protest against anything that would give a superficial sense of spiritual security. He faults Roman Catholicism for its 'new Sacrament of Penance' by which 'they did contrive, without more cost, to restore men, however fallen, to the same state of undisturbed security in which God had by Baptism placed them. Penance became a second Baptism.' At the same time he warns against an 'opposite course' with the 'same result:' 'The blood of Christ is indeed all-powerful to wash away sin; but it is not at our discretion, at once, on the first expression of what may be a passing sorrow, to apply It.'[121] Rather, the Church should preserve 'a reverent silence, not cutting off hope, and yet not nurturing an untimely confidence, or a presumptuous security'.[122] These themes from Tract 68 were taken up again in the *Letter to the Bishop of Oxford*. There, Pusey mitigated some of his criticism of Rome, conceding that as the decayed remnants of the Patristic system of discipline, the Roman use of confession retains at least shadowy indications of the depth of sin and the holiness of God, though in practice it was used superficially.[123] But he continues to attack the 'modern system' which

by God, the real-life consequences of sin remain. Thomas Mozley, *Reminiscences: Chiefly of Oriel College and the Oxford Movement* (London: Longmans, Green, 1882), 2:146–9; Calhoun, 'Conversion', 181–2.

    118. Pusey, *Baptism 1*, 72, quoting Lk. 15.13.
    119. Pusey, *Baptism 1*, 62.
    120. Pusey, *Baptism 1*, xiii.
    121. Pusey, *Baptism 1*, 58–9. Cf. Forrester, *Pusey*, 198. *Pace* Forrester, Pusey maintained this belief even in (and after) his 1846 sermons on absolution: 'Such a re-creation there cannot again be … In Baptism, sins are suddenly and painlessly blotted out through grace; deep sins after Baptism are forgiven, but upon deep contrition which God giveth: and deep contrition is, for the most part, slowly and gradually worked into the soul.' Pusey, 'Entire Absolution I', 223.
    122. Pusey, *Baptism 1*, xiv.
    123. Pusey, *Oxford*, 84–7.

stifles continually the strong emotions of terror and amazement which God has wrought upon the soul, and 'healing slightly the wound' which He has made, makes it often incurable; [which] makes peace rather than holiness, the end of its ministrations, and by an artificial wrought-up peace, checks the deep and searching agony, whereby God, as in a furnace of fire, was purifying the whole man.[124]

For this reason Pusey would later emphasize that penitential acts are not 'payment' for sin but a means of nourishing ongoing penitence.[125] He encouraged the regular use of private confession; but, even late in life, he insisted that it be infrequent so as to avoid overshadowing the deep inner workings of repentance.[126] This is due, largely, to the distinction he made between God's forgiveness in absolution and the longer-term fruits of repentance. While 'the restoration, on the part of God … is complete', 'the effect of sin upon the soul may often be to be worked out by sorrow and toil; the forfeited crown and larger favour of Almighty God to be gained by subsequent self-denial or suffering for Him or devoted service. But we have the very craving of our hearts.'[127]

Pusey insists that there can be no second baptism – literally, or in effect. Rather, repentance is itself a fruit of baptismal union with Christ. It is 'our Baptism in the Blood of Christ, which renders that repentance effectual'.[128] Even the sharp language Pusey uses to describe the bitterness of repentance is because it is, in part, a 'participation of His utter hatred of sin'.[129] The transformation and labour of repentance, aside from our willingness in it, is the work of God. God is the physician, 'probing the diseased and ulcerous part "to the very dividing of soul and body"' with a 'healthful severity'.[130] Although we are 'wearied and wasted by manifold wanderings, our steps unsteady through our many falls, *ourselves* to follow Him', Christ the good shepherd 'layeth [us] on His shoulders, rejoicing'. And Christ carries the faithful in this work of repentance, through the incarnation and union with him.

---

124. Pusey, *Oxford*, 87–8.
125. Pusey, 'Entire Absolution II', 29–37. Practically, this means that penances are to be undertaken for their psychological and spiritual effect, rather than for their severity; in his spiritual direction Pusey often chastised those to whom he was writing for excessive practices, discouraged sterner disciplines as impractical and regularly emphasized the need for moderation. Pusey to Sr Clara, 23 May 1846, LBV 76; 12 April 1873, LBV 77.
126. Pusey to Sr Clara Maria, n.d. [1877] in LBV 125, Pusey to Sr Clara, [April] 1882 in LBV 77; cf. Pusey, *Richards*, 134–6.
127. Pusey, 'Entire Absolution I', 35, 54.
128. Pusey, *Baptism 1*, 54, 63–5.
129. Pusey, *Baptism 1*, 79–80.
130. Pusey, *Oxford*, 96.

He bowed Himself from heaven to earth; He stooped to our lowliness; He folded us in love in His Bosom; in His lowliness on His shoulders which bare the Cross, He bare us; there would He have us lay down our sins; there would He have us rest our wearied limbs and our aching hearts; with His own pierced Hands would He hold us; there would He admit us nigh, … there would that thorn-crowned Head incline towards us, melt our stony heart with His look of tenderness, and cleanse us anew with that Precious Blood … Not to Angels only hath He given thee in charge, to bear thee up, but He Himself hath folded thee around Himself, hath bound thee like an ornament around His Neck, hath clothed Himself with thy mortality, that with thee, as part of Himself, 'His Body and His Bones,' He might ascend again to the Bosom of the Father, and Himself rejoicing, amid the rejoicing choirs of Angels, bring thee into the joy of thy Lord.[131]

One of the central realities of union with Christ, in both justification and sanctification, is love. Repentance, as the outgrowth of that union, is likewise a process of growing in love.

Deep sins after Baptism are forgiven, but upon deep contrition which God giveth: and deep contrition is, for the most part, slowly and gradually worked into the soul, deepening with deepening grace, sorrowing still more, as, by God's grace, it more deeply loves; grieved the more, the more it knows Him Whom it once grieved, and through that grief and love inwrought in it by God, the more forgiven.[132]

The model for this is the penitent woman of Luke 7.36-50. Noting that 'because she loved much, her sins are forgiven', he asks, 'But He Who gave to a sinner such love, shall we wonder that He received the love He gave? First, love made her offer to her Redeemer all which she had hitherto abused to sin, and then through her offering He kindled in her new love'. In this offering to God, 'the lips which she had profaned', became, when she kissed Christ's feet, 'the very instruments of her acceptance … her sins had separated her from God; now she may touch Him'. Instead of anointing her own beauty, she anoints Christ, weeping and wiping his feet with her hair: not only her wealth but her very self is given, as an expression of penitent love.[133] The following practical exhortation recalls Pusey's social concerns: the penitent is called to imitate her by self-denial ('at times at least, and in proportion to the form of their love') and to 'shew love to Christ's poor, in order in them to shew love to Himself'.[134]

---

131. E. B. Pusey, 'Hopes of the Penitent', in SR, 250–1; cf. Lk. 15.4-7, Ps. 91.11-12, Eph. 5.30-1, Gen. 2.23.
132. Pusey, 'Entire Absolution I', 23.
133. E. B. Pusey, 'Loving Penitence', in SR, 8–9. The penitent woman has traditionally been identified with Mary Magdalene, and Pusey throughout this sermon identifies her as such. This interpretation, however, is no longer accepted in current biblical scholarship.
134. Pusey, 'Loving Penitence', 17.

This, in turn, helps to distinguish between the 'sharp anguish' of early repentance and the 'purified and deepened' repentance which is Pusey's true concern. Purified repentance passes beyond self-loathing and fear of judgement, to the sorrow of love which sees that it has offended its beloved.

> By the very order of God with the soul … continued sorrow is not only the condition of continued pardon, but the very channel of new graces, and of the renewed life of the soul. Sorrow, as it flows on, is more refined, yet deeper. To part with sorrow and self-displeasure would be to part with love; for it grieveth, and is displeased because it loves.[135]

And yet, because this sorrow flows from love, 'the sting of sorrow is removed'.[136] The Church should 'hold out the prospect of peace, but as God's gift through the deepening of repentance; not to cut short His work … but to direct to His mercies in Christ', for

> not peace, but salvation is our end; but peace also He, the God of peace, will bestow, as He sees most healthful for them, according to the evenness and consistency of their course; clouding it, if they are remiss or halting; renewing it, when they humble themselves and press onward; and in all cases bestowing upon us more than we deserve, for His sake 'Who is our Peace'.[137]

And the offer of absolution

> is not to replace penitence … but to secure its fruits; not to diminish sorrow for past sin, but to make it joyous; not to offer easy terms, but to invite to the yoke of Christ, easy, but as freeing thee from the heavy yoke of sin; easy, because He Who placeth it upon thee, shall by it uphold thee.[138]

At the foot of the cross, the penitent finds sorrow 'sweeter than all other joy'.[139]

While union with Christ is doctrinally important for Pusey, it also has significant practical implications. Union with Christ requires the pursuit of holiness; and even when holiness is lost through sin, union with Christ is again the foundation of repentance. Throughout, however, the overarching theme is love, for in Christ the Christian is united to the God who *is* love. As this emphasis on divine love shows, the heart of Pusey's theology is not in his denunciations of sin, or any supposed harshness – those are merely the corollaries of his belief in the reality of God's redeeming work, not just in the next life but in this, which sin rejects. But the true heart of Pusey's theology is the exceeding depth of God's love for humanity,

---

135. Pusey, 'Entire Absolution I', 23–4.
136. Pusey to Maria, 16 May 1828, LBV 23; given in Forrester, *Pusey*, 61.
137. Pusey, *Oxford*, 96, quoting Eph. 2.14.
138. Pusey, 'Entire Absolution I', 55; cf. Mt. 11.28-30.
139. Pusey, 'Looking unto Jesus', 180.

realized in the incarnation of Jesus, in his union with the redeemed and in the infinite expanse of grace given to those who love him.[140] Pusey was speaking of the grace given to penitent love when he said, 'He giveth according to our longing. He Himself hath said, "Open thy mouth wide, and I will fill it:" the greater our longing for His grace, the larger His grace. His Infinite Love has no bounds, but the narrowness of our souls, which, if we crave it, He will enlarge.'[141] It is both fitting and poignant that he would echo those words in the weeks before his death.

> Each day is a day of growth. God says to you, 'Open thy mouth, and I will fill it.' Only long. He does not want our words. The parched soil, by its cracks, opens itself for the rains from Heaven and invites them. The parched soul cries out for the living God.
> Oh then long and long and long, and God will fill thee. More love, more love, more love![142]

***

The previous chapter focused on Pusey's treatment of allegory and the way in which that discussion generated a theological vision of the whole creation's participation in Christ, its archetype. This chapter, in turn, has discussed Pusey's teaching on union with Christ, which, as the fulfilment of the incarnation, is the centre of the entire participatory order in creation. This discussion has encompassed both doctrinal subjects such as faith, justification and the glorification of the body, as well as Pusey's practical teaching on Christian holiness and repentance. These twin aspects of Pusey's teaching on union with Christ, however, are intimately connected. The pursuit of practical holiness, through Christian works of mercy, is the lived realization of God's justifying declaration, and the means by which the faithful grow in faith; and thereby (since 'faith is instead of eyes') it is also the means by which their eyes are opened to see Christ in all things. But the grace of union is not given apart from the created order; rather, the sacral potential of creation is concentrated in the dominical sacraments, as the vehicles of this communion. Baptism, as this chapter has discussed, is the new birth into this life of union, and all these gifts inhere in it. But birth is followed by nourishment and growth, and the nourishment of the baptismal gift is the particular grace of the Eucharist.

---

140. This is not to deny a certain austerity in Pusey's attitudes on repentance, especially in the earlier years of the Oxford Movement; but it is important to consider the evolution of his attitudes for a complete picture of his spirituality. In one telling account, Sister Clara, who was under his spiritual direction from the 1840s, recalls that early in his ministry as a confessor he would insist that penitents kneel on the bare stone, forbidding the use of a cushion. In his later years, however, 'Dr. Pusey would *himself offer* a cushion for persons to kneel on, in confession.' Sister Clara, Reminiscences of Dr Pusey, in LBV 78, emphasis Sister Clara's.

141. Pusey, 'Entire Absolution I', 53, quoting Ps. 80.11.

142. Pusey to Sr. Clara, 22 August 1882, LBV 77, quoting Ps. 80.11; cf. Isa. 55.10-11.

Chapter 4

COMMUNION AND THE REAL PRESENCE

Pusey's eucharistic teaching is perhaps the aspect of his theology for which, today, he is best known. He was the champion of Tractarian doctrines in the eucharistic controversies and ritualist trials which began in the 1850s. More importantly for the purposes of this study, he wrote extensively on the subject. In addition to relevant material in the 'Types', he produced several eucharistic sermons – including the famous 'condemned sermon' of 1843 – and two lengthy historical treatises in defence of his doctrine; eucharistic themes also recur throughout his sermons on other subjects. In Pusey's theology, the Eucharist stands, with baptism, above the rest of the sacramental order of creation as a means of communicating union with Christ. However, while the water of baptism, in conveying union with Christ, also participates in its own rich network of natural and biblical symbolism (including Christ's own baptism, death and resurrection), the Eucharist adds a further dimension. The eucharistic elements, like the water of baptism, share in a network of associated natural and biblical symbolism, which signifies the grace conveyed in the sacrament. But they also, Pusey emphasizes, participate themselves (really, not just symbolically) in the body and blood of Christ, through Christ's own words at the last supper (and 'the word of God', as Pusey said with regard to justification, 'is power'). This aspect of the Eucharist has, of course, become a particularly fraught subject in the history of theology. The emphasis of this chapter is therefore different than the last. In Pusey's thought, the purpose of the Eucharist, as its elements suggest, is to nourish the life given in baptism. Therefore much of what he emphasizes with regard to the eucharistic grace of communion (holiness, repentance and so forth) has already been treated in the previous chapter. The weight of this chapter's discussion, rather, concerns the proper 'location' of Pusey's eucharistic theology among the schools of thought that have emerged from the historical debate regarding the real presence. The mistaken tendency to read Tractarian eucharistic theology – including Pusey's – through the lens of later Anglo-Catholicism has meant that Pusey is often interpreted as introducing into Anglicanism the Roman Catholic doctrine of transubstantiation. This chapter, however, argues that Pusey is more accurately understood as developing, through the principles of his 'sacramental vision', the high church tradition's Reformed doctrine of the real presence.

Eucharist and communion

The common feature of baptism and the Eucharist in Pusey's thought is that they both impart union with Christ. In contrast to lesser mysteries, the two dominical sacraments are not merely 'means of grace', but specifically 'instruments of knitting the soul to Christ', 'the appointed channels for applying the Atonement to the soul, the communication of Himself and His life'.[1] But whereas baptism is given by God as the beginning of the life of faith, the Eucharist is for its growth. 'Baptism gives, the Holy Eucharist preserves and enlarges life. Baptism engraffs into the true Vine; the Holy Eucharist derives the richness and fullness of His life into the branches thus engraffed. Baptism buries in Christ's tomb, and through it He quickens with His life; the Holy Eucharist is given not to the dead, but to the living.'[2] The mode of Christ's indwelling differs as well. 'Christ dwells in us in a twofold way, spiritually and sacramentally. By His Spirit, He makes us the temples of God; by His Body and Blood, He is to our bodies also a source of life, incorruption, immortality.'[3] In baptism, we receive the Holy Spirit, the Spirit of Christ, in our souls; in the Eucharist, we receive his body and blood into our bodies.

As we should expect, allegory plays a key role in Pusey's eucharistic teaching. The Passover is a prominent eucharistic type, as is the 'pure offering' (Mal. 1.11); these, however, as sacrificial types, will be discussed in Chapter 6. But the 'pure offering' (i.e., the grain offering or *mincha*) in particular shows Pusey's interest in the relation of the eucharistic elements to eucharistic types. Old Testament references to bread and wine (sometimes with oil) as 'gladdening man's heart' foreshadow the Eucharist.[4] Beyond biblical references there are natural types to consider. The 'nourishing' character of the Eucharist comes from an allegorical understanding of the bread and wine: the bread and wine of the Eucharist are food; food nourishes, and so the elements signify *through their matter* the spiritual nourishment given in the sacrament.[5] This is particularly the case with the bread: 'The seed corn, which is His Flesh, gives life by its death; as bread, again, His Body, it nourishes to Life eternal'; and, referring to the analogy of one bread and one body in 1 Corinthians 10.17, 'so again, this one image pourtrays [sic] to us the mysterious connexion between the Body of Christ, which is His Flesh, and the Body of Christ, which is the Church, and how, by partaking of that Body, we ourselves become what we partake of'.[6]

---

1. Pusey, *Jelf*, 39–40.
2. Pusey, 'Comfort', 4.
3. Pusey, 'Presence of Christ', 69. That is, we become 'temples' of the Holy Spirit in baptism, receiving Christ indirectly through the mediation of the Spirit (not directly in the sacrament), whereas in the Eucharist we receive Christ directly, in his own body and blood.
4. Pusey, *London*, 148–9.
5. Pusey, 'Comfort', 4.
6. Pusey, *London*, 148–9.

But the wine also has its symbolism. As noted in Chapter 1, Pusey put a great deal of emphasis on lay reception of the cup, which was withheld in Roman Catholicism; a part of his objection is the insistence that since Christ instituted the sacrament in two kinds, each element must have its own associated grace. Pusey rejects the Roman arguments concerning concomitance (that the body and blood of Christ are fully present in both elements) as 'miserable and rationalistic arguments in divine mysteries' and insists that 'to obey is better than sacrifice' (1 Sam. 15.22).[7] But whereas the bread conveys spiritual nourishment (as the element suggests), the natural symbolism of the wine suggests that its particular grace is one of joy, or spiritual inebriation.[8] The spiritual and the worldly are, as ever, opposed to one another; so in contrast to 'transport' or 'ecstasy' of worldly pride or success,

> The gift vouchsafed in the Holy Communion must be altogether of a different kind, because it is not the stirring up of the human spirit, but the union of the Divine, the Presence of the Redeemer within the soul, when the soul is silent, not acting upon itself, but 'caught up', present with its Lord, because 'one with Him', penetrated with Him and His Divinity, when in solemn words which have been used, the soul is 'transfigured' by His Holy Presence in it.[9]

Therefore, this inebriation should lead to sobriety, rather than confusion; forgetfulness of the world, of sin and of sorrow; and should issue in works of love and righteousness.[10]

Despite the distinction between baptism as the beginning of the Christian life, and the Eucharist as its nourishment, the gifts of life, love and practical holiness towards which these types point are much the same, because they are founded, in both sacraments, on union with Christ. God *is* life; Christ, the second person of the Trinity, is God, and therefore has life in himself. In the incarnation he united his living deity to his human body. So, in receiving Christ's body sacramentally, we receive into our own bodies his life and his divinity, for our own transformation. 'Receiving Him into this very body, they who receive Him, receive life, which shall pass over to our decaying flesh.'[11] Commenting on the latter verses of John 6, Pusey

---

7. Pusey, *Oxford*, 135–44. Pusey discusses the Council of Constance, Session 13 (cf. Council of Trent, Session 21, Chapter 21), which holds that administration in one kind does not deprive the recipients of 'any grace *necessary to salvation*' (emphasis Pusey's); Pusey reads this as a tacit admission that the laity are deprived of *some* grace by the practice and challenges the right of any human institution to determine what grace is or isn't necessary, that God has ordained. A parallel argument (though in milder language) is given in *London*, 161–4.

8. Pusey, *London*, 145–55.

9. Pusey, *London*, 155–6.

10. Pusey, *London*, 160–1.

11. Pusey, 'Comfort', 8–9.

writes, 'His flesh was life-giving, because he Himself had life'; 'this endless life passed over to us, through our eating His flesh and drinking His blood – words which have their adequate fulfilment in the mysteries of the Holy Eucharist ... "The Spirit quickeneth." The life-giving Spirit, or Deity, which is life, made that sacred flesh wherewith it was united life-giving.'[12] Christ's 'inherent life ... is transmitted on to us also, and not to our souls only, but our bodies also, since we become flesh of His flesh, and bone of His bone'.[13]

Again, with the gift of life comes the gift of love. We are to be 'caught up within the influence of the mystery of that ineffable love' within the life of the Trinity.[14] God's love is the answer to human love, which is the true longing of the human heart and the true goal of religion. Moral perfection, even if it were attainable, would not satisfy the yearnings of human nature. The human heart can only be satisfied by love for God; yet love is unsatisfied if it cannot see its beloved. Even sight, however – blessed gift though the beatific vision may be – cannot fully satisfy love, if it does not end in union.[15] This is also true of knowledge. 'Knowledge, not even the knowledge of God, can never be the whole of man. For man is formed in the image of God, and "God is love." '[16] 'Only from God could we have this longing for God'; in fulfilment of this longing, and as a foretaste of our final communion with him, we have God's gift of himself in the sacraments.[17]

Love, however, is tied to holiness. As the Eucharist is both the gift and the consummation of love for God, it is therefore both the gift and the consummation of holiness more generally. It nourishes all the blessings given in baptism; but in this nourishment it partakes of a dual character. There is, at least theoretically, the possibility of real and untarnished sanctity in the Christian life, of keeping unstained the white robes of baptism, and to such a 'saint', the communion of Christ's body and blood is the consummation of earth's highest joys. But to those pursuing the more sombre sanctity of repentance, the Eucharist is also a gift:

> What wraps the saint already in the third Heaven, may yet uphold us sinners, that the pit shut not her mouth upon us. The same reality of the Divine Gift makes It Angel's Food to the Saint, the ransom to the sinner. ... To him its special joy is that it is His Redeemer's very broken Body, It is His Blood, which was shed for the remission of his sins.[18]

The Eucharist partakes of Christ's death *for sinners*; Christ's flesh was given 'for the life of the world' (Jn 6.51) and thus, above all, for those who are dying through

---

12. Pusey, 'Will Ye?', 4.
13. Pusey, 'Comfort', 11.
14. Pusey, 'Comfort', 14.
15. Pusey, 'This Is My Body', 42–4.
16. Pusey, 'Will Ye?', 7, quoting 1 Jn 4.8, 16; cf. 1 Cor. 13.2.
17. Pusey, 'This Is My Body', 42; cf. 'Comfort', 18–19.
18. Pusey, 'Comfort', 18.

sin; Christ gave the sacramental cup of his blood, 'for the remission of sins' (Mt. 26.28).[19] In 'the communion of the blood of Christ' (1 Cor. 10.16), 'remission of sins is implied by the very words. For, if we be partakers of His atoning Blood, how should we not be partakers of its fruits?'[20] Nonetheless, a measure of holiness is also required in receiving communion. All of Pusey's eucharistic sermons emphasize the call to personal holiness.[21] However, in the 1843 sermon, he also emphasizes the corporate holiness of the Church: the Church's lack of sanctity shows the need for more frequent communions, so that the Church might grow in holiness; but at the same time, the corruption of the Church, set against the holiness required for communion, means that increased communions should not be rashly introduced.[22]

Real presence I: Pusey's reformed framework

This brief survey shows the interplay within Pusey's eucharistic theology of the unitive and allegorical themes already introduced. But in order to gain a proper understanding of Pusey's eucharistic thought, it is necessary to shift attention back to his theological continuity with and development of the old high church tradition. This stands in contrast to the widespread view that Pusey's teaching brought the Roman Catholic doctrine of transubstantiation into the Church of England.[23] The common view has had a damaging effect on Pusey's reputation: Anglo-Catholics may hail him as a restorer of true doctrine, but it has not befriended him to Evangelicals; and in terms of scholarly interest, having such a prominent element of Pusey's work classified as the replication, within Anglicanism, of a eucharistic theory which had already been developed elsewhere has rendered him more of an historical curiosity than a figure of interest in his own right.

Given the prevalence of this view, the claim made at the beginning of this chapter – that Pusey's understanding of the Eucharist is better seen as a development of Reformed eucharistic doctrine – may seem startling. The grounds for it, however, are straightforward: Pusey was raised in the high church tradition and grounded his theology in the Prayer Book. Both of these sources shared a broadly Calvinian understanding of the Eucharist, and so it is there that we should

19. Pusey, 'Comfort', 19–24.
20. Pusey, 'Comfort', 23.
21. Pusey, 'Presence of Christ', 10–12, 69–74; 'Will Ye?', 20–4; 'This Is My Body', 46–7. Pusey frequently singles out sexual sin for his attention, which may strike the modern reader as awkward; but this is less surprising when it is remembered that these sermons were delivered to young male university students.
22. Pusey, 'Comfort', 27–32.
23. See, e.g., W. H. Mackean, *The Eucharistic Doctrine of the Oxford Movement: A Critical Survey* (London: Putnam, 1933), 121–2; Owen F. Cummings, *Eucharistic Doctors: A Theological History* (New York: Paulist Press, 2005), 248–50.

look for the roots of Pusey's eucharistic theology.[24] Pusey's persistent criticisms of transubstantiation (discussed in Chapter 1) fit naturally within this perspective; they should not be dismissed.[25] That it has become common practice to do so is generally due to the overlapping assumptions that Pusey should be read through the lens of later Anglo-Catholicism, and that Newman's theological mutations were normative for the other Tractarians. It has already been argued, however, that both approaches produce serious distortions in our understanding of Pusey's theology.[26]

It should be acknowledged that Pusey's discussions of both the Eucharist and baptism contain many arguments which are framed as anti-Calvinist polemic. On the face of it, this would seem to contradict the interpretation I offer here. There are, however, other considerations which suggest a more complex relationship beneath the surface. In the preface to the first part of the *Enquiry*, Pusey's explanation of the 'Evangelical' (i.e., Lutheran) and 'Reformed' churches in Germany describes the latter as 'such as agree in the doctrine of the Lord's Supper with ourselves'.[27] As late as 1833, he held a high opinion of Calvin – Newman had to restrain him from calling the reformer a 'saint'![28] At the end of his life, he concluded years of wrestling with Protestant eucharistic theologies by stating his preference for Calvin over Luther.[29] Indeed, he insisted throughout his life that his eucharistic doctrine simply *was* a high church reading of the Prayer Book Catechism taught him by his mother.[30] These factors suggest that Pusey's attacks are aimed primarily

---

24. The high churchmen, though sometimes called 'Arminians' by opponents, are perhaps best described as simply non-Calvinist Reformed, as many of the defining points of strictly Arminian *or* Calvinist theology were censured by their characteristic reticence. Nockles, *Context*, 31–2; Van Mildert, *Sermons*, 1:94–114.

25. Pusey did recognize some similarities between his understanding of Anglican eucharistic doctrine and that of Rome, and thought them capable of fruitful dialogue; but he was always clear that the two were not identical. See discussion in Chapter 1 under 'The Reformation and Rome'.

26. It may be argued, as a third option, that Pusey should be seen as reviving the Patristic doctrine of the Eucharist. That Pusey was strongly influenced by the Fathers is, of course, without question; but his patristic reading was not (as it were) inscribed on a blank slate. Rather, his patristic influences were taken up into his inherited high church framework.

27. Pusey, *Enquiry I*, xiv. His sermon for Christmas the same year contains an unremarkable statement of high church eucharistic doctrine, which is, if anything, vaguely virtualist in character; while I argue below that this position is continuous with Pusey's later views, the sermon nonetheless does not, *pace* Liddon (and Douglas, who accepts Liddon's assessment), 'clearly foreshadow' Pusey's later teachings. Pusey, Sermon for 25 December 1828, Pusey Early Sermons MSS, Pusey House; Liddon, *Life*, 1:192; Douglas, *Eucharistic Theology*, 35.

28. Liddon, *Life*, 1:232–4; cf. Pusey, *Cathedral Institutions*, 54, 73.

29. Pusey, 'Introductory Essay', 39–40.

30. Liddon, *Life*, 1:7. There *is* observable development in Pusey's thought beyond the 'old' high church position, but despite his exaggeration to the contrary, Pusey's attribution

at Calvin*ists* in his own day; Pusey's statements about Calvin himself, on the other hand, when carefully analysed, show an evolving understanding that moves far beyond his ham-handed description, in 1836, of the Genevan magister as merely Zwingli's systematizer.[31] More importantly, these nuances raise the question of how the *structure* of Pusey's eucharistic theology relates to that of Calvin, an inquiry which might shed further light on this relationship.

The old high churchmen have typically been classified as holding either 'receptionist' or 'virtualist' views: that is, as holding that the faithful communicant receives communion with Christ in the *act* of receiving the Eucharist (not, however, as conveyed by or present in the elements themselves), or else receives the benefits or 'virtues' of Christ's body and blood in receiving the Holy Communion – but not Christ's body and blood directly.[32] One example of the former is, in fact, the pre-Tractarian Keble, who wrote in an early edition of *The Christian Year* that Christ is received 'in the heart, / not in the hands' (later grudgingly amended to 'in the heart, / *as* in the hands').[33] Waterland, in the eighteenth century, has also been classed as a receptionist.[34] Van Mildert appears to have been a virtualist, holding that 'most of the Reformed Churches' – including the Church of England –

---

of the origin of his thought should not be dismissed. Douglas's suggestion that Pusey's statement should be interpreted allegorically, with Lady Pusey's catechesis as a type foreshadowing Pusey's developed thought, is intriguing, but suggests a more dramatic shift in Pusey's eucharistic theology than my analysis would indicate. Douglas, 'Pusey, Poetry, and Eucharistic Theology', 98–9.

31. Pusey, *Baptism 1*, 107–14. Cf. *Oxford*, 172; *English Church*, 209; 'This Is My Body', 15–20. Pusey's understanding of Calvin shows a clear progression from this point: in 1839, he distinguished Calvin from Zwingli, though holding that their theories tended to the same end; in 1857, he links Calvin to an understanding of spiritual communion in the Eucharist, omitting Zwingli; in 1871 Zwingli alone is singled out for holding a merely symbolic understanding of the Eucharist. Despite this evolution, Pusey's understanding of Calvin must be counted as a weak point in his scholarship, although this might be partially excused since Pusey never had the personal motivations to engage with Calvin which led him into a deeper knowledge of Lutheranism and Roman Catholicism, and the deleterious influence of contemporary Calvinist polemics on Pusey's reading of Calvin was likely not helped by Pusey's acquaintance with Lutheranism. However, Palmer notes in 1838 that Calvin's 'language was very strongly in favour of the real presence, though it is questionable whether his doctrine was really consistent with it', in contrast with Zwingli. Robert Wilberforce also distinguishes between Zwingli and Calvin, though he classes Calvin as a virtualist. This suggests that Wilberforce's subsequent reference to a 'Zuinglo-Calvinistic system' in the 1552 Prayer Book (a term also used on occasion by Pusey) is less a confusion of the two reformers than a pejorative for a particular position. Palmer, *Treatise*, 1:293; R. I. Wilberforce, *The Doctrine of the Holy Eucharist* (London: John and Charles Mozley, 1853), 122–3, 137–49, 438–9.

32. Nockles, *Context*, 236–8; Härdelin, *Eucharist*, 126–8.

33. Härdelin, *Eucharist*, 129.

34. Härdelin, *Eucharist*, 126–8.

while they declare the elements of bread and wine to remain unchanged, and deny the body and blood of Christ to be *corporally* present, acknowledge them nevertheless to be *mystically* and *sacramentally* present; that is, they acknowledge, that, by virtue of the spiritual grace which accompanies the elements, they convey to the penitent and faithful communicant the full and actual benefits of our Lord's death upon the cross.[35]

Such, at least, are the definitions which have been used to classify these perspectives, and in some degree to divide them. If these positions are viewed descriptively, however, there are a number of shared characteristics between these positions which also occur in Pusey, suggesting that it may be more appropriate to think in terms of a sliding scale of overlapping weaker and stronger theories of the real presence, rather than in polemically loaded classifications. This can be seen in comparing Pusey to Waterland and, indeed, to Calvin.[36] Each shows a realism about union with Christ and its benefits, as communicated by the sacrament. This is balanced by several shared concerns: the continuation of the bread and wine as real material elements, the presence of Christ's body in heaven (the '*extra Calvinisticum*') and the necessity of faithfulness in receiving. With these caveats, however, these positions are emphatically *affirmations* made against lower views of the Eucharist. Calvin, though sharing some concerns with Zwingli, is often antagonistic to him.[37] Similarly, Waterland's weighty *Review of the Doctrine of the Eucharist* was, primarily, a rebuttal of the latitudinarian Benjamin Hoadly's memorialist doctrine. Likewise, in a postscript to a shorter work, Waterland sharply censures the radical virtualist John Johnson of Cranbrook (1662–1725), pointedly affirming the centrality of the words of institution to eucharistic doctrine (Johnson taught a real *immediate* presence of the Holy Spirit in the Eucharist, and only a *mediated*, virtual presence of Christ's body).[38] Pusey agreed with this

---

35. Van Mildert, *Sermons*, 1:102; emphasis Van Mildert's. The language of a 'mystical' or 'sacramental' presence, as we shall see, is appropriated by Pusey, albeit to a different theological end.

36. Calvin is used here primarily due to his prominence in the Reformed tradition and Pusey's evolving attitude towards him. His influence on Anglicanism, however, is more complicated than this use might suggest. The most prominent continental reformers in England during the Edwardian Reformation were Bucer and Vermigli, and through the Elizabethan period much of the English church appears to have maintained closer ties to Zurich than to Geneva. Calvin's influence grew, however, during the seventeenth century, and by the eighteenth his stature was such that English divines such as Waterland engaged extensively with his work. See Diarmaid MacCulloch, 'The Latitude of the Church of England', in *Religion and Politics in Post-Reformation England*, ed. Kenneth Fincham and Peter Lake (Woodbridge, Suffolk: Boydell, 2006), 41–59.

37. Kilian McDonnell, *John Calvin, the Church, and the Eucharist* (Princeton, NJ: Princeton University Press, 1967), 94–95.

38. Daniel Waterland, 'The Sacramental Part of the Eucharist Explained', in *Works*, 5:185–270; John Johnson, *The Unbloody Sacrifice, and Altar, Unvailed and Supported*, in *The*

tradition, both in its affirmation of a real communion of Christ's body and blood, and in its caveats about faithful receiving, the materiality of the elements, and the physical location of Christ's body in heaven. However, whereas Pusey draws a clear connection between communion and Christ's eucharistic presence, the older high churchmen were more reticent.[39] Van Mildert, for example, rejected speculation beyond the general views given above: theorizing about the nature of Christ's presence in the Eucharist was an unfruitful topic, tending only towards controversy. Calvin, in contrast to the English high churchmen, *does* offer a more developed theory of Christ's presence in the Eucharist, though one markedly different from Pusey's; this provides a fruitful point of comparison between the two.

For the moment, however, the structural similarities between Pusey and the high churchmen should be stated more fully. Both emphasize sacramental communion with Christ. For Pusey, this is the foundation of belief in the real presence. 'Since we receive' the body and blood of Christ, 'they must be there, in order that we may receive them'.[40] This, he thought, was the clear teaching of the Prayer Book Catechism, which emphasizes both the 'inward part' of the sacrament (the body and blood of Christ) and its 'benefit' (communion); the Prayer Book language of communion provides several of Pusey's arguments for the real presence.[41] So too, the final language of the Articles of Religion rejected an earlier denial of the 'reall and bodilie' presence of Christ, instead using language inspired by Lutheranism, but shifting its emphasis to make increased faith a secondary benefit to God's invisible working within the communicants.[42] Article 28's rendering of 1 Corinthians 10.16 as a 'partaking' of Christ's body and blood emphasizes the 'eaten' nature of the sacrament; with Alexander Knox (and supported by a parallel usage in the Wittenberg Concord), Pusey interprets the article's words 'given, taken, and

Theological Works of the Rev. John Johnson (Oxford: John Henry Parker, 1847), 1:226–322, esp. 272–3.

39. This may explain why high church contemporaries of Pusey were divided on his teaching. Some thought his language excessive; the doctrinal charges concerning Pusey's 1843 sermon on the Eucharist were in fact brought by an anti-Tractarian high churchman, Godfrey Faussett. Others (such as Phillpotts and Edward Churton) supported him. Palmer's position is similar to Pusey's. See Nockles, *Context*, 239–40; Palmer, *Treatise*, 1:401–6; cf. Liddon, *Life*, 2:314.

40. Pusey, 'Presence of Christ', 21–2.

41. Pusey, *English Church*, 161–6 on the Prayer Book Catechism, 167–83 on the Communion Service. Cf. Christopher Cocksworth, 'The Presence of Christ in the Eucharist and the Formularies of the Church of England', *Journal of Ecumenical Studies* 35, no. 2 (1998): 200.

42. Pusey, *English Church*, 194–6. Pusey's principal objection to the Lutheran conception of the Eucharist is the equivalence of word and sacrament, both as primarily means of increasing faith.

received' to mean that Christ's body and blood are 'given' by the priest, 'taken and received' by the communicants.[43]

Throughout this line of argument, Pusey's underlying conviction is that the Articles are properly read through the Catechism and Liturgy – both because instruction in the Church of England would have begun with the Catechism, continued with liturgical participation, and engaged the Articles only upon University matriculation; and because 'it is the order of nature and of grace, that our prayers are the interpreters of the Articles'.[44] Something of this process can be seen in Pusey's own development, as belief in a real communion (taught by the Catechism and liturgy) clearly preceded any definite doctrine of the real presence: in his sermon for Christmas 1828, Pusey describes the elements as 'symbols' for 'the renewal of the memory of Christ's death' – showing no clear doctrine of the real presence. However, they not only increase love for God but are 'that means by which in a more special manner ... we become partakers of Christ'.[45] Despite having defended the doctrine of the real presence to the Bishop of Oxford in 1839, four years later Pusey (by his own admission) *assumed* the doctrine of the real presence while preaching on the benefits of eucharistic *communion*.[46] Pusey's later eucharistic sermons insist on the real presence, but only as a means of emphasizing the reality of communion with Christ, in opposition to pantheistic 'communion'.[47] His ultimate preference for Calvin over Luther was for the same reason. In Pusey's analysis (not necessarily accurate on either count), Calvin taught a real communion without a real presence, and Luther a real presence without a real communion. While both positions fall short of a real presence with a real communion, Pusey held that the communion, as the end of the presence, is the

---

43. Pusey, *English Church*, 198–204. The argument from Knox also occurs, with other elements of Pusey's articulation of the formularies, in *Oxford*, 125–8 and *London*, 39–40.

44. Pusey, *English Church*, 183–6.

45. Pusey, Sermon for 25 December 1828, in 'Pusey Early Sermons MSS'.

46. Pusey thought his eucharistic doctrine fell squarely within the doctrinal spectrum of the Church of England, and theologically, this may have been the case. Politically, however, this can only be seen as a naïve miscalculation of the tempest surrounding the Tractarian party following the publication of Tract 90: it was Pusey's unguarded assumption of his own continuity with earlier high church eucharistic theology that led to the sermon's delation before the University and its subsequent condemnation. Later eucharistic sermons which reflect the same doctrine but which are more careful in its articulation passed without incident – the day after his 1853 sermon on the Eucharist, he noted, in a letter to Keble, the observation of the principal of Brasenose College [Richard Harington]: 'They cannot attack him this time. He has guarded himself too well.' Pusey, preface to *US I*, vi–vii; 'Entire Absolution I', 3. Pusey to Keble, 17 January 1853, in LBV 104.

47. See above, Chapter 3, under 'Baptism and regeneration'. The sermon cited in that section's discussion of pantheism versus sacramentalism ('Will Ye Also Go Away?') is primarily concerned with the eucharistic presence.

more important of the two – and so, in the end, he preferred Calvin's eucharistic theology to Luther's.[48]

The allegorical principles which undergird Pusey's 'sacramental vision' also contribute to his argument. Allegory applies particularly to the Old Testament; the institutions of the New Testament are not 'figurative' and do not point beyond themselves in the same way as the institutions of the Law. Accordingly, while the allegorical meaning of the Old Testament is built on the foundation of the literal meaning, in the New Testament the literal meaning *is* the spiritual reality.[49] 'The Blood of the Old Testament was a shadow, not in itself, but in its value. It was the real, although unavailing, blood of bulls and goats, picturing that the Atonement should be through the shedding of the Precious Blood of Christ. But the picture itself was real blood.' And so, at the Last Supper, 'Why should we think that He brought in a mere shadow, less expressive than those which He abolished?'[50] This is not to say that there is no figurative language in the New Testament; but Pusey argues that the words of institution have neither the correct grammatical structure (i.e., the 'figure' follows the subject; grammatically, Christ's body would be a figure of bread, not bread a figure of his body) nor the stylistic markers that would indicate a figurative meaning (e.g., use in a parable, or explicit identification as an allegory).[51] Pusey argues that grammatical analysis points not to a figurative meaning but to the reality of the gift given in the sacrament. The present participles, 'is given', 'is broken', 'is shed', indicate that the institution of the Eucharist was the inauguration of the Passion, and so shares in it. 'Hereby [Christ] seems as well to teach us that the great Act of His Passion then began … then did He "consecrate" Himself … and all which followed, until He commended His Blessed Spirit to the Hands of His Heavenly Father, was One protracted, willing, Suffering.'[52] So, as Pusey argued some years later, Christ's body and blood were present 'by anticipation' 'under those visible forms, which our Great High Priest, antedating the violence' of the crucifixion, 'consecrated by the words "This is My Body, this is My Blood."'[53] Still, this inauguration of the Passion in the Eucharist, the reality foreshadowed by the Old Covenant sacrifices, ultimately returns to communion: 'what else could the Apostles think, but that our Lord meant, that it was really and truly, and, in a Divine way, His Blood, and that they *now* [i.e., at the Last Supper] and henceforth should in a new and nearer way be united with Him and live by Him, as He Himself had promised?'[54]

48. Pusey, *Fathers*, 37–40; 'Introductory Essay', 39–40; cf. Naumann, 'Eucharistic Theologies', 220–3; Brilioth, *Eucharistic Faith*, 142–3; McDonnell, *John Calvin*, 241–6, 260–2.
49. De Lubac, *Medieval Exegesis*, 1:232–8.
50. Pusey, 'Presence of Christ', 27–8.
51. Pusey, 'Presence of Christ', 28–33.
52. Pusey, 'Comfort', 20–2.
53. Pusey, 'Will Ye?', 11–12.
54. Pusey, 'Presence of Christ', 27–8; emphasis mine.

Literalism, however, cuts both ways. Christ refers to the bread and wine as his body and blood; but afterwards refers to the cup as 'the fruit of the vine' (Mt. 26.28-29). Likewise Paul, discussing eucharistic communion, explicitly calls the bread not only the body of Christ but *bread* (1 Cor. 10.16, 11.26-28). If the words of institution must be taken literally, so too must these.

> If one might be taken figuratively, so might the other. If, as the Genevan school would have it, the words 'this is My Body' were figurative, or if, as Roman Divines say, St. Paul's words were figurative, 'the bread which we break', it would be but consistent to say with some modern sectaries, that the words 'so let him eat of that bread, and drink of that cup', are figurative too.[55]

There is further support in the Fathers, for whom the eucharistic presence in the *continuing* elements provided arguments against Docetism and Apollinarianism; and in the technicalities of substance metaphysics, where nourishment is provided by the substance rather than the accidents, yet the Fathers insisted that we are nourished by the eucharistic elements (i.e., by their substance, which remains after consecration). Pusey then closes his argument, comparing the Fathers' language on the Eucharist with their language on the incarnation and baptism: words denoting change or becoming are used of all three, yet no one supposes that God changed in the incarnation, or that we cease to be human after baptism; neither is the 'change' in the consecrated elements a *physical* change (i.e., a change in their nature or substance).[56] 'Holy Scripture, taken in its plainest meaning, affirms both that the outward elements remain, and still that there is the real Presence of the Body of Christ' – or, as he puts it elsewhere, the 'coexistence' of Christ's body and blood with the bread and wine.[57] Scripture does not speak in comprehensive theoretical statements, Pusey argues, but by addressing particular points in different places, which must be read in light of one another: the humanity and divinity of Christ, for instance, are taught in different places in Scripture.[58] So, as to the Eucharist, 'Our Blessed Lord does not say, "this is a figure of My absent Body," nor does He say, "This has altogether ceased to be bread, and is the same Body in the same way, as that which you see with your bodily eyes;" but simply, "This is My Body."'[59]

---

55. Pusey, 'Presence of Christ', 21–2, 33–4.
56. Pusey, 'Presence of Christ', 36–47.
57. Pusey, 'Presence of Christ', 14, 21–2; *Fathers*, 2–4. Pusey borrows 'coexistence' from Occam and uses it in preference to 'consubstantiation' to describe Luther's view of the real presence, the latter term being both pejorative in its origins and misleading in its suggestion of a 'consubstantiality' of Christ's body with the elements. Pusey does not, *pace* Douglas, see 'consubstantiation' as a pejorative for transubstantiation, but for views which teach the 'coexistence' of Christ's body with the elements, which he found not only in Luther but (more importantly) in the Fathers. Cf. Douglas, *Eucharistic Theology*, 144.
58. Pusey, 'Presence of Christ', 19–21.
59. Pusey, 'Presence of Christ', 21.

This is, however, beyond human explanation. Pusey cites Christ's passing through the door of his tomb and his entering the closed upper room after the resurrection, as well as his birth *illaesa virginitate*, as similar instances of the 'coexistence' of Christ's body and blood with another material substance; yet in each case, as Christ's body 'passed, it must have been in the same place, penetrating, but not displacing them. Still less need we ask, by what law of nature that Sacramental Presence can be, which is not after the order of nature, but is above nature'.[60] 'Christ hath said, "This is My Body;" He saith not, by what mode. We believe what He, the Truth, saith. Truth cannot lie. How He bringeth it to pass, we may leave to His Omnipotency.'[61]

Pusey's insistence on the ineffability of Christ's presence in the Eucharist is, in fact, one of the most constant aspects of his eucharistic teaching. In 1828, he argued that the communion was analogous to medicine or food; the inner workings of each need not be understood to have their benefit.[62] Late in life he would argue again that failing to understand the forces of nature, or mysteries uncovered by science, does not lead to their rejection; so our inability to understand God's sacramental actions need not lead to denial of the real presence.[63] The Jews, in St John's Gospel, ask of Jesus, 'How can this man give us His Flesh to eat?' (Jn 6.52). Pusey comments, 'He never answereth; and we, if we are wise, shall never ask how they can be elements of this world and yet His Body and Blood. But how they give life to us, He does answer.'[64] 'He does not explain' how we are to partake of him; 'but again He deepens His teaching, and tells them, in terms explicit although as yet unexplained, of that fulness [*sic*] of life and closeness of union with Himself

---

60. Pusey, 'Presence of Christ', 22–4. Each of these illustrations is borrowed from Patristic sources, given in *Fathers*, 56–60. Pusey's point here is that, even in the resurrection, Christ's body was naturally and locally present, yet in these instances from before his ascension, such events were possible through the power of his divinity; it is thus even less problematic for his body to coexist with another material substance when it is sacramentally (*not* naturally and locally) present.

61. Pusey, 'Presence of Christ', 22–3. Pusey's insistence on the reality of both the eucharistic elements and of Christ's presence has been classed by Brian Douglas as philosophical 'moderate realism', in contrast to both nominalism and an immoderate or carnal realism. Both nominalism and immoderate realism can be related conceptually to 'flat' or univocal approaches to ontology. Douglas, however, does not pursue that discussion (though he does note similarities between Pusey's eucharistic theology and that of Catherine Pickstock, one of the central figures in Radical Orthodoxy's critique of univocal ontology). While 'moderate realism' accurately captures certain aspects of Pusey's thought, it is unclear how that classification relates to my interpretation of Pusey's 'sacramental vision' (particularly with regard to its complexity) and it obscures the specifically Reformed roots of Pusey's thought. Douglas, *Eucharistic Theology*, 49–70.

62. Pusey, Sermon for 25 December 1828, Pusey Early Sermons MSS.

63. Pusey, 'This Is My Body', 13–14.

64. Pusey, 'Comfort', 7.

which He would give to His own'. Though many leave, because pride insists on understanding, the humility of the apostles is answered in the Eucharist. 'But how that Body which was to be broken, that Blood which was to be shed, should ... be present ... this remained as much a mystery as before.'[65]

There are here a number of elements that reflect the broader principles undergirding Pusey's sacramental vision. The arguments he gives for the 'coexistence' of Christ's body and blood with the elements echo his insistence on a 'comprehensive' reading of Scripture, as well as his understanding of doctrine as providing boundaries rather than positions. Likewise, his insistence on mystery as to the manner of the eucharistic presence reflects the resistance to over-definition, which emerged from his earlier critique of rationalism. Most importantly, however, Pusey's insistence on the reality of the eucharistic elements after consecration reflects the principle at the heart of his 'sacramental vision', namely, that the concreteness of the material creation is God's chosen ordinary means of communicating both revelation and grace. As 'the type were nothing, except in as far as it ... is the medium of conveying the archetype to the mind, so neither can the archetype be conveyed except through the type. Though the consecrated element be not the sacrament, yet neither can the soul of the Sacrament be attained without it.'[66] According to the principles of Pusey's 'sacramental vision', it is not a question of real bread or real body. Rather, if there is no real bread, there is no real body, either.

As a matter of placing Pusey's eucharistic theology in its correct theological location, however, his position needs to be viewed not only in terms of its internal consistency but in light of the post-Reformation debates about the Eucharist. Here, his argument for the continuation of the eucharistic elements also places him firmly in the Protestant camp. A second qualification to his belief in the real presence puts him more specifically within the Reformed tradition of eucharistic theology: the insistence that 'the natural Body and Blood' of Christ 'are in Heaven'.[67] This language, drawn from the Declaration on Kneeling in the end of the Communion Service, became a central point in Tractarian discussions of the Eucharist, due to its apparent incompatibility with their teaching. Pusey emphasizes, however, that the 1661 version prohibits only belief in a 'corporal' mode of Christ's presence, in contrast to the 'real and essential' presence prohibited in 1552; rubrics directing reverence towards the consecrated elements, on the other hand, indirectly teach the real presence.[68] Similarly, Pusey argues

---

65. Pusey, 'Will Ye?', 11–12.

66. Pusey, 'Types', 23–4.

67. The '*extra calvinisticum*', as it is commonly known, despite its name, is held by most non-Lutherans; Pusey recognizes, for instance, that it is also the teaching of Trent. It is, however, specifically its *conjunction* with the (Protestant) emphasis on the continuing reality of the elements that locates Pusey's eucharistic theology in the Reformed tradition. Pusey, *London*, 53–4; *English Church*, 318–29; cf. Naumann, 'Eucharistic Theologies', 171.

68. Pusey, *English Church*, 222–39.

that the reception of Christ's body and blood 'only after an heavenly and spiritual manner' (Article 28) is directed solely against carnal conceptions of the eucharistic presence.[69] However, he contrasts the proscribed 'natural' or 'corporal' presence of Christ with a sacramental presence, which 'is not circumscribed, not local, not after the mode of a body, but spiritual only and Sacramental'.[70] Human bodies, understood as 'natural' or physical entities, have certain properties, including presence in a particular place at a particular time. Christ's body, in this sense, is at God's right hand in heaven.[71] 'Sacramentally', however – a word which expresses 'not our knowledge, but our ignorance' – Christ's body is nonetheless present in the Eucharist.[72]

This conception of Christ's sacramental presence shows a high degree of continuity from the late 1830s onwards, although it also shows a certain degree of development. In his *Letter to the Bishop of Oxford* (1839), Pusey describes his belief,

> that in the Communion, there is a true, actual, though Spiritual (or rather the more real, because Spiritual) Communication of the Body and Blood of Christ to the believer through the Holy Elements; that there is a true, real, spiritual, Presence of Christ at the Holy Supper; more real than if we could, with Thomas, feel Him with our hands, or thrust our hands into his side; that this is bestowed upon faith, and received by faith, as is every other Spiritual gift, but that our faith is but a receiver of God's real, mysterious, precious, Gift; that faith opens our eyes to see what is really there, and our hearts to receive it; but that It is there independently of our faith.[73]

Here we can see that Pusey does not yet describe the presence as 'sacramental' but as 'spiritual'. 'Spiritual', however, does *not* mean subjective, or emotional, or 'to the soul of the believer'; rather Christ's presence 'is there independently of our faith'. Therefore, 'spiritual' means, primarily, *after the nature of a spirit*, not materially or corporally. A second sense, however, can be gleaned from Pusey's capitalization. 'Spiritual', when capitalized, appears to be a reference to the Holy

---

69. Pusey, *English Church*, 198–204.

70. Pusey, *London*, 53.

71. Note the title of Pusey's 1867 sermon, 'Jesus *at the Right Hand of God*, the Object of Divine Worship', in *Lenten Sermons, Preached Chiefly to Young Men at the Universities, between A.D. 1858–1874* (London: A. D. Innes, 1893), 438–64 (hereafter *LS*); emphasis mine.

72. Pusey, 'Presence of Christ', 22; cf. *Jelf*, 48; *London*, 49–56. Contrast with Robert Wilberforce, who applies Newman's understanding of Christ's resurrection appearances as involving the loss of material phenomena (discussed in Chapter 2 under 'Allegory and the Sacramental Vision') to the mode of the eucharistic presence, whereas Pusey applies a materialist understanding of those appearances to the coexistence of the elements. R. I. Wilberforce, *Eucharist*, 152–9.

73. Pusey, *Oxford*, 128.

Spirit; so *communion* with Christ is, in some sense, enabled by the Spirit; this reflects the relation between baptism and the Eucharist.[74] Christ is present in the Eucharist, therefore, in 'spiritual' rather than material form, as a 'gift' of the Spirit.[75]

This distinction, however, is somewhat confusing – an instance of Pusey's difficult 'full-formed accuracy'. Moreover, a 'spiritual' presence is open to subjective interpretations. As a result, Pusey clarified his language in 1853.

> The Presence, of which our Lord speaks, has been termed Sacramental, supernatural, mystical, ineffable, as opposed *not* to what is real, but to what is natural. The word has been chosen to express, not our knowledge, but our ignorance; or that unknowing knowledge of faith, which we have of things Divine, surpassing knowledge. We know not the manner of His Presence, save that it is not according to the natural Presence of our Lord's Human Flesh, which is at the Right Hand of God; and therefore it is called Sacramental. But it is a Presence without us, not within us only; a Presence by virtue of our Lord's words, although to us it becomes a saving Presence, received to our salvation, through our faith.[76]

Here, Christ's presence independent of our faith becomes more clearly 'without us' in addition to his presence 'within us'; 'spiritual' presence is replaced by 'Sacramental'. This is synonymous with the primary meaning of 'spiritual' in the earlier work – in fact, 'spiritual' is used (un-capitalized) to describe the real presence at another point in the 1853 sermon – but 'sacramental' is a less ambiguous term with regard to possible subjective or psychologizing interpretations.[77] However, this change in language also reflects another shift in Pusey's thought. Sacramental communion is now contrasted with spiritual communion: 'It is not a Presence simply in the soul of the receiver, as "Christ dwells in our hearts by faith;" or as, in acts of Spiritual, apart from Sacramental, Communion, we, by our longings, invite Him into our souls.'[78] This distinction between internal, spiritual communion and external, sacramental communion allows each to be given a valid place in the Christian life, whereas if

---

74. Pusey's point is *not* (as in Newman) the 'unreality of material phenomena' in comparison with spiritual reality, but that the acts of the Holy Spirit are more real than natural occurrences. Cf. Newman, *Apologia*, 140-1; *Justification*, 255-6; and see above in Chapter 3, under 'Allegory and the Sacramental Vision'.

75. Mark Garcia notes that for Calvin, 'a specific (non-corporeal) view of presence requires a correspondingly similar (spiritual) view of communion', and so 'the question of the mode of eucharistic presence naturally involved the question of the mode of eucharistic communion'. Pusey's reasoning appears to operate on similar principles, but with some reticence as to the potentially subjective understanding of 'spiritual communion' with reference to the Eucharist. Garcia, *Life in Christ*, 153.

76. Pusey, 'Presence of Christ', 21-2.

77. Pusey, 'Presence of Christ', 10. This is the point behind Pusey's qualified acceptance of the 'real objective presence'.

78. Pusey, 'Presence of Christ', 21-2. Cf. Sr Clara, Reminiscences, in LBV 78; Pusey, Rule in Pusey to Keble, 7 December 1846, LBV 102; Pusey to Sr. Clara Maria, 3 February

both were 'Spiritual', either might eclipse the other. It also clarifies the roles of the two sacraments, baptism as giving the gift of the Holy Spirit and thereby a mediated communion with Christ, the Eucharist giving an immediate communion of Christ's own body and blood; baptism planting the seed of spiritual renewal, the Eucharist emphasizing also the renewal of our bodies – though it would be mistaken to make this difference more than one of emphasis or propriety.[79] It would be too crude to read Pusey as assigning one sacrament to the Spirit and one to the Son. Rather, instead of replicating baptismal communion in the Eucharist, this distinction clarifies the primary and secondary roles of each person in the sacraments: the 'indwelling' of the Spirit in baptism makes us 'members of' the 'Son'; while in the Eucharist the Spirit serves a preparatory role (our souls must 'be prepared by repentance, faith, love, through the cleansing of His Spirit, for His Coming') and communion with Christ feeds the inner fire of the Holy Spirit, which was received in baptism.[80]

***

This chapter has, so far, argued that Pusey's eucharistic theology should be considered, not as an import of Roman Catholic or 'merely' Patristic theology, but as a development of the Reformed eucharistic theology of the earlier high church tradition. Two points of comparison – with Waterland, as the foremost theologian of the eighteenth-century high church tradition, and with Calvin, as the most prominent figure in Reformed theology – can further elucidate the nature of this connection. Waterland, as a representative of the high church tradition which formed Pusey's own theology, provides the narrower comparison, and thus the better starting point for this discussion.

Like Pusey, Waterland emphasizes the reality of communion as the fundamental gift of the Eucharist. As the duty of communion encompasses all Christian duties, so it procures all the spiritual privileges given in Christ.[81] Beyond mere privileges, however, there is also a 'communication from God, and a participation by us, of Christ's *crucified* body directly, and of the body *glorified* consequentially'.[82] Like Pusey, he insists on a real presence of Christ mediated by the elements. He does not make Pusey's inference from the reality of communion; but he does emphasize the meaning of the words of institution in much the same fashion. Mere remembrance is accomplished by the words, 'Do this in remembrance of me.' That Christ adds, 'This is my body', 'This is my blood', indicates something more. But to say that

---

1875, LBV 125; Pusey to Sr Clara, 11 May 1844, LBV 76. It is likely that this distinction was driven in part by his engagement, over the 1840s, with Counter-Reformation Catholic spiritual writers. Certainly, a continual spiritual communion of the sort now popularized as 'practicing the presence of God' is a major feature of Pusey's spirituality.

79. Pusey, 'Comfort', 4; 'Bliss of Heaven – Glory of the Body', 301–4.

80. Pusey, 'Presence of Christ', 10, 21–2. Cf. Chapter 6.

81. Daniel Waterland, *A Review of the Doctrine of the Eucharist, as Laid Down in Scripture and Antiquity*, in *Works*, 4:470–1.

82. Waterland, *Review*, 579; emphasis Waterland's.

we receive Christ's body and blood '*in power and effect*, or *in virtue and energy*', however, is to confuse the nature of what we receive, and the meaning of the word, 'body'. But (as with Pusey) the bread and wine remain, and the presence of Christ's body in heaven must be maintained. The bread and wine are not 'really and literally that body in the same *broken* state as it hung upon the cross', which would displace the crucifixion from history; nor are they 'literally and properly' 'our Lord's *glorified body*, which is as far distant from us, as *heaven* is distant'.[83] Instead, Waterland uses a series of analogies to relate the elements to Christ's body and blood. Royal regalia is not kingship, but coronation makes one a king; a title deed is not property, but transference of the deed conveys the property.[84] Since God has decreed that the eucharistic elements are to serve as the 'deed' of our union with Christ, 'then those outward symbols are, though not *literally*, yet *interpretively*, and to all *saving* purposes, that very body and blood which they so represent *with effect*'.[85]

Although these analogies provide a weaker understanding of the real presence than Pusey's direct affirmation, it is not mere symbolism. This can be seen in Waterland's critique of Reformation-era eucharistic theology. Medieval understandings of the Eucharist were too carnal; Luther did not go far enough in his corrections, while Calvin achieved the right balance, but was (in Waterland's estimation) somewhat confused. Whereas Calvin holds that the believer is raised to heaven to receive Christ, Waterland argues that this receiving is earthly, in the sacrament: 'the *natural* body is *there given*, but *not there present* ... The *mystical union* with our Lord's *glorified* body is *there* (or in that service) strengthened, or *perfected*; as a *right* may be given to a *distant* possession: and such *union* as we now speak of, requires no *local* presence of Christ's body.'[86] On the other hand, Zwingli over-corrected; against his denial of a real presence, Waterland maintains that 'though there is no *corporal presence* yet there is a *spiritual* one, exhibitive of Divine *blessings* and *graces*: and though we *eat* not Christ's *natural* glorified body in the Sacrament, or out of it, yet our *mystical union* with that very body is strengthened and perfected in and through the Sacrament, by the operation of the *Holy Spirit*'.[87] This 'spiritual presence', which Waterland contrasts with a 'corporal' one, appears to be roughly congruent to Pusey's concept of a 'sacramental presence'.

Waterland's understanding of eucharistic communion, however, shows how Pusey's development moved him beyond the older high churchmen. Waterland distinguishes between spiritual and sacramental receiving of Christ, but in a way that differs from Pusey. John 6, in his interpretation, refers to *spiritual* rather than

---

83. Waterland, *Review*, 573; emphasis Waterland's.
84. Waterland, *Review*, 571–2.
85. Waterland, *Review*, 574; emphasis Waterland's.
86. Waterland, *Review*, 599–600; emphasis Waterland's.
87. Waterland, *Review*, 609; emphasis Waterland's. Note that Waterland appears, in his references to a 'corporal presence' and to Christ's 'natural body', to be interpreting the Declaration on Kneeling in much the same way as Pusey.

sacramental feeding on Christ, because only worthy recipients receive life as the passage indicates. To receive Christ sacramentally is merely to receive the signs of communion (i.e., the signs of Christ's body and blood), while true communion is spiritual; sacramental communion is the 'ordinary' means of spiritual communion, but God may give other means.[88] Union with Christ is mediated by the Holy Spirit: Waterland even argues that patristic language of the Spirit's descent on the elements is imprecise, and should be more accurately understood as the Spirit's descent on the communicants *in receiving* the elements.[89] Waterland's emphasis on the Spirit as the agent of union with Christ bears a strong resemblance to Pusey's position in 1839, although even at that time Pusey's language is subtly stronger. The subsequent evolution of Pusey's thought which we have seen, however, moves him beyond this point of similarity. But in contrast to Waterland's theory, Pusey's developed position has a twofold advantage: as the 'ordinary means' of spiritual communion in Waterland's theory, the Eucharist is in danger of becoming secondary to baptism (i.e., as merely its extension), while simultaneously more 'subjective' non-liturgical 'spiritual communion' (as a kind of devotional act) appears to be tacitly discouraged, as secondary to liturgical action and 'extraordinary' in the Christian life rather than normative. Pusey's distinction between communion with Christ by the Spirit in baptism and immediate communion in the Eucharist, balances the two sacraments as being distinct and complementary, while giving value to both the public devotion of eucharistic participation and the more private life of prayer.

The most obvious difference between Pusey and Waterland, however, is one of tone. Pusey's fervid language is wedded to an adamant insistence on Christ's presence *with us*, not only spiritually but sacramentally. Waterland, by contrast, takes a more descriptive approach. He is clearer than Pusey in his explanations – Christ's dual presence in heaven and in the sacrament is left a paradox in Pusey, whereas Waterland's analogy to other 'effective signs' partially addresses the problem; but the explanation rings hollow compared to the paradox. In part, this may be because Waterland resorts to legal metaphors, while Pusey is more apt to speak of communion in biblical language which evokes marriage and new creation.[90] But beyond this, Waterland's eucharistic theory lacks motion: Christ

---

88. Waterland, *Review*, 535–9. Note that Waterland is here using 'sacramental' to mean *pertaining to the sacramental signs*, whereas Pusey uses the same term to refer to a mode of Christ's presence *by which he is present in the sacramental signs*.

89. Waterland, *Review*, 530, 609. Waterland's opposition to any action of the Spirit on the elements is curious; it may have roots in a partisan reaction to the controverted 'usages' (including the *epiclesis*) practiced within the non-juring schism (formed by high church clergy who could not, in conscience, swear the oath of supremacy to William III – or later, the Hanoverian monarchs – while James II or his nearer successors remained alive). Or, it may stem from opposition to the views of John Johnson of Cranbrook, noted above. See also Richard Sharp, 'New Perspectives on the High Church Tradition: Historical Background 1730–1780', in Rowell, *Tradition*, 11–13.

90. See discussion in Chapter 3 under 'Faith, justification and glorification'.

is securely in heaven, we are firmly on earth, and the Spirit mediates between the two. But for Pusey, Christ comes near to us in the Eucharist.

A brief overview of Calvin's eucharistic theology will lay the foundation for the remaining discussion of this chapter. Despite Tractarian assertions to the contrary, Calvin is not, in fact, a 'virtualist'; rather, he insists on the real presence, but labours intensely to demolish any overly materialistic conception of it and is concerned to draw the believer's gaze away from the mere elements, to the reality they convey.[91] There are differences: Calvin emphasizes that the Eucharist is a part of the Christian's broader partaking of Christ by faith through the Holy Spirit; this contrasts with the high church Anglican views of Pusey and Waterland, who see the sacraments more specifically as the *ground* of that communion. (The contrast is particularly sharp after Pusey introduces the distinction between spiritual and sacramental communion.)[92] And beyond a difference of emphasis, there is one of orientation. Calvin's real presence is, like that of Waterland and Pusey, brought about by the Holy Spirit. But this is not the downward motion of Pusey's theory, bringing heaven near to earth; nor is it the static mediation between heaven and earth found in Waterland. For Calvin, the role of the Holy Spirit 'bridges heaven and earth, bringing believing communicants to heaven to feed on Christ'.[93] Julie Canlis notes that whereas Calvin would not rethink the nature of the human body – hence the *extra calvinisticum* – 'he was willing to rethink presence'.[94] The weakness of Waterland's static view is he is *not* willing to rethink presence; Pusey, on the other hand, clearly *is* rethinking presence, though in a way that differed from Calvin. For Calvin, Christ is present because of our spiritual translation to heaven; for Pusey, Christ is present *to us*, though sacramentally, not naturally. Calvin's concept retains a spatial element to presence, while making it non-physical, whereas for Pusey, presence is neither strictly spatial nor physical. It has

---

91. Calvin, *Institutes*, 4.17.1–4, 12–15; McDonnell, *John Calvin*, 241–6; Julie Canlis, *Calvin's Ladder: A Spiritual Theology of Ascent and Ascension* (Grand Rapids, MI: Eerdmans, 2010), 159; cf. R. I. Wilberforce, *Eucharist*, 32–43, 137–49; Garcia notes, however, that Calvin's clarity about the presence of Christ *himself* is a late development; earlier writings do include some ambiguity as to 'virtue'. Garcia, *Life in Christ*, 153, 161, 165–8.

92. Calvin, *Institutes*, 4.17.5–8, 33; Canlis, *Calvin's Ladder*, 162–3, McDonnell, *John Calvin*, 184.

93. Calvin, *Institutes*, 4.17.10, 18, 31; McDonnell, *John Calvin*, 260–2; Garcia, *Life in Christ*, 163–4. While Calvin does insist, 'we do not think it lawful for us to drag [Christ] from heaven', he hesitates at insisting on a particular theory – so long as readers allow that an 'upward' motion in the sacrament does not negate Christ's presence. Together with the upward elements, discussed in the following section, that qualify the 'downward' dynamic of Pusey's eucharistic theology, this emphasizes that the 'direction' of sacramental action discussed here, despite its influence on the respective structures of their eucharistic theologies, is a matter of personal tendency and should not be mistaken as a more fundamental difference of doctrine.

94. Canlis, *Calvin's Ladder*, 116–17.

been suggested that Calvin, in attempting to mediate between Nestorianism and Eutychianism, is not entirely successful in avoiding the former, and constrains Christ's humanity to a particular place without allowing a role for his divinity.[95] Whatever may be the case for Calvin, Pusey clearly avoids such difficulties. A non-local presence, however, is a difficult concept, and to call it 'sacramental' because of our ignorance, however appropriate or even necessary, does not help to explain it.

Real presence II: Ascent and descent

The upward motion of Calvin's eucharistic theology, however, introduces the final discussion of this chapter. Pusey departed from Waterland (and thus from a view we might consider widespread among the older high churchmen), with regard to the Holy Spirit's role in eucharistic communion. However, there were two other points on which he ultimately differed from a more traditional high church view: namely, eucharistic adoration and the reception of Christ by the wicked. Pusey's position on these doctrines is formed by his emphasis on Christ's descent, his coming *to us*, to live *in us*, in the sacrament, which contrasts with both Waterland's static view and Calvin's understanding of the Christians being caught up to heaven.

Eucharistic adoration, for Pusey, resulted from an inference much like that which grounded his belief in the real presence. Pusey had argued from communion to the real presence, that if we receive Christ, he must be *there* for us to receive him.[96] But if Christ is present, it follows that he is to be adored. Pusey draws a favourite quotation from Lancelot Andrewes, that '*Christ Himself, the Substance of the Sacrament*, in and with the Sacrament; out of and without the Sacrament wheresoever He is, is to be adored.'[97] The Declaration on Kneeling is no obstacle: as already discussed, it is not a 'corporal' presence of Christ's 'natural' body that is being adored, and Pusey thought it ridiculous that anyone would even consider adoring the *elements* rather than Christ.[98] Accordingly, he insisted on changes to W. J. E. Bennett's *Plea for Toleration* of ritualism to reflect adoration of Christ present 'under the form of bread and wine' rather than adoration of the elements as Christ's 'visible Presence' in the Church.[99]

95. McDonnell, *John Calvin*, 214–19.
96. Pusey, *English Church*, 166.
97. Pusey, *English Church*, 312–37, esp. 316–17; emphasis Pusey's.
98. Pusey, *English Church*, 318–26. The same position is argued at length by Keble, *On Eucharistical Adoration*, 2nd edn (Oxford: John Henry and James Parker, 1859).
99. W. J. E. Bennett, *A Plea for Toleration in the Church of England* (London: J. T. Hayes, 1867), 3, 14; compare 3rd edn (1868), iii–iv and 3, 14. Bennett was charged with doctrinal error in his teaching on the Eucharist, but was acquitted in the Court of Arches (1870) and subsequently on appeal to the Judicial Committee of the Privy Council (1872) because he had adopted Pusey's language in the second edition. The phrase, 'under the form of bread and wine', is taken from the notice at the end of the first Book of Homilies; Pusey's defence

The question of reception by the wicked is more intricate, partly because of the apparent doctrinal prohibition in Article 29, 'Of the Wicked which eat not the Body of Christ', and in part because of the Reformed perspective this article exhibits, which was ingrained in the Tractarians. Their resistance to believing that the wicked in some way receive Christ in the Eucharist was not merely a matter of deference to authority, but an inherited theological trait. This can be seen both in Pusey's developing understanding of this doctrine and ultimately in Keble's resistance to Pusey's eventual conclusions on the subject. Until 1856, Pusey shared Keble's position that although Christ was 'objectively' present in the Eucharist, his presence was withdrawn from unworthy receivers; but in that year, having reconsidered the matter because of the Denison case, he altered his position.[100] Keble, however, resisted this change, and for more than two months they exchanged letters on the matter: ultimately agreeing to respect their differences of opinion, as neither position imperilled the central reality of Christ's presence in the Eucharist, though they both found the disagreement painful.[101]

The focus of this exchange – which ranged into patristic interpretations, textual criticism of patristic works, and the patristic scholarship of the article's framers – was the apparent conflict between John 6.53-56 ('He that eateth my flesh, and drinketh my blood, dwelleth in me, and I in him') and 1 Corinthians 11.27 ('whosoever shall eat this bread, and drink this cup of the Lord, unworthily, shall be guilty of the body and blood of the Lord'). In the interpretation which Pusey had held, and which Keble maintained, the wicked are guilty of receiving impenitently a consecrated *symbol* of Christ's body and blood, but not *directly* guilty of violating Christ's body and blood, which had been withdrawn from them.[102] Pusey did not find this satisfactory: Paul's language was too direct. While there are many offences that might be committed of impenitence or irreverence, even with regard to hearing the Gospel itself, none of these receives the singular distinction of making the offender 'guilty of the body and blood of the Lord'.[103] In order to reconcile the two passages, Pusey redeploys

of the phrase as a defining Anglican doctrine may seem forced, but it had earlier been held as such by Palmer. Pusey, *English Church*, 4-7; Palmer, *Treatise*, 1:389.

100. George Anthony Denison was a high churchman, connected to Oriel College (and thereby, indirectly, to the Tractarians) and with some sympathy for Tractarian teachings. He nevertheless remained outside of Tractarian circles. He was prosecuted for his position on the real presence in 1854-8; his views were at first condemned, but the initial ruling was overturned on appeal for technical causes. Pusey and other Tractarian and ritualist leaders mounted a vigorous defence of Denison's doctrine during the case, with which, however, Denison did not fully cooperate. See Pusey to Keble, 22 June 1856, LBV 104.

101. Pusey to Keble, 15 August to 10 October 1856, LBV 104; Keble to Pusey, 20 August to 8 October 1856, LBV 99. Given in Liddon, *Life*, 3:460-9.

102. Keble to Pusey, 1 August 1853 and 26 August 1856 (among others), LBV 99; Pusey to Keble, 19 August 1856, LBV 104; Pusey, *London*, 41. Compare with Waterland's understanding of the real presence and 'sacramental' communion, discussed above under 'Real presence I: Pusey's reformed framework'.

103. Pusey, *English Church*, 293-300.

an argument from his discussion of the coexistence of Christ's presence with the eucharistic elements: Scripture speaks 'to the point', not by means of giving complete systematic statements. So, John 6.54 does not mean that anyone who eats the sacramental body and blood of Christ, in any way and without qualification, has eternal life.[104] Rather, the references in that passage to 'eating' must be to a *manner* of eating, specifically, whereby Christ dwells in us and we in him. Article 29, which holds that the wicked are 'in no wise partakers of Christ' though they receive the sacrament, is interpreted in the same way.[105] His conclusion (suggested to him by Döllinger's writing on hell), is that 'Christ, although He could not dwell in their souls, could be present, as their Judge. God is present in Hell.'[106]

Despite Pusey's acknowledged change of position, the foundations of his later view are clearly laid in his earlier work. The dangers of receiving unworthily were used to argue, by analogy, the dangers of adult baptism under false pretences in 1835.[107] In 1839, the contrast between unworthy receiving and other offenses is used as an argument in defence of the real presence.[108] The 'manifold teaching' and 'different bearings' of God's single acts, which in 1843 allow for Christ's presence in the Eucharist to be both the 'joy of the saint' and the 'comfort to the penitent', provide the principle by which he may also be present as 'judge of the wicked'.[109] In 1851, Pusey took up the question directly; while he states that Christ's presence is withdrawn, he adds that 'it must in some sense be the Body and Blood of Christ, since the very ground why those who profaned the Lord's Supper, "ate and drank condemnation to themselves" is, according to Holy Scripture, that they did "not discern the Lord's Body"', and continues with an early form of the argument that to 'eat' (in Article 29 and Jn 6) is to eat 'beneficially'.[110] The very nature of this argument, however, reminds us of the larger backdrop of Pusey's eucharistic theology: the *purpose* of the sacrament is the *beneficial* receiving of Christ's body and blood, that he may 'dwell in us and we in him', nourishing the growth in

---

104. Pusey, *English Church*, 300–7.

105. Pusey, *English Church*, 250–7; *London*, 41–2; Pusey to Keble, 29 September 1856, LBV 104. Pusey argues that the text of the article ('partakers', cf. Heb. 3.14), like the passage from John, refers specifically to an eating with the stated effect, and argues that no more than this was intended by the framers of the article (*English Church*, 257–93). Arguing that his position was permitted by the Articles was of particular importance, as this issue had drawn attention during the Denison case, and Abp. Sumner had declared his opinion that positions similar to Pusey's were proscribed. Pusey challenged the authority of Sumner's declaration, by making his views known and offering to resign his professorship if Sumner's opinion were to be upheld as binding.

106. Pusey, *English Church*, 307–8; Letter to Keble, 19 August 1856, LBV 104.

107. Pusey, *Baptism 1*, 172–3.

108. Pusey, *Oxford*, 129.

109. Pusey, 'Comfort', 1, 7. The implication, when these are taken together, is that the whole Christ is present in his *person*, not merely in certain aspects of his *work*.

110. Pusey, *London*, 42–4.

holiness presupposed by both sacraments. Receiving the sacrament unworthily, without repentance, is only so grave a matter because it is an offense against God's love. Although the warning of God's judgement is present, Pusey's call to holiness in preaching on the Eucharist emphasizes rather the immensity of God's love, his self-giving, and the greatness of the gift of his indwelling.

***

Pusey's conception of God's love as descending *to* the Church is at the heart of his understanding of adoration and reception by the wicked. Among the many other gifts imparted by communion, 'the fervour of divine love' *is* 'that our Lord Jesus Christ, not in figure, but in reality, although a spiritual reality, does give Himself to us, does *come* to be in us'.[111] He is to be adored in the Eucharist, because he has *come*, and is *here*; he is present to (and, in a sense, received by, though to judgment rather than salvation) the wicked, because he has *come* and is *here*, as truly as in the incarnation and at the Last Judgment, although he is present 'sacramentally', not in his natural, physical body.[112] The absence of these emphases in Waterland is explained simply by the fact that Christ does not come to us – the Holy Spirit makes him present, but Christ nonetheless remains in heaven. Waterland's static view leaves a feeling of distance between Christ and the believer. But a more interesting contrast may be supplied by comparison with Calvin, whose upward dynamic achieves a similar nearness to Pusey's, though the motion of the sacrament is in the opposite direction.

Not surprisingly, given the high church heritage of Pusey's theology and the Reformed influence on that tradition's understanding of the Eucharist, Pusey and Calvin share much in common. The central fact of the Eucharist, which determines all subsequent considerations, is communion with Christ: Christ's body – not in itself, but united to his divinity – is a source of life to our bodies. As such, because Christ has promised to give us his body and blood in the Eucharist, we receive in the sacrament not 'a vain and empty sign' but 'the reality' of that gift.[113] Even in

---

111. Pusey, 'Presence of Christ', 10; emphasis mine.

112. Cf. Nockles, *Context*, 242. Keble appears to share Pusey's understanding of the Eucharist except on the point of reception by the wicked; here, it is to be suspected that he was held back from affirming Pusey's position by his fundamentally conservative nature, as this is a more dramatic departure from received Anglican tradition than the other points, which, however, entail it. The Tractarian understanding of the real presence can be argued from Scripture and an exact reading of the formularies; while adoration (in the Tractarian sense, which is primarily concerned with the disposition of the communicant in receiving communion, and not – as in Roman Catholicism and later Anglo-Catholicism – connected with extra-liturgical devotion) has precedent in, for instance, the oft-quoted words of Andrewes, and is at least unscathed by a precise reading of the Declaration on Kneeling. Pusey's understanding of reception by the wicked, however, though faithful to the letter of the Article, nonetheless exceeds the mainstream position of the high church tradition, although Pusey was preceded in his position on this subject by Denison.

113. Calvin, *Institutes*, 4.17.8–10.

defending the 'figurative' role of the Eucharist, Calvin is at pains to distinguish the sacrament, which 'not only symbolizes the thing that it has been consecrated to represent ... but also truly exhibits it' from human symbols, which are 'images of things absent rather than marks of things present'.[114] This is balanced in the same way Pusey was to do later: Calvin insists on a spiritual presence of Christ's body, which is physically present in heaven, and on the continuing reality of the elements.[115] For Calvin, however, John 6.48-58 teaches that Christ's nourishment of our souls is a general reality of the Christian life; this is particularly symbolized and instanced in the Eucharist, but the Eucharist is not the central focus of the passage.[116] And so, like Waterland after him (and indeed, like Pusey's initial position), Calvin's emphasis falls on the mediating role of the Spirit; however, in contrast to Waterland, and in common with Pusey, the Eucharist is not static, but an interpenetration of heaven and earth. Whereas Pusey emphasizes descent, for Calvin, the motion of the Eucharist is upwards; the communicant is caught up into heaven, where Christ is, to receive him.[117] Pusey's early (1839) dismissal of this as merely psychological is unfair: Calvin insists that there is 'no place for the sophistry that what I mean when I say Christ is received by faith is that he is received only by understanding and imagination'.[118]

In part, these contrasts reflect each writer's historical context. The seventeenth century saw a social transition, reflected in architecture, from the great hall, where nobles gathered in the midst of their people, to the withdrawing room, where they gathered apart.[119] Calvin's eucharistic theology suggests Christ 'in the great hall' – elevated, perhaps, over his people, but not beyond reach of an intercourse wherein one might ascend the dais to his nearer presence. Waterland, by contrast, seems to represent a Christ of the withdrawing room – at once present and removed, his presence felt through his actions rather than known in his person. Pusey, meanwhile, reflects the Romantic fascination with the immanence of

---

114. Calvin, *Institutes*, 4.17.21.

115. Calvin, *Institutes*, 4.17.11-12, 26-32, 43-50. David Steinmetz notes that Calvin's 'spiritual real presence' was 'an apparent oxymoron that bemused and annoyed Calvin's Lutheran critics'. The same paradox may be felt in Pusey's 'sacramental presence'. Calvin's rejection of a 'mixture, or transfusion of Christ's flesh with our soul' is principally directed against a local inclusion of Christ's body in the elements, also rejected by Pusey. Nonetheless, it sits uncomfortably with Pusey's notion that 'we become "flesh of His flesh, and bone of His bone"' (Gen. 2.23). Pusey's stronger conception of communion is likely formed, at least in part, by his frequent use of this allegory to convey New Testament themes of new creation and union with Christ. David Steinmetz, *Taking the Long View* (Oxford: Oxford University Press, 2011), 123.

116. Calvin, *Institutes*, 4.17.4.

117. Calvin, *Institutes*, 4.17.18, 31.

118. Pusey, *Oxford*, 132-3; Calvin, *Institutes*, 4.17.11.

119. John Morrill, *Stuart Britain: A Very Short Introduction* (Oxford: Oxford University Press, 2000), 84.

the sublime – a poetic influence rather than a social one, but no less a matter of historical context. In Calvin and Pusey, their emphases are also determined by the very different views to which they are opposed: for Calvin, a superstitious form of belief in the real presence; for Pusey, a rationalist disbelief. It is not surprising, then, that their forms of argument move in opposite directions, even though their respective understandings of the real presence are structurally similar.

However, although these differences in perspective may be influenced by historical context, they nonetheless have doctrinal consequences. For Calvin, both eucharistic presence and communion result from the Spirit's action in lifting us to heaven. For Waterland, although the Spirit is the mediator of *communion*, the question of *presence* is more ambiguous: the Spirit does not act on the elements, and although Christ's presence is not clearly tied to the elements (it is not entirely distinct, either), his argument on this front relies exclusively on the words of institution, not on any inferred action of the Spirit. Pusey appears to have inherited this tradition. From the start, he has a stronger emphasis on the connection of the presence with the elements than either Waterland or Calvin, but his mode of argument follows Waterland in emphasizing the words of institution rather than a mediating role for the Spirit, with regard to Christ's *presence* in the Eucharist. This sets the stage, however, for a shift to a *communion* of Christ's body and blood in virtue of that presence, rather than by the mediation of the Spirit – although it is enabled by, and nourishes, a life of Spiritual communion. However, Pusey and Calvin share a dynamic and intimate sense of Christ's presence in the Eucharist, which is lacking in Waterland; Pusey restores this aspect of the Eucharist, though he does so by continuing further in the direction which Waterland had set.

Despite the underlying structural similarities between all three, the divergence between Calvin's upward dynamic in the Eucharist and Pusey's own position is a point on which Pusey could be sharply polemical. 'We need not then (as the School of Calvin bids men) "ascend to Heaven, to bring down Christ from above," for He is truly present' in the earthly Eucharist; 'Our Dear Lord in His glorious Body does ever, in the Presence of the Father, make Intercession for us: His Meritorious Sacrifice and Passion live on there … But to us He hath given the communion of His Body, not in Heaven as yet, but here on earth.'[120] Despite such remarks, however, Pusey nonetheless retains several strong upward aspects in his eucharistic teaching. One rhapsodic passage echoes Calvin's image of gazing into heaven:

> O if we could, but for one moment, see, with St. Stephen, heaven opened, what should we behold, adored by Cherubim and Seraphim, the Joy of all the heavenly Intelligences, the Mystery above all mysteries, on which they ever gaze, in which they behold the Divine Love more and more unfolded to them, as they long to look into it, what but that sacred form of Jesus, irradiating heaven with the glory of the Indwelling Godhead? … Oh, sursum corda, sursum corda! One

120. Pusey, 'Presence of Christ', 22; 'This Is My Body', 25–6.

earnest, steadfast, piercing, longing, loving gaze into Heaven, will reveal to thee more than all the world's disputing, nay, than any argument, for 'flesh and blood will not reveal' it unto thee but 'thy Father which is in heaven'. Blessedness will it be beyond all bliss, blessedness above all created joy, for it is the fruit of the Infinite love of Jesus, the foretaste of the eternal joy of thy Lord, when, with God-given faith, thou canst say, I love thee, O only salvation of my soul; for thou hast redeemed me by Thy Blood, my Lord and my God. THOU, me!'[121]

Though not an explicitly eucharistic passage – it is a lament of doctrinal controversy, in a (controversial) sermon on the atonement – the 'foretaste' of heavenly joy and its accompanying gift of love have strong eucharistic overtones.[122] But elsewhere Pusey speaks more directly of sacramental ascent. 'It was then, as having been hallowed by baptism, (and that, as connected with the incarnation of our Lord, "through the vail, that is to say, His Flesh,") that St. Paul taught, that we might venture to draw near towards those heavens, where our ascended Lord now is, and which He had "opened to all believers." '[123] So, too, the Eucharist 'wraps the saint already in the third heaven'. Here, however, we come near to the root of his polemical vigour, because the same Eucharist 'may also uphold us sinners'.[124] Language of ascent, for Pusey, is closely connected with sanctification; the point of Christ's *descent* in the Eucharist is his mercy towards those for whom such heights seem dizzyingly far; the grace of the sacraments 'comes down', so to speak, so that it might raise us up to heaven.[125] The presence of such an upward motion in Pusey's eucharistic thought, however, should encourage us not to press the distinction too far.

It has been claimed that Pusey's understanding of eucharistic adoration and the reception of Christ by the wicked results from the 'downward' motion of his eucharistic theology. The comparison between Pusey and Calvin reinforces this point. God is the agent for both descent and ascent, and while Pusey cites Christ's appearances to Stephen and Paul as instances of his presence on earth while bodily in heaven, Calvin explains the same through Christ's gift of 'a clarity of vision to

---

121. Pusey, 'The Doctrine of the Atonement' 261–2; cf. Calvin, *Institutes*, 4.17.18:

> If we are lifted up to heaven with our eyes and minds, to seek Christ there in the glory of his Kingdom, as the symbols invite us to see him in his wholeness, so under the symbol of bread shall we be fed by his body, under the symbol of wine we shall separately drink his blood, to enjoy him at last in his wholeness.

122. The sermon is discussed extensively in Chapter 5, under 'Atonement and union'.
123. Pusey, *Baptism 2*, 186.
124. Pusey, 'Comfort', 14–15; cf. 'Presence of Christ', 10, where he describes the Eucharist as 'the heaven of those whose conversation is in heaven', though this is specifically because 'our Lord Jesus Christ … does give Himself to us, does *come* to be in us' (emphasis mine).
125. See also Pusey's views on the Christian life as oblation (an upward dynamic), discussed in Chapter 6, under 'Baptism, sacrifice and communion'.

pierce the heavens'.[126] Both attempt to represent the sacramental interpenetration of heaven and earth; both emphasize God's grace; both are, in fact, rooted in Christ's renewal of humanity through the incarnation. Upward and downward dynamics are, in a sense, matters of perspective; a question of which side of the eucharistic conjunction of heaven and earth one chooses to emphasize: Calvin emphasizes the effect of God's grace in exalting humanity; Pusey emphasizes his humility in giving us himself. But they differ dramatically in their consequences. If Christ is present to the faithful because they have been caught up to heaven, he cannot be adored as if on earth; if receiving him requires being raised to heaven by the Spirit, the wicked by definition cannot. If, on the other hand, he is in some sense present here on earth, he should be adored here, and may be present even to those who cannot receive him. But despite these differences, there is nonetheless a correlation between the intimacy of Christ's presence and the danger of unworthy receiving, which draws Pusey and Calvin closer together. Calvin holds a stronger view than Waterland and Keble in this respect: they would agree with him that, although Christ is not received without faith, he is nonetheless offered to the unworthy.[127] But whereas they hold that the wicked receive condemnation as violating the sign of a holy thing, Calvin goes further still, suggesting that the very grace offered in it is a poison to them.[128] This is only a step away from Pusey's affirmation that to the wicked Christ is present as judge – and as near to that position as one might come within an upward-moving eucharistic theology.

But Pusey's emphasis on a downward dynamic in the Eucharist also sheds light on his understanding of divine love. The fundamental reality of God's relationship with us, for Pusey, is his descent to us in humility. Pusey's vision of God's love is of a love which reaches out to us, lifting us indeed, but coming down from his throne to do so – not just once, in the incarnation, but daily. Pusey's calls to loving humility are, in fact, a call to embody divine love – whether in addressing individuals or the structures of society.[129]

***

Returning to a broader perspective, Pusey's eucharistic doctrine can now be regarded in the larger context of his theology. The Eucharist is a complement to baptism, furthering and nourishing the baptismal union with Christ. Such an understanding of the relation between the two sacraments is not only drawn from tradition but is supported by the symbolism of the eucharistic elements as food. The truth of the Eucharist is not, therefore, in the reduction of the sacrament to

126. Pusey, 'This Is My Body', 13–15; Calvin, *Institutes*, 4.17.29.
127. Calvin, *Institutes*, 4.17.33, 40.
128. Calvin, *Institutes*, 4.17.40.
129. Cf. Richard Holloway, 'Social and Political Implications of the Oxford Movement', in Wright, *Lift High the Cross*, 30–45; John Macquarrie, 'Theological Implications of the Oxford Movement', in Wright, *Lift High the Cross*, 27–8.

pure symbol or simple presence, but in the coexistence of the eucharistic bread and wine with the body and blood of Christ – a body and blood which are present here, though in their 'natural' form they remain in heaven.

Thus, the structure of Pusey's eucharistic thought points out both his indebtedness to earlier high church positions and his willingness to move beyond them. Even when compared to Calvin, there is something of a family resemblance, though Pusey is clearly in a very different (perhaps even eccentric) part of the Reformed heritage. But the differences even between Pusey and Calvin are derived primarily from the different dynamics used to structure otherwise similar understandings of union with Christ: while acknowledging that these differences are far-reaching in their consequences, we should also, perhaps, try to see beyond the polemics of nineteenth-century controversies, including Pusey's own, to acknowledge their similarities. Pusey's eucharistic doctrine, therefore, provides a strong case for questioning the view that Tractarian theology is a divergence from, rather than a development of, the earlier Reformed heritage of the Church of England.

More important for this study, however, is the fact that Pusey's belief in the real presence is one of the fullest expressions of his sacramental vision. It might, in theory, be questioned whether his insistence on the continuation of the material elements and his deference to the Declaration on Kneeling are merely lip service to the Anglican formularies. What demonstrates his sincerity is the fact that these beliefs, whatever their historical derivation, are firmly rooted in his wider theology. Indeed, his notion of the 'coexistence' of the elements with the body and blood of Christ fulfils his vision of creation: '*logoi* proceeding from and setting forth the *logos*'. In the Eucharist, elements of creation are suffused, not merely with grace or meaning but with their maker, foreshadowing the time when God in Christ will fill all things.

Chapter 5

SACRIFICE AND THE ATONEMENT

This study has argued that Pusey's theology should be understood, at its roots, as an attempt to address, within a doctrinally orthodox framework, the disjunction within Christianity between doctrine and practice – a disjunction which, he thought, had fatally weakened the faith and sown the seeds of rationalism. This led him to the recovery from the Fathers of a 'sacramental vision' for theology, in which he reinterprets the earlier Anglican high church tradition through a particular emphasis on allegorical hermeneutics and the doctrine of union with Christ. So far, this discussion has introduced Pusey's use of allegory and his understanding of communion (the latter particularly in relation to his development of high church sacramental doctrine). The final topic in this investigation is Pusey's theology of sacrifice. Here, Pusey's conviction, that what Christ does *for us*, he also does *in us*, serves both to unite (in practice) and to distinguish (for purposes of this discussion) the doctrine of the atonement and a practical theology of the Christian life: while Christ's death on the cross and living self-oblation in heaven are *for us*, that sacrifice is also realized *in us*, as members of his body. These two aspects of Pusey's consideration of sacrifice describe, roughly, the respective subjects of this chapter and the next. In both, the elements of allegory and communion which have already been identified in Pusey's thought are fully present.

This chapter focuses on Pusey's doctrine of the atonement. Pusey's treatment of this doctrine continues a high church tradition of interpreting the Cross through the use of sacrificial types. Pusey's indebtedness to this tradition of interpretation is particularly evident in his earlier works, culminating in the 'Lectures on Types and Prophecies'. He goes on, however, to combine that sacrificial understanding of the Cross with a doctrine of recapitulation. Pusey develops this synthesis in a later sermon, in which his primary concern is to defend a sacrificial model of the atonement. What is at stake in that sermon, however, is not merely the viability of the older tradition, but the participation of sacrificial types in their archetype – a participation which is both integral to the biblical witness and to a theology in which sacrifice is not the antithesis of God's love, but its end and fulfilment in humanity.

The atonement and the sacrificial types

The doctrine of the atonement has a complex history, and the character of Anglicanism is such that much of this complexity has existed in it, not only over time but all at once – a statement as true in Pusey's day as in our own. So, in order to situate Pusey's doctrine of the atonement, a brief historical survey is necessary. One common account follows. According to the earliest prominent theory of the atonement, the devil has the right to punish humanity because of sin; Christ takes the place of humanity, but being sinless and divine, defeats the devil, who thereby loses his claim. This theory, even at the peak of its influence, faced a number of difficulties, especially the question of whether the 'ruse' of the incarnation by which Satan was defeated made God a deceiver, leaving Satan in the right. By the eleventh century, there was need of an alternative. This was provided in Anselm's *Cur Deus Homo?*, which reinterprets the doctrine within the model of feudal justice: God's honour has been offended by human sin, making 'satisfaction' necessary through some form of recompense. Humanity, even if free from sin, could only ever offer what was due to God and is therefore incapable of offering any compensation. Therefore, Christ made the satisfaction on our behalf, being both perfect and divine – that is, owing nothing himself, infinite in honour and glory, and therefore able to make the compensation necessary to give satisfaction for sin. This became the dominant theory of the medieval period. By the time of the Reformation, however, theories of justice had changed, and with them the doctrine of the atonement, to a penal model emphasizing punishment instead of satisfaction: Christ died to bear our punishment, so that we might be redeemed. In the early seventeenth century this theory was again modified: Christ died not to bear the punishment that was actually due to the whole of humanity, but to demonstrate God's justice and his hatred of sin (the 'rectoral' or 'governmental' theory). Finally, in the late nineteenth and early twentieth centuries (though anticipated in the medieval period by Abelard), legal theory shifted to a more rehabilitative model, and once again atonement theory moved with it. According to the 'moral' theory, Christ's death is an example of love and holiness, either for our imitation or in which we participate through *theosis*.[1]

---

1. See Timothy Gorringe, *God's Just Vengeance: Crime, Violence and the Rhetoric of Salvation* (Cambridge: Cambridge University Press, 1996), esp. 26–7, 45–6; L. W. Grensted, *A Short History of the Doctrine of the Atonement* (Manchester: Manchester University Press, 1920), esp. 7–8; Stephen R. Holmes, *The Wondrous Cross: Atonement and Penal Substitution in the Bible and History* (London: Paternoster, 2007), 6–7. Gorringe argues that these theories were not only influenced by the prevailing legal thought of the time they emerged but were produced to provide religious justification for those legal systems. Grensted, on the other hand, attributes this dependence on legal theory to St Paul, whose own perspective is 'profoundly affected by the legal bias of his mind'. *Pace* Grensted, Holmes observes that Paul, like the rest of the New Testament, shows a 'mixing of metaphors' in

In England, however, several factors combined to prevent the dominance of any particular theory, making the interpretation of this doctrine by the nineteenth century relatively complex. The English church maintained contacts with continental reformers, so both the penal and the rectoral theories gained some currency. The comprehensive nature of the Church, however, allowed both to coexist; and, moreover, a conservative tendency in English theology, reinforced by the Prayer Book, preserved a strong role for satisfaction theory. Local culture also played a role: in the eighteenth century, the dominant image of God came to be the magistrate, charged with enforcing the law, but capable of exercising mercy. Within this framework, Christ's intercession receives the primary emphasis. Substitution of one victim for another would be considered unjust, but Christ's sufferings and obedience merit a reward, and so his pleas on our behalf are granted. This, too, can be traced to the influence of the legal system: The laws of this period provided for extensive use of the death penalty, but this was rarely applied; moreover, many clergy were themselves rural magistrates, making the analogy an easy one.[2] By the nineteenth century, the situation was still more complicated, as various theories occupied different portions of the intellectual landscape. Satisfaction retained official status in the Church of England. The rectoral theory remained prominent, as Gorringe emphasizes with regard to its influence on the Scottish theologian John McLeod Campbell; among Pusey's influences, a very moderate statement of this theory can be found in the sermons of his undergraduate tutor, Thomas Vowler Short.[3] Meanwhile, in the broader cultural consciousness, penal theory became so prevalent as to influence social theory and economics.[4] The intercession of Christ remained important as well, though shorn of its explicitly magistratial imagery – it is a recurring theme in Pusey's discussion of the eucharistic sacrifice, and was the topic of one of his sermons on 'comforts to the penitent' meant to address the objections to his teaching on post-baptismal sin.[5] And, as I will argue, the theological reticence of the high church tradition introduced an alternative theory

---

discussing redemption. Note especially Paul's use of sacrificial language in, for example, Rom. 3.25, 12.1; 1 Cor. 5.7, Eph. 5.2.

2. Gorringe, *God's Just Vengeance*, 170–82; see especially the discussion of John Balguy, 170–2. The similarities of this view to the rectoral theory are apparent: Christ is not a substitute for us in receiving punishment, and the emphasis is on the role of the divine magistrate in displaying both justice and mercy. However, redemption does not come through Christ's work as an exemplar – rather, he merits forgiveness for us as a reward.

3. Gorringe, *God's Just Vengeance*, 197–204, 206; T. V. Short, *Sermons on Some Fundamental Truths of Christianity* (Oxford: J. Parker, 1829), 27–33, 381–3, 389–92.

4. Hilton, *Age of Atonement*, 33, 81–9.

5. Pusey, preface to *US I*, v; cf. *Eleven Addresses during a Retreat of the Companions of the Love of Jesus, Engaged in Perpetual Intercession for the Conversion of Sinners*. (Oxford: James Parker, 1868), 57–60. The sermon in question was one of a number that were lost prior to publication.

to those outlined above, in which Christ's death and intercession is seen in the ritual context of the Old Testament, rather than in the realm of legal transaction.

For Pusey in particular, however, the investigation should begin in 1830, with the second part of the *Enquiry*. In discussing an early form of the distinction between official and received doctrine – here the system *of* a church, versus the system *in* a church – one of Pusey's examples is the Anselmian tradition of satisfaction. The doctrine *of* the Church is simply that Christ died for our sins; but the theory of satisfaction was widely held *in* the Western church as an explanation of that doctrine. As long as satisfaction is understood to be only an explanation, it is innocuous and may indeed be helpful; but danger creeps in when what ought to be only an explanation *in* a given church is made the doctrine *of* that church – that is, when one 'model' for a doctrine is followed in a way that excludes others (i.e., univocally). With complementary perspectives silenced, the explanation risks obscuring the true doctrine, while giving 'advantage' to Christianity's detractors, and putting a 'stumbling block in the way of many an enquirer'.[6]

> It is very different ... whether the great doctrine of the atonement be presented to the mind simply, as it is in Scripture, as a proof of God's great love to the world, of his love for men, while they were yet sinners, at the same time that he condemned sin; or whether it be clogged with the scholastic appendage, that it was *necessary* that an infinite satisfaction should first be made to God's justice before he *could* pardon us.[7]

This 'clogging' effect, among other things, suggests the opposition between God's mercy and justice; and while the theory of satisfaction may be edifying for some individuals, Pusey fears it has been the parent of reactions against orthodox Christianity, as well as a barrier by which the soul's 'efforts to grow in the love of God have been impeded by the early predominance given to the fear of Him'.[8]

This position, far from being 'liberal' (as some readers have thought), in fact puts Pusey very close to the high church tradition. He had sent drafts of this volume to Bishop Blomfield of London, in which his language rejecting this 'infinite satisfaction' of God's justice was very possibly stronger than that eventually published. Blomfield's response on this point was balanced: he insists that satisfaction is the doctrine of the Church of England (the term is used in the Communion Service), but then goes on to dismiss 'infinite satisfaction' as a meaningless phrase of human theorizing and defines 'satisfaction' as meaning only that God '*judged it enough*, that Christ should die, instead of *our* suffering that punishment'.[9] This line of interpretation is also reflected by Van Mildert, who held

---

6. Pusey, *Enquiry II*, 41–5.
7. Pusey, *Enquiry II*, 93; emphasis Pusey's.
8. Pusey, *Enquiry II*, 93–4.
9. Blomfield to Pusey, Letter of 4 January 1830, in LBV 40; emphasis Blomfield's.

that, as with the Eucharist, it is unhealthy and irreverent to press the specifics of the atonement too far:

> It is hardly to be expected that we should be able to clear up every difficulty respecting the necessity or efficacy of *vicarious suffering*. Neither may it be possible for us to affix so clear and definite a meaning to the word *satisfaction*, when applied to the propitiation of the Father by our Lord's death and sacrifice, as may preclude cavils and disputes. We know only that it has produced the effect which the word *satisfaction* implies, in that it has been accepted by the Almighty as a sufficient expiation for sin.[10]

Likewise, Van Mildert rejects questions of why satisfaction was necessary or 'how it was rendered efficacious', as well as inquiries into the relationship between God's infinite mercy and justice, or the necessity of the cross. He admits that such speculations may have their place, either in increasing veneration of the mystery of the cross in 'pious and sober-minded men' or for apologetic purposes, but beyond those limited ends, maintaining the simple teaching of the Gospel, 'that "Christ died, the just for the unjust;" and that "when we were enemies, we were reconciled to God by the death of his son," must surely be sufficient'.[11] Here we see the same three points later echoed by Pusey: a general aversion to overly detailed speculation on the atonement, an allowance that such theorizing may have a limited role in personal edification and the absolute rejection of any 'necessity' that might interfere with the freedom of God's mercy.

***

This reticence about theories of the atonement, however, raises a question. The atonement is a central doctrine in Western Christianity; but if theorizing on it is discouraged, how does one speak of it? L. W. Grensted notes that 'exponents of the sacrificial aspect of Christ's death have never been wanting in the Church, though their language has seldom been developed into a definite theory, and it is interesting to notice how often the Anselmic satisfaction theory has itself tended to revert to sacrificial phrases and ideas'.[12] In fact, however, what the high church tradition demonstrates is a very regular use of sacrificial imagery, not just by 'reversion' but by deliberate choice. As the earlier discussion of allegory suggests, such imagery is not, indeed, liable to 'definite theories' – for Pusey, this would be its attraction! – but there is sufficient evidence to establish a clear pattern of reliance on sacrificial types in preference to more legal theories (if not entirely uninfluenced by them).

Although the older high churchmen are generally cautious in their use of Old Testament types, this is one area where biblical precedent allows it. So, in

---

10. Van Mildert, *Sermons*, 1:100–1; emphasis Van Mildert's.
11. Van Mildert, *Sermons*, 1:101–2.
12. Grensted, *Atonement*, 7.

one place, Van Mildert establishes Christ's role as mediator and intercessor by elaborating on the pagan and Hebraic patterns of priesthood, which are fulfilled in Christ's self-offering.[13] In another, he argues that the purpose of the Law was not only to preserve the Jews from idolatry but also 'to prepare them, by a typical and figurative service, for the acceptance of that one great atonement for sin to be effected by the promised seed'.[14] The sacrificial system of the Old Covenant 'taught, in the clearest manner, that momentous truth, that guilt could only be done away by some vicarious atonement offered up as a propitiation for sin'.[15] 'It was an intermediate dispensation between the giving of the promise and the fulfillment of that promise, shewing most clearly, by the very nature of its enactments and provisions, the guilt of sin and the necessity of a Redeemer.'[16] '[Paul] represents the Passover to have been a symbol of redemption through the blood of Christ. He raises the dignity of the Levitical sacrifices, by asserting them to have been figurative of our Lord's expiatory sacrifice upon the Cross.'[17]

The appeal to sacrificial types as models for the atonement is even stronger a generation earlier, in Jones of Nayland. Like Van Mildert after him, Jones shows an interest in the priesthood as a type of Christ, though he goes further in drawing a parallel between the life of the High Priest within the courts of the temple as a sort of living self-offering and Christ's self-offering to God within the true tabernacle in heaven.[18] With specific regard to sacrifice, he uses the description of Christ as the 'Lamb of God' to recall the sacrifices of Isaac and the Passover lamb, arguing that God provided in Christ 'another substitute of Isaac and of all mankind ... who should taste of death for every man, and take away the sins of the world' and interpreting the Exodus as foreshadowing redemption from the slavery of sin.[19] Likewise, he summarizes the doctrine of Christ's sacrifice with relation to the Law:

> 1. That Christ is what the passover was, a lamb taken from the flock of his people. 2. That he was a sacrifice, put to death as an offering to God. 3. That this was done *for us*, for our redemption and deliverance from the divine wrath, as the passover was sacrificed for the redemption of the Hebrews, when the first born of Egypt were destroyed.[20]

Still earlier in the eighteenth century, the same interest in sacrifice appears in Waterland's sermon, 'Christ's Sacrifice of Himself Explained'. As the title suggests,

---

13. Van Mildert, *Sermons*, 1:422.
14. Van Mildert, *Sermons*, 1:212.
15. Van Mildert, *Sermons*, 1:215.
16. Van Mildert, *Sermons*, 1:220.
17. Van Mildert, *Sermons*, 1:217–18.
18. Jones, *Figurative Language*, 91–9, 107–10, 351; *Sermons on Various Subjects and Occasions*, ed. William Henry Walker (London: C. J. G. and F. Rivington, 1830), 2:320.
19. Jones, *Sermons*, 2:83–90.
20. Jones, *Figurative Language*, 91–2; drawing on Heb. 9.24-25 and 1 Cor. 5.7; emphasis in original.

he dwells here on notions of sacrifice rather than on legal theories of the atonement. Although Waterland has 'just a hint of penal language', he refuses 'to dogmatize upon so mysterious a subject'.[21] Instead, he emphasizes that sacrifice is a gift to God, and that it was especially the obedience of Christ that was pleasing to God, while (showing some influence from the rectoral theory) he suggests that Christ's sacrifice can be understood (if not explained) as an appropriate means of our redemption, first in preserving the glory, holiness and justice of God in requiring satisfaction for offenses, and second in making our redemption dependent on someone other than ourselves, thereby encouraging humility.[22] The frequent association of sacrifice with the victim's death is not emphasized, emerging only in Waterland's insistence that Christ's humanity alone was offered (because divinity cannot suffer), and in the moral imperative that follows from Christ's sacrifice, 'to sacrifice the *old man*'.[23]

***

This brief survey, despite going no earlier than Waterland, should suffice to show that there is a tradition in high church Anglicanism which relies more heavily on sacrificial than on legal imagery when speaking of the atonement. Before returning to Pusey, however, we should consider his mentor, Charles Lloyd, whose lectures on Romans provide a clear foundation for aspects of Pusey's later thought. In addition to the views on post-baptismal sin already discussed in Chapter 1, there is a dual structure in Lloyd's soteriology similar to that later seen in Pusey: 'Our justification is ascribed to the death – to the very blood of Christ – our future salvation to his resurrection'; shortly thereafter, resurrection is equated with Christ's presence in heaven.[24] This justification is not 'effected – declared – or known, until he sat down on the right hand of his Father, and presented his sacrifice in heaven'.[25] Thus, the ascension – Christ's entry into the heavenly sanctuary (Heb. 9.24-25) – is especially important. This draws on the sacrifices of the Day of Atonement: the bull is killed, but the atonement is not made until its blood is sprinkled on the mercy seat; and so Christ's atonement for humanity is made not in his death, but when, having died, he is enthroned in heaven.

Pusey's own understanding of the types which foreshadow the atonement has, of course, much in common with his high church predecessors. But his treatment is much more complex, due to his sophisticated understanding of allegory. His preface to the major discussions of sacrifice in the 'Lectures on Types and Prophecies' places it firmly within a network of other images, all related to Christ's saving work:

> It had been perhaps misleading, had vicarious death and conquest over death been exhibited together: each was taught separately, that they might

---

21. Grensted, *Atonement*, 264–6.
22. Waterland, 'Christ's Sacrifice', 737–41, 743–4.
23. Waterland, 'Christ's Sacrifice', 740, 744–5.
24. Lloyd, 'Romans', 5.10-11.
25. Lloyd, 'Romans', 5.10.

be taught purely: in that, as in Isaac, only an emblem of death, or in Moses, a punishment for their sakes but not vicarious: in the slain beasts vicarious, but not propitiatory: in the bronze serpent propitiatory, but not vicarious; all were to be united in Him who came in the likeness of sinful flesh and a sacrifice for sin to condemn sin in the flesh (Rom. 8.3).[26]

Though the role of the Law was to teach (Pusey is reinterpreting *torah*, 'teaching', within his allegorical framework), its role was preparatory in illuminating each element distinctly. The relationships between the types can only be seen in Christ; and indeed the fullness of their interrelations can only be known to God, who created them.[27] This is one dimension of these networks; another side can be seen in his treatment of the Levitical priesthood, where the single image itself symbolizes

---

26. Pusey, 'Types', 89, 102–4. Pusey uses both propitiation and expiation to describe the effects of sacrifice, following an established pattern in earlier Anglican theology. This may have roots in the Authorized Version, which differentiates between Old Testament כפר, 'atonement', and New Testament ἱλαστήριον, ἱλασμός, 'propitiation'. Some, such as Van Mildert (quoted earlier in this section), appear to use both interchangeably. Others, however, make a subtle distinction. Butler, followed by Edward Maltby (a latitudinarian, Pusey's tutor after Eton and later Bishop of Durham), distinguishes between Christ's sacrifice as propitiatory, and the Old Testament sacrifices as expiatory. Waterland admits that the Eucharist can be called propitiatory, in a qualified or 'lax' sense, like any good work which pleases God, but only Christ's sacrifice is *properly* propitiatory (pleasing to God) or expiatory (effective to remove sin). Pusey's use reflects both of these elements. In the 'Types', Pusey contrasts the Day of Atonement with the Passover as signifying respectively expiation and sorrow as opposed to freedom and joy; subsequent (commemorative) Passovers are propitiatory, 'as was all sacrifice ... appointed by God'. And, 'as they were propitiatory', so by analogy the Eucharist is 'well pleasing' (the passage is discussed in greater depth in Chapter 6, under 'Sacrifice and the Eucharist'). Later references to expiation are rare, but in 1844 he describes penance as expiation on the basis of Prov. 16.6. Propitiation, however, is prominent in his discussions of the eucharistic sacrifice: he identified himself with a tradition which understood propitiation to mean 'rendering God propitious' – favourable or gracious – and insisted that the Eucharist was in this sense propitiatory, although it was not *a propitiation*, which can only be said of Christ (similar to Waterland's 'lax' and 'proper' uses). This more positive sense of propitiation should not be confused with that of, for example, de la Taille (noted in this chapter under 'Atonement and union', and discussed more fully in Chapter 6 under 'Sacrifice and the Eucharist') for whom propitiation is reparatory bloodshed required for forgiveness. An awareness of such differences in interpretation is reflected in the manuscript of the 'Types': translating '*propitiorium*' in a passage from Bellarmine, Pusey had half-written, then crossed out, 'propitiatory', before deciding 'expiatory' was more accurate. Pusey, *Jelf*, 68; *London*, 20–2; 'Types', 104; Pusey to Sr. Clara, 7 June 1844, LBV 76; Butler, *Analogy*, 258; Edward Maltby, *Sermons* (London: T. Cadell, 1819–22), 1:171–2; Waterland, 'Christian Sacrifice', 126, 148–9; 'Distinctions', 280–2.

27. Pusey, 'Types', 91–2.

many things. It was not only an institution but a symbol of the holiness of God's chosen people; as a type, it foreshadowed not only the priesthood of Christ, but the holiness of the Church, and the 'future spiritual offices' of the Church's ministry.[28]

His discussion of sacrifice, however, focuses primarily on the two great festivals of the Day of Atonement and the Passover. Pusey sees the broader sacrificial system as deriving from these ceremonies – unfortunately allowing their significance as types to marginalize other rites, whereas according to his own theory, allowing an independent significance to *each* element of the sacrificial system would provide for a more complex array of relationships between the significance of the various sacrifices, and thereby a deeper range of symbolic meaning in each.[29] In Pusey's discussion of the two great rites of the Old Testament, however, the Passover is closely linked with the Eucharist; it will therefore be considered in the following chapter. His discussion of the Day of Atonement, however, is focused on the Christian understanding of atonement. This reflects, again, Lloyd's influence. Lloyd's parallel with the ascension, however, is shifted across the symbolic network associated with sacrifice to become another element associated with the Eucharist: although its imagery is from the Day of Atonement, the eternal reality of Christ's self-offering in heaven allows a connection with the repeated 'commemorative' nature of the Eucharist which Pusey draws from the Paschal type. Pusey's emphasis in the 'Types' falls instead on the instructive nature of the Atonement rituals, as seen particularly in the pair of goats: one sacrificed as a sin offering, the other sent away bearing the sins of the people. Drawing on Cyril of Alexandria, Pusey interprets the two goats as foreshadowing Christ's death and resurrected life. 'We hear death and life joined in the work of atonement: death for atonement to God, life for complete remission. The symbol speaks almost in the words of St. Paul, "He died for our sins, and rose again for our justification. He ever liveth to make intercession for us."'[30] But, although the type is instructive, and even redeems from the penalties of the Law, it was nonetheless imperfect, as shown in its repetition and the continued reign of sin: it 'had no life to impart', was 'outward and inadequate and transitory'.[31] Spiritual redemption was needed, which is found in Christ.

> Far different was it, when the real sacrifice was made … this was *adequate*, on account of the infinite dignity of Him, who offered it, the Eternal Son of God; it was inward, because He was the Son of Man also … He became Son of Man that we might be sons of God; and having by His sacrament made us members of Himself, his sufferings become ours, yea we share all which is His, His death, His sufferings, His life, because we are *in* Him of whom we have been made members; *in* whom we are accepted, *in* whom we have redemption (*in*, not

---

28. Pusey, 'Types', 93.
29. Pusey, 'Types', 96, 100.
30. Pusey, 'Types', 97, citing Rom. 4.25 and Heb. 7.25.
31. Pusey, 'Types', 97–8. The passage relies heavily on Heb. 8.1–9.14.

merely *by*, nor *through* nor 'for the sake of' but '*in*'), in whom we have been chosen, yea *in* whom we are.³²

This passage illustrates how Pusey's understanding of Christ's sacrifice is shaped by his 'for us–in us' duality, being both external to us and realized within us through his sacramental indwelling. This internal aspect of sacrifice will be discussed in the following chapter. But the interaction between sacrifice and union with Christ in Pusey's theology also has its effect on how the external aspect of sacrifice is understood.

Atonement and union

Pusey explores this interaction more deeply in his University Sermon, 'The Doctrine of the Atonement'. In this sermon, Pusey maintains a traditional position, but re-thinks most of the arguments made to support it. On a superficial reading, the sermon appears to state a straightforward Anselmian understanding of the atonement as satisfaction; but careful attention shows that such an interpretation produces contradictions within the sermon itself. While Pusey insists (with Anselm) that the cross is the cause for our forgiveness and the means of our satisfaction, Anselm's arguments are either rejected or altered by Pusey's theological emphasis on communion. In the end, Pusey argues, the atonement is not so much about humanity's redress to an offended God, as about God's restoration of wounded humanity; and God's justice, and the satisfaction made to it, must be redefined accordingly.

In this sermon, Pusey is arguing against the position that 'the Satisfaction was … rather the cause than the fruit of the love of God for his creature man' – a position which Pusey attributes incidentally to 'the Arian poet' John Milton.³³ Pusey's arguments are not directed against Milton, however, but against his Christ Church colleague Benjamin Jowett, which he makes clear when he responds to Jowett's argument that union with Christ makes a vicarious atonement impossible. This response includes a lengthy quotation from Karl Friedrich August Fritsche, as 'one, who studied for many years the teaching of St. Paul, but, alas! apparently as a scholar only, studying St. Paul as he might *any other book*', but who concluded that 'vicariousness' was indeed Paul's teaching – a not-so-subtle jab both at Jowett's position in *Essays and Reviews*, and at his depth of biblical scholarship.³⁴ In fact,

---

32. Pusey, 'Types', 98, citing Eph. 1.4, 6-7; emphasis Pusey's. In the MS, 'His sacrament' replaces 'Baptism', which is struck out.

33. Pusey, 'Atonement', 232–4.

34. Pusey, 'Atonement', 254–60, emphasis added. The appeal to read Scripture like 'any other book' was the centrepiece of Jowett's contribution to *Essays and Reviews*. Benjamin Jowett, 'On the Interpretation of Scripture', in *Essays and Reviews*, 338; *The Epistles of St. Paul to the Thessalonians, Galatians, and Romans* (London: John Murray, 1894), 2:47–51.

Pusey is responding to Jowett throughout the sermon, as an early footnote makes clear, in which Pusey quotes Jowett's commentary on St Paul, with explanatory interpolations, as the full statement of the problem to be addressed:

> The doctrine of the Atonement ... has often been explained in a way at which our moral feelings revolt. God is represented as angry with us, for what we never did [original sin]. He is ready to inflict a disproportionate punishment on us for what we are, [sinners by our own actual sins]. He is satisfied by the sufferings of His Son in our stead. Christ is a victim laid on the altar to appease the wrath of God. He is further said to bear the infinite punishment of infinite sin. When He had suffered or paid the penalty, God is described as granting Him the salvation of mankind in return.[35]

Pusey passes over several of Jowett's sentences, however: after 'in our stead', he omits reference to the imputation of Adam's sin and Christ's righteousness; and both before and after 'Christ is a victim ... to appease the wrath of God', he omits statements linking Christ's death with the Old Testament sacrifices. The omitted statements appear to be points with which Pusey agrees; he quotes the portions that he criticizes in his sermon. This continued belief that Christ's death should be understood through the sacrificial types suggests, as his conclusion will show, that this sermon is implicitly an attempt to rescue a sacrificial interpretation of the atonement from Jowett's harshly negative portrayal.

Pusey's response builds on two foundational points: the unity of the persons of the Trinity in mind, will and action; and the hypostatic union of Christ's divinity and his humanity. While his actions may be attributable to either his human or his divine nature, they are actions of Christ's one *person*, and therefore acts of the Triune God, known and decided upon in eternity. So Jowett's (and Milton's) separation between the wrathful Father and the redeeming Son is impossible to maintain – redemption is as much an act of the Father's love as the Son's.[36] Such a correction goes a long way towards rebutting the misinterpretations Pusey is addressing, but the claim at stake, that union with God and sacrifice are incompatible, has not yet been addressed. Thus, this clarification merely serves as an introduction, and it is in the remainder of the sermon that Pusey's reinterpretation of traditional satisfaction theory comes to full bloom.

Next, Pusey rejects the idea that Christ's death was in any way *necessary*. With Anselm and the tradition that follows from him, he admits that 'sin has a sort of infinity of evil, as being done against the Infinite Majesty of the All-holy God'.[37]

---

35. Pusey, 'Atonement', 234–5; quoting Jowett, *Epistles*, 2:317; bracketed words are Pusey's insertions.

36. Pusey, 'Atonement', 232–4.

37. Pusey, 'Atonement', 236–7; cf. Anselm, *Cur Deus Homo?*, in *Anselm of Canterbury: The Major Works*, ed. Brian Davies and G. R. Evans (Oxford: Oxford University Press, 1998) 1.13, 1.20–21, 2.6.

However, he rejects any necessity in God, insisting instead on divine freedom. And so, he acknowledges positively the positions which hold that God might have forgiven sin without satisfaction, or on 'the imperfect satisfaction of a holy but mere man', or on the perfect satisfaction of one mere human, *accepted for* humanity though not in itself adequate for all humanity – a major contrast with Anselm, who acknowledges God's freedom from *external* constraint, but insists that the *internal* self-consistency of God's justice makes adequate recompense a necessary requirement of forgiveness.[38] But for Pusey, the 'way, which God has chosen, is eminent in these things, that no other way could so impress on us the heinousness of sin and the holiness of God, or the love of God for us, sinners as we are, or could so issue in the renewal of our nature and our union with God'.[39]

We can see here some influence from the rectoral theory of the atonement, in that Christ's death on the cross is, in a way, educational, as a demonstration of God's nature. But it is not, as in the rectoral theory, 'to demonstrate God's justice and his hatred of sin'; rather, it is the *gravity* of sin against God, and God's love for us, that are taught by the cross. The point that truly merits attention, however, is Pusey's emphasis on 'the renewal of our nature'. It is in this context that Pusey continues his argument:

> You know what you were by nature, aliens from God, at enmity with God, turned away and (it is the Scripture term) 'haters of God'. Man could not redeem man, because he had himself that great debt upon him. Man, even if one were created anew, free from that original stain and in a state of grace, could not redeem man, because he owed himself and all which he was, already to God. This, then, is what is meant by the doctrine of satisfaction: not that God was under any necessity to redeem man, but that, if He did, for the redemption of the whole race of man there was needed a Divine Redeemer.[40]

Here again we hear echoes of Anselm; but once more, Pusey has shifted the thrust of his argument away from the traditional satisfaction theory. For Anselm and those who followed him, the concern was redemption from punishment for sin.[41] However, Pusey has just been arguing that forgiveness and freedom from punishment are of God's free grace, not constrained by any necessity, even the necessity of a divinely made satisfaction. So he cannot here be speaking about forgiveness; rather, the clue lies in his emphasis on what we are by *nature*, and our need for a renewed nature – humanity needs to be redeemed, not from punishment

---

38. Pusey, 'Atonement', 235–6; cf. Anselm, *Cur Deus Homo?*, 1.12, 1.19–20; David Brown, 'Anselm on Atonement', in *The Cambridge Companion to Anselm*, ed. Brian Davies and Brian Leftow (Cambridge: Cambridge University Press, 2004), 284.

39. Pusey, 'Atonement', 237.

40. Pusey, 'Atonement', 240–1, quoting Rom. 1.30.

41. Cf. Anselm, *Cur Deus Homo?*, 1.11. See also 2.6, for comparison with Pusey's argument.

but from sin and its corruption.[42] This theme grows stronger as Pusey goes on. We ought to offer our whole selves to God, but are unable to do so; Pusey describes this inability as a 'sickness' or 'wound' in need of a physician.[43] So, despite outward similarities to Anselm, Pusey's underlying thought is in fact closer to the maxim of Gregory Nazianzen, 'that which He has not assumed He has not healed; but that which is united to His Godhead is also saved'.[44] The post-Anselmian tradition came to use 'satisfaction' in a more punitive sense – as, for instance, in the early twentieth-century Roman Catholic theologian Maurice de la Taille, who defined it as *punishment*, required together with propitiation (reparation) for forgiveness, by removing the debt and the guilt of sin.[45] Pusey appears to have redefined 'satisfaction' according to an earlier patristic sense, close to that of Tertullian, who understands it in terms of returning to a right relationship with God.[46] Despite the differences regarding the freedom of God's forgiveness noted above, on this point Pusey appears closer to Anselm than later interpreters such as de la Taille: for Anselm too, *satisfaction* is more concerned with compensation for the neglected worship properly due to God, than with punishment.[47]

In Pusey's early correspondence with Blomfield, he had expressed difficulties with the notion of the cross as an 'infinite satisfaction' made to God's justice. Blomfield had insisted on both satisfaction and its connection with God's justice, but allowed some flexibility as to the meaning of both terms. Pusey revisits this point, and, just as he had reshaped the idea of satisfaction, he now goes on to offer a new, reoriented understanding of God's justice. After describing the sickness

---

42. Elsewhere, Pusey holds that we are redeemed (primarily) *from* 'an endless antipathy and rebellion and loss of God, our only Good' *to* the beatific vision – the fullness of joy and love in union with God, and the full knowledge of God's love. Pusey, 'Jesus, the Redeemer, and His Redeemed', in *LS*, 422–8.

43. Pusey, 'Atonement', 241–2.

44. Gregory Nazianzen, 'Epistle to Cledonius the Priest, Against Apollinarius', in *Nicene and Post-Nicene Fathers*, ed. Philip Schaff and Henry Wace (Peabody, MA: Hendrickson, 1994), 2nd series, 7:440.

45. Maurice de la Taille, *The Mystery of Faith: Regarding the Most August Sacrament and Sacrifice of the Body and Blood of Christ*, trans. Joseph Carroll and P. J. Dalton (New York: Sheed and Ward, 1940), 1:10–11.

46. Tertullian, *On Repentance*, in *Ante-Nicene Fathers*, ed. Alexander Roberts, James Donaldson and A. Cleveland Coxe (Peabody, MA: Hendrickson, 1994), 3:663–4 [§8]. Tertullian is credited with introducing the term to theology, with reference to repentance for post-baptismal sin: for instance, connecting 'satisfaction' with the return of the prodigal son to his father. The likely source of the term's ambiguity lies in its different uses in Roman law: 'Tertullian's doctrine of "satisfaction" may have come from Roman private law, where it referred to the amends one made to another for failing to discharge on obligation, or from Roman public law, which enabled the term to be interpreted as a form of punishment.' Jaroslav Pelikan, *The Christian Tradition* (Chicago: University of Chicago Press, 1971), 1:147.

47. David Brown, 'Anselm', 290–5.

of sin, cured by Christ the physician, he continues, 'And in that remedy, God so willed that His own justice should be shown, as well as his mercy and tender love … And yet how depth answereth to depth! The depths of God's aweful Justice and holiness stream forth in His aweful love.' Pusey goes on to clarify his meaning, that God's righteousness is shown primarily in making righteous.[48] Paradoxically, the essence of God's justice is not punishment, but forgiveness:

> From first to last, St. Paul's theme is the righteousness of God Himself. It had to be explained how God could be righteous and yet forgive sin. It is not, as elsewhere, the love of God, although God's love shines not even in Heaven itself with such a divine tender lustre, as from the Cross. It is the 'righteousness of God', which had been made manifest. To the unseared conscience the forgiveness of sin is a greater mystery than sin itself. We are, alas! too much at home with sin to be surprised at any thing about it. Damnation is no mystery to the soul which feels separate from God. Darkness transelemented into light, hate transformed into love, ghastliness of sin transformed into the beauty of holiness, deserved displeasure issuing into the overpowering, sin-forgiving, sin-annihilating love of God, this is the mystery of mysteries, which 'Angels desire to look into', which man could scarcely dare believe.[49]

This is not to say that God's justice has nothing to do with punishment, however. Punishment is due to sin. 'It was to God's just judgment, that our lives were forfeited.' But, 'what was justly due to our sins, Christ paid; the punishment that we deserved, Christ bore. For Christ, the Innocent, Who owed nothing, took the place of us the guilty'.[50] This is how Pusey defines the vicarious 'satisfaction to the Divine justice'.[51] But, as has been noted, Pusey saw no necessity for *someone* to be punished, in order for God to forgive; and redemption is not primarily from punishment but from sin. So the fact that Christ 'took the place of the guilty' becomes first and foremost an expression of love, freely given. There are echoes once again of the patristic understanding of satisfaction as Pusey draws the sermon to a close: Man, even in his perfection, owes 'himself and all which he was' to God; yet 'we were all sinners, and had nothing to offer'.[52] But 'God so loveth the service of our free will that it lay in the plan of salvation which He chose, that Jesus should with His Human Will choose freely to offer Himself as a Sacrifice for sin.'[53] Just as Tertullian links satisfaction with the return of the prodigal to his Father, Pusey links satisfaction – or as he puts it elsewhere in the sermon, 'propitiatory sacrifice' – with the restoration of human self-offering to God. To this, Pusey adds that because the offering of the divine Son

48. Pusey, 'Atonement', 242–5.
49. Pusey, 'Atonement', 243–4.
50. Pusey, 'Atonement', 246.
51. Pusey, 'Atonement', 246.
52. Pusey, 'Atonement', 240–2.
53. Pusey, 'Atonement', 260–1.

of God is infinite, Christ is able not only to offer sacrifice on his own account but to fill up all that is lacking on the part of humanity because of sin.[54] 'The infinite love of the satisfaction of Jesus remedies that quasi-infinity of evil, which sin has from "the infinity of the Divine Majesty, against which the contempt of disobedience offended, and the infinite good which is forfeited, which is, God." '[55]

***

Pusey's understanding of the atonement, then, rejects the *necessity* of satisfaction for God's forgiveness. In so doing, he redefines satisfaction as the restoration of right relationship with God, rather than a recompense to avert punishment, and reorients the definition of God's justice away from the punishment of sin, towards its fulfilment in redeeming love. The cross is God's freely chosen means of forgiveness, not the necessary precondition for it; Christ bears the punishment due to sin as the expression of God's love, while he restores humanity's self-denying and self-giving relationship of love, obedience and sacrifice towards God, by giving of himself even unto death. Because he chose death freely as man, humanity is restored in him (recapitulated); because he is God, his self-offering is sufficient for all mankind.

Pusey's reinterpretation of satisfaction theory demonstrates the elements in his thought which this study has already brought forward. The sacrificial theme which he inherited from the high churchmen is the culminating point of his reflections on satisfaction and divine justice; their adherence to this biblical type in preference to legal models may well have provided the doctrinal flexibility which allowed Pusey's redefinitions. These modifications themselves are rooted in his sacramental vision: Pusey insists that Christ's death be interpreted in a way which preserves the theological viability of the sacrificial types, as pointing to the cross; but he also insists that such a sacrificial understanding of Christ's death be understood in light of our own participation in Christ (and thus, to recall the linguistic elements in his thought pointed out in Chapter 2, not only must the integrity of the sacrificial model for the atonement be preserved, but its interaction with the unitive model should be not only acknowledged but embraced). Meanwhile, Pusey's emphasis on divine love, which redirected his understanding of the atonement away from penal concerns, similarly affected his understanding of hell: his last major work begins with the premise that we can be separated from God's presence, but never his love – hell is not the loss of God's love, but hatred of it.[56]

Viewed against the wider background of nineteenth-century theology, however, Pusey's interpretation of the atonement also demonstrates his role as a transitional figure in nineteenth-century English theology. The beginning of the century showed the variety of satisfaction, penal and rectoral theories recounted above; by the end of the century, the moral theory was finally gaining respectability as a major interpretation of the atonement. Despite a long-standing history as a complement

---

54. Pusey, 'Atonement', 242–3, discussing Rom. 3.21-26.
55. Pusey, 'Atonement', 242, quoting Bernard, *On the Nativity*, Sermon 3.
56. Pusey, *Everlasting Punishment*, 2–5.

to other aspects of the atonement, earlier attempts to emphasize this perspective (by Abelard and Faustus Socinus) attracted widespread condemnation; acceptance ultimately came with works such as R. C. Moberly's *Atonement and Personality*, which combined the earlier attention to moral renewal with a greater emphasis on the work of the Holy Spirit and the indwelling of Christ. Pusey's reorientation of an 'external' model of the atonement towards Christ's indwelling makes him a transitional figure between the two.

Moberly, however, is an interesting figure to consider with regard to the Tractarians' role in this evolution: growing up, his father's parish neighboured Keble's, and the two families were on visiting terms; he went on to become a contributor to *Lux Mundi*, a volume which attempted to wed Tractarian theology to an endorsement of modern critical scholarship. But beyond these connections, there are specific similarities between his argument and the teaching of the Oxford Movement. Moberly demonstrates a strong emphasis on union with Christ, as mediated by the sacraments (shared by the Oxford Movement generally); his understanding of the eucharistic presence is very similar to Pusey's.[57] Beyond this, the Tractarian concern with *phronesis* shows itself in his rejection of reason as a mere 'infantile' playing with logic, in favour of a pre-Enlightenment emphasis on wisdom and the discernment of truth, the full realization of which requires submission to and communion with God.[58] In an ingenious extension of this principle, Moberly rejects freedom as the ability to choose *anything*; rather, free will is the ability to act in such a way as to make the action truly one's own, which is determined by the way in which character and discernment have been formed.[59]

As to Pusey's own influence, Moberly has inherited his understanding of penitence as an expression of love. However, the related idea of Christ as the perfect penitent, repentant on our behalf though not for himself, goes beyond anything Pusey suggests; for Pusey, penitence, though it may (and indeed should) characterize the corporate life of the Church, is never a characteristic of the sinless Christ.[60] Nonetheless, the 'absolute and irreparable' 'antithesis of righteousness against unrighteousness' (in Moberly's words) is a common theme in Pusey.[61] And in matters more closely related to the atonement itself, similarities between the two are evident in Moberly's assertion that forgiveness is not earned, but freely given, and in the belief that 'objective' and 'subjective' aspects of the atonement are complementary and linked to one another by the gift of the Holy Spirit – although in Moberly, this is more a reflection on the history of the doctrine than the structural

57. Robert Campbell Moberly, *Atonement and Personality* (New York: Longmans, Green, 1906), 154–205, 254–76.

58. Moberly, *Atonement and Personality*, 234, 242.

59. Moberly, *Atonement and Personality*, 222. For another Tractarian perspective foreshadowing Moberly, see R. I. Wilberforce, *The Doctrine of the Incarnation*, especially pp. 9–114 on 'Christ, the Pattern Man'.

60. Moberly, *Atonement and Personality*, 28–30, 117–31.

61. Moberly, *Atonement and Personality*, 14.

principle found in Pusey.⁶² There are also differences: Moberly allows more of a mind–body dualism than Pusey would have, in suggesting that bodily sickness, unlike sin, is not truly a sickness of the self; and he betrays a progressive note when he suggests that the truths of past ages have been surpassed by the 'mature consciousness' of modern man.⁶³ Despite these differences, however (and some of them are more with Pusey in particular, than with the Tractarians generally), Moberly clearly carries on the theological heritage of the Oxford Movement, and at least indirectly of Pusey himself.⁶⁴

What especially marks Pusey as a transitional figure, however, is his modification of a more traditional external account of the atonement in a way that accounts for its inward realization, harmonizing Christ's work for us and in us. While some acknowledgement of internal change has always accompanied the doctrine of the atonement, Pusey has clearly shifted strongly in that direction. But he has not exchanged one for the other: rather, he repeatedly insists on holding both together. Even *within* those aspects of Christ's death which are 'for us', there are both recapitulatory elements which prepare the way for what is internal, and aspects which are more 'purely' external. Christ's self-offering restores humanity's proper sacrifice to God, but it is also the means and expression of God's forgiveness, distinct from his inward renewal, and it is such because Christ takes on the punishment due to human sin. As such, it forms a parallel to his understanding of justification: even if the inward and outward aspects are in fact (if not in definition) inseparable, justification is *both* outward declaration and inward transformation. Set against the overall shift in nineteenth-century theology, from predominantly external theories in the beginning of the century, to a greater acceptance of moral theories at the century's end, Pusey's fusion of the two puts him at a pivotal point in nineteenth-century theology.

In terms of Pusey's own theology, however, the blend of sacrifice and communion seen in his theology of the atonement is not merely a compromise (or the midpoint in a transition) between old theology and new. It is, rather, the fruit of his sacramental vision. If the sacrificial rites of the Old Testament are not merely historically convenient illustrations, but '*logoi* proceeding from and setting forth the *logos*', they cannot simply be dismissed on a theological whim. Rather, their participation in Christ's archetypal self-offering makes their preservation as types necessary both to the integrity of the biblical witness and to any well-rounded understanding of the atonement. The linguistic nature of allegory, however, entails that sacrificial models of the doctrine exist in dialogue with, and should therefore be shaped by, other models, including those based on a notion of communion with Christ. Thus, sacrifice not only informs the doctrine of Christ's death *for us* but also provides the end and fulfilment, through participation in him, of his work *in us*.

62. Moberly, *Atonement and Personality*, 58–63, 136–53.
63. Moberly, *Atonement and Personality*, 32, 50.
64. In some respects, the differences with Pusey noted here mark Moberly's thought as sharing some commonalities with Newman; see in Chapter 2, under 'Allegory and the Sacramental Vision'.

Chapter 6

SACRIFICE AND THE SACRAMENTS

The previous chapter examined the way in which Pusey's sacramental vision combines a reliance on sacrificial types with his emphasis on union with Christ to produce an understanding of the atonement as a restorative, rather than a retributive, sacrifice. This chapter continues that discussion: on the cross, Pusey argues, Christ restored humanity's right offering to God *for us*; but that same sacrifice must also be realized *in us*; and while Christ's work *for us* is associated, in Pusey, with his incarnate acts, his work *in us* centres on the sacraments. Accordingly, this chapter will examine the way in which elements of older high church theology, combined with Pusey's allegorical reading of Scripture and his characteristic emphasis on union with Christ, connect Christ's sacrifice with the dominical sacraments. With regard to the Eucharist this is expected – although Pusey's doctrine, derived from earlier Anglican tradition which again is shaped by its appeal to Old Testament types, is very different from a classic Roman Catholic presentation of the eucharistic sacrifice. But there is a sacrificial aspect to baptism as well. This is less obvious and receives no explicit discussion in Pusey's work; but a careful study of the imagery and types he uses to discuss the sacrament reveals a pattern of thought in which the Christian's life-in-Christ itself becomes sacrificial.

Although the obscure nature of this discussion (particularly with regard to baptism) might suggest it is merely a curiosity of Pusey's thought, it is not so. John Boneham notes that the Tractarians on occasion veiled their discussion of the most profound doctrines in allegory, in order to keep their principle of 'reserve', and this appears to be just such a case.[1] This subject goes to the very roots of Pusey's theology. Participation in Christ lies at the very heart of Pusey's sacramental vision; yet participation, for Pusey, is ultimately concerned, not merely with ontological or hermeneutical theory but with a *life* which participates in the sacrificial death-and-resurrection of Jesus Christ. Indeed, if (as Pusey maintains) doctrines cannot be properly understood when engaged, as it were, from the 'outside', the only true understanding of Christ's sacrifice is through the Christian's living self-oblation in him; and it is in the sacraments, as they unite the faithful to Christ *in* his sacrifice, that this living self-oblation is most fully realized.

---

1. Boneham, 'Tractarian Theology', 274.

Sacrifice and the Eucharist

In the 'Lectures on Types and Prophecies', Pusey's discussion of the eucharistic sacrifice in many ways runs parallel to his handling of the atonement. Once again, he begins with Abraham; but with Abraham's tithe to Melchizedek rather than with the sacrifice of Isaac. Whereas Isaac and Melchizedek – the victim and the priest – are types of Christ, Abraham is a type of the Church. Accordingly, Christ (corresponding to Melchizedek) is the priest of the eucharistic offering, and Abraham's tribute suggests that the Church offers its sacrifice through him.[2] The 'shewbread' within the holy place foreshadowed the Eucharist, 'in that it was an "unbloody offering," accompanied with frankincense, the representation of prayer, that it was continually before the Lord, that it was offered by the whole congregation ... that it was eaten, in the holy place, and by men only who were at all events ritually holy and purified for the partaking of it – the priests', parallel to the continuous offering of bread and wine, with prayer, by the Church; and, while the table of incense told of the sacrifices by which it was hallowed on the Day of Atonement, the 'shewbread' echoed the Passover, as an offering of bread (recalling the unleavened bread) that was to be 'eaten entire', like the Passover lamb (Exod. 12.10).[3] Again, the 'meal offering' in particular – especially when accompanied by a drink offering – foreshadows the Eucharist by its very elements; and just as in the Eucharist, those elements symbolize our spiritual nourishment by God; though not, in the Old Covenant, actually conveying it. Pusey draws particular attention to Malachi's prophecy of a 'pure offering' (1.11) as foretelling the offering of the Eucharist by Gentiles, in contrast to the Jewish sacrifices at Jerusalem.[4]

However, whereas Pusey's principal type of the atonement was the ritual of the Day of Atonement, its counterpart in his discussion of the Eucharist is the Passover. While both solemnities represent liberation from death by 'similar vicarious suffering', 'the one represented humiliation, the other joy; the one the expiation of sin, the other the setting free of the sinner'.[5] But the Passover, unlike the Day of Atonement, 'partakes of a double character'; it had not only an annual celebration but also a single historic event to which the annual celebration referred, and this duality produced a slight difference in the nature of the Paschal celebration when compared to the Day of Atonement. The first Passover was, in the strictest sense, a vicarious sacrifice: the lamb was slaughtered in place of the first-born children of Israel, and through this sacrifice Israel won redemption from bondage. 'The other passovers [sic]', however, 'were also sacrifices, but rather sacrifices commemorative of a vicarious sacrifice, than in themselves strictly vicarious. Their main office was to keep in mind that first sacrifice ... Yet these subsequent Passovers were not only *feasts* but sacrifices, and "feasts upon a sacrifice."' These subsequent sacrifices were

---

2. Pusey, 'Types', 72–3.
3. Pusey, 'Types', 111.
4. Pusey, 'Types', 112–14; cf. *Minor Prophets*, 2:471–4.
5. Pusey, 'Types', 102.

'*commemorative* and representative only of a vicarious sacrifice, yet although no longer vicarious, still propitiatory, as was all sacrifice, and all shedding of blood, appointed by God'.[6] It is through this duality that the Passover prefigures the Eucharist:

> As those subsequent Passovers were commemorations of the first, so is the Lord's Supper of the death of Christ; as they were commemorative and not vicarious, so is this; as they furnished sustenance, so does this; as they yet were propitiatory to God, so is the offering of the elements, as shewing forth the death of our Redeemer and Intercessor, well pleasing to Him.[7]

Pusey emphasizes, however, that the commemoration in the Eucharist is distinct from the element of sacramental participation.

> As in the Passover, so in the Eucharist; first that whereof the sacrifice consists, in the Passover, the lamb, in the Eucharist, the bread and wine, both alike symbolic of the Body and Blood of Christ, are first offered to God. ... Then God gives them back in nourishment to His people, only to the Jews in type, to Christians in reality, to the Jews the nourishment of the body, to Christians to the strengthening and refreshing of the soul also, through the Body and Blood of Christ.[8]

This distinction, however, is perhaps better seen as clarifying two aspects of a single eucharistic movement, than as separating two discrete events: he wishes to set forth two connected and mutually dependent aspects of the eucharistic celebration, rather than to sever or homogenize them. Although Pusey laments the tendency of some Protestants to collapse the commemoration into the act of communion, he also notes that the fathers make a close link between the 'one sacrifice of the cross' and 'our daily refreshment through Christ's blood, derived from it'; while 'from their vivid perception of the relations between the several Christian truths', they 'glide imperceptibly from the mention of the one to the other, or speak of the one under the form of the other'. The root of this, he notes – quoting Ambrose – is Christ's presence in the symbols with which the commemoration is offered. 'Although Christ does not now seem to be offered, yet he is offered on earth, when the body of Christ is offered'; indeed, Christ himself makes the offering, 'inasmuch as his word', recited by the priest, 'sanctifies the sacrifice which is offered'.[9]

6. Pusey, 'Types', 102–3; emphasis Pusey's.
7. Pusey, 'Types', 103.
8. Pusey, 'Types', 104.
9. Ambrose, *Enarrationes in* xii. *Psalmos Davidicos* (Ps. 38.25), quoted in Pusey, 'Types', 107. Pusey appears to have held this doctrine into the late 1860s: in *The Minor Prophets*, he refers to celebrations of the Eucharist as 'those sacrifices ... made on our Altars, as a memorial'. Given this evidence, it is most likely that he maintained the view described here throughout his life. Nonetheless, his understanding of the eucharistic sacrifice becomes

This discussion of the Passover provides the foundation for Pusey's understanding of the Eucharist as a 'commemorative sacrifice'. This concept, however, allows for the interaction of the two main sacrificial types, because the Paschal event commemorated in the Eucharist is also the Christian Day of Atonement. This is the point at which we see the influence of Lloyd's understanding that the atonement is fulfilled in Christ's offering of his sacrifice in heaven.[10] Pusey connects this imagery from the Day of Atonement with the Passover, emphasizing that our commemoration is not only internal, but an external act before God; it is performed not only in words but symbolically, through our actions and through the eucharistic bread and wine. 'It is no small thing that we present unto God in figure, that whereof Christ our great High Priest presents the reality continually – the figure or memorials of that sacrifice, which was offered for the sins of the world.'[11] This theme is picked up in Tract 81, where, after reviewing the eucharistic allegory of the Passover, he describes the commemoration as 'offering the memorials of that same sacrifice which He, our great High-Priest, made once for all, and now being entered within the veil, unceasingly presents before the Father'.[12] Within this framework, eucharistic commemoration flows naturally into communion: 'They first offered to God His gifts, in commemoration of that His inestimable gift, and placed them on His altar here, to be received and presented on the Heavenly Altar by Him, our High Priest; and then, trusted to receive them back, conveying to them the life-giving Body and Blood.'[13] So, as baptism begins and the Eucharist nourishes the Christian life, the Christian's baptismal participation in Christ's self-offering appears to be enacted, and thereby strengthened, in the Eucharist. And, parallel to the life–death duality Pusey emphasizes in the Day of Atonement, the faithful gain life in the Eucharist through participating in Christ's offering of his death. Both 'participations', however (or more accurately, both aspects of the Christian's one participation in Christ), are mediated to us through the central idea of the commemorative sacrifice.

Supporting this, however, is Pusey's vision of union with Christ, not merely as individuals but as the Church.

---

difficult to trace in later years. *London* defends the description of the eucharistic offering as, in a limited sense, 'propitiatory', but other statements are either concise affirmations of *a* eucharistic sacrifice, shaped by political considerations and too brief for doctrinal exposition; or they are dialectical discussions of Protestant and Roman Catholic writers, which avoid direct statement of his own views. Pusey, *Minor Prophets*, 2:472; *London*, 20–36; 'Will Ye?', 26–7; *Eirenicon I*, 25–31; *Eirenicon III*, 88–90.

10. Discussed in Chapter 5 under 'The atonement and the sacrificial types'.

11. Pusey, 'Types', 106. See also *Eleven Addresses*, 57–8. It is notable that the appeal to Christ's entry into the holy place, so central to Lloyd's thought on the atonement, appears not in Pusey's direct treatment of the atonement but primarily in his eucharistic teaching.

12. Pusey, *Eucharistic Sacrifice*, 5.

13. Pusey, *Eucharistic Sacrifice*, 6.

It is not accidental that the Christian Church is called by the same as the Eucharist – the Body of Christ; for Christ dwelleth in the Church, and it visibly exhibits Him, and He imparteth Himself through the Eucharist as the outward and visible sign; and the Priest, in presenting the sacred symbols of Christ's passion, presenteth them as the tokens of God's loving-kindness to the Church, which is a part of Christ and in Christ. Where Christ is, there in a measure is His Church; the Church is to share in the sufferings of Christ, not vicariously, but as part of Him; the Church is offered and presented by Christ, to the Father. In one way, there is then a difference between the offering of the symbols of Christ's Body and of His mystical Body, the Church; in another they take place together, and may be well opposed to other sacrifices. And so in the Old Testament, the sacrificer offered himself, and his sacrifice, as supplying what was lacking in himself; so also in the New Testament not only is Christ typically offered, but the Church also.[14]

There is a careful balance to be preserved, however. Augustine, for instance,

> neither identifies the sacrifice of the Cross with that of the Altar, nor that of the members of Christ with the Head, although he speaks as one who saw them to be intimately blended together; and the fact that he would seem to have blended what one might term the two extremes of interpretation, sufficiently shews that he did in fact confound neither.

Rather, he 'does not mean so to identify these sacrifices, as to merge in the lower the mystery of the higher, but rather represents the lower as contained within the mystery of the higher'.[15] The Eucharist is not the cross, but participates in it; the cross is not the Eucharist, but contains it. The self-offering of the Church participates in, and is contained by, the self-offering of Christ. There is a paradox, that although Christ suffered vicariously *for us*, we share in his sufferings 'not vicariously, but as part of Him', through his work *in us*. Yet as Christ's work *for us* centres on the cross, and his work *in us* flows from the new life of the resurrection, ultimately we come around to the life–death duality found in the Day of Atonement. Christ offers his death for us; we offer to God our new life, through his death. 'We have offered up "ourselves, our souls and bodies," on the Altar of His Cross, as "a reasonable, holy, and living Sacrifice" unto God, to be united with His Atoning Sacrifice, and consumed by the Fire of His Love.'[16]

***

Just as Pusey's emphatic realism about Christ's presence in the Eucharist has been mistaken for the Roman Catholic doctrine of transubstantiation, so too his doctrine

---

14. Pusey, 'Types', 107–8.
15. Pusey, 'Types', 108.
16. E. B. Pusey, 'Increased Communions', in *Par. S. I*, 325, quoting the Prayer Book Communion Service's paraphrase of Rom. 12.1.

of the eucharistic sacrifice has been taken as a replication within Anglicanism of Roman Catholic doctrine. It has been shown, however, that his *rapprochement* with Rome regarding the real presence was nonetheless characterized by very 'protestant' concerns, even late in his life; and comparison with Waterland and Calvin showed the Reformed lineage evident even in Pusey's fully developed understanding of the real presence. The same pattern appears here: comparison with a classic Roman Catholic articulation of the eucharistic sacrifice shows how strongly Pusey differs from such a theoretical framework, while Waterland is again much closer.[17]

A Roman Catholic perspective from a few decades after Pusey's death is provided by Maurice de la Taille, in *The Mystery of Faith*.[18] He begins by distinguishing between sacrifice as an act of worship ('latreutic', containing elements of both thanksgiving and petition) and as an act of propitiation.[19] Propitiation, as de la Taille defines it, requires blood: the death of the victim symbolizes both the restoration of the spiritual order over the physical and the fact that the consequence of sin is death. As propitiation only becomes necessary in consequence of sin, the latreutic sense of sacrifice is primary, and its essential feature is not death, but the act of offering. Given the reality of sin, however, the propitiatory aspect of sacrifice becomes ubiquitous, and the immolation of the victim becomes inextricably linked with the offering.[20] 'The victim IS EITHER OFFERED TO BE IMMOLATED, OR IS OFFERED BY IMMOLATION, OR IS OFFERED AS IMMOLATED.'[21] This is then followed by God's acceptance of the offering – symbolized in the Old Testament by placing the sacrifice on the altar, or by its burning – and a partaking of the sacrifice, which signifies both God's answer to our prayers and our corporate fellowship with him.[22] Understood in this *schema*, Christ's

17. Cf. Calvin, *Institutes*, 4.18.10, 16. Calvin – to follow up on the discussion of his eucharistic theology in Chapter 4 – does not offer an extended comparison, because he does not accept a eucharistic sacrifice; this is primarily because, unlike Waterland (discussed below), he does not permit varying classes of sacrifice. However, he interprets 'sacrifice', in patristic discussion of the eucharist, as a kind of shorthand for 'commemoration of a sacrifice', and he also insists on a 'thank offering' which comprises the entire Christian life. While this falls short of a 'commemorative sacrifice' *by which* the Christian life is offered, it nonetheless displays a clear resemblance to the views of Waterland and Pusey discussed here.

18. De la Taille's discussion, in fact, marks the beginning of a turn in Roman Catholic thought to a position which ultimately emphasized the participation of the Eucharist in Christ's sacrifice – and which thus came to some resemblance of Pusey, although it arrives by a different route. Nonetheless, de la Taille is early enough in the twentieth century, and close enough to the beginning of this shift, to suggest Pusey's differences from Roman Catholic theology in the nineteenth century. E. L. Mascall, *Corpus Christi: Essays on the Church and the Eucharist* (London: Longmans, Green, 1953), 89–108.

19. De la Taille, *Mystery*, 1:1–10. De la Taille's definition of 'propitiation' differs substantially from Pusey's. See discussion in Chapter 5, n. 26.

20. De la Taille, *Mystery*, 1:10–11.

21. De la Taille, *Mystery*, 1:14; emphasis his.

22. De la Taille, *Mystery*, 1:15–22.

self-offering signifies 'the dedication of the human race to God and the alienation of the human race from sin', while as the perfect and highest possible offering it is 'the most effective to appease the divine majesty'.[23] Christ's sacrifice is perfect, in part, because it is voluntary, which requires that he was living when the sacrifice was made; so the suffering of his Passion, as leading to his Death, is the sacrifice, rather than the death itself; that is, Christ offers himself 'to be immolated'.[24] Both the resurrection and the ascension mark God's acceptance of Christ's sacrifice.[25] De la Taille emphasizes, however, that in order fully to be a sacrifice, there must be a clear act of offering. Although Christ's suffering and death constitute his *immolation*, the only explicit act of *offering* among the events of the Passion is in the Last Supper.[26]

Here, de la Taille finds specific references to offering in the separate mention of Christ's body and blood – symbolizing Christ's death – in the institution of the Eucharist; and especially in the statements that Christ's blood is shed 'for many', 'for the remission of sins' – which indicate a propitiatory intent. In addition, he draws an analogy with the Passover, as initiating a covenant; and with Melchizedek's offering of bread and wine, which he interprets through John 6.51-59: 'Therefore, before Christ was to give His Flesh with the bread as food, He was to give it over to death in sacrifice, for the life of the world; and He was to give it as bread.'[27] Beyond these analogies to the Old Testament, Judas's betrayal (the initiating event of the Passion) occurred at the Supper; and Jesus' High Priestly Prayer (Jn 17) links the Supper with the Passion. Christ's prayer, 'Let this cup pass from me', reflects that having offered himself in the Supper, he was from then on bound to be immolated in the Passion.[28] So, in the Last Supper there is a representative slaying of Christ, which constitutes a real offering of his future immolation.[29] As offering and immolation together form a single sacrifice, the symbolic offering of the bread and wine is united to the real offering of Christ's body and blood; the bread and wine are not merely symbolic, but actually show what they represent, and so Christ's body and blood must be truly present in the eucharistic elements, as much at the Last Supper as in the Eucharist.[30]

However, if the sacrifices of the Old Testament were offered *by* immolation, and in the Last Supper Christ offered himself *to be* immolated, in the Eucharist, Christ is offered by the Church *as* immolated, eternally God's accepted victim in heaven. In this, the Eucharist differs from Christ's offering of himself in the Passion as foretelling differs from commemoration – although, de la Taille insists, 'it is one

23. De la Taille, *Mystery*, 1:34, 36–8.
24. De la Taille, *Mystery*, 1:40–1.
25. De la Taille, *Mystery*, 1:185–201.
26. De la Taille, *Mystery*, 1:41–6.
27. De la Taille, *Mystery*, 1:51–115; quotation 110.
28. De la Taille, *Mystery*, 1:117–25.
29. De la Taille, *Mystery*, 1:51.
30. De la Taille, *Mystery*, 1:136–53.

and the same thing to offer the Body of Christ as having suffered and died in the Passion, as to offer the Passion and death of the Body; it is the same to offer Christ as Victim of a past immolation, as to offer that immolation itself'.[31] More importantly, whereas Christ is the true priest, the Church's priesthood is derived from his, and so the Passion and the Eucharist relate to each other as a principal sacrifice which has 'propitiatory and latreutic power', and a subordinate sacrifice, which applies to us the effects of that primary sacrifice.[32] The sacrificial nature of the Mass is further supported by arguments that it offers the same victim of the Passion by offering Christ; that in it, communicants partake of the same sacrificial victim; that Christ is, in heaven, an eternal victim just as he is the eternal priest; and finally, that as Christ's offering was accepted by God in the resurrection and ascension, the sanctification and future glorification imparted by communion indicate that we partake of his body.[33]

In contrast to de la Taille, Waterland's understanding of the eucharistic sacrifice relies on the distinction between material and spiritual sacrifices. This is not, as it might seem, a division between the external and internal, or the physical and the psychological. Rather, it is an expression of the distinction between type and fulfilment: the 'spiritual' is 'serving God in *newness* of *spirit*, not in the *oldness* of the *letter*'.[34] There is some tension here, however. Although the word 'spiritual' may be applied to material things (as the 'spiritual body' in 1 Cor. 15.44), the 'spiritual sacrifice' is not material, which would risk collapsing the distinction between type and antitype.[35] Rather, what is 'spiritual' pertains to God's redeeming work in the New Covenant, especially his renewing work within us and the actions that flow from it. The Eucharist is a spiritual sacrifice, which is performed outwardly, with material things; but the bread and wine themselves are not spiritual sacrifices.

This emphasis on the *action* of offering allows for a broader concept of sacrifice: all Christian acts done to God – whether of good works, prayer or self-denial – are spiritual sacrifices.[36] This does not, however, deprive the Eucharist of its central place. While the good works of Christians can be described as sacrifices of self to God in a general sense, the Eucharist is emphatically the Church's sacrifice of itself – the good works of Christians are gathered up in the Eucharist.[37]

---

31. De la Taille, *Mystery*, 2:23–4.

32. De la Taille, *Mystery*, 2:24–6.

33. De la Taille, *Mystery*, 2:93–184; cf. 1:195–201.

34. Waterland, 'Christian Sacrifice', 124; emphasis Waterland's.

35. Waterland, 'Distinctions', 267–8; cf. 'Christian Sacrifice', 143–7; 'Christ's Sacrifice', 740. Elsewhere, Waterland objects further that the analogy between the Eucharist and Old Testament grain-offerings fails in that there is no portion reserved for God; accordingly, he faults others who taught a material sacrifice of the eucharistic elements for conflating the *offering* of the elements (to be consecrated for communion) with *sacrifice*, which is a gift to God.

36. Cf. Waterland, 'Distinctions', 234–59, 276–7. Cf. 1 Sam. 15.22, 'to obey is better than sacrifice, and to hearken better than the fat of rams'.

37. Waterland, 'Distinctions', 282–4.

So, among the actions before the consecration of the bread and wine, there is the offering of alms, which gathers within the corporate offering of the Church the individual spiritual sacrifices of charity. In the prayers following the consecration, there is 'the offering up Christ's *mystical body*, the Church, or *ourselves* a part of it, as an holy, lively, reasonable *sacrifice* unto God: a sacrifice represented by the outward *signs*, and conveyed, as it were, under the *symbols* of bread and wine'.[38] The offering of the whole Church naturally includes the individual offerings of its members; in keeping with the threefold eucharistic offering just described, it seems likely that Waterland understands the Prayer Book's adjectives 'holy, lively, reasonable' to indicate the holiness and devotion of individual Christians, their charitable actions in the world, and the service of their wills to God.

The fact that the Church's offering is the offering of Christ's mystical body, however, points to the centrality of Christ's sacrifice and its eucharistic commemoration. This begins with a direct correlation between Christ's sacrifice and that of the individual Christian: his sacrifice calls us to our own, sacrificing the '*old man* with the *affections* and *lusts*' while instead living to God, together with the 'spiritual sacrifices' of prayer, praise and charitable acts.[39] While the distinction between 'new' and 'old' sacrifices is generally between the spiritual sacrifices of the new covenant and the typical sacrifices of the old, Waterland notes that Augustine particularly calls Christ's sacrifice on the cross *the* 'new' sacrifice – and so our own offerings are, in some sense, derived from that great self-offering.[40] The Eucharist, however – the Church's self-offering as the body of Christ – is also the commemoration of his singular sacrifice, '*offering to view*' before 'God, angels, and men, under certain *symbols*, the *death, passion*, or *sacrifice* of Christ', while 'pleading the merit' of Christ's sacrifice, with praise and thanksgiving, 'in behalf of ourselves and others'.[41] This commemoration, however, reflects the characteristic ambiguity of Waterland's account. Insofar as it is a *commemoration*, it is more a means of relating us to Christ's redemptive sacrifice and applying its benefits to us, than it is itself a 'proper' sacrifice, and it can be called a sacrifice only as a figure of speech. As the commemoration itself, however, is an act of faithful obedience to God, and incorporates the Church's self-offering as the body of Christ, it *is* a 'proper' sacrifice, though one of thanksgiving rather than of redemption.[42] This coincidence of the commemorative sacrifice with – and, in some sense, its incorporation within – the self-offering of the Church leads to a unity between the two sacrifices. Whereas Christ himself is the primary altar of Christian sacrifice,

> His table here below is a secondary *altar* in two views; first, on the score of our *own* sacrifices of *prayers, praises, souls*, and *bodies*, which we offer up from

---

38. Waterland, 'Christian Sacrifice', 182–3; emphasis Waterland's.
39. Waterland, 'Christ's Sacrifice', 744–5; emphasis Waterland's.
40. Waterland, 'Distinctions', 260–2.
41. Waterland, 'Christian Sacrifice', 183; emphasis Waterland's.
42. Waterland, 'Christian Sacrifice', 138–40; 'Distinctions', 284–96.

thence; secondly, as it is the *seat* of the consecrated *elements*, that is, of the *body* and *blood* of Christ, that is, of the *grand sacrifice*, symbolically represented and exhibited, and spiritually there *received*; received by and with the *signs* bearing the name of the *things*.[43]

In this union of the sacrifices of Christ and the Church, our offering is, in a sense, added to Christ's, just as in the Old Testament, grain and libations were added to the daily sacrifice of a lamb. The sacrifices we offer on earth as we plead his sacrifice are added to the sacrifice which he pleads in heaven, 'not to *heighten the value* of it, which is already infinite, but to *render ourselves capable of the benefits* of it', by uniting us to it. 'So may the *sacrifice* of Christ be *commemorated*, and *our own sacrifices* therewith *presented*, be considered as *one sacrifice* of the *head* and *members*, in union together'; and, being united to Christ's self-offering, our own is made acceptable to God.[44]

***

Waterland provides a useful comparison with Pusey, not least because there are other writers among the high churchmen and their seventeenth-century forebears who are much closer to Pusey's position. Tract 81 (for which Pusey wrote the introduction) contains several writers who use the paschal type, just as Pusey does, to explain the 'commemorative sacrifice', while Waterland himself does not; and Pusey is clearly sympathetic to the line of Anglican thought connecting the eucharistic sacrifice with the elements, which Waterland rejects.[45] What unites Pusey and Waterland, however, is what appears to be an underlying, characteristically Protestant concern to preserve the uniqueness of Christ's sacrifice, which can be observed in their conceptions of both sacrifice and the nature of eucharistic commemoration: Pusey and Waterland both distinguish firmly between the sacramental and sacrificial aspects of the Eucharist in a way de la Taille does not. These principles shape an understanding of eucharistic participation in Christ's sacrifice very different from de la Taille's.

Regarding the nature of sacrifice itself, de la Taille emphasizes the act of *offering*, while Waterland picks out the nature of sacrifice as a gift to God. Pusey, unsurprisingly, does not offer a precise definition, but his language repeats the idea of a 'gift' as well. Aside from some terminological differences, these three views can be seen, thus far, as more or less synonymous. Differences emerge, however, when a specifically propitiatory sacrifice is considered. For de la Taille, the main aspect of propitiation is bloodshed, which receives so much emphasis that it becomes

---

43. Waterland, 'Distinctions', 296; emphasis Waterland's.
44. Waterland, 'Christ's Sacrifice', 745–6; emphasis Waterland's.
45. Although Waterland himself does not pursue the paschal allegory as a means of explaining the 'commemorative sacrifice', two of his sources for this discussion do. Waterland, 'Christian Sacrifice', 134–40; cf. excerpts of Buckeridge and Brevint, in [Pusey/Harrison], *Eucharistic Sacrifice*, 83–92, 190–200.

as necessary to sacrifice as offering (even if this necessity is practical, rather than intrinsic). For both Waterland and Pusey, the bloodshed of the Old Testament sacrifices is principally a type foreshadowing Christ's death, rather than an essential feature of propitiatory sacrifice. Waterland allows some consideration of bloodshed in Christ's sacrifice, but his emphasis is rather on Christ's obedience, as sacrifice is, for him, above all an inward action or disposition, although often (and particularly on the cross) enacted outwardly. Pusey's emphasis on vicarious suffering lends his perspective a more concrete and physical flavour than Waterland's. However, his tendency to extend Christ's vicarious suffering not only through the Passion, but even as far back as the divine humility shown in the incarnation, makes Christ's death the focal and climactic act that defines his sacrificial work, rather than the sole essential element in it.[46] So, in contrast to de la Taille's entanglement of offering and immolation, both Waterland and Pusey retain a view of sacrifice emphasizing solely the act of offering, even if it is a life (or death) being offered. De la Taille's three-part definition of propitiatory sacrifice seems forced, especially as his subsequent argument on the necessity of the eucharistic presence for the efficacy of the cross has overtones of a misguided anti-Protestant polemic. By contrast, Pusey and Waterland, unburdened by the 'necessity' of immolation, are free to present the Passion as a single continuous act of self-offering, and the Eucharist as the Church's self-offering derived from it, without being forced to argue, counterintuitively, that offering *for immolation* and offering *as immolated* are identically sacrificial.

There is a further difference among the three positions as to the nature of the eucharistic commemoration. De la Taille's position rests on a strong doctrine of the real presence: Christ, the victim of the Passion, is present to be offered in the Mass; and therefore the Mass, by offering the same victim, offers the same sacrifice. In contrast, both Waterland and Pusey rely on the notion of a commemorative sacrifice, so that what is offered is not, in the strictest sense, the same as what was offered in the Passion, but participates in it.[47] The contrast between them lies in their answers to the question, what is the 'commemoration' in the Eucharist that participates in the Passion? For Waterland, the bread and wine are not 'sacrifices', and so cannot be the commemoration offered to God; the offering lies, rather, in the verbal commemoration of the prayer of consecration.[48] Pusey, on the other

---

46. Pusey, 'Christ Risen our Justification', 217; *Eleven Addresses*, 25–6; 'God with Us', 49–52. The cross *is* essential, together with the resurrection, for Pusey's understanding of *theosis*.

47. See Pusey, 'Types', 105–9. Pusey acknowledges that the real presence strengthens the significance of the eucharistic sacrifice; but in the introduction to Tract 81 he cites transubstantiation as one of two major contributing factors in late medieval distortions of a true doctrine of the eucharistic sacrifice. *Eucharistic Sacrifice*, 7–10.

48. Cf. Waterland, 'Christian Sacrifice', 123, 182–4. Waterland does not specifically state *what* in the Communion Service constitutes the commemoration, so it is conceivable that it could lie in the communion. However, the more likely candidate is the prayer of consecration, given his categorization of various offerings associated with (but not constitutive of) the eucharistic sacrifice by their position relative to it, as well as his distinction between sacrament and sacrifice.

hand, holds that the commemoration is made in the bread and wine, as symbols of Christ's Passion, and is impatient with Waterland's delicate ambiguity.[49] For both, however, this emphasis on commemorative action or symbols is closely connected to a clear distinction between the Eucharist as *sacrifice* and as *sacrament* (though both writers see these dimensions as closely related).[50] With regard to de la Taille, it is tempting to suspect that sacramental union with Christ is a distant consideration. It is probably unfair to draw too strong a conclusion from the near-omission of this element from a work specifically on the *sacrificial* aspect of the Eucharist, and he does admit (however briefly) that we partake of Christ in the Eucharist. However, one cannot help but note that a work entitled *The Mystery of Faith* identifies that 'mystery' as the sacrifice of Christ on the cross and in the Eucharist, while partaking is only mentioned as proof that there is a sacrifice we partake of.[51] In connection with this, however, it can be noted that de la Taille's structure is ultimately self-defeating. Forced to concede – despite their supposed structural identity – that an offering *after* the event of immolation is necessarily secondary to the offering leading immediately to that immolation, the eucharistic sacrifice becomes merely the means of applying the primary sacrifice. Seen through his attack on Protestants for believing only a partaking and not a true sacrifice in the Eucharist, this conclusion appears, at best, ironic.[52]

This, however, raises the question of participation. As we have seen, de la Taille describes the Eucharist as a re-offering of Christ's sacrifice; this re-offering is the means of appropriating its benefits. This structure leaves little room for participation in Christ's self-offering; and indeed, such considerations are absent from his work; the nearest topic is his extended discussion of how to compute the value of the Mass, based on how the infinite value of Christ's sacrifice presented therein is limited by the devotion of those offering it.[53] This contrasts sharply with Pusey and Waterland. Pusey holds that the eucharistic

---

49. Pusey, 'Types', 108–9; cf. Waterland, 'Christian Sacrifice', 134–40, 143–7. It should be noted that Pusey's emphasis on the bread and wine as sacrificial offerings is well within the high church tradition, despite Waterland's antipathy to the notion. Pusey's position appears to be a synthesis of the two schools Waterland describes, which emphasize, respectively, the offering of the bread and wine, and the offering of a commemoration.

50. Pusey, 'Entire Absolution I', 3–4; Waterland, 'Christian Sacrifice', 123.

51. This is not, perhaps, too surprising, when we consider that de la Taille was writing in an era when non-communicating Masses would still have been frequent within Roman Catholicism.

52. De la Taille, *Mystery*, 1:20–2; 2:24–6; cf. R. I. Wilberforce, *Eucharist*, 349. Wilberforce appears to be closer to de la Taille than Pusey is: he defines sacrifice not just as offering but as an offering which involves 'the slaughter of that which is offered'. Like Pusey, the eucharistic sacrifice is connected with Christ's intercession, but it is in virtue of the real presence and as mediated through Christ's natural body in heaven that the Church participates in Christ's sacrifice, not through a carefully defined commemorative participation (364, 389–92).

53. De la Taille, *Mystery*, 2:223–320.

sacrifice is propitiatory, but overwhelmingly because it commemoratively 'pleads the sacrifice' of Christ to the Father.[54] Waterland goes even further to maintain that, insofar as this commemorative action is propitiatory, it is *not* a sacrifice (it is pleasing to God as an act of obedience, but it is not strictly an offering); it is only a sacrifice in the sense that it is *not* propitiatory (in the sense that it is offered, it is to give thanks and praise, not to win God's favour). For both, the primary means of appropriating the benefits of the cross is receiving communion. The Eucharist, considered as a sacrifice, is therefore free to hold a different significance.

As Waterland puts it, the Eucharist is 'a *federal* rite between God and man', which therefore has both a gift from God to the Church, and a gift from the Church to God; it is both a sacrament and a sacrifice.[55] The sacrificial aspect of the Eucharist, as a gift to God, must have something mysterious about its effects; at least with regard to its effect on the congregation that participates in the offering, it pertains to their disposition. It does not add to the sacrifice of Christ, but 'renders us capable of it', or makes us able to receive it. As an act of obedience to God, the commemoration opens the hearts of the faithful to receive his grace in the sacrament; and especially as the eucharistic offering incorporates the practical faithfulness of the whole Church, it can be seen as both the preparation for and the fulfilment of God's grace. This much is Waterland's position, and this much Pusey, too, accepts – adding only a much firmer insistence on the commemorative sacrifice, as made through the symbolic materials of bread and wine.[56] For both, the intertwining of commemoration and self-oblation is rooted in the Church's baptismal union with Christ, as members of his body. In this respect, the primary difference lies in the contrast between Waterland's reticence – he only mentions this once – and Pusey's mystical fervour, where the minor sacrifices incorporated into the eucharistic offering are quickly passed over to allow a greater emphasis on our participation in Christ's offering.

---

54. For Pusey, all sacrifices offered to God are, in some sense, pleasing to him; but (parallel to other hierarchies of analogy and participation in Pusey's thought) the sacrifice of the Church *as* Christ's body, in union with and pointing towards his self-offering, is propitiatory in such a way that other offerings are not propitiatory by comparison. Compare especially with Pusey's hierarchy of sacramental participation, discussed in Chapter 2 under 'Allegory and the Sacramental Vision', and his treatment of Christian and non-Christian virtue, given in Chapter 3 under 'Holiness, sin and repentance'.

55. Waterland, 'Christian Sacrifice', 123, emphasis Waterland's. This approach (like Pusey's, which is similar) is more intuitive than attempting, with de la Taille, to make the application of Christ's work (i.e., God's gift to us) the primary effect of the Church's sacrifice to God.

56. Pusey, 'Types', 107–9.

Baptism, sacrifice and communion

As expected, Pusey's understanding of the eucharistic sacrifice points back towards baptism: the eucharistic self-offering of the Church as the Body of Christ is not only founded on the baptismal gift of union with Christ, but raises the question of whether that union itself may carry a sacrificial significance. Once more, Pusey's high church heritage and theology of communion come together within his sacramental vision to shape his treatment of the topic. Pusey adopts Waterland's theme of Christian fidelity, though he displaces it from a eucharistic to a baptismal context, which emphasizes union with Christ through the gift of the Holy Spirit. He consistently discusses baptismal fidelity, however, through the medium of sacrificial types drawn from the Old Testament; and the allegorical tapestry that he thus weaves illustrates a vision in which this same fidelity, as it expresses the pentecostal gift received in baptism, is revealed as the living sacrifice of the Christian.

While sacrifice is discussed more overtly with regard to the Eucharist, the timeline of Pusey's work suggests that his understanding of our baptismal union with Christ provides the starting point for his understanding of sacramental participation in Christ's sacrifice. The 'Types' were written in 1836, and Tract 81 was published in 1838, but it was in 1835, in Tract 68's discussion of post-baptismal sin, that we find the first reference to this idea. Contrasting Christian penitence with the ideal sanctity of the baptized, Pusey writes,

> Since we have no longer a whole burnt-offering to lay upon God's altar, let us the more diligently 'gather up the fragments which remain', and which, for His Son's sake, He wills 'not to be lost'; content, whatever the road may be, so it but end in Heaven; thankful if, although we cannot have the reward of those who have 'followed the Lamb whithersoever He goeth', we may yet be accounted but as the least in the kingdom of Heaven, or as hired servants in our Father's house.[57]

---

57. Pusey, *Baptism 1*, 79–80, referring to Jn 6.12, Rev. 14.4, Mt. 5.19 and Lk. 15.19. Taken together, these quotations and allusions suggest a deeper dimension to Pusey's theology here than occurs at the surface of the text: the broader context of the verse from Revelation includes reference to an ideal of Christian celibacy, while the reference to John 6 suggests that (per the argument of this chapter) the vocation to repentance includes its expression in the eucharistic offering, and the father's welcome of the prodigal in Luke assures the reader of God's joy in receiving penitents. *Baptism 1* predates the first of Williams's tracts on 'reserve' by roughly two years, but this effectively 'reserved' mode of writing – with deeper meanings accessible to readers who are more familiar with the biblical text and who are willing to reflect upon the allusions – both illustrates the Tractarian practice of reserve prior to its articulation in Williams's tracts, and (coming as it does in Pusey's first major contribution upon his full adherence to the Oxford Movement) suggests that for Pusey, 'reserve' only reinforced a natural tendency in his theology.

The Christian life is a 'whole burnt offering'; sin defiles the sacrifice and scatters the sacrificial fire, and the work of penitence is one of gathering up the coals and fanning them once again into flame.

In the second edition of *Baptism*, Pusey connects Christ's baptizing 'with the Holy Spirit and with fire', both to the necessity of the Passion and ascension (with their sacrificial overtones), and with the renewal of God's presence in humanity – a baptism in which Christ, 'as God, shed forth abundantly that Spirit, Which had again in His sacred person resumed His dwelling in man'.[58] Pusey's discussion draws on Exodus 40.29-34 and 2 Chronicles 7.1-2, where sacrifice is linked to the presence of God in the Tent of Meeting and in the Temple, and in the latter case (as also in 1 Kings 18.38) with the descent of fire from heaven upon the sacrifice – it is the 'burnt offering', specifically, that is consumed. If the descent of heavenly fire upon the sacrifice as a sign of God's acceptance is read allegorically of the Holy Spirit's descent in tongues of flame at Pentecost, the following interpretation emerges. Christ's self-offering – as the fulfilment of all sacrifices, and therefore not only a sin-offering, but a whole burnt offering as well – is accepted by God, in consequence of which the Holy Spirit fills his temple, the Church; and yet also, as the Church is 'in Christ', it is united to the self-offering of his humanity, and the fire of heaven descends on the faithful (the Holy Spirit, at Pentecost and in baptism) to show God's acceptance of that offering.[59]

This interpretation is reinforced by scattered statements throughout Pusey's sermons. The strongest example comes from an Easter sermon published in 1848. 'Blessed whosoever, with the incense of prayer and the oil of charity, is feeding that Sacred Flame, which descended from Heaven, and mounteth thither again.' 'Ye sought Him, not to embalm His lifeless Body, but longing to offer to Him what He will accept "as a sweet-smelling savour," yourselves, with the fragrance of good works, which, "without money and without price," ye have bought of Him.'[60] These lines reiterate the sacrificial imagery first established in the work on baptism. The descent of heavenly fire, although framed in sacrificial language, also refers to the Holy Spirit, as Pusey connects the 'Sacred Flame' with personal devotion and works of charity.[61] He also refers indirectly to the Eucharist: although the language of fire descending from heaven is specific to the burnt offering, incense

---

58. Pusey, *Baptism 2*, 243. 'Dwelling' alludes to Jn 1.14, and thence to the Tabernacle as the sign of God's presence in Israel.

59. Cf. Pusey, 'Types', 112–13. In Exod. 40.29, Moses offers not only a burnt offering but also a grain offering, which suggests eucharistic as well as baptismal implications.

60. Pusey, 'Christ Risen Our Justification', 227–8, 229–30; quoting Isa. 55.1.

61. Cf. Pusey, 'Entire Absolution II', 42. Here, the 'rekindling' of devotion and good works in repentance becomes the grounds of evangelism. The 'tokens of penitence' – earnestness, zeal against sin and longing for God – 'must first burn within, then without; first consume self as an offering to God, then burst abroad in the burning longing for his glory; first, His "Spirit of burning" [Isa. 4.4] within, then that "fire upon earth," [Lk. 12.49] which He would have "kindled"'.

and oil are the accompaniments of the grain offering (a eucharistic type), which *together* ascend as 'a sweet savour to the LORD' (Lev. 2.1-2). This bears a strong resemblance to Waterland's understanding of the eucharistic sacrifice. The descent and ascent of the heavenly flame appear to reiterate the pattern of grace shown in the incarnation and ascension: as in Christ God became man, and man was taken into God, so the gift of the Holy Spirit descends to unite us to Christ, and sanctifying us, bears the fruits of our sanctification up to heaven as we are drawn into ever closer participation in Christ. Finally, the reference to 'embalming' Christ brings in the death–life duality that forms the central point of *theosis*: dying with Christ to sin, and living to God in him. This is much the same as the previous image of descent and ascent, as Christ's death was the nadir of the incarnation's descent, and it is the resurrected Christ who ascends; in baptism, the gift of the Holy Spirit coincides with our dying to sin, while our subsequent life to God *is* the process of sanctification that is borne up as a 'sweet-smelling savour'.

Although the language is less explicitly sacrificial, the image of fire for holiness appears again in his later eucharistic sermons. So, in 1853, Pusey writes,

> This is the comfort of the penitent, the joy of the faithful, the Paradise of the holy, the Heaven of those whose conversation is in Heaven, the purity of those who long to be partakers of His holiness, the strengthening of man's heart, the renewal of the inward man, the fervour of Divine love, spiritual peace, *kindled* hope, assured faith, *burning* thankfulness, – that our Lord Jesus Christ, not in figure, but in reality, although a spiritual reality, does give Himself to us, does come to be in us.[62]

Again, in 1871, 'Prepare your souls, my sons, and so receive Him Who is your Life; He will dwell in you, and Himself will strengthen you: in darkness, He will enlighten you, for He is light … He, the living coal which the Seraph touched not with his hands, will be a living *Fire* of love within you.' And, even after sin, 'Jesus will not forsake the soul, though it has forsaken Him. Repentance will restore the forfeited grace and the union with God and Jesus. Each devout Communion will be fresh life and light and *fire* of love: each will be fresh power to love Him, and to contain His Love, yea Himself, eternally.'[63] Although the 'fire' here is Christ's eucharistic presence, not the Holy Spirit, the sacrificial portrayal of the Christian's growth in holiness remains the same. The imagery of fire appears again at the very end of his life, once more when speaking of the source of human (and especially Christian) love in God: 'Love is indeed a wonderful thing, and yet it would be more wonderful, if it were not; since love is of God, a spark out of the boundless, shoreless Ocean of His Fire of love.'[64]

62. Pusey, 'Presence of Christ', 10; emphasis mine.
63. Pusey, 'This Is My Body', 46–7; emphasis mine. The image of the coal (Isa. 6.6) for the Eucharist is derived from Ephraim Syrus. Pusey, *Fathers*, 119–31; Rowell, 'Ephraim', 113–17.
64. Pusey to Sr Clara, 22 August 1882, LBV 77.

Most of the sacrificial allusions in Pusey's work speak of this transformative, irradiating power of divine love, but there are a handful of allusions to sacrifice in his earlier *Plain Sermons*, which are of a different character. Sacrifice is here, as in his later work, something which relates to Christian holiness; but the emphasis is rather on self-denial and dying with Christ than on subsequent life in him. So, 'St. Paul … while setting forth the free grace of the Gospel, insists on the self-denial, and sacrifices, and sufferings of the Gospel.' Later, he cautions that 'we must not measure sacrifices by what seems great in the eyes of men' and insists that regardless of whether we find joy in it (though, he thinks, many will), 'every one has something to give up, as a sacrifice to God; and so every one has some cross, which he may thus take, and thus be doubly blest, both for bearing his Cross and lending to the Lord'.[65] In another sermon from the same volume, he questions contemporary standards of Christian living, asking, 'Where [is] the Gospel measure of self-denying, self-sacrificing charity?'[66] Here, 'sacrifice' is used synonymously with self-denial and suffering. But, as with the later instances we have just considered, these too are sacrifices *to God*, done for the sake of holiness.

This more austere aspect of internal sacrifice serves as a reminder that repentance, for all that it is turning *to* God in love, is also turning *away* from sin, and therefore, turning away from 'the world, the flesh, and the devil'. Pusey even goes so far as to describe life apart from God in terms of union with Satan.

> The reality of the Indwelling of the Divine Spirit in those who obey Him, throws an awful light on the reality of that of which our Lord also spake, the indwelling of the evil spirit in those who obey *him*. 'They dwell there'; a sevenfold spirit of evil as opposed to the One, but sevenfold, Spirit of Truth; so that as the souls of the saints are led by the indwelling 'Spirit', and He rules their life, exalts their senses, fills their minds, sanctifies their thoughts, is the Author of their actions, so in the souls of those who have emptied themselves of Him, Satan dwells, rules their actions, prompts their words, moves their limbs, is at last the living Death within them, filling their every part, is the spirit, whom their soul and body obey.[67]

A little later, he concludes, 'Between these two, then, lies the course of men; here only are we two selves; hereafter unity is to be restored, wholly good or wholly evil; either all to be transfigured into the glory of our Lord, or all to be debased to hell; all to be spiritual, or all carnal.' For the present, however, our carnal nature is at odds with our spiritual nature, and we are set against ourselves.[68] It is a stark choice between two kinds of life; and of the two, one must be growing, the other

---

65. Pusey, 'The Cross Borne for Us, and in Us', 2, 17.
66. Pusey, 'Victory over the World', 84.
67. Pusey, 'The Transfiguration of Our Lord the Earnest of the Christian's Glory', 231, quoting Lk. 11.26.
68. Pusey, 'The Transfiguration of Our Lord the Earnest of the Christian's Glory', 233.

dying. The stern interpretation of the Christian's internal sacrifice evident in Pusey's earlier thought should certainly be considered in light of his development and the severity evident in early Tractarian spirituality, which, however, was moderated with time. Pusey's growing emphasis on divine love is, as I have argued, a characteristic of his mature theology. Nonetheless, the primary image of the Christian life as a burnt offering predates the *Plain Sermons* by several years, and there is a logical continuity between the austerity Pusey emphasizes in those sermons, and the fervid mysticism that flowers in the 1840s.[69] It is, after all, *on the cross* that God's love shines with 'a divine tender lustre' greater even than is seen in heaven; and if the Christian life is a participation of that sacrifice, mortification of self and love for God must necessarily inhere in one another.[70]

The final passage to consider is a brief allusion to sacrifice in the *Sermons on Repentance* delivered at St Saviour's, Leeds, where Pusey opens one sermon with the image of the martyrs under the altar in Revelation 6.9. Taking up the sacrificial imagery of the passage, Pusey describes them as 'souls, under the shadow of the Altar of God, to Whom they had offered their lives a sacrifice acceptable to Him, in union with His in Whom and through Whom they suffered'.[71] But their cry, 'How long?' is a statement of longing for the final perfection and glorification of humanity in the general resurrection, which is the fulfilment of union with Christ. Again, sacrifice blends with communion. This time, however, the conjunction comes not through holiness, either as a consuming fire of divine love or as self-denial, but through actual bloodshed. Pusey does not elaborate on the image, but it suggests a connection between martyrdom and a broader conception of sacrifice. In particular, it suggests Cyprian's notion of 'white martyrdom' through asceticism, and Gregory the Great's description of this 'ascetic suffering' as a sacrificial flame – a theme which connects with Pusey's views on the Christian life (and indeed the incarnation itself) as sacrificial, even if not expressed in quite these words.[72] In Pusey's treatment, however, it is the holiness of the divine indwelling that constitutes the sacrificial flame, fed and manifested by asceticism – the flame is not asceticism itself.

As these passages show, the sacrificial language appearing in the two editions of *Baptism* is not an isolated image, used for a moment and then discarded; it is rather the foundational statement of a structural image in Pusey's thought. The ascended Christ offers himself as the new Adam in heaven; in acceptance of his offering, the fire of the Holy Spirit descends on his earthly mystical body in the

---

69. Closely related to asceticism and self-denial is Pusey's emphasis on works of mercy; these are described as sacrifices well into his maturity. Pusey, *Minor Prophets*, 1:66–8, 2:84, 240.

70. Pusey, 'Atonement', 243–4.

71. Pusey, 'Bliss of Heaven – Glory of the Body', 289.

72. Isabelle Kinnard, '*Imitatio Christi* in Christian Martyrdom and Asceticism: A Critical Dialogue', in *Asceticism and its Critics*, ed. Oliver Freiberger (Oxford: Oxford University Press, 2006), 131, 141.

waters of baptism, to transform the Church and to sanctify it. To be united to Christ in baptism is for the old self to be consumed by the fire of divinity; daily fidelity is both the means by which the Christian is refined by this fire from heaven and the choice continually to give oneself in love as a sacrificial gift to God. Indeed, the recurrence of this imagery is so frequent that this theme of sacrificial transformation can even be seen where no sacrificial language is overtly used. The water of baptism conveys the fire of the Holy Spirit; the water for which the parched soul longs (to recall Pusey's last letter to Sr Clara) is the fire of divine love. 'More love, more love, more love!' is, for Pusey, a cry of self-offering to God. It is as much the desire and fulfilment of self-sacrifice as it is the goal and realization of union with Christ, because growth in Christ *is* the sacrificial transformation by, and into, the fire of divine love.[73]

This latent sacrificial dimension of baptism provides the context for Pusey's discussion of the eucharistic sacrifice. The Eucharist is a sacrifice, both because the bread and wine are offered as a commemoration before God of Christ's sacrifice, and because that symbolic offering *by* the Church is also an offering *of* the Church, which participates in the self-offering of Christ through union with him. It was at the Last Supper that Christ, 'as a Priest, did … offer Himself without spot to God', beginning a *single* act of offering which included all that followed. And so in the Holy Communion he is received, not simply as the glorified source of life, after and (in a sense) apart from the cross; but especially as he was – and is – in that offering of himself to the Father, by and in which he is glorified and gives life to the world.[74] The earthly commemoration points to and 'pleads' the sacrifice of Christ, which is the perfect self-offering of renewed humanity, whereas the offering of the Church is imperfect, but taken up in Christ's perfection. Just as the Eucharist is both the joy of the saint and a comfort to the penitent in communion, its sacrificial dimension also shares in the eschatological tension of being in Christ through baptism, though not yet perfected in him. Moreover, as the offering of the Church, the Eucharist becomes the focal and climactic act that defines the Christian life of sacrifice. Understood in terms of *phronesis*, the liturgical act of offering, in Christ, the life of Christian fidelity increases and reinforces the fidelity of the sacrificial life-in-Christ. This connection between Christian fidelity and the eucharistic sacrifice is present as much in Pusey as in Waterland, though in Pusey it is more implicit, in keeping with the Tractarian emphasis on reserve. Nonetheless, Pusey's

---

73. Pusey to Sr Clara, 22 August 1882, LBV 77. Pusey points out that the penitent life may indeed be more acceptable to God than a life unstained by sin: 'Only be it an ardent, kindled, fiery life, which willeth not that any of its dross, any thing dead, remain unconsumed.' The sentiment is similar to a saying of Joseph of Panephysis, when asked by Abba Lot what he could do beyond his various disciplines: 'Then the old man stood up and stretched his hands towards heaven. His fingers became like ten lamps of fire and he said to him, "If you will, you can become all flame."' Pusey, 'Entire Absolution I', 54; Benedicta Ward, *Sayings of the Desert Fathers*, 103.

74. Pusey, 'Comfort', 21–2.

understanding of the eucharistic sacrifice as the focal point for the offering of the Christian life does seem to have been handed on to younger generations of Tractarians: Moberly and Charles Gore, at the end of the century, both discuss the eucharistic sacrifice in ways clearly shaped by Pusey's doctrine.[75]

The centrality of participation to the sacrificial aspect of the sacraments highlights the way in which this discussion forms a counterpart to Pusey's understanding of the atonement. Pusey relied heavily on sacrificial imagery in thinking about the atonement, and the central feature of his treatment of that doctrine is the restoration of humanity's right relationship of self-sacrificial love for God, which was realized in Christ. Seen together with his understanding of sacrifice in the Eucharist and in baptism, Christ's sacrifice *for us* in the atonement and *in us* through our sacramental participation are two sides of a single sacrificial motif, one aspect included in the larger themes of Christ's work in recapitulating and divinizing humanity. Just as Christ was righteous and obedient on our behalf that we might become righteous and obedient, and just as Christ was raised on our behalf that we might share his resurrected life, so Christ restored the sacrificial self-giving of humanity in love to God, that through the sacraments we might offer ourselves in him to God.

That Pusey would emphasize a sacrificial dimension in communion is itself of note, as the classic forms of *theosis* only emphasize death to sin and new life in Christ; in some cases participation has even been set (as indeed by Jowett, discussed in the previous chapter) in opposition to sacrifice and the atonement. Pusey is able to fuse these two approaches to soteriology, however, because of the principles of his sacramental vision: the inherent complexity of meaning and truth, the polyvalence of images which renders them capable of complex signification, and the centrality of Christ as the source, and ultimate reference, of all things. The Old Testament provides a rich network of sacrificial images, with Christ at the centre: because Christ is both the paschal lamb and the great high priest, the eucharistic commemoration of his sacrifice participates in his one eternal oblation of himself in heaven; because the Church is his body, *it* is consumed by the heavenly fire of the Holy Spirit which descends in acceptance upon that offering. Pusey navigates these connections with a creative agility, but this vision of the Christian life is not merely an exercise in the utility of his sacramental vision. It is, in fact, the resolution of his theological project and the culmination of his sacramental vision: the integration of doctrine and practice through the use of sacrificial types by which Christ himself – the archetype – illuminates the Christian life.

75. R. C. Moberly, *Ministerial Priesthood: Chapters (Preliminary to a Study of the Ordinal) on the Rationale and Meaning of Christian Priesthood*, 2nd edn (London: John Murray, 1899), 251–61; Charles Gore, *The Body of Christ: An Enquiry into the Institution and Doctrine of Holy Communion* (London: John Murray, 1901), 210–14.

Conclusion

RECLAIMING PUSEY FOR THEOLOGY

This study has argued that Pusey's theological project was driven, from the beginning, by the search for, and ultimately the development of, his sacramental vision of theology. The evidence does not support theories which propose one or more 'revolutions' in his thought. Rather, he presents a consistent, if evolving, concern to develop an alternative to a disputatious conception of theology, which saw the discipline as concerned primarily with the proof of polemical or apologetic points, and which he criticized as theologically narrow and disconnected from Christian practice. In search of an alternative, he turned to the principles of patristic allegory (and with it, an understanding of creation as participating in Christ), from which he sought to recover a renewed vision of theology. This vision is expressed in Pusey's theological use of biblical and natural types, and in his doctrinal emphasis on the gift of union with Christ, which is communicated in the sacraments. The same gift of communion, however, unites the Christian to a participation in Christ's sacrifice, which is fulfilled in the Christian life and expressed, above all, in the Eucharist, as the Church's commemorative sacrifice.

In this conception of the Christian life, Pusey appears to have resolved the original concern articulated in the *Enquiry*: his sacramental vision is thus, at least within his own theology, a success. But this study opened with a broader question of Pusey's relevance to theology today. Pusey's reputation, I argued, suffered from problems of appeal, access and scholarly interest. The first two, however, are not generally insurmountable obstacles within academia; and the foregoing study will, together with other recent work on Pusey, hopefully go some distance towards alleviating them.

The problem of Pusey's scholarly interest, however, is a more serious one: scholars will study a figure who is unappealing or obscure, as long as that individual is seen as interesting; but a person who is thought uninteresting, no matter how admirable or intellectually accessible, will remain largely unstudied. The particulars of the case for Pusey's originality and theological insight have been laid out in the preceding chapters. As this is the principal point in question, however, I wish to go beyond these particulars to outline, in broad strokes, the larger case for Pusey's place in theology, under two headings.

The first point (and the less intricate of the two) is the integrative nature of his theology, which results from his sacramental vision. This study has emphasized, throughout, the degree to which Pusey's theology is deeply rooted in the earlier high church tradition, despite the extent to which he reshapes it. His reshaping of the earlier tradition, however, puts him at a pivot point between eighteenth-century high churchmanship and later Anglo-Catholicism. Thus, while the preceding discussion has given the greatest weight to the tradition which Pusey was developing, it has also noted (albeit briefly) later instances in which Pusey foreshadowed later Anglo-Catholics – whether Farrer's emphasis on concreteness in signification, Moberly's communion-driven understanding of the atonement, or the interpretation (in both Moberly and Gore) of the eucharistic sacrifice as the corporate self-oblation of the Church-in-Christ; and of course beyond these instances there is Pusey's role as an important, though not the sole, influence in the emergence of the broader Anglo-Catholic emphases on union with Christ and the eucharistic presence. Beyond these specifically doctrinal influences, there are signs of a deeper influence, particularly in the school (including Gore and Moberly) associated with the volume *Lux Mundi*. This is not to say that Pusey's theological vision was preserved whole: Liddon was correct to observe that Gore, in his partial acceptance of biblical criticism, had abandoned Pusey's reliance on Church tradition; though he too, in flatly opposing tradition to criticism, missed some of the nuanced irony – and with it, the push to deeper principles – that had allowed Pusey's rigour as a critical scholar to coexist with his acceptance of allegory.[1] Nonetheless, both Gore and Moberly also borrow from Liddon forms of argument which derive from Pusey.[2] From a later generation,

---

1. *Lux Mundi* (1889) was a volume of essays, edited by Charles Gore, which served as a theological manifesto for a group of younger Tractarians (sometimes referred to as 'Liberal Catholics', though the term is often used more to denote a trajectory of differing positions than as a precise denominator for this group), under the heading of 'The Religion of the Incarnation'. It is best known for Gore's essay, 'The Holy Spirit and Inspiration', in which Gore (who was at the time principal of Pusey House) argued for a moderate version of *kenosis* in order to reconcile Jesus' references to the authorship of the Old Testament texts with the insights of critical scholarship. Liddon (who had played the chief part in the founding of Pusey House) was aghast, arguing that Gore's position effectively did away with Pusey's principles regarding the authority of Church tradition in interpreting the Old Testament text. Charles Gore, 'The Holy Spirit and Inspiration', in *Lux Mundi: A Series of Studies in the Religion of the Incarnation*, ed. Charles Gore, 2nd edn (New York: E. and J. B. Young, 1890), 313–62. Liddon to Gore, 26 October and 1 November 1889; and Liddon to Lord Halifax [Charles Lindley Wood], 14 January 1890, in *Lux Mundi* Papers, Pusey House.

2. Thus, following Liddon, Gore and Moberly argue for a conception of the priesthood as *expressing* the priesthood which the Church derives from its union with Christ, and that 'sacerdotalism' is only offensive because a robust, *lived* understanding of the priesthood of the whole Church has been lost. This not only draws out specific ecclesiological implications from Pusey's understanding of union with Christ but also reflects an 'inverted sacramentalism' parallel to Pusey's understanding of grace and works, and echoes his argument that 'low' views of the sacraments tended to derive from a 'low' view (and practice) of the Christian life. H. P. Liddon, 'Sacerdotalism', in *Sermons Preached before*

Michael Ramsey, in *The Gospel and the Catholic Church*, includes a passage on the German church which reads very nearly as a synopsis of the *Enquiry*, once again suggesting (though not, in this case, proving) Pusey's influence.³ These instances, taken together, make a strong case for Pusey's historical interest and importance. Beyond this historical case, however, Pusey's location *between* the old high church tradition and later Anglo-Catholicism – and thus (at some risk of oversimplifying) incorporating both broadly 'Protestant' and 'Catholic' concerns with regard to, for instance, justification, the atonement and the Eucharist – gives his theology a complexity which can challenge one-sided treatments of these topics, not only within Anglicanism (of whatever stripe) but beyond.

Beyond these demonstrations of Pusey's creativity and historical interest, however, it is possible to sketch (if not, in this space, to work out in detail) ways in which his work may have a continuing or even an increased relevance for theology in the twenty-first century. Pusey was sceptical of the claim that reason was a neutral and unprejudiced faculty; he rejected simplistic approaches to the language and meaning of Scripture, and repudiated 'progress' in favour of tradition. Each point of these rejections reflects a deep criticism of the intellectual assumptions of the 'modern' mindset, which in turn raises the question of Pusey's relation to similar critiques in our own day. Indeed, postmodern perspectives insist that reason is contextual, and favour complexity of meaning over a reductionist simplicity.⁴ Likewise, contemporary approaches to theology (whether 'postmodern' or not) share many of his concerns, even if they differ in their solutions. Recent critiques read similarly to the *Enquiry* in tracing the rise of secular philosophies to an 'epistemological crisis' fostered by theological controversy over the supposedly 'plain' meaning of Scripture, and the critical quest for the history behind the canon of Scripture has been recognized as responsible for fragmenting the canon, destroying its literal meaning and draining it of theological significance; meanwhile, the role of tradition is increasingly appreciated as transmitting communal understanding and stimulating new reflection, rather than merely perpetuating the dated (or worse, prejudiced and oppressive) ideas of the past.⁵

---

the University of Oxford, Second Series (Oxford: Rivingtons, 1879), 198–9; Charles Gore, *The Ministry of the Christian Church* (London: Rivingtons, 1889), 83–6, 338; Moberly, *Ministerial Priesthood*, 96–7. Cf. Pusey, 'Presence of Christ', 12; *Baptism 2*, 188–90.

   3. A. M. Ramsey, *The Gospel and the Catholic Church* (Peabody, MA: Hendrickson, 2009), 170–2.

   4. Kevin J. Vanhoozer, 'Theology and the Condition of Postmodernity: A Report on Knowledge (of God)', in *The Cambridge Companion to Postmodern Theology*, ed. Kevin J. Vanhoozer (Cambridge: Cambridge University Press, 2003), 8, 10–11.

   5. Kevin J. Vanhoozer, 'Scripture and Tradition', in Vanhoozer, *Postmodern Theology*, 150–5; *The Drama of Doctrine: A Canonical-Linguistic Approach to Christian Theology* (Louisville, KY: Westminster John Knox, 2005), 7–8; Alister McGrath, *Genesis of Doctrine*, 81–92, 180–5.

Beyond these broad commonalities, however, Pusey's critique and the vision of theology he subsequently recovers from the Fathers more closely resemble arguments found in the twentieth-century French *nouvelle théologie* and, at the turn of the twenty-first century, Radical Orthodoxy (itself influenced by the former). To these might be added other theologians who are outside these schools but are nonetheless informed by them (as, for example, this study has referred to Hans Boersma); but to avoid over-complicating the comparison this discussion will focus only on the two larger movements. Like Pusey, each begins with a critique of flawed approaches to theology (concerned, in part, with the dis-integration of faith and practice), which is resolved by a sacramentally oriented 'turn to the Fathers'. But it is not merely the broad outline which shows similarities: the handling of the particular points also echoes Pusey. Thus, the *nouvelle théologie* aimed to establish a 'third way' in theology between the compromised orthodoxy of neo-Thomism (together with its associated hermeneutic methods) and modernism.[6] Radical Orthodoxy begins with a critique of 'apologetic' approaches to theology which are compromised by the way in which they adopt modern philosophical categories inimical to Christianity in their quest to oppose secularism.[7] These concerns are answered by a patristic *ressourcement* which centres on the recovery of a sacramental or participatory ontology which both engages the concreteness of human thought and avoids the pitfalls of univocal theories of being and meaning. Within this framework, the *nouvelle théologie* (particularly as represented by de Lubac and Daniélou) prioritizes discussion of patristic exegesis and natural symbolism; Radical Orthodoxy, in contrast, finds in the Fathers (and especially in Augustine) a source for epistemology and cultural analysis.[8] Pusey anticipates these views in his attempt to find a 'third way' between 'orthodoxism' and rationalism, and in his rejection of a flat 'apologetic' reading of Scripture; his resulting *ressourcement* of patristic theology, as Chapter 2 has shown, focuses primarily on hermeneutics, but does so from an epistemologically driven (if unsystematic) perspective. Beyond this framework, there are further commonalities: tradition as the necessary context for theological activity, a complex understanding of truth, the priority of faith and/or the affections over reason; and, with particular respect to Radical Orthodoxy, the assertion that the only true alternative to Christianity is a pantheistic nihilism, together with an insistence on 'bodiliness' or concreteness rather than abstraction as the foundation of knowledge.[9]

6. Boersma, *Nouvelle Théologie*, 2–3, 96, 215. The *nouvelle théologie* saw Neo-Thomism as 'courting secularism', to which it was nominally opposed, in its acceptance of the division between nature and grace.

7. Smith, *Radical Orthodoxy*, 32–7.

8. Boersma, *Nouvelle Théologie*, 149–59, 171–2. Smith, *Radical Orthodoxy*, 46–7.

9. Boersma, *Nouvelle Théologie*, 109–12, 152–4, 164; Smith, *Radical Orthodoxy*, 66, 146–53, 224–9, 244–5; D. Stephen Long, 'Radical Orthodoxy', in Vanhoozer, *Postmodern Theology*, 126–7, 139–40. For Pusey's argument on pantheism as the true opponent of Christianity, see Chapter 3, under 'Baptism and regeneration'; for the relationship of Pusey's views to Radical Orthodoxy's parallel claims concerning nihilism, see Chapter 3, n. 45. The

Despite this wide range of commonalities, there are nonetheless key differences between Pusey and these later movements. Pusey would, no doubt, have some qualified reservations (for instance) with regard to Radical Orthodoxy's use of postmodern continental philosophy: he was keenly aware of the way that adopting a mode of discourse not congenial in itself to the sacramental vision of theology risks clouding one's perception of it; though he himself also, as seen in *Daniel*, flexed his considerable critical muscle precisely for the purpose of exposing higher criticism.[10] A more important difference, however, is that the *nouvelle théologie* and Radical Orthodoxy benefit from a deeper historical analysis in their critique, and greater technical clarity in their respective appropriations of the Fathers. This is in part a matter of historical development: their studies simply come later. But there is also a sense in which their discussions are in a sense second order: they seek to explain and argue, analytically, for the perspectives they set forth, and thus inevitably remain, to some extent, outside them. Pusey, on the other hand, may be less clear – but this stems in part from the fact that he *inhabits* the sacramental vision more than he speaks *about* it, which lends his theology a synthetic and even (in a sense) an experimental character.[11] Taken as a whole, however, both the broad commonalities Pusey shares with these perspectives and the differences between them suggest the possibility of a fruitful dialogue between these schools and Pusey's theology.

The most significant contrast, however, is that Pusey's 'sacramental vision' favours linguistic analysis over metaphysics. Pusey's discussion of language is, once again, strikingly avant garde: his conception of types as images in dynamic networks of signification has clear similarities to the understanding of language, in contemporary semiotic theory, as a shifting system of signs; though, for Pusey, this indicates constant growth in meaning and the complexity of 'definite' but multifaceted truth, rather than the perpetual misunderstanding and relativism emphasized by deconstructionist theories.[12] This linguistic turn of thought is, perhaps, unsurprising in a scholar who was not only an adept and intuitive linguist, but whose professorship was specifically concerned with the *language* of the Old Testament. It also, however, draws him into dialogue with a second group of perspectives which focus on the linguistic nature of theology.

---

difference noted there between Pusey's psychological framework and Radical Orthodoxy's emphasis on ontology reflect, in part, the analytic/synthetic distinction noted in the next paragraph.

10. See discussion in Chapter 1 under 'The German Enquiry and the renewal of theology'. Radical Orthodoxy sees Postmodernism as fulfilling (and thus, to an extent, exposing) the tendencies of Modernism, and uses it accordingly – much like Pusey's use of higher criticism in *Daniel*. Smith, *Radical Orthodoxy*, 67–8, 91–3, 140–2.

11. That is, his inhabiting of the sacramental vision is 'experimental', not as seeking novelty or discovery, or as flitting from one theory to the next, but as a matter of practice rather than theory.

12. Graham Ward, 'Deconstructive Theology', in Vanhoozer, *Postmodern Theology*, 78–9.

These perspectives – respectively, grammatical, narrative and dramatic accounts of theology – again begin by criticizing the problematic divide between propositional and experiential approaches to Christianity. Within these accounts, doctrine functions as a regulative grammar or story which both forms – or, in Vanhoozer's dramatic account, is literally enacted by – the Christian experience and makes sense of it.[13] Grammatical and narrative theories also incorporate an understanding of tradition as the inherited (but evolving) 'culture' which shapes, and is conveyed by, the language/narrative of the community. Vanhoozer, in contrast, emphasizes the fallibility of traditions and criticizes the cultural account of tradition as tending to relativism and lacking a robust Christological and Pneumatological emphasis. He therefore prefers to ground his account of doctrine-as-drama on the canon of Scripture, which provides a fixed text that is nonetheless capable of varied dramatic interpretations.[14]

'Orthodoxism' and 'pietism', in Pusey's *Enquiry*, are roughly analogous to 'propositional' and 'experiential' approaches to Christianity, and the necessity of an enacted or embodied faith is central to his theology. In contrast with grammatical, narrative or dramatic models, however, Pusey's sacramental vision appeals to poetry, with its high saturation of imagery – because images (as Vanhoozer says of dramas) '*show* rather than tell', and because the density and interplay of poetic images allow them to speak beyond themselves in a way dry propositions cannot – and with more inward power.[15] Tradition is, of course, central to Pusey's theology; but here his account provides a way through the debate. He acknowledges the tendency of individual traditions to degenerate through self-obsessed 'formularism'. The view of tradition connected with Pusey's understanding of consent in the Fathers, however, if seen in light of his theology of baptism, the indwelling of Christ, and the connection between sanctification and phronesis, provides the Christological and Pneumatological (and therefore non-relativistic) account of tradition which Vanhoozer finds lacking in the cultural definition. Though Pusey does not himself provide this articulation, it is possible to draw out of his theology an account of tradition as the reading (and re-reading),

---

13. George A. Lindbeck, *The Nature of Doctrine: Religion and Theology in a Postliberal Age*, 25th anniversary edn (Louisville, KY: Westminster John Knox, 2009), 18–27, 65–70; Stephen Crites, 'The Narrative Quality of Experience', in *Why Narrative? Readings in Narrative Theology*, ed. Stanley Hauerwas and L. Gregory Jones (Eugene, OR: Wipf and Stock, 1997), 85–6; Vanhoozer, *Drama*, 7–8, 16–17.

14. Vanhoozer, *Drama*, 163; 'Scripture and Tradition', in Vanhoozer, *Postmodern Theology*, 160–4.

15. Vanhoozer, *Drama*, 48, 309–10; McGrath, *Genesis*, 17–19, 67–9. Inevitably, the communication of theology is primarily *verbal* – spoken or read – and if it is to be enacted by its audience, it must first move them to do so. *Pace* Vanhoozer, a poetic account of doctrine need not be *merely* subjective; but it insists on a subjective dimension, precisely because it is that element which draws the audience into the account and moves them to action.

through history, of Christ's revelation in Scripture, by the body of Christ, with the mind of Christ.[16] This, in turn defines 'embodied faith': not merely enactment, but a living participation in the body of Christ, through penitent love and self-denial, which fans the indwelling fire of the Holy Spirit.

Pusey, then, may have greater contemporary relevance than many might at first suspect; and these brief comparisons also suggest that we may be in a better position now to understand his theology, than interpreters in the century after his death. The 'Types', which do so much to reveal these patterns in the rest of Pusey's thought, were suppressed after his death as potentially scandalous, and even during his life he was hesitant to publicize them, due to the possible reaction. Now, they fit easily within a number of hermeneutical and theoretical discussions. In addition to the comparisons in twentieth- and twenty-first-century theology discussed here, others writing on Pusey have drawn parallels with Jean Luc Marion, Yves Congar, and Rowan Williams.[17] The number of comparisons available suggests that Pusey's sacramental vision does, indeed, anticipate certain key issues in twentieth- and twenty-first-century theology, and continues to offer fruitful engagement to those who wrestle with these problems today.

Despite the recent increase in interest, however, it remains the case that Pusey has been very little studied; much more work remains to be done, both as to his role in the Oxford Movement and on him individually. With regard to his context in the Oxford Movement, this study indicates two areas for future scholarship to consider. It is true that the Oxford Movement cannot be understood without attention to its broader dimensions outside Oxford; but this approach needs a complement in correcting the unbalanced scholarly obsession with Newman.[18] The deep philosophical differences between Pusey and Newman point out the distortion introduced by understanding the Movement solely through one figure, and suggest that in the future, studies which allow greater individuality to the protagonists of the Movement might provide a deeper insight into its diversity. Similarly, Pusey's connections with the old high churchmen demonstrate the error of viewing the Tractarians through the lens of later Anglo-Catholicism. While the links between the old high church tradition and the Oxford Movement have been increasingly emphasized in more recent scholarship, Pusey's theology – including

---

16. Cf. Boersma, *Scripture as Real Presence*, 222–3. Boersma notes, with relation to the 'Types', that Pusey was concerned to set forth a Christological, rather than an historical, reading of prophecy. If the same distinction is transferred to ecclesiology, it might be observed that both the cultural-linguistic accounts of tradition, and Vanhoozer's canonical-linguistic critique, present an historical understanding of the Church and its tradition, whereas Pusey provides the framework for a Christological account of both.

17. Douglas, 'Pusey's "Lectures"', 200; McCormack, 'History', 20; Geoffrey Rowell, 'Europe and the Oxford Movement', in *The Oxford Movement: Europe and the Wider World 1830–1930*, ed. Stewart J. Brown and Peter B. Nockles (Cambridge: Cambridge University Press, 2012), 162.

18. Herring, *Oxford Movement*, 2–4.

even some observed similarities with Calvin – suggests a further argument for seeing the Catholicism of the Oxford Movement as an evolution of the Protestant heritage of the Church of England, rather than a departure from it.

Scholarship on Pusey himself is, in many ways, still in its infancy, and there are many opportunities for further research. As noted in the first chapter, a fresh and in-depth look at Pusey's development is much needed. Beyond this, however, Pusey's correspondence with Keble is extensive, offering many fruits, and the differences between him and Newman, mentioned in Chapters 1 and 2, bear further exploration. Outside strictly religious matters, Pusey's political involvements were extensive, but have gone nearly untouched, and his energetic involvement in University affairs has only received brief treatment.[19] With regard to Pusey's theology, even those topics which have been written on, here or elsewhere, are far from having been exhausted: his sacramental theology and his theology of Scripture are broad fields, and although Westhaver's study is a valuable contribution, the 'Types' is itself a rich enough document to sustain much further investigation. Pusey's ascetical theology has received less attention, but his letters of spiritual direction and his theology of repentance both merit engagement, and McCormack has suggested a study of Pusey's theology of joy.[20] Finally, Pusey's theory of 'formularism' and his views on Church unity suggest a compelling theological account of the Church and its history. His teaching on hell, however, is likely to be of only historical interest: despite the enthusiasm of Liddon (or rather, his editors), his volume on the topic has not aged well beyond the controversy for which it was written.[21]

Pusey was not the mere reactionary and grim ascetic portrayed in his caricatures. On the contrary, he was a man of ecstatic spirituality united with considerable critical ability and wise caution; though conservative, his positions were not born of mere traditionalism, but of a deep criticism of the often unexamined assumptions on which biblical and theological scholarship has 'progressed'. Yet faced with the problems his critique exposed, he went on to wrestle with these problems, and developed a vision of theology which provided him with the foundation for rich, imaginative and often subtle thought, while avoiding the pitfalls of modern assumptions. This sacramental vision was, arguably, well ahead of his time: it anticipated, and still has much to contribute to, contemporary conversations about the very nature of theology. It is time, therefore, to reclaim Pusey for theology.

---

19. Alan Livesly, 'Regius Professor of Hebrew', in Perry Butler, *Pusey Rediscovered*, 71–118; Ellis, 'University Reform', 298–331.

20. McCormack, 'History', 20–3.

21. Liddon, *Life*, 4: 344–59. Liddon died before writing the fourth volume, which was written from his notes by his editors; the opinions contained in it are likely theirs. Pusey himself thought his work on hell was 'an odd mish-mash' of material and excessively dry. Geoffrey Rowell, *Hell and the Victorians: A Study of the Nineteenth-Century Theological Controversies Concerning Punishment and the Future Life* (Oxford: Clarendon Press, 1974), 143.

BIBLIOGRAPHY

Pusey – Published works

I. Major works, sermon collections, tracts, and selected pamphlets

Works listed in original publication order, following the appendix in Liddon, *Life*, 4:395–446, except where otherwise noted.

[1828] *An Historical Enquiry into the Probable Causes of the Rationalist Character Lately Predominant in the Theology of Germany*. London: C. and J. Rivington, 1828.
[1830] *An Historical Enquiry into the Causes of the Rationalist Character Lately Predominant in the Theology of Germany. Part II. Containing an Explanation of the Views Misconceived by Mr. Rose, and Further Illustrations*. London: C. J. G. and F. Rivington, 1830.
[1833] *Remarks on the Prospective and Past Benefits of Cathedral Institutions, in the Promotion of Sound Religious Knowledge and of Clerical Education*. 2nd edn. London: Roake and Varty, 1833. Reprint, University of California Libraries.
[1834] 'Thoughts on the Benefits of the System of Fasting, Enjoined by Our Church'. TFT 18. 3rd edn. London: J. G. and F. Rivington, 1838.
[1835] 'Supplement to Tract XVIII. On the Benefits of the System of Fasting Prescribed by Our Church'. TFT 66. New edn. London: J. G. and F. Rivington, 1838.
[1835] *Scriptural Views of Holy Baptism*. TFT 67–9. London: J. G. and F. Rivington, 1836. Internet Archive.[1]
[1835] *Subscription to the Thirty-nine Articles: Questions Respectfully Addressed to Members of Convocation on the Declaration Proposed as a Substitute for the Subscription to the Thirty-nine Articles*. Oxford: J. H. Parker, 1835.
[1836] 'An Earnest Remonstrance to the Author of the Pope's Letter'. TFT 77. London: J. G. and F. Rivington, 1839.
[1838] *Testimony of Writers of the Later English Church to the Doctrine of the Eucharistic Sacrifice, with an Historical Account of the Changes Made in the Liturgy as to the Expression of that Doctrine*. TFT 81. London: Gilbert and Rivington, 1837.[2]
[1838] *The Confessions of St. Augustine*. Translated by E. B. Pusey. Everyman's Library. London: J. M. Dent, n.d. [Originally published London: J. G. and F. Rivington and Oxford: John Henry Parker as vol. 1 of the Library of the Fathers].

---

1. The publication history of this work is somewhat complex; for details, see notes at Liddon, *Life*, 4:397–8.
2. Pusey wrote the introduction; the *catena* was compiled by Benjamin Harrison. Despite the 1837 publication date listed on the first edition, the tract was in fact released in 1838. Imberg, *Authority*, 37–8.

[1839] *A Letter to the Right Rev. Father in God, Richard, Lord Bishop of Oxford, on the Tendency to Romanism Imputed to Doctrines Held of Old, as Now, in the English Church*. Oxford: J. H. Parker, 1839.

[1839] *Scriptural Views of Holy Baptism, as Established by the Consent of the Ancient Church, and Contrasted with the Systems of Modern Schools*. TFT no. 67. 4th edn. London: J. G. F. and J. Rivington, 1840. Reprint, New York: AMS Press, 1969.

[1841] *The Articles Treated on in Tract 90 Reconsidered, and Their Interpretation Vindicated in a Letter to the Rev. R. W. Jelf, D. D., Canon of Christ Church*. Oxford: John Henry Parker, 1841.

[1841] Vol. 3 of *Plain Sermons, by Contributors to the 'Tracts for the Times'* [edited by Isaac Williams and W. J. Copeland]. London: J. G. F. and J. Rivington, 1841.[3]

[1842] *A Letter to His Grace the Archbishop of Canterbury, on Some Circumstances connected with the Present Crisis in the English Church*. 3rd edn. Oxford: John Henry Parker, 1842.

[1845] *A Course of Sermons on Solemn Subjects Chiefly Bearing on Repentance and Amendment of Life*. Oxford: John Henry Parker, 1845.[4]

[1848] *Sermons during the Season from Advent to Whitsuntide* [later editions retitled *Parochial Sermons*, vol. 1, *For the Season* …]. 4th edn. Oxford: John Henry Parker, 1852.

[1849] *Marriage with a Deceased Wife's Sister Prohibited by Holy Scripture, as Understood by the Church for 1500 Years*. Oxford: John Henry Parker, 1849.

[1850] *The Church of England Leaves Her Children Free to Whom to Open Their Griefs. A Letter to the Rev. W. U. Richards, Minister of All Saints, St. Mary-le-Bone*. 2nd edn. Oxford: John Henry Parker, 1850.

[1850] *The Royal Supremacy Not an Arbitrary Authority but Limited by the Laws of the Church, of which Kings are Members*. Oxford: John Henry Parker, 1850.

[1851] *A Letter to the Right Hon. and Right Rev. the Lord Bishop of London, in Explanation of Some Statements Contained in a Letter by the Rev. W. Dodsworth*. 7th edn. Oxford: John Henry Parker, 1851.

[1853] *Parochial Sermons*. Vol. 2. 3rd edn. Oxford: John Henry Parker, 1857.

[1854] *Collegiate and Professorial Teaching and Discipline: In Answer to Professor Vaughan's Strictures, Chiefly as to the Charges against the Colleges of France and Germany*. Oxford: John Henry Parker, 1854.

[1855] *The Doctrine of the Real Presence, as Contained in the Fathers from the Death of St. John the Evangelist to the Fourth General Council*. Oxford: John Henry Parker, 1855. Reprint, Nabu.

[1857] *The Councils of the Church from the Council of Jerusalem A.D. 51, to the Council of Constantinople A.D. 381, Chiefly as to Their Constitution, but also as to Their Objects and History*. Oxford: John Henry Parker, 1857.

[1857] *The Real Presence of the Body and Blood of Our Lord Jesus Christ the Doctrine of the English Church*. Oxford: James Parker, 1869.

---

3. Republished, with some alterations, as *Parochial Sermons*. Vol. 3. Oxford: James Parker, 1873.

4. Pusey edited the collection. Of nineteen sermons, ten were his own, while the remainder were contributed by other Tractarians; all but two, however, were preached by Pusey. Liddon, 2:497.

[1859] *Nine Sermons, Preached before the University of Oxford, and Printed Chiefly between 1843–1855*. New edn. Oxford: James Parker, 1879. Reprint, Kessinger.
[1860] *The Minor Prophets*. 2 vols. New York: Funk and Wagnalls, 1888–9.[5]
[1864] *Daniel the Prophet*. 3rd edn. London: James Parker, 1869.
[1865] *The Church of England a Portion of Christ's One Holy Catholic Church, and a Means of Restoring Visible Unity. An Eirenicon, in a Letter to the Author of 'The Christian Year'*. Oxford: John Henry and James Parker, 1865.
[1865] Preface. In *Tract XC. On Certain Passages in the XXXIX Articles, by John Henry Newman, with a historical preface by the Rev. E. B. Pusey, D.D. (revised) and Catholic Subscription to the XXXIX Articles Considered in Reference to Tract XC, by the Rev. John Keble, M.A.* London: Walter Smith.
[1867] 'Introductory Essay'. In *Essays on Re-union* [edited by Frederick George Lee], 1–62. London: Gilbert and Rivington, 1867.
[1868] *Eleven Addresses during a Retreat of the Companions of the Love of Jesus, Engaged in Perpetual Intercession for the Conversion of Sinners*. Oxford: James Parker, 1868.
[1869] *First Letter to the Very Rev. J. H. Newman, D.D.* [= *Eirenicon, Part II*]. Oxford: James Parker, 1869.
[1870] *Is Healthful Reunion Impossible? A Second Letter to the Very Rev. J. H. Newman, D.D.* [= *Eirenicon, Part III*]. Oxford: James Parker, 1870. [Editions after 1876 retitled *Healthful Reunion as Conceived Possible before the Vatican Council*].
[1872] *Sermons Preached before the University of Oxford between A.D. 1859 and 1872*. Oxford: James Parker, 1872.
[1874] *Lenten Sermons, Preached Chiefly to Young Men at the Universities, between A.D. 1858–1874*. London: A. D. Innes, 1893.
[1876] *On the Clause 'And the Son,' in Regard to the Eastern Church and the Bonn Conference. A Letter to the Rev. H. P. Liddon, D.D., Ireland Professor of Exegesis, Canon of S. Paul's*. Oxford: James Parker, 1876.
[1880] *Ten Sermons Preached before the University of Oxford between 1864–1879, Now Collected into One Volume, and a Sermon Preached at the Opening of Keble College on S. Mark's Day, 1876*. Oxford: James Parker, 1880. Reprint, Kessinger.
[1880] *What Is of Faith as to Everlasting Punishment? In Reply to Dr. Farrar's Challenge in His 'Eternal Hope,' 1879*. 3rd edn. Oxford: James Parker, 1880.
[1882] *Parochial and Cathedral Sermons*. London: A.D. Innes, 1892.
[1884?] *Parochial Sermons Preached and Printed on Various Occasions, Now Collected into One Volume*. London: Walter Smith, 1884.

II. Cited Sermons

'Bliss of Heaven – Glory of the Body'. In *SR*, 289–308.
'Bliss of Heaven, "We Shall Be Like Him"'. In *SR*, 255–71.
'Bliss of Heaven, "We Shall See Him as He Is"'. In *SR*, 272–88.
'The Christian the Temple of God'. In *Par. S. I*, 344–58.
'Christ Risen Our Justification'. In *Par. S. I*, 216–31.
'The Cross Borne for Us, and in Us'. In *Pl. S.*, vol. 3, 1–18
'The Doctrine of the Atonement'. In *US II*, 232–62.

---

5. Published in six parts, 1860–77; Liddon, *Life*, 4:418.

'Entire Absolution of the Penitent'. Oxford: James Parker, 1866. In *US I*, xx + 64 pp., paginated individually.
'Entire Absolution of the Penitent. Sermon II. Judge Thyself, That Thou Be Not Judged of the Lord'. 3rd edn. Oxford: John Henry Parker, 1857. In *US I*, 46 pp., paginated individually.
'Faith'. In *Par. S. II*, 1–20.
'God's Condescending Love in Restoring Man by His Own Indwelling'. In *PCS*, 459–71.
'God Is Love'. In *Parochial Sermons … on Various Occasions*. 28 pp., paginated individually.
'God with Us'. In *Par. S. I*, 47–60.
'The Holy Eucharist a Comfort to the Penitent'. Oxford: John Henry Parker, 1843. In *US I*, viii + 93 pp., paginated individually.
'Hopes of the Penitent'. In *SR*, 237–54.
'The Incarnation, a Lesson of Humility'. In *Par. S. I*, 61–75.
'Increased Communions'. In *Par. S. I*, 309–29.
'Jesus, the Redeemer, and His Redeemed'. In *Lenten Sermons*, 421–36.
'Jesus at the Right Hand of God, the Object of Divine Worship'. In *Lenten Sermons*, 437–65.
'Justification'. Oxford, John Henry Parker, 1853. In *US I*, 50 pp., paginated individually.
'Looking unto Jesus, the Groundwork of Penitence'. In *SR*, 173–91.
'The Love of God for Us'. In *PCS*, 439–50.
'Loving Penitence'. In *SR*, 1–18.
'The Mystery of the Trinity, the Revelation of Divine Love'. In *PCS*, 493–502.
'The Presence of Christ in the Holy Eucharist'. Oxford: James Parker, 1871. In *US I*, vii + 74 pp., paginated individually.
'Progress Our Perfection'. In *SR*, 309–29.
'Prophecy, a Series of Miracles Which We Can Examine for Ourselves'. In *US II*, 53–77.
'The Resurrection of Christ, the Source, Earnest, Pattern of Ours'. In *PCS*, 451–8.
'The Sacredness of Marriage'. In *Par. S. II*, 387–94.
'This Is My Body'. Oxford: James Parker, 1871. In *US III*, 47 pp., paginated individually.
'The Transfiguration of Our Lord the Earnest of the Christian's Glory'. In *Pl. S.*, vol. 3, 223–240.
'Union with Christ Increased through Works Wrought through Him'. In *SR*, 211–36.
'The Value and Sacredness of Suffering'. In *Pl. S.*, vol. 3, 291–309.
'Victory over the World'. In *Pl. S.*, vol. 3, 74–86.
'Will Ye also Go Away?' Oxford: James Parker, 1880. In *US III*, x + 28 pp., paginated individually.

Pusey House archives

I. Liddon Bound Volumes

Maria R. Barker to Pusey (1827–8). LBV 21. Transcribed by Mary Maude Milner (hereafter MMM).
Pusey to Maria R. Barker [Pusey]. LBV 23–4. MMM.
Bishop Blomfield to Pusey. LBV 40.
Keble to Pusey, vol. 1 (1823–50). LBV 50.
Bishop Phillpotts to Pusey (1844–64). LBV 59.

Pusey to Liddon, vol. 2 (1871–9). LBV 68.
Pusey to Sr Clara [Clarissa Powell]. 3 vols (1843–82). LBV 76–8. MMM.
Keble to Pusey, vols 2–4 (1846–66). LBV 98–100. MMM.
Pusey to Keble, 7 vols (1823–66). LBV 101–7. MMM.
Pusey to Bishop Lloyd. LBV 108. Transcribed by [Catherine Lloyd?].
Pusey to Sr Clara Maria [Hole] (1874–82). LBV 125. MMM.

II. Other collections

Pusey. 'Lectures on Types and Prophecies of the Old Testament'.
Pusey Early Sermons MSS.
Pusey Papers – E. B. P. Biblical MSS
Pusey Papers – Notebooks
Lux Mundi Papers

Other primary sources, 1800–83

Acts of the Diocesan Synod, Held in the Cathedral Church of Exeter, by Henry, Lord Bishop of Exeter, on Wednesday, Thursday, and Friday, June 25, 26, 27 of the Year of Our Lord 1851. London: John Murray, 1851.

Badeley, Edward. *Substance of a Speech Delivered before the Judicial Committee of the Privy Council, on Monday the 17th and Tuesday the 18th of December, A.D. 1849, upon an Appeal in a Cause of Duplex Querela, between the Rev. George Cornelius Gorham, Clerk, Appellant, and the Right Rev. Henry, Lord Bishop of Exeter, Respondent*. London: John Murray, 1850.

Bennett, William J. E. *A Plea for Toleration in the Church of England, in a Letter to the Rev. E. B. Pusey, D.D., Regius Professor of Hebrew, and Canon of Christ Church, Oxford*. London: J. T. Hayes, 1867.

Bennett, William J. E. *A Plea for Toleration in the Church of England, in a Letter to the Rev. E. B. Pusey, D.D., Regius Professor of Hebrew, and Canon of Ch. Ch. Oxford*. 3rd edn. London: J. T. Hayes, 1868.

Declaration Concerning Confession and Absolution. London: English Church Union Office, 1873.

Essays and Reviews. 2nd edn. London: John W. Parker, 1860. Reprint, Cornell University Library.

Froude, Richard Hurrell. 'Essay on Rationalism, as Shown in the Interpretation of Scripture'. In *Remains of the Late Reverend Richard Hurrell Froude, M.A.: Fellow of Oriel College, Oxford*, edited by J. Keble and J. H. Newman, part 2, vol. 1:1–64. London: J. G. and F. Rivington, 1839.

Hansard's Parliamentary Debates. London: C. C. Hansard, 1829. n.s. 21.

Jowett, Benjamin. *The Epistles of St. Paul to the Thessalonians, Galatians and Romans: Essays and Dissertations*. Edited by Lewis Campbell. 2 vols. London: John Murray, 1894.

Jowett, Benjamin. 'On the Interpretation of Scripture'. In *Essays and Reviews*, 330–433.

Keble, John. 'Hell'. In Pusey, ed., *Sermons on Repentance*, 88–103.

Keble, John. 'National Apostasy Considered in a Sermon, Preached in St. Mary's Oxford before His Majesty's Judges of Assize on Sunday, July 14th, 1833'. London: A. R. Mowbray, 1931.
Keble, John. *On Eucharistical Adoration*. 2nd edn. Oxford: John Henry and James Parker, 1859.
Keble, John. *On the Mysticism Attributed to the Early Fathers of the Church*. TFT no. 89. London: J. G. F. and J. Rivington, 1841.
Liddon, H. P. 'Sacerdotalism'. In *Sermons Preached before the University of Oxford: Second Series, 1868–1879*, 183–202. Oxford: Rivington's, 1879.
Maltby, Edward. *Sermons*. 2 vols. London: T. Cadell, 1819–22.
Mozley, J. B. *Essays Historical and Theological*. 2 vols. New York: E. P. Dutton, 1879.
Mozley, Thomas. *Reminiscences: Chiefly of Oriel College and the Oxford Movement*. 2 vols. London: Longmans, Green, 1882.
Newman, John Henry. *Apologia pro vita sua and Six Sermons*. Edited by Frank M. Turner. New Haven, CT: Yale University Press, 2008.
Newman, John Henry. *Autobiographical Writings*. New York: Sheed and Ward, 1957.
Newman, John Henry. *An Essay in Aid of a Grammar of Assent*. Garden City, NY: Image Books, 1955.
Newman, John Henry. *An Essay on the Development of Christian Doctrine*. London: Longmans, Green, 1900.
Newman, John Henry. 'The Gospel, a Trust Committed to Us'. In *Parochial and Plain Sermons*, 389–400.
Newman, John Henry. 'The Indwelling Spirit'. In *Parochial and Plain Sermons*, 365–74.
Newman, John Henry. *Lectures on Justification*. 3rd edn. London: J. G. F. and J. Rivington, 1840. Reprint, BiblioLife.
Newman, John Henry. *The Letters and Diaries of John Henry Newman*. Edited by Gerard Tracey. Oxford: Clarendon Press, 1995.
Newman, John Henry. *A Letter to the Rev. E. B. Pusey, D.D. on His Recent Eirenicon*. London: Longmans, Green, Reader, and Dyer, 1866. Reprint, Bibliobazaar.
Newman, John Henry. 'Mysteries in Religion'. In *Parochial and Plain Sermons*, 358–64.
Newman, John Henry. *Parochial and Plain Sermons*. San Francisco: Ignatius, 1997.
Newman, John Henry. *Remarks on Certain Passages in the Thirty-Nine Articles*. TFT no. 90. 4th edn. London: J. G. F. and J. Rivington, 1841.
Palmer, William. *A Narrative of Events Connected with the Publication of the Tracts for the Times, with an Introduction and Supplement Extending to the Present Time*. London: Rivington, 1883.
Palmer, William. *Origines Liturgicae, or Antiquities of the English Ritual, and a Dissertation on Primitive Liturgies*. 2 vols. Oxford: University Press, 1832.
Palmer, William. *A Treatise on the Church of Christ: Designed Chiefly for the Use of Students in Theology*. 2 vols. 3rd edn. London: J. G. F. and J. Rivington, 1842.
Perceval, A. P. *A Collection of Papers Connected with the Theological Movement of 1833*. London: J. G. F. and J. Rivington, 1842.
[Phillpotts], Henry. *A Pastoral Letter to the Clergy of the Diocese of Exeter, on the Present State of the Church*. London: John Murray, 1851.
Rose, Hugh James. *A Letter to the Lord Bishop of London, in Reply to Mr. Pusey's Work on the Causes of Rationalism in Germany; Comprising Some Observations on Confessions of Faith, and Their Advantages*. London: C. J. G. and F. Rivington, 1829.

Rose, Hugh James. *The State of the Protestant Religion in Germany; in a Series of Discourses Preached before the University of Cambridge*. Cambridge: J. Smith, Printer to the University, 1825.
Rose, Hugh James. *The State of Protestantism in Germany, Described: Being the Substance of Four Discourses Preached before the University of Cambridge in 1825*. 2nd edn, enlarged, with appendix. London: C. J. G. and F. Rivington, 1829.
Short, Thomas Vowler. *Sermons on Some of the Fundamental Truths of Christianity*. Oxford: J. Parker, 1829.
Short, Thomas Vowler. *A Sketch of the History of the Church of England to the Revolution of 1688*. Oxford: S. Collingwood, Printer to the University, 1832.
Strauss, David Friedrich. *The Life of Jesus Critically Examined*. Translated by George Eliot. Edited by Peter C. Hodgson. 4th edn. Philadelphia: Fortress Press, 1972.
Van Mildert, William. *Sermons Preached before the Honourable Society of Lincoln's Inn, from the Year 1812 to the Year 1819*. 2 vols. Oxford: S. Collingwood, Printer to the University, 1831.
Wilberforce, Robert Isaac. *The Doctrine of Holy Baptism, with Remarks on the Rev. W. Goode's 'Effects of Infant Baptism'*. 2nd edn. London: John Murray, 1849.
Wilberforce, Robert Isaac. *The Doctrine of the Holy Eucharist*. London: John and Charles Mozley, 1853.
Wilberforce, Robert Isaac. *The Doctrine of the Incarnation of Our Lord Jesus Christ, in Its Relation to Mankind and to the Church*. London: John Murray, 1848.
Williams, Isaac. *On Reserve in Communicating Religious Knowledge*. Parts 1–3. TFT 80. London: J. G. and F. Rivington, 1838.
Williams, Isaac. *On Reserve in Communicating Religious Knowledge*. [Conclusion]. TFT 87. 2nd edn. London: J. G. F. and J. Rivington, 1840.
Williams, Rowland. 'Bunsen's Biblical Researches'. In *Essays and Reviews*, 50–93.

Works on Pusey

Published volumes, journal articles, and PhD theses primarily on Pusey. Individual essays in published volumes listed in General Bibliography.

Brown, David. 'Pusey as Consistent and Wise: Some Comparisons with Newman', *Anglican and Episcopal History*, 7 (2002): 328–49.
Butler, Perry, ed. *Pusey Rediscovered*. London: SPCK, 1983.
Calhoun, John Clay. 'Edward Bouverie Pusey's Theology of Conversion'. PhD diss., Drew University, 1993. ProQuest Dissertations and Theses.
Cobb, Peter. *Doctor Pusey*. London: Church Literature Association, 1983.
Douglas, Brian. *The Eucharistic Theology of Edward Bouverie Pusey: Sources, Context and Doctrine within the Oxford Movement and Beyond*. Leiden: Brill, 2015.
Douglas, Brian. 'Pusey and Scripture: Dead End or Fertile Ground?'. *New Blackfriars*, 101, no. 1096 (November 2020): 698–715.
Douglas, Brian. 'Pusey and Transubstantiation: An Exploration of His Thinking and Ecumenical Implications'. *New Blackfriars* 101, no. 1091 (January 2020): 85–100.
Douglas, Brian. 'Pusey, Poetry and Eucharistic Theology'. *St Mark's Review* 238 (2016): 87–105.

Douglas, Brian. 'Pusey's "Lectures on Types and Prophecies of the Old Testament": Implications for Eucharistic Theology'. *International Journal of Systematic Theology* 14 (2012): 194–216.
Douglas, Brian, and Jane Douglas. 'Pusey and the Romantic Poets: Some Links to Eucharistic Theology'. *New Blackfriars* 98, no. 1077 (2016): 539–54.
Forrester, David. *Young Doctor Pusey: A Study in Development*. London: Mowbray, 1989.
Galilee, David. 'Pusey: A Forgotten Text?'. *Theology* 78 (1975): 196–202.
Geck, Albrecht, ed. *Autorität und Glaube: Edward Bouverie Pusey und Friedrich August Gotttreu Tholuck im Briefwechsel (1825–1865)*. Göttingen: V und R Unipress, 2009.
Geck, Albrecht. 'The Concept of History in E. B. Pusey's First Enquiry into German Theology and Its German Background'. *Journal of Theological Studies*, n.s. 38 (1987): 387–408.
Geck, Albrecht. 'Friendship in Faith: Edward Bouverie Pusey und Friedrich August Gottreu Tholuck im Kampf gegen Rationalismus und Pantheismus'. *Pietismus und Neuzeit: Ein Jahrbuch des neueren Protestantismus* 27 (2001): 91–117.
Grafton, Charles Chapman. *Pusey and the Church Revival*. Milwaukee: Young Churchman, 1908.
Larsen, Timothy. 'Anglo-Catholics: E. B. Pusey and Holy Scripture'. In *A People of One Book: The Bible and the Victorians*, 11–42. Oxford: Oxford University Press, 2011.
Larsen, Timothy. 'E. B. Pusey and Holy Scripture'. *Journal of Theological Studies*, n.s. 60 (2009): 490–526.
Liddon, Henry Parry. *The Life of Edward Bouverie Pusey, Doctor of Divinity, Canon of Christ Church; Regius Professor of Hebrew in the University of Oxford*. 3rd edn. Edited by J. O. Johnston and Robert J. Wilson. 4 vols. London: Longmans, Green, 1893.
Lough, A. G. *Dr. Pusey: Restorer of the Church*. Oxford, 1981.
Matthew, H. C. G. 'Edward Bouverie Pusey: From Scholar to Tractarian'. *Journal of Theological Studies*, n.s. 32 (1981): 101–24.
Naumann, Jonathan Charles. 'The Eucharistic Theologies of Nineteenth Century Anglican and Lutheran Repristination Movements Compared'. PhD thesis, University of Glasgow, 1990. EThOS.
Prestige, Leonard. *Pusey*. London: Philip Allan, 1933.
Russell, George W. E. *Dr. Pusey*. The English Churchman's Library. London: A. R. Mowbray, [1913].
Savile, Bourchier Wrey. *Dr. Pusey: An Historic Sketch; with Some Account of the Oxford Movement during the 19th Century*. London: Longmans, Green, 1883.
Strong, Rowan, and Carol Engelhardt Herringer, eds. *Edward Bouverie Pusey and the Oxford Movement*. London: Anthem, 2012.
Trench, Maria. *The Story of Dr. Pusey's Life*. London: Longmans, Green, 1900.
Westhaver, George. 'The Living Body of the Lord: E. B. Pusey's "Types and Prophecies of the Old Testament"'. PhD thesis, University of Durham, 2012. Durham E-Theses Online.

General bibliography

Allchin, A. M. *Participation in God: A Forgotten Strand in Anglican Tradition*. Wilton, CT: Morehouse-Barlow, 1988.

Allchin, A. M. 'Pusey: The Servant of God'. In Perry Butler (ed.), *Pusey Rediscovered*, 366–90.

Allchin, A. M. 'The Theological Vision of the Oxford Movement'. In Coulson and Allchin (ed.), *Rediscovery*, 50–75.

Allchin, A. M. 'The Understanding of Unity in Tractarian Theology and Spirituality'. In Rowell (ed.), *Tradition*, 227–37.

Andrews, Robert M. 'High Church Anglicanism in the Nineteenth Century'. In Strong, *Partisan Anglicanism*, 141–64.

Anselm. *Cur Deus Homo?* In *Anselm of Canterbury: The Major Works*, edited by Brian Davies and G. R. Evans, 260–356. Oxford: Oxford University Press, 1998.

Avis, P. D. L. 'The Shaking of the Seven Hills'. *Scottish Journal of Theology* 32 (1979): 439–55.

Baker, William J. *Beyond Port and Prejudice: Charles Lloyd of Oxford, 1784–1829*. Orono: University of Maine at Orono Press, 1981.

Boersma, Hans. *Heavenly Participation: The Weaving of a Sacramental Tapestry*. Grand Rapids, MI: Eerdmans, 2011.

Boersma, Hans. *Nouvelle Théologie and Sacramental Ontology: A Return to Mystery*. Oxford: Oxford University Press, 2009.

Boersma, Hans. *Scripture as Real Presence: Sacramental Exegesis in the Early Church*. Grand Rapids, MI: Baker Academic, 2017.

Boersma, Hans. *Seeing God: The Beatific Vision in Christian Tradition*. Grand Rapids, MI: Eerdmans, 2018.

Boneham, John. 'Tractarian Theology in Verse and Sermon'. In Stewart J. Brown, Nockles, and Pereiro (ed.), *Handbook*, 271–86.

Braaten, Carl E., and Robert W. Jenson, eds. *Union with Christ: The New Finnish Interpretation of Luther*. Grand Rapids, MI: Eerdmans, 1998.

Brilioth, Yngve. *The Anglican Revival: Studies in the Oxford Movement*. London: Longmans, Green, 1933.

Brilioth, Yngve. *Eucharistic Faith and Practice Evangelical and Catholic*. Translated by A. G. Hebert. London: SPCK, 1930.

Brilioth, Yngve. *Three Lectures on Evangelicalism and the Oxford Movement*. Oxford: Oxford University Press, 1934.

Brown, David. 'Anselm on Atonement'. In *The Cambridge Companion to Anselm*, edited by Brian Davies and Brian Leftow, 279–302. Cambridge: Cambridge University Press, 2005.

Brown, Stewart J., and Peter B. Nockles, eds. *The Oxford Movement: Europe and the Wider World 1830–1930*. Cambridge: Cambridge University Press, 2012.

Brown, Stewart J., Peter B. Nockles, and James Pereiro, eds. *The Oxford Handbook of the Oxford Movement*. Oxford: Oxford University Press, 2017.

Butler, Joseph. *The Analogy of Religion, Natural and Revealed, to the Constitution and Course of Nature*. In *The Works of Bishop Butler*, edited by David E. White. Rochester, NY: University of Rochester Press, 2006. 147–314.

Calvin, Jean. *Institutes of the Christian Religion*. Edited by John T. McNeill. Translated by Ford Lewis Battles. Library of Christian Classics. London: SCM Press, 1961.

Cameron, J. M. 'Newman and the Empiricist Tradition'. In Coulson and Allchin, *Rediscovery*, 76–96.

Canlis, Julie. *Calvin's Ladder: A Spiritual Theology of Ascent and Ascension*. Grand Rapids, MI: Eerdmans, 2010.

Carter, Grayson. 'The Evangelical Background'. In Stewart J. Brown, Nockles and Pereiro, *Handbook*, 38–50.
Chadwick, Henry. 'The History of the Oxford Movement: 150 Years On'. In Wright, *Lift High the Cross*, 46–81.
Chadwick, Owen. *The Spirit of the Oxford Movement: Tractarian Essays*. Cambridge: Cambridge University Press, 1990.
Chadwick, Owen. *The Victorian Church*. 2nd edn. 2 vols. London: Adam and Charles Black, 1970.
Chapman, Mark P. *The Fantasy of Reunion: Anglicans, Catholics, and Ecumenism, 1833–1882*. Oxford: Oxford University Press, 2014.
Chapman, Mark. 'Pusey, Alexander Forbes, and the First Vatican Council'. In Strong and Herringer, *Edward Bouverie Pusey*, 115–32.
Church, R. W. *The Oxford Movement: Twelve Years, 1833–1845*. London: Macmillan, 1891.
Cobb, Peter G. 'Leader of the Anglo-Catholics?'. In Perry Butler, *Pusey Rediscovered*, 349–65.
Cocksworth, Christopher J. *Evangelical Eucharistic Though in the Church of England*. Cambridge: Cambridge University Press, 1993.
Cocksworth, Christopher. 'The Presence of Christ in the Eucharist and the Formularies of the Church of England', *Journal of Ecumenical Studies* 35, no. 2 (1998), 197–209.
Coulson, John and A. M. Allchin, eds. *The Rediscovery of Newman*. London: Sheed and Ward, 1967.
Crites, Stephen. 'The Narrative Quality of Experience'. In Hauerwas and Jones, *Narrative*, 65–88.
Crouse, Robert D. '"Deepened by the Study of the Fathers": The Oxford Movement, Dr. Pusey, and Patristic Scholarship', *Dionysius* 7 (1983): 137–47.
Cummings, Owen F. *Eucharistic Doctors: A Theological History*. Mahwah, NJ: Paulist Press, 2005.
Denison, Keith. 'Dr Pusey as Confessor and Spiritual Director'. In Perry Butler, *Pusey Rediscovered*, 210–30.
Driver, S. R. *The Book of Daniel*. The Cambridge Bible for Schools and Colleges. Cambridge: University Press, 1900.
Dudley, Martin, and Geoffrey Rowell, eds. *Confession and Absolution*. Collegeville, MN: Liturgical Press, 1990.
Ellis, Ieuan. 'Pusey and University Reform'. In Perry Butler, *Pusey Rediscovered*, 298–331.
Farrer, Austin. *The Glass of Vision*. Westminster: Dacre Press, 1948.
Faught, C. Brad. *The Oxford Movement: A Thematic History of the Tractarians and Their Times*. University Park: Pennsylvania State University Press, 2003.
Ffoulkes, E. S. *A History of the Church of S. Mary the Virgin Oxford, the University Church: From Domesday to the Installation of the Late Duke of Wellington Chancellor of the University*. London: Longmans, Green, 1892.
Ford, David F. 'System, Story, Performance: A Proposal about the Role of Narrative in Christian Systematic Theology'. In Hauerwas and Jones, *Narrative*, 191–215.
Forrester, David W. F. 'Dr. Pusey's Marriage'. In Perry Butler, *Pusey Rediscovered*, 119–38.
Frappell, Leighton. '"Science" in the Service of Orthodoxy: The Early Intellectual Development of E. B. Pusey'. In Perry Butler, *Pusey Rediscovered*, 1–33.
Garcia, Mark A. *Life in Christ: Union with Christ and Twofold Grace in Calvin's Theology*. Eugene, OR: Wipf and Stock, 2008.

Geck, Albrecht. 'From Modern-Orthodox Protestantism to Anglo-Catholicism: An Enquiry into the Probable Causes of the Revolution in Pusey's Theology'. In Strong and Herringer, *Edward Bouverie Pusey*, 49–66.

Geck, Albrecht. 'Pusey, Tholuck, and the Reception of the Oxford Movement in Germany'. In Stewart J. Brown and Nockles, *Oxford Movement*, 168–84.

Gore, Charles. *The Basis of Anglican Fellowship in Faith and Organization*. London: A. R. Mowbray, 1914.

Gore, Charles. *The Body of Christ: An Enquiry into the Institution and Doctrine of Holy Communion*. London: John Murray, 1901.

Gore, Charles. 'The Holy Spirit and Inspiration'. In *Lux Mundi: A Series of Studies in the Religion of the Incarnation*, edited by Charles Gore, 315–62. 2nd edn. New York: E. and J. B. Young, 1890.

Gore, Charles. *The Ministry of the Christian Church* [= *The Church and the Ministry*]. London: Rivingtons, 1889.

Gorringe, Timothy. *God's Just Vengeance: Crime, Violence and the Rhetoric of Salvation*. Cambridge: Cambridge University Press, 1996.

Greenacre, Roger. Preface to Dudley and Rowell, *Confession*, ix–xii.

Greenfield, Robert Harvie. 'Such a Friend to the Pope'. In Perry Butler, *Pusey Rediscovered*, 162–84.

Gregory Nazianzen. 'Epistle to Cledonius the Priest against Apollinarius'. In Philip Schaff and Henry Wace, eds. *Nicene and Post-Nicene Fathers*. 2nd series, vol. 7:439–43. Peabody, MA: Hendrickson, 1994. Christian Classics Ethereal Library.

Grensted, L. W. *A Short History of the Doctrine of the Atonement*. Manchester: Manchester University Press, 1920.

Härdelin, Alf. 'The Sacraments in the Tractarian Spiritual Universe'. In Rowell, *Tradition*, 78–95.

Härdelin, Alf. *The Tractarian Understanding of the Eucharist*. Uppsala: Almquist & Wiksells, 1965.

Hauerwas, Stanley, and L. Gregory Jones, eds. *Why Narrative? Readings in Narrative Theology*. Eugene, OR: Wipf and Stock, 1997.

Heen, Erik M., and Philip D. W. Krey, eds. *Hebrews*. Ancient Christian Commentary on Scripture, edited by Thomas C. Oden, New Testament 10. Downers Grove, IL: InterVarsity Press, 2005.

Herring, George. *What Was the Oxford Movement?* London: Continuum, 2002.

Herringer, Carol Engelhardt. 'Pusey's Eucharistic Doctrine'. In Strong and Herringer, *Edward Bouverie Pusey*, 91–113.

Hilton, Boyd. *The Age of Atonement: The Influence of Evangelicalism on Social and Economic Thought 1785–1865*. Oxford: Oxford University Press, 1988.

Holmes, Stephen R. *The Wondrous Cross: Atonement and Penal Substitution in the Bible and History*. London: Paternoster, 2007.

Holloway, Richard. 'Social and Political Implications of the Oxford Movement'. In Wright, *Lift High the Cross*, 30–45.

'An Homily Wherein Is Declared That Common Prayer and Sacraments Ought to Be Ministered in a Tongue That Is Understood of the Hearers'. In *Certain Sermons, or Homilies, Appointed to be Read in Churches in the Time of the Late Queen Elizabeth, of Famous Memory*, 325–38. London: Prayer-Book and Homily Society, 1852.

Hooker, Richard. *Of the Laws of Ecclesiastical Polity*. In *The Works of that Learned and Judicious Divine Mr. Richard Hooker*, edited by John Keble, 1:121–3:468. 7th edn. Oxford: Clarendon Press, 1888.
Imberg, Rune. *In Quest of Authority: The 'Tracts for the Times' and the Development of the Tractarian Leaders, 1833–41*. Lund: Lund University Press, 1987.
Jasper, David. 'Pusey's "Lectures on Types and Prophecies of the Old Testament"'. In Perry Butler, *Pusey Rediscovered*, 51–70.
Jones, William. *A Course of Lectures on the Figurative Language of the Holy Scripture, and the Interpretation of It from Scripture Itself*. London: J. F. and C. Rivington, 1787.
Jones, William. *Sermons on Various Subjects and Occasions*. Edited by William Henry Walker. 2 vols. London: C. J. G. and F. Rivington, 1830.
Jupp, Roger. '"Nurseries of a Learned Clergy": Pusey and the Defence of Cathedrals'. In Perry Butler, *Pusey Rediscovered*, 139–61.
Kinnard, Isabelle. '*Imitatio Christi* in Christian Martyrdom and Asceticism: A Critical Dialogue'. In *Asceticism and Its Critics*, edited by Oliver Freiberger, 131–52. Oxford: Oxford University Press, 2006.
Lakoff, George, and Mark Johnson. *Metaphors We Live By*. With a new afterword. Chicago: University of Chicago Press, 2003.
Laud, William. 'The Answer of the Most Reverend Father in God, William, Lord Archbishop of Canterbury, to the Speech of the Lord Say and Seal, Touching the Liturgy'. In *Works*, 6:83–146.
Laud, William. *A Relation of the Conference between William Laud, Late Archbishop of Canterbury, and Mr. Fisher the Jesuit, by the Command of King James, of Ever Blessed Memory*. Vol. 2 of *Works*.
Laud, William. *The Works of the Most Reverend Father in God, William Laud, D.D., Sometime Archbishop of Canterbury*. 6 vols. Oxford: John Henry Parker, 1847–57.
Levis, R. Barry. 'Defining the Church: Pusey's Ecclesiology and Its Eighteenth-Century Antecedents'. In Strong and Herringer, *Edward Bouverie Pusey*, 67–89.
Lindbeck, George A. *The Nature of Doctrine: Religion and Theology in a Postliberal Age*. 25th anniversary edn. Louisville, KY: Westminster John Knox, 2009.
Livesley, Alan. 'Regius Professor of Hebrew'. In Perry Butler, *Pusey Rediscovered*, 71–118.
Long, D. Stephen. 'Radical Orthodoxy'. In Vanhoozer, *Postmodern Theology*, 126–45.
Louth, Andrew. *Discerning the Mystery: An Essay on the Nature of Theology*. Oxford: Oxford University Press, 1983.
Louth, Andrew. 'The Nature of Theological Understanding: Some parallels between Newman and Gadamer'. In Rowell, *Tradition*, 96–109.
Louth, Andrew. 'The Oxford Movement, the Fathers, and the Bible'. *Sobornost* 6 (1984): 30–45.
Lubac, Henri de. *Medieval Exegesis: The Four Senses of Scripture*. 3 vols. Trans. Mark Sebanc and E. M. Macierowski. Grand Rapids, MI: Eerdmans, 1998–2009.
Lyte, Maxwell. *A History of Eton College (1440–1910)*. 4th edn. London: Macmillan, 1911.
MacCulloch, Diarmaid. 'The Latitude of the Church of England'. In *Religion and Politics in Post-Reformation England*, edited by Kenneth Fincham and Peter Lake, 41–59. Woodbridge, Suffolk: Boydell, 2006.
Mackean, W. H. *The Eucharistic Doctrine of the Oxford Movement: A Critical Survey*. London: Putnam, 1933.
Mackley, Robert. 'Dr Pusey and the SSC'. In *In This Sign Conquer: A History of the Society of the Holy Cross 1855–2005*, edited by William Davage, 54–62. London: Continuum, 2006.
Macnab, K. E. 'Editing Liddon: From Biography to Hagiography?'. In Strong and Herringer, *Edward Bouverie Pusey*, 31–48.

Macquarrie, John. 'Theological Implications of the Oxford Movement'. In Wright, *Lift High the Cross*, 13–29.
Macy, Gary. *The Banquet's Wisdom: A Short History of the Theologies of the Lord's Supper*. New York: Paulist Press, 1992.
Macy, Gary. *The Theologies of the Eucharist in the Early Scholastic Period: A Study of the Salvific Function of the Sacrament According to the Theologians c. 1080–1220*. Oxford: Clarendon Press, 1984.
Mascall, E. L. *Corpus Christi: Essays on the Church and the Eucharist*. London: Longmans, Green, 1953.
McAdoo, H. R. *Anglicans and Tradition and the Ordination of Women*. Norwich: Canterbury Press, 1997.
McCormack, Ian. 'The History of the History of Pusey'. In Strong and Herringer, *Edward Bouverie Pusey*, 13–30.
McDonnell, Kilian. *John Calvin, the Church, and the Eucharist*. Princeton, NJ: Princeton University Press, 1967.
McGrath, Alister E. *Iustitia Dei: A History of the Christian Doctrine of Justification*. Third edn. Cambridge: Cambridge University Press, 2005.
McGrath, Alister E. *The Genesis of Doctrine: A Study in the Foundation of Doctrinal Criticism*. Grand Rapids, MI: Eerdmans, 1997.
McGrath, Francis. *John Henry Newman: Universal Revelation*. Macon, GA: Mercer University Press, 1997.
Moberly, Robert Campbell. *Atonement and Personality*. New York: Longmans, Green, 1906.
Moberly, Robert Campbell. *Ministerial Priesthood: Chapters (Preliminary to a Study of the Ordinal) on the Rationale and Meaning of Christian Priesthood*. 2nd edn. London: John Murray, 1899.
Morrill, John. *Stuart Britain: A Very Short Introduction*. Oxford: Oxford University Press, 2000.
Morris, Jeremy. *The High Church Revival in the Church of England: Arguments and Identities*. Leiden: Brill, 2016.
Murray, Scott R. 'Luther in Newman's "Lectures on Justification"'. *Concordia Theological Quarterly* 54 (1990): 155–78.
Newsome, David. 'Justification and Sanctification: Newman and the Evangelicals'. *Journal of Theological Studies*, n.s. 15 (1964): 32–53.
Nockles, Peter. 'The Oxford Movement: Historical Background 1780–1833'. In Rowell, *Tradition*, 24–50.
Nockles, Peter. *The Oxford Movement in Context: Anglican High Churchmanship 1760–1857*. Cambridge: Cambridge University Press, 1994.
Nockles, Peter. 'Pusey and the Question of Church and State'. In Perry Butler, *Pusey Rediscovered*, 255–97.
O'Donnell, Gabriel. 'The Spirituality of E. B. Pusey'. In Butler, *Pusey Rediscovered*, 231–54.
Parker, Kenneth L. 'Tractarian Visions of History'. In Stewart J. Brown, Nockles and Pereiro, *Handbook*, 151–65.
Pelikan, Jaroslav. *The Christian Tradition*. 5 vols. Chicago: University of Chicago Press, 1971.
Pereiro, James. '"A Cloud of Witnesses": Tractarians and Tractarian Ventures'. In Stewart J. Brown, Nockles and Pereiro, *Handbook*, 111–22.
Pereiro, James. *'Ethos' and the Oxford Movement: At the Heart of Tractarianism*. Oxford: Oxford University Press, 2008.

Pereiro, James. 'The Oxford Movement and Anglo-Catholicism'. In Strong, *Partisan Anglicanism*, 187–211.
Pereiro, James. 'The Oxford Movement's Theory of Religious Knowledge'. In Stewart J. Brown, Nockles, and Pereiro, *Handbook*, 185–99.
Perry, John F. 'Newman's Treatment of Luther in the Lectures on Justification'. *Journal of Ecumenical Studies* 36 (1999): 303–17.
Pickering, W. S. F. 'Anglo-Catholicism: Some Sociological Observations'. In Rowell, *Tradition*, 153–72.
Prickett, Stephen. *Romanticism and Religion: The Tradition of Coleridge and Wordsworth in the Victorian Church*. Cambridge: Cambridge University Press, 1976.
Prickett, Stephen. 'Tractarianism and the Lake Poets'. In Stewart J. Brown, Nockles and Pereiro, *Handbook*, 67–78.
Ramsey, A. M. *The Gospel and the Catholic Church*. Peabody, MA: Hendrickson, 2009.
Rowell, Geoffrey. 'The Anglican Tradition: From the Reformation to the Oxford Movement'. In Dudley and Rowell, *Confession*, 91–119.
Rowell, Geoffrey. 'Europe and the Oxford Movement'. In Stewart J. Brown and Nockles, *Oxford Movement*, 153–67.
Rowell, Geoffrey. *Hell and the Victorians: A Study of the Nineteenth-Century Theological Controversies Concerning Eternal Punishment and the Future Life*. Oxford: Clarendon Press, 1974.
Rowell, Geoffrey. '"Making [the] Church of England Poetical": Ephraim and the Oxford Movement'. *Hugoye* 2 (1999): 111–29.
Rowell, Geoffrey, ed. *Tradition Renewed: The Oxford Movement Conference Papers*. Allison Park, PA: Pickwick, 1986.
Rowell, Geoffrey. *The Vision Glorious: Themes and Personalities of the Catholic Revival in Anglicanism*. Oxford: Oxford University Press, 1983.
Saward, John. *Perfect Fools: Folly for Christ's Sake in Catholic and Orthodox Spirituality*. Oxford: Oxford University Press, 1980.
Scupoli, Lorenzo. *The Spiritual Combat*. Mesa, AZ: Scriptoria, 2009.
Seitz, Christopher. *Figured Out: Typology and Providence in Christian Scripture*. Louisville, KY: Westminster John Knox, 2001.
Selby, Robin C. *The Principle of Reserve in the Writings of John Henry Cardinal Newman*. Oxford: Oxford University Press, 1975.
Sharp, Richard. '"The Communion of the Primitive Church"? High Churchmen in England *c*. 1710–1760'. In Stewart J. Brown, Nockles and Pereiro, *Handbook*, 23–37.
Sharp, Richard. 'New Perspectives on the High Church Tradition: Historical Background 1730–1780'. In Rowell, *Tradition*, 4–23.
Sheridan, Thomas L. 'Newman and Luther on Justification'. *Journal of Ecumenical Studies* 38 (2001): 217–45.
Skinner, S. A. *Tractarians and the 'Condition of England': The Social and Political Thought of the Oxford Movement*. Oxford: Oxford University Press, 2004.
Smith, James K. A. *Introducing Radical Orthodoxy: Mapping a Post-Secular Theology*. Grand Rapids, MI: Baker Academic, 2004.
Soloway, R. A. *Prelates and People: Ecclesiastical Thought in England 1783–1852*. London: Routledge and Kegan Paul, 1969.
Soskice, Janet Martin. *Metaphor and Religious Language*. Oxford: Clarendon Press, 1985.
Steinmetz, David. *Taking the Long View*. Oxford: Oxford University Press, 2011.
Strange, Roderick. 'Reflections on a Controversy: Newman and Pusey's "Eirenicon"'. In Perry Butler, *Pusey Rediscovered*, 332–48.

Strong, Rowan, ed. *Partisan Anglicanism and Its Global Expansion, 1829–c. 1914*. Vol. 3 of *The Oxford History of Anglicanism*, edited by Rowan Strong. Oxford: Oxford University Press, 2017.
Strong, Rowan. 'Pusey and the Scottish Episcopal Church: Tractarian Diversity and Divergence'. In Strong and Herringer, *Edward Bouverie Pusey*, 133–48.
Taille, Maurice de la. *The Mystery of Faith: Regarding the Most August Sacrament and Sacrifice of the Body and Blood of Christ*. 2 vols. Translated [by Joseph Carroll and P. J. Dalton]. New York: Sheed and Ward, 1940–50.
Teale, Ruth. 'Dr Pusey and the Church Overseas'. In Perry Butler, *Pusey Rediscovered*, 185–209.
Tertullian. *On Repentance*. In *Ante-Nicene Fathers*, edited by Alexander Roberts, James Donaldson and A. Cleveland Coxe, 3:657–66. Peabody, MA: Hendrickson, 1994. Christian Classics Ethereal Library.
Toon, Peter. 'Anglicanism in Popish Dress'. In Rowell, *Tradition*, 173–84.
Toon, Peter. *Evangelical Theology 1833–1856: A Response to Tractarianism*. Atlanta, GA: John Knox, 1979.
Torrance, Alan J. *Persons in Communion*. Edinburgh: T&T Clark, 1996.
Vanhoozer, Kevin J., ed. *The Cambridge Companion to Postmodern Theology*. Cambridge: Cambridge University Press, 2003.
Vanhoozer, Kevin J. *The Drama of Doctrine: A Canonical-Linguistic Approach to Christian Theology*. Louisville, KY: Westminster John Knox, 2005.
Vanhoozer, Kevin J. 'Scripture and Tradition'. In Vanhoozer, *Postmodern Theology*, 149–69.
Vanhoozer, Kevin J. 'Theology and the Condition of Postmodernity: A Report on Knowledge (of God)'. In Vanhoozer, *Postmodern Theology*, 3–25.
Varley, E. A. *The Last of the Prince Bishops: William Van Mildert and the High Church Movement of the Early Nineteenth Century*. Cambridge: Cambridge University Press, 1992.
Wakefield, Gordon S. '"A Mystical Substitute for the Glorious Gospel"? A Methodist Critique of Tractarianism'. In Rowell, *Tradition*, 185–98.
Ward, Benedicta, trans. *The Sayings of the Desert Fathers: The Alphabetical Collection*. Kalamazoo: Cistercian, 1975.
Ward, Benedicta. 'A Tractarian Inheritance: The Religious Life in a Patristic Perspective'. In Rowell, *Tradition*, 215–25.
Ward, Graham. 'Deconstructive Theology'. In Vanhoozer, *Postmodern Theology*, 76–91.
Warner, Martin. *Philosophical Finesse: Studies in the Art of Rational Persuasion*. Oxford: Oxford University Press, 1989.
Waterland, Daniel. 'The Christian Sacrifice Explained'. In *Works*, 5:121–84.
Waterland, Daniel. 'Christ's Sacrifice of Himself Explained; and Man's Duty to Offer Spiritual Sacrifice Inferred and Recommended'. In *Works*, 5:737–46.
Waterland, Daniel. 'Distinctions of Sacrifice'. In *Works*, 5:231–96.
Waterland, Daniel. 'Regeneration Stated and Explained According to Scripture and Antiquity, in a Discourse on Titus III. 4, 5, 6'. In *Works*, 4:425–58.
Waterland, Daniel. *A Review of the Doctrine of the Eucharist, as Laid Down in Scripture and Antiquity*. In *Works*, 4:459–802.
Waterland, Daniel. 'The Sacramental Part of the Eucharist Explained, in a Charge delivered in part to the Clergy of Middlesex at the Easter Visitation, 1739'. In *Works*, 5:185–230.
Waterland, Daniel. 'A Summary View of the Doctrine of Justification'. In *Works*, 6:1–39.

Waterland, Daniel. *The Works of the Rev. Daniel Waterland, D.D., Formerly Master of Magdalene College, Cambridge, Canon of Windsor, and Archdeacon of Middlesex.* Edited by William Van Mildert. 3rd edn. 6 vols. Oxford: University Press, 1856.

Weil, Louis. 'The Tractarian Liturgical Inheritance Re-assessed'. In Rowell, *Tradition*, 110–19.

Westhaver, George. 'Mysticism and Sacramentalism in the Oxford Movement'. In Stewart J. Brown, Nockles, and Pereiro, *Handbook*, 255–270.

William of St. Thierry. *The Golden Epistle of Abbot William of St. Thierry.* Translated by Walter Shewring. London: Sheed and Ward, 1973.

Wright, J. Robert, ed. *Lift High the Cross: The Oxford Movement Sesquicentennial.* New York: Forward Movement Publications, 1983.

INDEX

absolution 22, 24, 26–7, 86–8, 115, 117
Allchin, A. M. 3, 9
allegory (hermeneutic) 59–62, 90–2, 120, 129, 167, 187, 190
   complexity allowed by 58, 153, 155–6, 165
   and creation 70–1, 81
   integrating faith and life 48, 54, 62–4, 88–9
   see also imagery, language, Scripture, types
analogy 58 n.12, 71–2, 81, 179 n.54
Anglo-Catholicism 4, 6, 11, 50, 119, 123–4, 142 n.112, 188–9, 193–4
Anselm 9, 150, 152–3, 158–61
Articles of Religion 45–6, 75, 127–8, 140–1; *see also* doctrine
asceticism; *see* self-denial
atonement 66, 101, 149–51, 153–5, 157, 163–5, 170
   moral theory of 150, 163, 165
   penal theory of 150–1, 155
   rectoral theory of 150–1, 155, 160
   sacrificial model for (*see* Day of Atonement, sacrifice, types: sacrificial)
   satisfaction 150–3, 155, 158–63
Augustine 32, 59, 69 n.64, 75, 77 n.102, 98 n.45, 102 n.64, 113 n.116, 171, 175, 190

baptism 87–8, 96, 101, 110, 119, 130, 192
   and communion 92–4, 112–15, 118–20, 135
   and Eucharist 118–20, 137
   and holiness 89, 94, 145
   as removing sin 23, 114
   and sacrifice 170, 180–2, 184–6
   types of 90–1, 119
   unworthy receiving of 94–6
   see also absolution, communion, holiness, justification, sin: post-baptismal, regeneration, repentance
beatific vision 106–7, 122, 161 n.42
bishops; *see* episcopacy
Blomfield, Charles James 27, 31, 43, 152, 163
body and blood of Christ
   'coexistence' with eucharistic elements 130–2, 141, 146–7
   concomitance of 121
   in heaven 126–7, 132–4, 136, 138, 147, 155
   see also Eucharist, real presence
body, human 106–7, 121–2, 183–4, 186
Boersma, Hans 3, 63 n.31, 77, 190, 193 n.16
Brilioth, Yngve 4, 98
Brown, David 2, 11, 83 n.128
Butler, Joseph 65–6, 156 n.26

Calhoun, John Clay 2, 4, 96–7
Calvin, Jean 124–5, 128–9, 194
   baptism 90 n.2
   eucharistic sacrifice 172 n.17
   real presence 125–7, 134 n.75, 135–6, 138–9, 142–6
Calvinism 90 n.2, 124–5, 130
Chadwick, Owen 6, 10
Chapman, Mark 2, 83 n.128
Charity; *see* love
Christian life 40, 47–8, 53, 63, 89, 93, 108, 110, 167, 179–87
   and faith 40, 47–9, 53, 63, 149, 186–7, 190, 192–3 (*see also* faith, *phronesis*)
   growth 64–8, 77, 86, 92, 94, 118, 120, 141–2, 182, 185 (see also *phronesis*)
   see also holiness, repentance, self-oblation

Church 43–5, 157, 164, 168, 170–1, 179, 181, 184–6, 193
  faith of 77, 101
  holiness of 123, 157
  unity of 108, 194
Church of England 23, 29–30, 32, 74, 128 n.46, 147, 152, 194
  catholicity of 35, 43–4, 108
  communion 10, 68, 86–7, 106, 164–5, 187–8, 192
    baptismal 34, 63, 77, 91–4, 99, 101–2, 104–5, 112–13, 120–1, 135, 180, 182
    eucharistic 119–21, 123, 126–32, 134–8, 141–2, 144, 146–7, 178–9
    and holiness 64, 66, 89, 108–9, 116–19, 167, 174
    and longing for God 97–9, 122
    and sacrifice 157–63, 167, 170–1
    spiritual 134–5, 137–8, 144
  concreteness 69–70, 72, 84–5, 89, 132, 190; *see also* allegory, creation, incarnation, sacraments
  confession 19, 22–4, 26–7, 36, 114–15
  consent (consensus), patristic 76–7, 80
    vs. systems 76
    see also tradition
Council of Trent 37, 46, 103, 132 n.67
creation 74, 81, 88, 104, 147
  as divine poetry/speech 71, 78–80
  sacramentality of 78, 98, 118–19, 132

Day of Atonement 155, 156 n.26, 157, 170–1
Denison, George Anthony 140, 141 n.105, 142
doctrine
  articles 39, 42, 45
  as boundary 45–6, 74, 76, 103–4, 132
  development of 77 n.104
  official vs. popular (received) 36, 152
Döllinger, Ignaz von 38, 141
Douglas, Brian 2, 37 n.85, 47 n.129, 50, 124 n.30, 131 n.61

ecumenism 3, 36–8
  'mutual explanation' 37, 46, 48, 74
  see also doctrine: as boundary

emotion 22, 103, 111–12, 114
'English Catholicism' 4, 35, 38; *see also* Church of England
episcopacy 42–4, 74
Essays and Reviews 32 n.65, 51 n.147, 158
Eucharist 19, 34, 87–9, 119–22, 129, 135, 137, 142, 145–7, 168, 171
  adoration 139, 142, 144–6
  cup, administration of 36, 38, 121
  elements/bread and wine 120–1, 126–7, 130, 132, 135–6, 138–9, 141, 143–4, 146–7, 170–1, 173, 176–9 (*see also under* body and blood of Christ)
  reception by the wicked 77 n.102, 140–2, 145–6
  types of 119–20 (*see also* Passover)
  words of institution 119, 126, 129–31, 135, 138, 144
  see also body and blood of Christ, communion, eucharistic sacrifice, real presence
eucharistic sacrifice 36, 46, 156 n.26, 157, 168, 171, 174, 176–82, 185–8
  and commemoration 169–70, 175–9, 185, 187 (*see also* Passover)
  propitiatory (*see under sacrifice*)
  and sacramental communion 169–71, 176, 178–9, 186
Evangelicalism 3–4, 27, 49, 93, 96–7, 114, 123
evangelism 31–33, 181 n.61
extra calvinisticum; *see* body and blood of Christ: in heaven

faith 77, 101–4, 118, 133–4
  basis of 57, 64
  relation to reason 57, 58 n.13
  psychology of 52, 67–70, 122, 189–90
  and works 102–4 (*see also phronesis*)
  see also knowledge of God/Christ
Farrer, Austin 73–4, 188
fasting 67, 110
Fathers (Church) 25, 75, 82, 130, 135
forgiveness 21–2, 24–6, 87, 105, 113–17, 122–3, 154–5, 158, 160, 163–5, 173
Formula of Concord 39 n.95, 45–6
'formularism' 33–5, 39, 42 (defined), 45, 47, 49–50, 54, 56, 76, 77 n.104, 108 n.89, 192, 194

Forrester, David 1, 2, 5, 7–8, 18–19, 21–3, 25–8, 33–4, 45
Froude, Richard Hurrell 17–18, 49

Geck, Albrecht 2, 40, 47 n.129
Gladstone, William Ewart 28 n.46, 31–2
Gore, Charles 186, 188
Gorham case 18, 27, 46, 96
grace 22–3, 106, 132, 160
 and sacraments 101, 104, 113, 145–7
 sanctifying 86–8, 94, 103
 of union with God/Christ 63, 92, 108
 see also communion, holiness, sacraments, sorrow for sin

Hampden, Renn Dickson 48, 76
hermeneutics; see allegory, imagery, Scripture
high church tradition 16 n.2, 42–3, 49
 atonement 152–3, 155, 188
 baptismal regeneration 93, 95–6
 Catholic Emancipation 17, 28–31, 36
 eucharistic theology 119, 123, 127, 128 n.46, 132, 135–6, 139, 142, 147, 172, 178 n.149
 foundation for Pusey's theology 10, 19–20, 25–7, 38, 89, 96–7, 123–4, 180, 189, 193
 Hackney Phalanx 16 n.2, 62 n.28
 Hutchinsonians 62
 reticence 61–2, 68, 124 n.24, 127, 151, 153, 179
 use of types 62, 88, 149, 153, 155, 163
 see also Blomfield, Denison, Gorham case, Hook, Jones, Knox, Lloyd, Palmer, Phillpotts, Rose, Van Mildert, Waterland
holiness 64, 66, 68, 77, 97, 105, 107–11, 115, 117–18, 174, 182–6, 192
 in baptism 94, 97, 109–10
 of the Church 108, 123
 in the Eucharist 121–3, 141–2, 145
 of God 114, 159–60, 162, 164
 non-Christian 109–10
Holy Spirit 134–5, 164, 192–3
 in the Eucharist 133–8, 143–4, 146
 renewing the Christian 99–102, 106, 108, 111, 120, 122
 and sacrifice 181–6

Hook, Walter Farquhar 26, 74–5
Hooker, Richard 43 n.113, 82
humility 110–12, 132, 146, 155, 177

idealism 81 n.120, 82–4, 133 n.72, 134 n.74
imagery 69–74, 77–9, 84, 146, 192
 networks of signification 58, 72–9, 88, 106, 119, 152, 155–8, 163, 165, 170, 186, 189, 191–2
 see also allegory, language, types
imagination 79–80, 88
incarnation 130, 142, 184
 humility of 110, 177
 sacramentality of 81, 85, 88–9,
 and salvation 99–101, 115, 118, 146, 182
 see also Jesus Christ: humanity and divinity of
inspiration 52, 58 n.14, 60, 109

Jesus Christ 73, 111, 192
 as 'archetype' 70–1, 73, 78, 82, 88–9, 132, 149, 156, 165, 186
 ascension of 99–100, 155, 157, 172–4, 181–2, 184
 blood of (see forgiveness)
 body of (see body and blood of Christ; Church)
 cross of 100, 105, 112, 117, 149, 153, 158, 162–3, 177, 184–5
 death of 101, 152, 155, 157, 159, 182
 divinity and humanity of 121–2, 139, 142, 155, 157, 159, 162–3, 181, 184–5
 dying with (see repentance, self-denial)
 intercession of 151–3
 Passion of 129, 171, 174, 181
 person of 141 n.109, 159
 priesthood of 157, 185
 presence of, in the Eucharist (see body and blood of Christ, real presence)
 in the poor 111
 resurrection of 100–1, 106–7, 155, 157, 173–4, 182
 righteousness of 91, 101, 104–6, 159, 186
 transfiguration of 106–7 (see also body, human)
 work 'for us' (see recapitulation, atonement); 'in us' (see theosis)

Jones, William (of Nayland) 62, 154
Jowett, Benjamin 158–9, 186
joy 8 n.29, 109, 116–17, 121–2, 141, 144–5, 168, 182–3, 185
judgement (divine) 24, 66, 68, 87–8, 142
justice, God's 152–3, 155, 158, 160–3
justification 91, 97, 103–6, 118, 155, 165, 186; *see also* baptism, communion

Keble, John 10, 17–18, 26, 44, 48–9, 55–6, 65–7, 71, 74, 78–9, 111, 164
   differences with Pusey 35, 60 n.21, 140, 142 n.112
   eucharistic theology of 125, 140, 142
   'National Apostasy' (Assize Sermon) 17, 30
knowledge of God/Christ 64, 73, 77, 102–3, 106–7, 118, 122, 134, 161 n.42
Knox, Alexander 105, 127

language 70–2, 129, 165, 190
   as theological paradigm 190–1
   see also imagery
Larsen, Timothy 3, 21, 50
Liddon, Henry Parry 1, 6, 188
   Life of Edward Bouverie Pusey, D.D. 1, 5–6
Lloyd, Charles 16–17, 25, 29–30, 36, 62 n.28, 155, 157, 170
longing for God 97–8, 118, 122; *see also* communion, psychology of faith
Louth, Andrew 77 n.106, 83 n.126
love 9, 12, 24–5, 64, 100, 102–3, 104 n.73, 110, 121, 161 n.42, 181–3, 193
   for God 64, 116–18, 122, 127, 145, 163–4, 184–6
   of God/Christ 87–8, 96, 111, 122, 142, 145–6, 149, 152, 158–60, 161 n.42, 162–3, 171, 184
     indwelling 107–9, 116–18, 185
   for the poor 111–12, 116, 184 n.69
Lubac, Henri de 60–1, 63 n.31, 82–3, 190
Luther, Martin 33–5, 47, 53, 124, 128–9, 130 n.57, 136
Lutheranism 34–5, 39, 43, 124
Lux Mundi 164, 188 n.1

marriage 86–8, 91
material phenomena; *see* idealism
materialism 81–2, 133 n.72

Matthew, H. C. G. 19–21, 34, 38, 42, 50
mercy 23, 68, 118, 145, 151–3, 162
Moberly, Robert Campbell 164–5, 186, 188
'modern orthodoxy' 40, 47, 53
Morris, Jeremy 7, 64 n.33

Neander, Johann August Wilhelm 25, 42
Newman, John Henry 10, 16–20, 25, 34, 37, 49, 65, 79, 95–6, 105, 124
   correspondence on transubstantiation 36–7, 84
   contrasted with Pusey 11, 30–1, 35, 44, 46, 68, 82–4, 107 n.85, 133 n.72, 134 n.74, 193
   Lectures on Justification 34
   statements about Pusey 6, 11, 19–20, 41, 55
   Tract 90 (*Remarks on Certain Passages*) 36, 46, 128 n.46
   see also idealism, objectivism
nouvelle théologie 190–1; *see also* Lubac, Henri de

obedience 105–6, 109, 163, 186
   of Christ 155, 177, 186
objectivism 82–4
   see also truth
'orthodoxism' 39–40, 47–9, 56–7, 93, 190, 192
Oxford Movement 1, 17–20, 26, 70 n.67, 164–5, 193
   interpretation of 10, 119, 124, 147
   and Pusey's development 19, 42, 48, 53
   Pusey's divergence from 66–8, 96
   theology of 44, 64–5, 140, 185–6
   see also Froude, Keble, Newman, Pusey, Williams

Palmer, William (of Worcester College) 20 n.10, 26, 49, 53, 124 n.31, 139 n.99
pantheism 98–9, 128, 190
participation 63–4, 82, 88, 115, 190, 193
   in Christ's death and resurrection 92, 150, 163, 167
   as sacrifice 180–1, 184–7
   of the Eucharist in the Passion 119, 129, 170–1, 175–9

Index

Passover 154, 156 n.26, 157, 168, 173
   as commemorative sacrifice 157, 168–70, 176 n.45
penance; *see* confession, repentance, self-denial
penitence; *see* repentance
Pentecost; *see* Holy Spirit
Phillpotts, Henry 27–8, 46, 95
phronesis 63, 65–6, 102–3, 164, 185, 192
   see also reserve
pietism 40, 42, 47, 49, 93, 192
poetry 69, 70 n.67, 71, 74, 79, 192
   divine (*see under* creation)
postmodernism 60, 189
practical Christianity; *see* Christian life
Prayer Book 123–4, 127–8, 151–2, 171, 175
   declaration on kneeling 132, 139
prophecy 51, 57, 74, 82, 106
Protestantism 22, 33, 38, 44, 103–4, 176, 178, 189, 194
Pusey, Edward Bouverie
   biographical 10 n.34, 16–18, 55
   Daniel the Prophet 19, 21, 50–2
   Eirenicon 3, 36–8, 46, 103
   Enquiry into ... the Theology of Germany 17, 33, 39–42, 189, 192
   and his development 19, 21, 38, 42–3, 45–52
   in his later theology 55–7, 62–3, 89, 93, 97, 152, 187
   'The Holy Eucharist a Comfort to the Penitent' 17, 123, 127 n.39
   influence of, in theology 5, 123, 147, 163, 186, 188–9
   last letter to Sr Clara 118, 182, 185
   'Lectures on Types and Prophecies' 6, 55–6, 58–9, 68–9, 98, 105–6, 149, 155–8, 168–9, 180, 193–4
   Letter to the ... Bishop of Oxford [Richard Bagot] 22–4, 114, 133
   reception of 2, 5–12
   relevance of (contemporary) 3–5, 54, 187, 193
   'revolution' theories of his development 18–23
   rule of life 8 n.29, 9 n.33, 66
   Scriptural Views of Holy Baptism (Tracts for the Times 67–9) 17, 25, 34, 55, 58–9, 67, 90, 93, 97, 114, 180–1, 184

   Sermons on Repentance 10, 18, 184
   social criticism 32–3, 111–12, 116
   spirituality of 8–10, 12, 111, 118 n.140, 134 n.78, 184 (*see also* communion, self-offering, sorrow for sin)
   theological consistency 15–16, 23–5, 27, 38, 46, 52–3
   theological project 47–9, 53–4, 124–5, 128, 136–7, 140, 187
   Tract 81 (*Testimony ... to the Doctrine of the Eucharistic Sacrifice*) 67, 170, 176, 180
Pusey, Maria (*née* Barker) 8, 17, 22, 32, 45, 66

Radical Orthodoxy 63 n.31, 69 n.64, 190–1
rationalism 38–40, 42–3, 47, 49, 52, 56, 58, 93, 132, 190
real presence 36, 46, 68, 77 n.102, 119, 122, 126–34, 139–47, 164, 173, 177, 182, 188
   motion of 137–8, 142–6
   'real objective presence' 83, 134 n.77, 140 (*see also* objectivism)
   receptionism 125–7
   'sacramental presence' 126, 133–4, 136, 139, 142
   virtualism 125–7, 136, 138
   see also body and blood of Christ, Eucharist
recapitulation 99, 104–6, 149, 158, 160–3, 165, 167, 171, 184–6
reform, ecclesiastical
   Church of England 30–1
   Church of Ireland 17, 30
Reformation 19, 22, 26, 35, 74–5
regeneration 25, 91, 93–5, 104, 109–10
   and conversion 96–7
   distinguished from renewal 96, 97 n.37
repentance 8–9, 22–3, 66, 105, 113–18, 122, 164, 180–3, 185 n.73, 193;
   see also sin: post-baptismal, sorrow for sin
reserve 64–8, 70 n.67, 167, 180 n.57, 185;
   see also *phronesis*
revelation 73, 85, 132, 193

Roman Catholic theology
  assumed of Pusey 10, 19, 22–3, 119, 123, 171
  Pusey contrasted with 142 n.112, 161, 172
  Pusey's engagement with 33, 35–8, 103–4, 114, 130
Romanticism 79, 80, 143
Rose, Hugh James 17, 20, 26, 38–9, 41–3, 45, 47, 52, 57
Rowell, Geoffrey 9, 25

sacraments 86, 97, 99, 164, 167
  in relation to types 81, 85, 92
  see also absolution, baptism, Eucharist, marriage
sacrifice 101, 149, 167, 174–5, 184
  and atonement, 151–2, 155–6, 159, 162–3, 165, 185
  expiation 153, 156 n.26
  and immolation 172–4, 176–8
  as offering 172–8
  and propitiation 153–6, 162, 169, 172, 176–7, 179
  see also eucharistic sacrifice, self-offering
Sanctification; *see* holiness
Scripture 52, 67, 73, 75, 91, 149, 152, 165, 192–3
  complexity and obscurity of 58–61, 64–5
  polemical interpretation of 56–7, 190
  speaks 'to the point' 130, 132, 141
  see also allegory, inspiration, revelation, types
self-denial 110, 115, 156 n.26, 183–4, 193; *see also* fasting
self-offering
  of Christ 154–5, 157, 165, 167, 170–1, 173, 175–81, 184–8
  Christian 155, 167, 170–1, 174–5, 179–87
  of the Church 171, 174–7, 179–82, 185, 187–8
  human 161, 163, 167, 173, 185
sin 21–4, 26, 93, 96, 114, 117, 152, 157, 159–64, 182–3

post-baptismal 23–6, 94, 96–7, 112–16, 181
sorrow for sin 9, 21–5, 116–18
suffering 10 n.34, 183
  vicarious 153, 155–6, 177
  and atonement 158, 162
symbolism; *see* imagery

Taille, Maurice de la 156 n.26, 161, 172–4, 176–8
theosis 99, 104–6, 149–50, 165, 167, 171, 182, 185–6
Tholuck, Friedrich August Gotttreu 42, 47
tractarians; *see* Oxford Movement
tradition 73, 75, 77, 80, 188–90, 192
transubstantiation 36–7, 84, 123–4
Trinity 87, 109, 122, 159
truth 82–3, 76 n.101, 190–2
types 59, 61, 70–3, 77–8, 80–2, 84–6, 88, 92, 132, 149, 155–6, 191
  historical 80, 82
  natural 63, 70, 77, 80, 82, 91, 94, 119–21, 187, 190
  priesthood 153–4, 156–7, 168
  sacrificial 153–4, 157, 159, 163, 165, 168, 170, 174–5, 177, 180–2, 186
  see also allegory, baptism, Day of Atonement, Eucharist, imagery, Passover, sacramentals

understanding; *see* knowledge of God/Christ
union with God/Christ; *see* communion

Van Mildert, William 29–30, 62 n.28, 68, 95, 125–7, 152–4, 156 n.26

Waterland, Daniel 62, 96, 172
  atonement 154–5, 156 n.26
  eucharistic sacrifice 174–80, 182, 185
  real presence 125–6, 135–9, 142–4
  regeneration 95–6
Westhaver, George 2, 61, 76, 82, 89
Wilberforce, Robert Isaac 36, 37 n.85, 49, 125 n.31, 133 n.72, 178 n.52
Williams, Isaac 64–6, 70 n.67
  on Pusey 67–8

www.ingramcontent.com/pod-product-compliance
Lightning Source LLC
Chambersburg PA
CBHW062222300426
44115CB00012BA/2178